CRISIS INTERVENTION AND COUNSELING BY TELEPHONE AND THE INTERNET

Third Edition

CRISIS INTERVENTION AND COUNSELING BY TELEPHONE AND THE INTERNET

Edited by

DAVID LESTER

The Richard Stockton College of New Jersey

and

JAMES R. ROGERS

The University of Akron

(With 24 Other Contributors)

CHARLES C THOMAS • PUBLISHER, LTD.
Springfield • Illinois • U.S.A.

Published and Distributed Throughout the World by

CHARLES C THOMAS • PUBLISHER, LTD.
2600 South First Street
Springfield, Illinois 62704

This book is protected by copyright. No part of
it may be reproduced in any manner without written
permission from the publisher. All rights reserved.

© 2012 by CHARLES C THOMAS • PUBLISHER, LTD.

ISBN 978-0-398-08828-6 (hard)
ISBN 978-0-398-08829-3 (paper)
ISBN 978-0-398-08830-9 (ebook)

Library of Congress Catalog Card Number: 2012018194

First Edition, 1973
Second Edition, 2002
Third Edition, 2012

With THOMAS BOOKS *careful attention is given to all details of manufacturing and design. It is the Publisher's desire to present books that are satisfactory as to their physical qualities and artistic possibilities and appropriate for their particular use.* THOMAS BOOKS *will be true to those laws of quality that assure a good name and good will.*

Printed in the United States of America
SM-R-3

Library of Congress Cataloging-in-Publication Data

Crisis intervention and counseling by telephone and the internet / edited by David Lester and James R. Rogers. -- 3rd ed.
    p. cm.
    Rev. ed. of: Crisis intervention and counseling by telephone / edited by David Lester.
    Includes bibliographical references and index.
    ISBN 978-0-398-08828-6 (hard) -- ISBN 978-0-398-08829-3 (pbk.) -- ISBN 978-0-398-08830-9 (ebook)
    1. Crisis intervention (Mental health services) 2. Hotlines (Counseling) I. Lester, David, 1942- II. Rogers, James R. III. Crisis intervention and counseling by telephone.

RC480.6.C7415 2012
362.28'81--dc23

2012018194

EDITORS

David Lester, Ph.D.
The Richard Stockton College of New Jersey
Galloway, New Jersey
lesterd@stockton.edu

James R. Rogers, Ph.D.
University of Akron
Akron, Ohio
jrrogers@uakron.edu

NEW CONTRIBUTORS

Karl Andriessen, MSuicidology
Suicide Prevention Program CMHC
Gent, Belgium
karl.andriessen@pandora.be

Cara Anna
New York City
caraesque@gmail.com

Laura A. Davidson, M.A.
University of Nevada, Reno
Reno, Nevada
ldavidso@unr.edu

William P. Evans, Ph.D
University of Nevada, Reno
Reno, Nevada
wevans@unr.edu

John F. Gunn III, M.A.
Rutgers University
Camden, New Jersey
john.gunn.3@gmail.com

Danielle R. Jahn, M.A.
Texas Tech University
Lubbock, Texas
danielle.jahn@ttu.edu

Karolina Krysinska, Ph.D.
KU Leuven – University of Leuven
Leuven, Belgium
Karolina.Krysinska@ppw.kuleuven.be

Barbara Medlock, R.N., M.S.N.
Portage Path Behavioral Health
Akron, Ohio
bmedlock@portagepath.org

Shelly Meyers, Ed.D.
The Richard Stockton College of New Jersey
Galloway, New Jersey
Shelly.Meyers@stockton.edu

Brian L. Mishara, Ph.D.
Université du Quebec à Montréal
Canada
mishara.brian@uqam.ca

Lorie L. Sicafuse, Doctoral Candidate
University of Nevada, Reno
Reno, Nevada
lsicafuse@unr.edu

Sarah C. Westen, B.S.
Union College
Schenectady, New York
sarah.westen@gmail.com

CONTRIBUTORS TO EARLIER EDITIONS

Gene Brockopp
Diane Blum
John Douds
Lee Ann Hoff
John Kalafat
Charles W. Lamb
Ann S. McColskey
Tim Williams
Dmitri Schustov
Vanda Scott
Gerladine Wilson
Lin Young

PREFACE

In 1973, Gene W. Brockopp (Executive Director of the Suicide Prevention and Crisis Intervention Service in Buffalo, New York) and David Lester (then Director of Research and Evaluation) edited a book on the use of the telephone for crisis intervention and counseling, with a particular focus on suicide prevention. In 2002, David Lester prepared a second edition of the book: *Crisis Intervention and Counseling by Telephone*.

Although knowledge about the suicidal individual was widely disseminated, the information and experience gained using the *telephone* as a treatment modality had not been codified, published, or disseminated. The first edition of *Crisis Intervention and Counseling by Telephone* sought to remedy this as we described the results of our experience with telephone counseling in our suicide prevention center in Erie County (New York), and we recruited others to contribute their experience. The book was well received, widely used, and a Japanese translation undertaken. The second edition updated knowledge about the use of the telephone as a medium for crisis intervention, and new chapters were solicited from experts in the field.

Not surprisingly, the field has changed tremendously since the second edition appeared. Not only has more research and writing appeared on crisis intervention by telephone, but the field has been radically altered by the advent of the Internet. The Internet has enabled online resources to become available for those in crisis but, more importantly, it has provided the means to provide crisis intervention and counseling via the Internet, both by e-mails and by instant messaging, in what is now know as *e therapy*.

It is clearly time for the third edition of *Crisis Intervention and Counseling by Telephone and the Internet* with James R. Rogers as co-editor. Many of the chapters in the first and second editions remain relevant and useful today, and they have been retained, albeit with editing on occasions and several additions. However, new chapters have been written for this third edition, and several chapters have been updated and rewritten. As before, the content of the chapters sometimes overlaps, but this overlap has not been eliminated in order that each chapter can stand alone as a complete essay.

We hope that this book will further stimulate interest and discussion of the telephone and the Internet as a mode of treatment, and we hope that it will prove useful for those setting up telephone and Internet counseling services and those in charge of centers already operating, especially in training and supervising those on the front-lines, the crisis interveners.

David Lester & James R. Rogers

CONTENTS

Page
Preface xi
Chapter

Part I
THE VARIETIES OF TELEPHONE SERVICE

1. Counseling by Telephone: An Overview – *David Lester* 5
2. A Survey of Telephone Counseling Services – *David Lester* 28

Part II
CRISIS INTERVENTION AND COUNSELING BY TELEPHONE

3. The Unique Contribution of Telephone Therapy – *Tim Williams and John Douds* 41
4. Crisis Intervention – *John Kalafat* 48
5. Responding to Suicidal Crises: The Crisis Intervention Approach – *James R. Rogers* 67
6. How Best to Help Suicidal Persons over the Telephone and Internet – *Brian L. Mishara* 74
7. Telephone Therapy: Some Common Errors and Fallacies – *Charles W. Lamb* 84
8. The Telephone Call: Conversation or Therapy – *Gene W. Brockopp* 89
9. Active Listening – *David Lester* 94
10. Cognitive Therapy Approaches to Crisis Intervention – *David Lester* 101
11. Transactional Analysis and Learned Helplessness Approaches to Crisis Counselling – *David Lester* 111
12. Gestalt Therapy Approaches to Crisis Intervention with Suicidal Clients – *Lin Young and David Lester* 120

Part III
PROBLEM CALLERS

13. The Obscene Caller – *Gene W. Brockopp and David Lester* 135
14. The Chronic Caller – *Gene W. Brockopp, David Lester, and Diane Blum* 159
15. Chronic Calls Placed to Suicide and Crisis Intervention Hotlines: Case Strategies for the Persistent Mentally Ill and Vulnerable – *Lorie L. Sicafuse, William P. Evans, and Laura A. Davidson*... 177
16. The Covert Cry for Help – *Gene W. Brockopp*.................. 194
17. The Silent Caller – *Vanda Scott, David Lester, and Gene W. Brockopp* 199
18. The Nuisance Caller – *Gene W. Brockopp* 211
19. The "One Counselor" Caller – *Gene W. Brockopp*............... 215

Part IV
SPECIAL TOPICS

20. Adolescents – *Sarah C. Westen*................................ 223
21. War Veterans – *Karolina Krysinska and Karl Andriessen*.......... 250
22. Rural Communities – *Danielle R. Jahn* 263
23. The Elderly – *John F. Gunn III* 274
24. Individuals with Disabilities on Campus – *Shelly Meyers*......... 286

PART V
BEYOND THE TELEPHONE CONTACT

25. Beyond the Telephone Contact – *Lee Ann Hoff* 295
26. Beyond the Phone Lines: New and Emerging Technologies in the Field of Crisis Intervention – *Laura A. Davidson, William P. Evans, and Lorie L. Sicafuse*....................... 309
27. Crisis Intervention by E-mail – *Geraldine Wilson and David Lester*... 323
28. Counseling the Client in Crisis by Letter – *Dmitri Schustov and David Lester* 331

Part VI
THE TELEPHONE COUNSELOR

29. The Case for Nonprofessional Crisis Workers – *Richard K. McGee and Bruce Jennings* 341

30. The Use of the Professional in Telephone Counseling – *Ann S. McColskey* 352
31. Selecting the Telephone Counselor – *Gene W. Brockopp* 363
32. Training Telephone Counselors – *John Kalafat* 371
33. Identifying and Responding to Burnout – *James R. Rogers and Barbara Medlock* 398

Part VII
EVALUATING TELEPHONE COUNSELING SERVICES

34. The Effectiveness of Suicide Prevention and Crisis Intervention Services – *David Lester* 411
35. Reflections from a Caller – *Cara Anna* 422

Name Index 429
Subject Index 443

CRISIS INTERVENTION AND COUNSELING BY TELEPHONE AND THE INTERNET

Part I

THE VARIETIES OF TELEPHONE SERVICE

Chapter 1

COUNSELING BY TELEPHONE: AN OVERVIEW[1]

DAVID LESTER

Telephone counseling was first used widely in the 1960s by suicide prevention and crisis intervention services as a means of providing immediate and inexpensive access to crisis intervention for those in distress. Since then, the telephone has been utilized for a variety of purposes by psychotherapists and by mental health clinics. In this chapter, I will review these uses and then discuss the unique qualities of counseling by telephone, together with the advantages and drawbacks of this medium for counseling.

The Use of Telephone in Counseling

There have been several books and articles discussing the use of the telephone for counseling and crisis intervention that provide broad overviews (Sanders & Rosenfield, 1998; Masi & Freedman, 2001; Mishara & Daigle, 2001; Krysinska & De Leo, 2007). Aronson (2000) has edited a book on the use of the telephone in psychotherapy, while Baker et al. (2005) have edited a book on the use of the telephone for providing support both in business as well as in health and medicine.

The telephone has been used as a means for counseling in a variety of services (Lester, 1977, 1995; Lester & Brockopp, 1973), including suicide pre-

---

[1] Despite the large number of references for this chapter, this overview mentions only a small proportion of the articles and books on the use of the telephone in crisis intervention and counseling. A full review would require another book!

vention centers, crisis intervention centers, teen hotlines, rape crisis counseling, rumor control hotlines, drug hotlines (Schmitz & Mickelson, 1972), parent hotlines (Newcomb et al., 1984), poison control centers (Broadhead, 1986), career counseling (Roach et al., 1983), sex information and counseling (Anon, 1972), sexual abuse (Pierce & Pierce, 1985), health care problems for elderly adults (Moreland & Grier, 1986), AIDS (Benedetti et al., 1989), and all kinds of "Dial-A-Need" hotlines (Goud, 1985). There has even been a nationally broadcast radio call-in show which, following ethical guidelines from the American Psychiatric Association, gave advice and made referrals but abstained from diagnosis and treatment (Ruben, 1986).

Services can be oriented toward providing crisis counseling, perhaps combined with referral to other community agencies or resources if long-term therapy is indicated, providing support (Weinberger et al., 1986), or providing information about the specific problem and the resources available for obtaining help (Sheerin, 1994). The service can be passive or active. For example, Iscoe, Hill, Harmon, and Coffman (1979) provided recordings on a campus counseling service telephone for dealing with specific problems such as anxiety and loneliness and information about therapy and the campus counseling center, a passive technique, while Ragle and Krone (1985) actively initiated calls to freshman students.

Recent papers have discussed the use of telephone counseling for children left at home while parents work (Guerney, 1991), those with eating disorders (Latzer & Gilat, 2000), students traumatized by war (Noy, 1992), survivors of Hurricane Katrina (Combs, 2007), bereaved families (Battin et al., 1975) and families providing palliative care (Wenk et al., 1993), and for providing continued supportive counseling for discharged psychiatric patients (Meyersberg, 1985), disadvantaged parents (Madoc-Jones et al., 2007), ex-smokers (Ossip-Klein et al., 1984) and workers in a welfare-to-work program (Schmidt & Austin, 2004). The telephone has been used to follow-up discharged patients (Schnelle et al., 1979), especially those who have attempted suicide (Vaiva et al., 2006), and to reduce the number of clients who fail to show for appointments at a mental health clinic (Hochstadt & Trybula, 1980). It has been used for behavioral assessment of the activities and experiences of clients (Weissman-Frisch et al., 1983) and to motivate clients to follow behavioral therapy regimens, such as those for quitting smoking (McFall et al., 1993). Psychosocial telephone counseling has been provided to patients recovering from cervical cancer (Nelson et al., 2008). Evans et al. (2000) provided a 24/7 crisis consultation service for patients treated for deliberate self-harm through which they could talk to a psychiatrist and which seemed to reduce demands for other health care services (although only 17% of those provided with the service used it).

Telephone has been used for "coaching," an action-oriented relationship between a coach and a client which focuses on where the clients are today and how they can achieve their goals. Weekly sessions last for 30 minutes or so with e-mail exchanges between sessions if there is a need.[2]

The telephone has also been used to provide consultation for counselors by their supervisors, both between sessions (Wolf et al., 1969) and during sessions (Rickert & Turner, 1978), for training mental health counselors (Connell & Smyer, 1986), and for encouraging adoption of new programs in institutions after conducting workshops in them (Fergus, 1979).

Some clients, such as aphasic patients and socially impaired clients, may require special training sessions with the telephone to enhance their attention and understanding of verbal telephone communications (Davidoff & Katz, 1985; Praderas & MacDonald, 1986).

Cell Phones and Smart Phones

In recent years, there have been efforts to extend crisis intervention to cell (mobile) phones. Chen et al. (2010) used cell phones to send messages to patients discharged after treatment for a suicide attempt in China. The patients received weekly messages of concern, and they reported that they found these messages helpful. In Sri Lanka, Marasinghe et al. (2012) went further and provided problem-solving therapy, meditation exercises, guidance for improving social support, and advice on alcohol and drug abuse via cell phones. Their experimental group reported a greater reduction in depression and suicidal ideation than the control group.

Some groups are developing free smart phone apps on suicide. The QPR Institute[3] has an informational app available (*The tender leaves of hope: Helping someone survive a suicide crisis*), and so has the Texas Youth Suicide Prevention Project.[4] The Departments of Defense and Veterans Affairs have developed *PTSD Coach* a free iPhone app for veterans.[5] Of course, many of the online services can now be accessed by smart phones. For example, the Samaritans in Massachusetts have set up *IM Hear* for high school students in Framingham (Massachusetts), an online messaging service staffed by peers.[6] Whittaker et al. (2012) developed a cell phone depression prevention intervention for adolescents that delivered two messages a day, based on cognitive behavioral therapy, including texts, videos and cartoons.

---

[2] Organizations which can refer clients to coaches include www.coachfederation.org, www.coachu.com, and www.mentorcoach.com.
[3] www.qprinstitute.com
[4] www.texassuicideprevention.org
[5] www.ptsd.va.gov/public/pages/ptsdcoach.asp
[6] www.samaritansusa.org/framingham.php

Nationwide Telephone Services

It is has long been a problem that every community with a crisis intervention or suicide prevention hotline has a different telephone number and, furthermore, not all communities are covered. The advent of nationwide hotlines has eliminated this problem. In the United States there is the National Suicide Prevention Lifeline (1-800-273-TALK), while in Australia, there is Lifeline Australia, carried by the major mobile phone carriers free of charge.

The Extent of Telephone Use

Miller (1973) surveyed psychiatrists and found that 97% used the telephone for handling emergencies, 45% used the telephone as an adjunct for face-to-face therapy, and 19% used the telephone as the primary mode of treatment. Not all those surveyed found the telephone easy to use for counseling, and Miller noted that therapists should explore their reactions to the medium and whether all types of problems can be handled in this way. For example, those surveyed by Miller found problems concerning anxiety more easy to handle over the telephone than problems concerning depression.

Rosenbaum (1977) found that 87% of the therapists he surveyed had used either telephones or correspondence to maintain contact with clients. Sometimes the therapist had moved, sometimes the client. Some clients refused transfer to new therapists, and the therapists felt constrained to maintain contact. Most saw the contact as merely supportive, but a minority did see the contact as an opportunity for further insights on the part of the client. Most charged no fee for brief calls (say, less than 10 minutes) but did charge for longer calls.

The Use of the Telephone by Specialty

As well as the crisis-oriented and information services mentioned above, the telephone has been used by therapists of various persuasions.

Behavior and Cognitive Therapy

Dubren (1977) used recorded messages for clients to reinforce their abstinence from smoking as part of a behavior therapy program, and Shapiro et al. (1985–1986) used taped messages to provide support and information and to suggest cognitive and behavioral coping strategies for ex-smokers.

McGlynn (1980) used personal telephone contact with clients in a treatment program for anorexia nervosa, and Smith (1978) used the telephone for assigning behavioral homework to treat obese patients and for checking on their progress. Taylor (1984) treated an agoraphobic by telephone who lived too far from the clinic to attend. Using implosive therapy techniques, the man was instructed to expose himself to anxiety-arousing stimuli and to rate his emotions on each occasion. Spevak and Richars (1980) used telephone follow-up to provide support and to review basic strategies for chronic nail-biters originally treated using cognitive therapy. McNamee et al. (1989) treated agoraphobics in their homes, using the telephone to transmit both relaxation and exposure treatment techniques.

Hypnosis

Owens (1970), a dentist, explored the effectiveness of inducing hypnosis by telephone with a number of his patients with whom he had used hypnosis before. He used a standard induction technique procedure in order to induce a mild level of hypnosis, and he was successful in all cases, as well as in two additional cases whom he had never previously hypnotized.

Hypnosis has been induced by telephone successfully by others (Gravitz, 1983). Leff (1969) treated a client for insomnia when she was unable to visit him at the office; Kroger (1969) treated a client for a serious hiccup problem; Stanton (1978) used relaxation and guided fantasy to treat obesity and examination anxiety; and Cooperman and Schafer (1983) used guided fantasy to calm a patient before surgery, to reduce post-operative leg pain, and to cope with unresolved grief.

Psychoanalysis

Robertiello (1972) reported two instances where he was unable to see his psychoanalytic patients, in one case because the patient was travelling and the other because the patient was ill and could not visit the analyst's office. He felt that the telephone made little difference in one case in which much of the content of the sessions was centered around the patient's dreams. In the second case, the use of the telephone facilitated the analysis since the transference neurosis of the patient had become so disruptive that the patient could not bear to be in the same room as the analyst. The telephone sessions made it easier for her to get in touch with her emotions and to reflect upon the transference, thereby helping to resolve it. Saul (1951) described telephone work with a client for whom the sessions by telephone diluted the strength of the transference.

Hymer (1984) used the telephone with two clients, one who began calling between face-to-face sessions and another who moved to a new city. Hymer noted that the typical transference feelings using the telephone are sometimes sexual ("Reach out and touch someone") and sometimes symbiotic regressions to the mother-infant bond. The analyst must be aware of this and monitor the changes in transference during and between telephone sessions.

There are also countertransference issues. Hymer was at first annoyed by the intrusions from one client, but she eventually became aware of the progress made by the client as a result of these telephone sessions and made them part of the ongoing therapy plan. Should the analyst not be able to cope with the telephone calls, such calls should be forbidden in the interests of the treatment.

Hymer's client who called between sessions had schizophrenia, and the telephone calls helped her develop important ego functions such as limiting the length of the call and planning for the time of day of the call. The client also began to trust the analyst as an object that might be constant (the analyst was "there" even when she could not be seen), and she became able to thank the analyst. She was also able to use the telephone calls as a safety valve and to strengthen her ability to verbalize her thoughts and feelings, and the calls replaced the wrist-cutting in which she had previously engaged.

Group Counseling

Rosenfield and Smillie (1998) reported the successful use of telephone conference for group therapy with women who had cancer and required support.

The Use of the Telephone for Special Problems

Anxious Clients

Therapists sometimes have very anxious clients, and those in crisis often call local crisis intervention services each day if they feel upset. Chiles (1974) suggested that therapists structure this behavior and have such clients call (or receive a call) regularly at specified times each day as a safety valve. He used this practice with a client who overate and drank every night, calling her regularly at 8:30 pm, a time each evening at which she felt particularly depressed.

Family Therapy

Hightower and Dimalanta (1980) use the telephone (combined with speakers) in the course of family therapy (1) to correct distortions which arise, for example, when one member is absent; (2) if some family members cannot attend a session; and (3) if the family cancels a meeting. To prevent family members trying to form alliances with one of the therapists, Hightower and Dimalanta recommended that all co-therapists participate in all telephone contacts.

Beebe (1968) used the telephone to help psychotic patients begin to reintegrate with their families. Psychiatric patients need to be prepared for return to the family situation, but full reintegration may be too stressful for both the patient and the family to cope with. For psychotic individuals, the telephone often provides the right amount of distance for the initial contacts. It permits contact without closeness, and it serves to curb the fantasies which take over when there is no communication between the patient and the family. Furthermore, the family feels involved with the patient and is permitted to help the patient, thereby relieving the guilt over how they might have contributed to the psychiatric illness. In one case of a youth who had been forced into the Navy by parents who had wanted to get rid of him, the patient became anxious, confused, and delusional, thinking that he had killed his mother. A telephone call home was a great relief to him and reduced the severity of the psychotic episode.

Physically Disabled Clients

Physically disabled clients may not be able to travel easily to therapists for face-to-face sessions. Evans and his colleagues have used conference telephone calls to conduct group therapy with the blind (Evans & Jaureguy, 1981a, 1981b; Jaureguy & Evans, 1983), with physically disabled rehabilitation clients (Evans et al., 1984), and with socially isolated and lonely elderly clients (Evans et al., 1982).

Resistant Clients

Taussig and Freeman (1988) noted that telephone contact was excellent for anxious, resistant, and disorganized clients who cannot cope with face-to-face sessions. The telephone calls are motivating if the therapist initiates the contact, and the calls provide the clients with visual anonymity and a safety valve for their feelings.

Grumet (1979) reported on a woman with schizophrenia whom he treated for ten years by telephone. In her initial office visits, she was tense and overstimulated so that little therapeutic movement occurred. She often ended visits in a rage, storming out in mid-session. She began making crisis calls, and Grumet agreed to let her have telephone contacts as well as face-to-face contacts, but within weeks, the face-to-face contacts ceased. During the ten years, the content of the telephone calls became more therapeutically productive, and the client was able to hold down a job and develop more healthy interpersonal relationships with others. Her diagnosis was downgraded to a personality disorder of mixed type.

Shepard (1987) described her work over a year and a half with two clients for whom it would have been difficult to have face-to-face sessions. One was disabled and the other had to care for two elderly relatives at home. However, neither client seemed to be able to cope with face-to-face sessions, and both found the telephone therapy sessions much more tolerable. Both were able to reveal personal thoughts and feelings over the telephone, and the therapist felt that both made considerable progress. Shepard saw her role as primarily supportive and increasing the self-understanding of the clients, but she felt that face-to-face sessions would be necessary to work though the transference issues, issues which the telephone sessions minimized.

Unreachable Clients

Hymer (1984) used the telephone for sessions when some of her clients could not reach her during a transit strike. Rosenbaum (1974) conducted therapy with one client for 19 years by telephone and letter after he moved to a different city, and he expected the contact to continue until either he or the client died! Ranan and Blodgett (1983) reported telephone therapy with one client who lived too far away from the clinic to attend and with another who was too phobic to drive to the clinic. This latter client had missed 75% of her appointments when scheduled for face-to-face sessions but, after switching to the telephone, never missed a session. She said that she had come to hate the therapist because he represented her problems, and the telephone had helped her overcome her resistance to therapy. In order to neutralize her anger, she imagined the therapist as she wanted him to look, and at home she could maintain her sense of self and lessen her anxiety over closeness. She had poor ego control, and the telephone contact supported her fragile ego defenses since she knew that she could not attack or hurt the therapist. However, as she progressed, she found it difficult to switch and come in to see the therapist for face-to-face sessions. Ranan and Blodgett felt that telephone therapy could be useful for paranoid, phobic, borderline, mistrustful, and anxious clients and those troubled by being too close to others.

The Unique Features of Telephone Counseling

There are many unique features to conducting therapy by telephone (Lester, 1977b).

Client Control

When a client walks into a therapist's office, the therapist has most of the power. There may be a receptionist to receive the client, the therapist may sit behind a desk, the client is in the therapist's "space," and there may be a difference in status evident in the therapist's clothes or in the office furnishings. It is difficult to terminate the contact since that involves standing up and walking out. In telephone contacts, on the other hand, the client is in his or her space, the visual cues to the therapist's status are eliminated, and termination of the session is accomplished by simply hanging up the telephone.

This equalization of power may produce anxiety in the therapist, but it may facilitate communication for the client. MacKinnon and Michaels (1970) reported the case of a client who was able to reveal disturbing thoughts she had about her therapist only when a snowstorm forced her to have a telephone session with him.

Client Anonymity

When calling crisis interventions services, the client can remain anonymous, and this may encourage greater self-revelation and openness of thoughts and feelings. Anonymity minimizes the threat of possible ridicule, abuse, censure, or hurt because of the therapist's evaluations and reactions. Common folklore says that it sometimes easier to talk openly to strangers (whom one will never see again) than to friends.

Technological advances, such as Caller ID, threatened this anonymity, but it is now possible to purchase services which block Caller ID, thereby restoring anonymity. The introduction of video-telephones will also impact on client anonymity.

Positive Transference

Since the therapist remains unseen and, sometimes, also anonymous, the client is more able to fantasize about the therapist. Although transference is sometimes counterproductive, it may be that clients are able to make of the therapist what they *need* (Williams, 1971), and this may be important for the client in distress who may not be able to tolerate the reality of the actual therapist.

Related to this freeing effect of the positive transference, the restriction of the therapy to auditory cues may expand the client's imagination to encompass new mental and emotional possibilities and give free rein to discern new vistas for living (Hymer, 1984; Miller, 1973).

Reduced Dependency

In crisis services, the employment of many counselors means that a client rarely talks to the same counselor twice, and so the client will develop a dependency upon the service rather than on one particular individual. This makes it possible for the client to tolerate a counselor leaving temporarily or permanently.

Accessibility and Immediacy

Most people have low-cost access to a telephone. This is critical for those in crisis, for the elderly and the infirm, and for those who have to leave town for a while. Crisis services which operate on a 24-hour basis also permit immediacy, and many therapists suggest that their clients use crisis services between therapy sessions should crises occur.

Miller (1973) suggested that the different properties of telephone therapy may appeal to particular kinds of clients. For example, the easy access may appeal to clients with dependency and oral needs who can reassure themselves that support is close at hand. Ambivalent clients (such as those with schizophrenia) can use the telephone to maintain distance and control in the therapeutic relationship. Hostile clients may be better able to express their emotions since they feel safer at a distance. The immediacy of the telephone contact may appeal to impulsive clients who cannot tolerate anxiety. Such clients may utilize the telephone too frequently, and the therapist may have to set firm limits on how much telephone contact will be permitted.

The telephone is a *machine*, a concrete object and impersonal. This mechanical property of the telephone may appeal to those who are obsessional and neurotic and to people with schizophrenia who may prefer relating to machines than to people. The telephone may also appeal to clients who want to remain anonymous or protect themselves. They may not trust the therapist and may be exploring the possibility of therapy before committing themselves to therapy, or they may use the telephone to reveal embarrassing and shameful thoughts and feelings.

Therapists can use the telephone actively. They can give support to insecure and unstable clients between regular face-to-face sessions. They can instruct impulsive clients to call whenever they feel in danger of acting upon their impulses. They can tell clients who block in face-to-face sessions to call whenever they recall the thought. They can suggest telephone sessions when difficult material comes up, and they can use the telephone to bring significant others into the treatment process or to evaluate the client more completely.

Battin et al. (1975) noted that there is still a stigma attached to seeing a therapist and that potential clients may feel ashamed to seek help. Telephone therapy may feel less shameful to such people. In discussing the use of the telephone for bereavement counseling, Battin et al. suggested that it may be better for the bereavement counselor to call the bereaved family since then the contact is more similar to a condolence call and so more acceptable to the survivors.

The Disadvantages of Telephone Counseling

Lester and Brockopp (1973) noted that the telephone is usually used for conversation. The danger, therefore, is that the habits of ordinary telephone usage distort the treatment sessions so that they become conversational rather than therapeutic. Therapists must be aware of this danger and guard against it.

Miller (1973) noted that therapists may feel less in control of the therapy when using the telephone. Clients can, of course, hang up, and the therapist cannot use the visual cues from the client available in face-to-face sessions. (Interestingly, one therapist who has written on telephone sessions is blind [Cooperman & Schafer, 1983].) Therapists may also feel that they are open to unreasonable demands by clients for their time.

The setting from which clients call the therapist and that in which the therapist receives the call can raise problems. Therapists may become annoyed when called at home but find calls more acceptable when at the office. Clients may find it difficult to call from some places. For example, one client found that calling from work led to the intrusion of her professional "personality" into the therapy session and blocked her ability to think and feel freely (Hymer, 1984).

Hymer (1984) commented upon the countertransference issues involved in telephone therapy, especially when clients call the therapist at unexpected and nonscheduled times. If therapists cannot overcome their irritation at the calls, such calls should perhaps be forbidden or, alternatively, planned and scheduled into the treatment process.

It might be that telephone counseling is less effective than face-to-face therapy. Though no controlled comparisons of client outcome have appeared, Antonioni (1973) did find similar levels of counselor empathy and client satisfaction for telephone and face-to-face therapy in the *initial* sessions. However, Daniel (1973) found that introverts preferred face-to-face sessions over telephone sessions, and so telephone therapy may not appeal to all clients.

In the community, the telephone is occasionally used by individuals to make obscene telephones calls to others for hostile and sexual purposes (Murray, 1967). Obscene calls are also made to telephone counseling services, and Lester (1973) has presented some suggestions for how such callers might be handled by therapists. Other problems, such as the chronic caller and the silent caller, have been discussed by Lester and Brockopp (1973). Crisis-oriented services raise questions as to whether paraprofessional staff can provide sound, ethical, and effective counseling (Lester & Brockopp, 1973).

Concerns have been raised about the availability of dial-a-need hotlines. Some have argued that the use of such hotlines illustrates a loss of "community" and increased alienation in the society, with the result that we do not turn to one another for help. They are quick-fix substitutes for meaningful human contact, and they are vulnerable to abuse (Goud, 1985). Goud also questioned whether hotlines create problems ("iatrogenic problems," caused by the treatment) as in the creation of chronic callers by crisis-oriented services (Lester & Brockopp, 1973).

Analogous Modes of Communication in Therapy

The use of the telephone for counseling introduces some distance into the therapist-client relationship. This distance can be present in other situations. Therapy and counseling can be conducted by letter, by computer, by e-mail, by tape recorder, and by television (Lester, 1977a). In each of these situations, some of the cues available to the face-to-face therapist are removed.

As is the case in telephone counseling, Lester noted that all of these situations affect the status of the client and the therapist because the client can more easily "tune out" or ignore the therapist. In a case using television and telephone for counseling, Nathan et al. (1968) made it necessary for both the client and the therapist to press a key at a reasonable rate in order to keep the sound and picture clear. If either reduced the rate of key-pressing, the picture and sound of the other faded.

In these situations, greater anonymity is possible, transference is likely to be different, and openness affected. In some of these situations, the tempo of the psychotherapy is slowed down, and this can have advantages for the client.

Lowinger and Huston (1955) had clients and therapists sit in different rooms and communicate simply by sound. The psychotherapy was judged to be effective, and eight of the clients developed a transference relationship with the psychotherapist. However, the transference was not as intense as usually found, and none of the clients used it to facilitate their resistance. Two patients walked around during the sessions, and one reported that she found it easier to concentrate on her problems without the psychotherapist being physically present.

Restricting the cues available to the client and the therapist is not new. After all, traditional psychoanalysis, by placing the analyst out of sight behind the client, restricted the visual cues for both. The traditional Roman Catholic confessional also restricted visual cues.

Issues Raised by Telephone Hotlines

The use of telephone counseling in crisis intervention and hotline services has raised several important issues, such as the selection, training, and evaluation of telephone counselors.

Counselor Selection

A few telephone crisis intervention services use trained professional counselors, but the majority use nonprofessional volunteers as counselors. Although psychological tests have been explored as possible screening instruments, including the California Psychological Inventory (King et al., 1980) and the Rokeach Value Survey (Mahoney & Pechura, 1980), most services rely on an interview and the volunteer's performance during training and early days as a counselor to select out poor counselors.

Training and Supervision

The training programs for nonprofessional volunteers typically involve 20 to 30 hours of classroom time. Occasional studies have explored whether a few hours devoted, for example, to empathy training, do indeed raise the level of empathic responding in counselors (Frauenfelder & Frauenfelder, 1984), but few studies have compared and contrasted alternative styles and content for training programs.

Losee et al. (1988) found that training for improved technical effectiveness in counselors improved the resolution of the problem for the caller but did not improve the caller's satisfaction with the call. Training for improved clinical effect resulted in the reverse, increasing caller satisfaction but leading to no improvement in problem resolution. More research like this would provide useful suggestions for improving the content of training programs for volunteers.

Walfish and Gesten (2008) discussed issues involved in supervising paraprofessionals in general, including those who work for crisis intervention services.

Staff Turnover and Burnout

Counselors in crisis intervention services often find the stress level high and, as a result experience, burnout and quit working at the service (Baron & Cohen, 1981; Cyr & Dowrick, 1991). Roberts and Camasso (1994) surveyed over 100 services and found that MSW-level social workers had the highest rate of turnover and that certain types of callers (such as child abuse victims and alcoholics) were especially stressful for counselors. Mishara and Giroux (1993) found that the stress level of volunteers was predicted by experience as a counselor, the urgency of the calls, and inappropriate coping mechanisms on the part of the counselor. As a result of these problems, some centers have set up special programs to assist their volunteers in coping with burnout in an effort to reduce the turnover of staff. Kinzel and Nanson (2000) have described education and debriefing strategies for coping with staff burnout and reducing staff turnover.

Who Uses the Service?

Watson et al. (2006) studied over 90,000 callers to Lifeline Australia, a national 24/7 telephone counseling service and found that only a small proportion of callers were in need of urgent suicide and crisis intervention. Only 2.6% of the callers had suicidal ideation. Lifeline had become a generalist service providing general social support. Bryant (1998) has described the calls made to a Vietnam veteran's telephone counseling service.

Larkin et al. (2011) studied who *would* call a suicide hotline by asking a random-digit-dial sample what they would do if they knew someone who was suicidal – call 911, call a suicide hotline, talk to family, call a psychiatrist, or go to an emergency room. Calling a suicide hotline was more likely for younger people, women, European Americans, those with a high school education or beyond, wealthier people (incomes > $30,000), those with medical insurance, and those living in the United States for more than 15 years. Larkin et al. noted that messages about suicide hotlines need to be tailored for specific populations if the service wants to increase the likelihood that they would use a suicide hotline.

Problem Callers

There are certain types of callers who cause counselors particular difficulties. Walfish (1983) found that some counselors found suicidal callers and obscene callers difficult to handle, and they also found anger, both in themselves and in the caller, a problem. Training programs typically give counselors specific training in handling problem callers, such as the obscene caller (Clark & Borders, 1984; Steley, 1990), the chronic caller (Barmann, 1980), and suicidal callers (Hinson, 1982).

Evaluation

The evaluation of telephone counseling remains the most important issue facing crisis intervention services (Lester, 1994; Chapter 33 in this book), especially since it is often claimed that such services have little effectiveness beyond referral and support (Hornblow, 1986). A recent issue of *Suicide & Life-Threatening Behavior* (2007, volume 37, issue 3, June) contained a special section with two articles by Brian Mishara and his team examining which counselor styles produced the best outcomes, two papers by John Kalafat and Madelyn Gould and their team on evaluating the outcomes of calls from suicidal and nonsuicidal individuals, and a final paper by Thomas Joiner and his team on establishing standards for assessing the suicidal risk in callers. All of these papers focused on the former United States national hotline (1-800-SUICIDE).

Follow-up studies, in which callers are contacted and asked to evaluate the service, typically find that the majority of callers are satisfied with the service (e.g., Gingerich et al., 1988). Tekavcic-Grad and Zavasnik (1987) found that counselors tend to be more critical of themselves than were the callers. Young (1989) asked callers to list helpful behaviors in their counselors, and the callers mentioned listening and feedback, understanding and caring, nonjudgmental support and directiveness. However, directiveness led to the most change in the callers' behavior. Reese et al. (2006) surveyed clients who had received counseling services from a private telephone counseling agency as part of an employee assistance program. Of those responding, 96% said that they would use the service again, and more than half (58%) preferred the telephone contact over face-to-face meetings. The most attractive features of the telephone service were convenience, control, and inhibition (for example, it was less scary).

Cooper et al. (2011) followed up clients who had been seen at an emergency department after an incident of self-harm and who were contacted after discharge by telephone, letters, and crisis cards. This follow-up was seen as a gesture of caring and alleviated feelings of loneliness. Contact from mental health specialists was preferred, preferably by telephone initially, although letters were helpful later.

A common technique for evaluating counselor performance is to have an actor make scripted calls to the center (Davies, 1982; Bryant & Harvey, 2000) or to listen in to actual calls (directly or from tape recordings) (Bonneson & Hartsough, 1987). For example, in a study where observers listened to actual calls, Mishara and Daigle (1992) found that the most common responses made by counselors were *acceptance*, followed by *orientation-investigation* (asking direct questions). Fourteen percent of the callers were judged to be less depressed by the end of the call, and some problem-resolution was present in 68% of the calls.

Bryant and Harvey (2000) used scripted calls to evaluate a telephone crisis intervention service for veterans and found that many of the volunteers had good counseling skills but lacked knowledge of the specific needs of veterans, such as post-traumatic stress and common veteran terminology. This supports those who argue that "like counseling like" is preferable.

Research

Research into hotlines is growing, exploring many issues. Some examples are presented in this section.

Who Volunteers

Paterson et al. (2009) compared students who volunteered for a hotline with students who did not and found that volunteers had higher levels of empathy and obtained higher Agreeable scores on the Big Five personality dimensions, but did not differ in mental health symptoms (in themselves or in family members).

Who Calls, Why and When?

Barber et al. (2004) explored gender differences in the themes presented by callers to a helpline. Young men referred to relationship breakdown more than young women, and men spoke of material hardship more. Women reported being victims of abuse more and referred to interpersonal and family problems.

Kolloerstrom and Steffert (2003) found that calls from women to a crisis-call center increased during the period of the full moon, but calls by men decreased. The proportion of calls from men increased on weekends.

Conclusions

Telephone therapy can be useful for particular types of clients and for many clients at some point during their therapy. Therapy by telephone has unique features which may be useful in helping clients make therapeutic progress.

Therapists should, therefore, give thought to how the telephone might be incorporated as a regular and planned part of the treatment program for some clients.

REFERENCES

Anon. (1972). Sex counseling over the telephone. *Sexual Behavior, 2*(8), 22–25.

Antonioni, D. T. (1973). A field study comparison of counselor empathy, concreteness and client self-exploration in face-to-face and telephone counseling during the first and second interviews. *Dissertation Abstracts International, 34B*, 866.

Aronson, J. K. (Ed.). (2000). *Use of the telephone in psychotherapy.* Northvale, NJ: Jason Aronson.

Baker, C. D., Emmison, M., & Firth, A. (2005). *Calling for help.* Amsterdam, The Netherlands: John Benjamins.

Barber, J. G., Blackman, E. K., Talbot, C., & Saebel, J. (2004). The themes expressed in suicide calls to a telephone help line. *Social Psychiatry & Psychiatric Epidemiology, 39*, 121–125.

Barmann, B. C. (1980). Therapeutic management of chronic callers to a suicide prevention center. *Journal of Community Psychology, 8*, 45–48.

Baron, A., & Cohen, R. B. (1982). Helping telephone counselors cope with burnout. *Personnel & Guidance Journal, 60*, 508–510.

Battin, D., Arkin, A., & Wiener, A. (1975). Telephone intervention in the therapy of bereaved families. *Journal of Thanatology, 3*, 43–47.

Beebe, J. E. (1968). Allowing the patient to call home. *Psychotherapy, 5*, 18–20.

Benedetti, P., Zaccarelli, M., Giulani, M., & di Fabio, M. (1989). The Italian AIDS hot-line. *AIDS Care, 1*, 145–152.

Bonneson, M. E., & Hartsough, D. M. (1987). Development of the Crisis Call Out come Rating Scale. *Journal of Consulting & Clinical Psychology, 55*, 612–614.

Broadhead, R. S. (1986). Directing intervention from afar: The telephone dynamics of managing acute poisonings. *Journal of Health & Social Behavior, 27*, 303–319.

Bryant, R. A. (1998). An analysis of calls to a Vietnam veteran's telephone counseling service. *Journal of Traumatic Stress, 11*, 589–596.

Bryant, R. A., & Harvey, A. G. (2000). Telephone crisis intervention skills. *Crisis, 21*, 90–94.

Chen, H., Mishara, B. L., & Liu, X. X. (2010). A pilot study of mobile telephone message interventions with suicide attempters in China. *Crisis, 31*, 109–112.

Chiles, J. (1974). A practical therapeutic use of the telephone. *American Journal of Psychiatry, 131*, 1030–1031.

Clark, S. P., & Borders, L. D. (1984). Approaches to sexual and sexually abusive callers. *Crisis Intervention, 13*, 14–24.

Cole, W. (2000). The (un)therapists. *Time, 156*(16), 95.

Combs, D. C. (2007). Mental health interventions by telephone with Katrina survivors. *Journal of Health Care for the Poor & Underserved, 18*, 271–276.

Connell, C. M., & Smyer, M. A. (1986). Telephone conference networks for training in mental health. *Gerontologist, 26*, 339–341.

Cooper, J., Hunter, C., Owen-Smith, A., Gunnell, D., Donovan, J., Hawton, K., & Kapur, N. (2011). "Well it's like someone at the other end cares about you." *General Hospital Psychiatry, 33*, 166–176.

Cooperman, S., & Schafer, D. W. (1983). Hypnotherapy over the telephone. *American Journal of Clinical Hypnosis, 25*, 277–279.

Cyr, C., & Dowrick, P. W. (1991). Burnout in crisis line volunteers. *Administration & Policy in Mental Health, 18*, 343–354.

Daniel, L. S. (1973). A study of the influence of introversion-extraversion and neuroticism on telephone counseling versus face-to-face counseling. *Dissertation Abstracts International, 34B*, 2300.

Davidoff, M., & Katz, R. (1985). Automated telephone therapy for improving auditory comprehension in aphasic adults. *Cognitive Rehabilitation, 3*(2), 26–28.

Davies, P. G. (1982). The functioning of British counseling hotlines. *British Journal of Guidance & Counseling, 10*, 195–199.

Dubren, R. (1977). Self-reinforcement by recorded telephone messages to maintain non-smoking behavior. *Journal of Consulting & Clinical Psychology, 45*, 358–360.

Evans, M. O., Morgan, G., & Hayward, A. (2000). Crisis telephone consultation for deliberate self-harm patients. *Journal of Mental Health, 9*, 155–164.

Evans, R. L., Fox, H. R., Pritzl, D. O., & Halar, E. M. (1984). Group treatment of physically disabled adults by telephone. *Social Work in Health Care, 9*(3), 77–84.

Evans, R. L., & Jaureguy, B. M. (1981a). Group therapy by phone. *Social Work in Health Care, 7*(2), 79–90.

Evans, R. L., & Jaureguy, B. M. (1981b). Telephone counseling with visually im-paired adults. *International Journal of Rehabilitation Research, 1981, 4*, 550–552.

Evans, R. L., Werkhoven, W., & Fox, H. R. (1982). Treatment of social isolation and loneliness in a sample of visually impaired elderly persons. *Psychological Reports, 51*, 103–108.

Fergus, E. O. (1979). Telephone change agentry in the diffusion of a program for the elderly. *Journal of Community Psychology, 7*, 270–277.

Frauenfelder, K., & Frauenfelder, J. (1984). The effect of brief empathy training for student hotline volunteers. *Crisis Intervention, 13*, 96–103.

Gingerich, W. J., Gurney, R. J., & Wirtz, T. S. (1988). How helpful are hotlines? *Social Casework, 69*, 634–639.

Goud, N. (1985). Dial-a-need hotlines. *Journal of Humanistic Education & Development, 24*(2), 76–80.

Gravitz, M. A. (1983). Early use of the telephone and recordings in hypnosis. *American Journal of Clinical Hypnosis, 25*, 280–282.

Grumet, G. W. (1979). Telephone therapy. *American Journal of Orthopsychiatry, 49*, 574–584.

Guerney, L. F. (1991). A survey of self-supports and social supports of self-care children. *Elementary School Guidance & Counseling, 25*, 243–254.

Hightower, N. A., & Dimalanta, A. S. (1980). Ma Bell. *Family Therapy, 7*, 147–151.

Hinson, J. (1982). Strategies for suicide intervention by telephone. *Suicide & Life-Threatening Behavior, 12*, 176–184.

Hochstadt, N. J., & Trybula, J. (1980). Reducing missed initial appointments in a community mental health center. *Journal of Community Psychology, 8*, 261–265.

Hornblow, A. R. (1986). The evaluation and effectiveness of telephone counseling services. *Hospital & Community Psychiatry, 37*, 731–733.

Hymer, S. M. (1984). The telephone session and the telephone between sessions. *Psychotherapy in Private Practice, 2*(3), 51–65.

Iscoe, I., Hill, F. E., Harmon, M., & Coffman, D. (1979). Telephone counseling via cassette tapes. *Journal of Counseling Psychology, 26*, 166–168.

Jaureguy, B. M., & Evans, R. L. (1983). Short term group counseling of visually impaired people by telephone. *Journal of Visual Impairment & Blindness, 77*(4), 150–152.

King, G. D., McGowen, R., Doonan, R., & Schweibert, D. (1980). The selection of paraprofessional telephone counselors using the California Psychological Inventory. *Journal of Community Psychology, 8*, 495–501.

Kinzel, A., & Nanson, J. (2000). Education and debriefing. *Crisis, 21*, 126–134.

Kolloerstrom, N., & Steffert, B. (2003). Sex difference in response to stress by lunar month. *BMC Psychiatry, 3*, #20, 1–8.

Kroger, W. S. (1969). Hypnotherapy for intractable post-surgical hiccups. *American Journal of Clinical Hypnosis, 12*, 1–4.

Krysinska, K., & De Leo, D. (2007). Telecommunication and suicide prevention. *Omega, 55*, 237–253.

Larkin, G. L., Rivera, H., Xu, H., Rincon, E., & Beautrais, A. L. (2011). Community responses to a suicidal crisis. *Suicide & Life-Threatening Behavior, 41*, 79–86.

Latzer, Y., & Gilat, I. (2000). Calls to the Israeli hotline from individuals who suffer from eating disorders. *Eating Disorders, 8*, 31–42.

Leff, J. A. (1969). An initial induction of hypnosis by telephone with treatment of anxiety. In D. Stern (Ed.), *Psychotherapy in nonpsychiatric specialities*, pp. 237–241. Springfield, IL: Charles C Thomas.

Lester, D. (1973). Telephone counseling and the masturbator. *Clinical Social Work Journal, 1*, 257–260.

Lester, D. (1977a). *The use of alternative modes for communication in psychotherapy.* Springfield, IL: Charles C Thomas.

Lester, D. (1977b). The use of the telephone in counseling and crisis intervention. In I. de Sola Pool (Ed.), *The social impact of the telephone*, pp. 454–472. Cambridge, MA: MIT Press.

Lester, D. (1994). L' efficacite des centres de prevention du suicide. *Santé Mental au Quebec, 19*(2), 15–24.

Lester, D. (1995). Counseling by telephone. *Crisis Intervention & Time-Limited Treatment, 2*, 57–69.

Lester, D., & Brockopp, G. W. (1973). *Crisis intervention and counseling by telephone.* Springfield, IL: Charles C Thomas.

Losee, N., Auerbach, S. M., & Parham, I. (1988). Effectiveness of a peer counselor hotline for the elderly. *Journal of Community Psychology, 16*, 428–436.

Lowinger, P., & Huston, P. (1955). Transference and the physical presence of the physician. *Journal of Nervous & Mental Disease, 121*, 250–256.

MacKinnon, R. A., & Michaels, R. (1973). The role of the telephone in the psychiatric interview. In D. Lester & G. W. Brockopp (Eds.), *Crisis intervention and counseling by telephone*, pp. 58–76. Springfield, IL: Charles C Thomas.

Madoc-Jones, I., Warren, E., Ashdown-Lambert, J., Williams, E., & Parry, O. (2007). Planned telephone support for disadvantaged parents in North Wales. *Child & Family Social Work, 12*, 316–325.

Mahoney, J., & Pechura, C. M. (1980). Values and volunteers. *Psychological Reports, 47*, 1007–1012.

Marasinghe, R. B., Edirippulige, S., Kavanagh, D., Smith, A., & Jiffry, M. T. M. (2012). Effect of mobile-based psychotherapy in suicide prevention. *Journal of Telemedicine & Telecare*, in press.

Masi, D., & Freedman, M. (2001). The use of telephone an on line technology in assessment, counseling, and therapy. *Employee Assistance Quarterly, 16*(3), 49–63.

McFall, S. L., Michiner, A., Rubin, D., & Flay, B. R. (1993). The effects and use of maintenance newsletters in a smoking cessation program. *Addictive Behaviors, 18*, 151–158.

McGlynn, F. D. (1980). Successful treatment of anorexia nervosa with self-monitoring and long distance praise. *Journal of Behavior Therapy & Experimental Psychiatry, 11*, 283–286.

McNamee, G., O'Sullivan, G., Lelliott, P., & Marks, I. (1989). Telephone-guided treatment for housebound agoraphobics with panic disorder. *Behavior Therapy, 20*, 491–497.

Meyersberg, G. (1985). The use of the telephone in psychiatric rehabilitation. *Nordisk Psykiatrisk Tidsskrift, 39*, 185–188.

Miller, W. B. (1973). The telephone in outpatient psychotherapy. *American Journal of Psychotherapy, 27*, 15–26.

Mishara, B. L., & Daigle, M. (1992). The effectiveness of telephone interventions by suicide prevention workers. *Canada's Mental Health, 40*(3), 24–29.

Mishara, B. L., & Daigle, M. (2001). Helplines and crisis intervention services. In D. Lester (Ed.) *Suicide prevention: Resources for the millennium*, pp. 153–171. Philadelphia: Brunner-Routledge.

Mishara, B. L., & Giroux, G. (1993). The relationship between coping strategies and perceived stress in telephone intervention volunteers at a suicide prevention center. *Suicide & Life-Threatening Behavior, 23*, 221–229.

Moreland, H., & Grier, M. (1986). Telephone consultation in the care of older adults. *Geriatric Nursing, 7*(1), 28–30.

Murray, F. S. (1967). A preliminary investigation of anonymous nuisance telephone calls to females. *Psychological Record, 17*, 395–400.

Nathan, P., Smith, S., & Rossi, A. (1968). Experimental analysis of a brief psychotherapeutic contact. *American Journal of Orthopsychiatry, 38*, 482–492.

Nelson, E. L., Wenzel, L. B., Osann, K., Dogan-Ates, A., Chantana, N., Reina-Patton, A., Laust, A. K., Nishimoto, K. P., Chicz-DeMet, A., du Pont, N., & Monk, B. J. (2008). Stress, immunity, and cervical cancer. *Clinical Cancer Research, 14*, 2111–2118.

Newcomb, A. F., Chenkin, C. G., Card, A. L., & Ialongo, N. S. (1984). Parent-line. *Professional Psychology, 15*, 75–81.

Noy, B. (1992). The open line for students in the Gulf War in Israel. *School Psychology International, 13*, 207–227.

Ossip-Klein, D. J., Shapiro, R. M., & Stiggins, J. (1984). Freedom Line. *Addictive Behaviors, 9*, 227–230.

Owens, H. E. (1970). Hypnosis by phone. *American Journal of Clinical Hypnosis, 13*, 57–60.

Paterson, H., Reniers, R., & Vollm, B. (2009). Personality types and mental health experiences of those who volunteer for helplines. *British Journal of Guidance & Counselling, 37*, 459–471.

Pierce, R. L., & Pierce, L. H. (1985). Analysis of sexual abuse hotline reports. *Child Abuse & Neglect, 9*, 37–45.

Praderas, K., & MacDonald, M. L. (1986). Telephone conversational skills training with socially isolated, impaired nursing home residents. *Journal of Applied Behavior Analysis, 19*, 337–348.

Ragle, J., & Krone, K. (1985). Extending orientation. *Journal of College Student Personnel, 26*(1), 80–81.

Ranan, W., & Blodgett, A. (1983). Using telephone therapy for unreachable clients. *Social Casework, 64*(1), 39–44.

Reese, R. J., Conoley, C. W., & Brossart, D. F. (2006). The attractiveness of telephone counseling. *Journal of Counseling & Development, 84*, 54–60.

Rickert, V. C., & Turner, J. E. (1978). Through the looking glass. *Social Casework, 59*(3), 131–137.

Roach, D., Reardon, R., Alexander, J., & Cloudman, D. (1983). Career counseling by telephone. *Journal of College Student Personnel, 24*(1), 71–76.

Robertiello, R. C. (1972). Telephone sessions. *Psychoanalytic Review, 59*, 633–634.

Roberts, A. R., & Camasso, M. J. (1994). Staff turnover at crisis intervention units and centers. *Crisis Intervention & Time-Limited Treatment, 1*, 1–9.

Rosenbaum, M. (1974). Continuation of psychotherapy by "long distance" telephone. *International Journal of Psychoanalytic Psychotherapy, 3*, 483–485.

Rosenbaum, M. (1977). Premature interruption of psychotherapy. *American Journal of Psychiatry, 134*, 200–202.

Rosenfield, M., & Smillie, E. (1998). Group counseling by telephone. *British Journal of Guidance & Counselling, 26*, 11–19.

Ruben, H. L. (1986). Reflections of a radio psychiatrist. *Hospital & Community Psychiatry, 37*, 934–936.

Sanders, P., & Rosenfield, M. (1998). Counselling at a distance. *British Journal of Guidance & Counseling, 26*, 5–10.

Saul, L. J. (1951). A note on the telephone as a technical aid. *Psychoanalytic Quarterly, 20*, 287–290.

Schmidt, C. M., & Austin, M. J. (2004). Utilizing hotline services to sustain employment. In M. J. Austin (Ed.), *Changing welfare services*, pp. 143–152. New York: Haworth.

Schmitz, M. B., & Mickelson, D. J. (1972). Hotline drug counseling and Rogerian methods. *Personnel & Guidance Journal, 50*, 357–362.

Schnelle, J. F., Gendrich, J., McNees, M. P., Hanna, J., & Thomas, M. M. (1979). Evaluation of outpatient client progress. *Journal of Community Psychology, 7*, 111–117.

Shapiro, R. M., Ossip-Klein, D. J., Gerrity, E. T., & Stiggins, J. (1985–1986). Perceived helpfulness of messages on a community-based telephone support service for ex-smokers. *International Journal of the Addictions, 20*, 1837–1847.

Sheerin, D. F. (1994). Telephone consultancy in adolescent psychiatry. *Irish Journal of Psychological Medicine, 11*, 15–20.

Shepard, P. (1987). Telephone therapy. *Clinical Social Work Journal, 15*, 56–65.

Smith, C. H. (1978). The effects of telephone prompting and programmed homework in behavioral treatment of the obese. *Dissertation Abstracts International, 39B*, 3007–3008.

Spevak, P., & Richars, C. S. (1980). Enhancing the durability of treatment effects. *Cognitive Therapy & Research, 4*, 251–258.

Stanton, E. E. (1978). Hypnotherapy at a distance through use of the telephone. *American Journal of Clinical Hypnosis, 20*, 278–281.

Steley, J. R. (1990). Sexually abusive callers in the context of crisis agencies. *Australian Journal of Marriage & Family, 11*(1), 19–27.

Taussig, J. E., & Freeman, E. W. (1988). The next best thing to being there. *American Journal of Orthopsychiatry, 58*, 418–427.

Taylor, I. (1984). Self-exposure instructions by telephone with a severe agoraphobic. *Behavioural Psychotherapy, 12*, 68–72.

Tekavcic-Grad, O., & Zavasnik, A. (1987). Comparison between counselors' and callers' expectations and their realization on the telephone crisis line. *Crisis, 8*, 162–177.

Vaiva, G., Durocq, F., Meyer, P., Mathieu, D., Philippe, A., Libersa, C., & Goudemand, M. (2006). Effect of telephone contact on further suicide attempts in patients discharged from an emergency department. *British Medical Journal, 332*, 1241–1245.

Walfish, S. (1983). Crisis telephone counselors' views of clinical interaction situations. *Community Mental Health Journal, 19*, 219–226.

Walfish, S., & Gesten, E. (2008). Supervision of paraprofessional human service workers. In A. K. Hess, K. D. Hess & T. H. Hess (Eds.), *Psychotherapy supervision*, pp. 246–262. Hoboken, NJ: John Wiley.

Watson, R. J., McDonald, J., & Pearce, D. C. (2006). An exploration of national calls to Lifeline Australia. *British Journal of Guidance & Counselling, 34*, 471–482.

Weinberger, M., Hiner, S. L., & Tierney, W. M. (1986). Improving functional status in arthritis. *Social Science & Medicine, 23*, 899–904.

Weissman-Frisch, N., Crowell, F. A., Bellamy, G. T., & Bostwick, D. (1983). A telephone interview technique for assessing living environments and lifestyles of retarded adults in community residential facilities. *Behavioral Assessment, 5*, 219–230.

Wenk, R., Alegre, C., & Diaz, C. (1983). Palliative care hotline in Argentina. *Journal of Pain & Symptom Management, 8*, 123–124.

Whittaker, R., Merry, S., Stasiak, K., McDowell, H., Doherty, I., Shepherd, M., Dorey, E., Parag, V., Ameratunga, S., & Rodgers, A. (2012). MEMO – A mobile phone depression prevention intervention for adolescents. *Journal of Medical Internet Research, 14*(1), e13.

Williams, T. (1971). Telephone therapy. *Crisis Intervention, 3*, 39–42.
Wolf, A., Schwartz, E., McCarthy, G., & Goldberg, I. (1969). Training in psychoanalysis in groups without face-to-face contact. *American Journal of Psychotherapy, 23*, 488–494.
Young, R. (1989). Helpful behavior in the crisis center call. *Journal of Community Psychology, 17*, 70–77.

Chapter 2

A SURVEY OFTELEPHONE COUNSELING SERVICES

DAVID LESTER

One of the first surveys of telephone counseling services was conducted by McGee, Richard, and Bercun (1973). McGee et al. did more than simply survey the services existing at that time. He also identified and discussed some of the issues related to setting up a telephone counseling service, and we will follow his format in this chapter.

Results of Three Surveys

McGee et al. surveyed 19 services in the southeastern part of the United States. McGee did not simply send these services a questionnaire for them to complete. Instead, he had members of his team call the centers and time how long it took before they were talking to a counselor. He found that some centers did not take calls directly but, instead, had an answering service answer the call and request the client's telephone number. The counseling service would then call the client back. When the team member had contacted a counselor, the team member would indicate that this was not an emergency call but rather a study of the services. The team member would then ask a series of questions about the service.

McGee identified eight different systems:

1. Calls are answered directly by the crisis counselor.

2. Calls are answered by an operator or receptionist in the center who then switches the call to a crisis counselor.

3. The call is answered by a commercial answering service which than forwards the call directly to the crisis worker.

4. The call is answered by a commercial service which takes the client's telephone number and notifies the crisis worker who then calls the client.

5. The call is taken by staff at a different agency who notify the crisis worker who then calls the client back.

6. The call is taken by staff in another agency who then give the client the crisis worker's telephone number for the client to call.

7. A recording informs the client of the telephone number of an available crisis worker.

8. There is no answer!

Some services used different systems for different times of the day and different days of the week. McGee et al. found that the mean time to get to a counselor for the eight systems ranged from six seconds for type 1 to 17 minutes and 35 seconds for type 5. McGee argued that crisis agencies should handle their own calls and not give this responsibility to other agencies, commercial or noncommercial.

Roberts (1970) sent a questionnaire to 28 suicide prevention agencies with emergency telephone numbers listed in telephone directories. The typical agency had a Board of Directors, and many had also Advisory Boards with members chosen for their expertise or position in the mental health field (such as psychiatrists, hospital administrators, and police chiefs). The typical agency had a director-coordinator, most commonly a mental health professional, but clergy and lay directors were occasionally found. The typical agency had a lack of bureaucratic structure, probably because of both the lack of well-developed hierarchical relationships among the staff and the use of volunteers.

All of the agencies maintained a 24/7/365 telephone service,[7] and most used a standard crisis intervention protocol for handling clients. The agencies publicized their availability using newspapers and magazines, public service announcements on television and radio, talks and speeches by the staff, the telephone directory, booklets and professional publications, and seminars for professionals in related fields (mental health and criminal justice). Less commonly used were information cards circulated among the public, church bulletins and newsletters, letters to community agencies, film specials, and placards in buses. Most of the agencies wanted to expand their services rather than create new services, but few carried out any sound evaluation of their services other than reporting the volume of clients handled during the year.

Roberts (1995) carried out a survey of 107 crisis intervention centers in the United States in 1986 to 1987. The most common objectives of these centers were suicide prevention, crisis intervention, referral, and community education. Less common were handling acute psychiatric emergencies, family violence intervention, and rape crisis work.

---

[7] A service operating 24 hours a day, seven days a week, every day of the year.

About a tenth did not provide full 24/7/365 coverage, but 55% offered face-to-face counseling and 33% had set up outreach services. About a half of the services were established in 1968–1970 and one-third in 1974–1987. Thirty-seven percent of the services were autonomous; only 11 % were housed in a hospital. The most common methods for informing the community were public information talks, newspaper ads and articles, radio announcements, television appearances, brochures and fliers, and telephone directory listings. The most common problems they handled were, in order, depression, substance abuse, suicide attempts, marital problems, and behavioral crises. All but one of the services surveyed provided orientation and in-service training for their staff. The training programs ranged from two hours to 112 hours, with an average of 38 hours.

The agency budgets ranged from $5,800 to $5 million, with funds coming most often from the United Way or from local governments. Other sources of funds were private donations, private foundation grants and, least commonly, client payments.

Roberts noted that few agencies surveyed were able to deal with the homeless, victims of violent crimes, or accident victims. The most common administrative problems reported by the agencies were insufficient funding and insufficient staff to handle the volume of clients.

International Coordination

Lester (2001) invited the directors of three international organizations to which telephone crisis centers can belong to describe the purpose and functions of their organizations.

Befrienders International

Befrienders International (BI) originated with The Samaritans, a crisis intervention service started in the United Kingdom 50 years ago by the Reverend Chad Varah (Scott, 2001).[8] It is now an umbrella organization with centers in 40 nations and over 40,000 trained volunteers. These volunteers provide about five million hours of care each year, which if paid for with the minimum wage in the United States would cost over 35 million dollars.

In addition to providing suicide prevention services, BI also provides training workshops and international conferences. As an organization, BI seeks to

---

[8] The Samaritans, Upper Mill, Kingston Road, Ewell, Surrey KT17 2AF, UK. The website is www.befrienders.org.

promote awareness of suicide and the means of prevention through the efforts of volunteers, to promote life-coping skills that will prevent suicide, to deploy services in regions where no services presently exist, to stimulate networks in the field of suicide prevention, and to develop and support existing suicide prevention services.

In recent years, BI has developed services to respond to disasters, such as the crash of a Pan Am passenger plane over Lockerbie (Scotland) in 1988 and the earthquake in Osaka (Japan) in 1995. BI has developed a program called Reaching Young Europe, which seeks to provide children with coping skills. BI has also utilized the Internet for crisis intervention by setting up an e-mail crisis intervention service.

The International Federation of Telephonic Emergency Services

The International Federation of Telephonic Emergency Services (IFOTES) grew out of efforts by Raynald Martin (who had started La Main Tendue in Geneva, Switzerland, in the late 1950s) to support other telephone counseling services in Europe (Bezencon, 2001).[9] Regular conferences are held, and a central office is located in Switzerland.

IFOTES has plans to provide more publications and pamphlets which would be useful to members, to establish services in other nations, especially South America, and to enable branches to exchange knowledge with one another.

Lifeline International

Lifeline began in Sydney, Australia, in 1964, but quickly became an international movement, with national committees in nations whose function is to establish crisis intervention services in their communities (Dominish, 2001). In some nations, the services carry the name Contact. Although Lifeline came out of a religious situation (the founder of the service in Sydney was a Methodist minister) and the sponsors of the services are frequently religious organizations (such as churches), clients are not exposed to any particular religious orientation.

Lifeline has established training manuals and organizational guidelines. In the future, Lifeline hopes to establish standards of good practice and to coordinate with national strategies to prevent suicide.

---

[9] IFOTES, 6 rue du Nord, 1180 Rolle, Switzerland. www.ifotes.org.

Issues

Cost

The first issue identified by McGee et al. was the cost. Providing maximum coverage for a telephone counseling service (24 hours a day, seven days a week, 365 days a year) does not necessarily entail additional cost if volunteers are used for the actual crisis intervention. The major cost is the office where people can be on duty, rent, office supplies, and basic utility services.

In McGee's 1973 survey, many centers felt unable to provide 24/7/365 coverage. These centers were forced to use an answering service which entails additional costs or an answering machine to inform callers when counselors would be on duty.

Staffing

A second issue is staffing. The majority of crisis intervention centers used, and still use, volunteer nonprofessionals, often called paraprofessionals. Providing 24/7/365 coverage, therefore, can require a volunteer pool of 50 to 100 volunteers. Since drop-out rates are sometimes high, this also entails continual recruitment and training programs to replenish the depleted pool of volunteers.

Some centers use professionals to answer calls during the daytime and volunteers in the evenings, at nights, and on weekends. Other centers prefer to use their professional staff for seeing clients in face-to-face counseling (if the center has a walk-in clinic) and for training and supervision of the volunteers. McGee et al. found some centers, however, that preferred to use the professionals to cover the "more serious" calls typically received at night and to use volunteers during the day.

Location

It is better to provide an office where the crisis interveners can take calls. This is especially important in the evenings, at nights, and on weekends. Calls can easily be switched to the homes of the crisis interveners, but there is a psychological difference in taking a call at home from taking a call in an office. At home, counselors are in a relaxed, nonworking environment. Crisis calls from clients can easily be seen, not necessarily consciously, as an unwelcome intrusion into the counselor's "safe" space. This perspective can influence how the counselor responds to the caller, usually in a counterproductive way.

On the other hand, for a volunteer to work, sometimes alone, in an office at night can be fear-provoking. At the center where I worked, even professionals experienced fear at night when working alone. One of our female social workers, taking calls alone one night, experienced acute anxiety when she had to respond to an obscene caller. She went and checked that all the doors to the office were locked, and she felt much more violated than had she received such a call during the day when other staff members were present. Eventually, at our center, the volume of calls quickly required the presence of at least two counselors at all times, and the presence of a co-worker alleviated this problem. It also helped to keep counselors awake and alert during the night, a time when volunteers, who have typically had a normal work day before coming to the center for the night shift, sometimes have to fight falling sleep. Before we were able to have two counselors on duty at all times, we did have one counselor fall asleep *during* a call with a chronic caller.

Record Keeping

Centers need to collect and store information on callers. Many clients call repeatedly, and it is crucial to be able to access information on these clients so that a treatment plan can be formulated which different counselors can implement. This is possible even if clients use pseudonyms, for the pseudonym can be used to identify the client.

Some clients present special problems. We had frequent calls from a young girl with schizophrenia who was a chronic wrist-cutter. The case file told counselors to talk to her about superficial matters for five to ten minutes and, when she was calmer, to urge her to try to go to sleep. Under no circumstances were the counselors to inquire about and discuss her fantasies or dreams, for this would in all likelihood increase her distress and probability of further wrist-cutting that night.

In other cases, we had chronic callers for whom we had devised treatment plans to help them improve their situation. It was imperative that counselors coordinated their approaches to these chronic callers and responded in a consistent manner.

Naming the Service

Berman (1998) noted that the name "Suicide Prevention Center" was rapidly disappearing. In 1969, a survey of agencies dealing with suicidal clients identified 53 out of 121 agencies with the name Suicide Prevention Center (44%). In 1997, the American Association of Suicidology directory of such services identified only 36 of 850 agencies using that name (4%).

Berman suggested that the term suicide was used in agency names in the past to galvanize the community, to attract volunteers, and to raise funds. Over time, however, agencies were able to justify funding with the volume of clients that they served. It was also feared that using the word suicide in the name of the agency might deter nonsuicidal clients from calling.

Some directors of services have noted that occasional clients feign suicidal motivation and behavior to justify calling and that many services want to address the problems of nonsuicidal clients as well as suicidal clients. Other service directors, however, feel that agencies specializing in suicide were needed in communities and that the volume of calls received by those agencies was typically great enough to justify their specialization.

Mishara and Daigle (2001) have noted that there is no research on whether it is better to focus the service specifically on suicide or not. Political and funding constraints should not also win out over the needs of the target populations.

Generic Versus Specific Lines

Many agencies have telephone crisis intervention services which seek to handle all types of crises, while others, more and more as time goes by, are set up to service particular types of clients. The clients may differ in problems (such as drug abuse, suicide, and sexual assault) or personal characteristics (such as lines for teenagers or for seniors, lines for homosexuals, and lines for women).

Typically, a telephone service for a specific clientele is set up when there is community interest in that particular clientele and when there are funds available, and they typically receive a high volume of calls.

At our center in Buffalo, at one point, we had four lines (suicide prevention, problems in living, teen hotline, and drug hotline) with four different telephone numbers. However, all calls went to the same counselors, who answered each call with the appropriate words depending which of ten lines lit up on their telephone. This is rare. Most services have separate funding, administrations, and counselors.

Generic Versus Specific Counselors

Can any counselor handle any kind of crisis and any kind of caller? For some mental health professionals, the answer to this question is "Yes" while for others, it is "No." Some services have "like counseling like," such as women's hotlines where the staff are women or gay hotlines where the staff are all gay. Others maintain that good crisis interveners can deal with any kind of client.

Standards

If services are advertised and the public encouraged to use them, then the centers have a responsibility to provide the services advertised with a high degree of quality. The counselors must be adequately trained and competent, they must be helpful to clients, and clients must be able to gain access to counselors quickly and easily.

At the present time, the American Association of Suicidology (AAS) accredits suicide prevention and crisis services in the United States. AAS has established a set of approved standards which services must meet for accreditation. The services must submit documentation of their services, and they are visited by a team of trained investigators who inspect the services.[10]

At the international level, Befrienders International (known in many nations as The Samaritans), which has established centers in over 40 nations, has annual conferences where staff from centers can meet, and has set up "twinning" programs between centers in different nations whose staff visit each other's center. In this way, Samaritan centers can be assumed to meet standards for providing adequate care.

Impact

Mishara and Daigle (2001) noted that resources are often scarce, and many services compete for limited funds for operation. Thus, services will be increasingly called upon to assess their impact on the community and confirm that they are meeting their stated goals. Services that rely on volunteers and minimal funding from government sources or private charities may be able to avoid formal evaluations and rely solely on reporting the number of clients using their services. But those services that receive private and government funds cannot escape the demands of the funding sources for evaluation to justify continued funding.

Telephone counseling and crisis intervention services must, therefore, clearly formulate and state their goals, and they must explore whether they have met these goals. Are the services effective or ineffective? Do they help all people, or do they harm some? Are some methods of intervention or types of service more effective than others?

---

[10] AAS, 5221 Wisconsin Avenue, NW, Washington DC 20015. The website is www.suicidology.org.

The Changing Population

Mishara and Daigle (2001) note that the elderly today grew up in an era when the use of the telephone was used primarily for business and emergencies, whereas younger adults and the youth today are accustomed to use the telephone for recreational conversation. This younger generation may also be more inclined to make use of counselors and psychotherapists. Therefore, there may be a tremendous increase in the demand for and use of telephone counseling and crisis intervention services, especially as this younger generation ages.

Changing Technology

At the present time, national telephone services are being introduced, often with a toll-free number, and these services may replace the local services. Such national services may be particularly advantageous in regions where local telephone calls are not free and where, therefore, other members of the household can view billing records and see to which people and agencies telephone calls have been placed. Mishara and Daigle point out, however, that such national services may ignore local cultural differences and lack local knowledge and so be less effective than locally-based services. Some national hotlines channel the calls to the crisis intervention center nearest to the caller rather than having a centrally located staff. This may alleviate the objection raised by Mishara and Daigle.

Mishara and Daigle (2001) noted that advances in technology impact telephone counseling services. Caller ID makes telephone counseling less anonymous and less confidential, although it is now possible to block Caller ID in some regions, so that one can make a telephone call and remain anonymous to the other person. Video telephones, when they become more widespread, may compound this problem.

The Internet, with its chat rooms, e-mail, and instant messaging, may also make the telephone obsolete. Later in this book, we explore the use of the Internet for crisis intervention and counseling, and Befrienders International has established a comprehensive service utilizing e-mail.

Should Suicide Prevention Be the Goal?

Lester (1992) argued that there may not be a need for suicide prevention telephone services. He noted that there is good evidence that childhood trauma, such as sexual abuse, greatly increase the likelihood that suicidal tendencies will appear later in life. If this is so, then perhaps suicide prevention efforts should focus on reducing the incidence of such childhood trauma and providing good mental health services for those traumatized. Most suicidal clients also have psychiatric disturbances. Thus, helping the suicidal client may involve treating their psychiatric disturbance.

Lester suggested, therefore, that those concerned with suicide prevention should simply join other mental health agencies in the community working on the basic social and individual problems, such as child abuse and depression, although he proposed this simply to be provocative and encourage debate on this issue.

In a similar vein, Mishara and Daigle (2001) noted that volunteers at telephone crisis intervention services are not equipped to treat those who are psychiatrically disturbed, yet mental health professionals and volunteers rarely communicate directly with one another about coordinating their services or about the care of individual clients. On the other hand, it may be better, Mishara and Daigle argued, that volunteers at telephone counseling services divorce themselves from the mental health profession since there is some stigma associated with the labeling and the techniques used by mental health professionals. The separation of roles also prevents the professionalization of lay volunteers, which may be for the good. However, this issue is one which merits greater debate.

Conclusion

The field needs a new, updated, comprehensive survey of suicide prevention and crisis intervention services in the United States and worldwide. It would be most useful to know the current state of the services provided. Furthermore, there needs to be much more examination of and debate about the issues raised in this chapter concerning the operation of suicide prevention and crisis intervention services. Arguments for and against each approach and each decision need to be fully explored so that services may make more informed choices in the future.

REFERENCES

Berman, A. (1998). Circumlocution office. *Newslink, 24*(3), 3.
Bezencon, E. (2001). The International Federation of Telephonic Emergency Services. In D. Lester (Ed.), *Suicide prevention: Resources for the millennium*, pp. 274–282. Philadelphia: Brunner-Routledge.
Dominish, C. (2001). Lifeline International and suicide. In D. Lester (Ed.), *Suicide prevention: Resources for the millennium*, pp. 282–284. Philadelphia: Brunner-Routledge.

Lester, D. (1992). Is there a need for suicide prevention? *Crisis, 13*, 94.

Lester, D. (Ed.). (2001). *Suicide prevention: Resources for the millennium*. Philadelphia: Brunner-Routledge.

McGee, R. K., Richard, W. C., & Bercun, C. (1973). A survey of telephone answering systems in suicide prevention and crisis intervention agencies. In D. Lester & G. W. Brockopp (Eds.), *Crisis intervention and counseling by telephone*, pp. 24–40. Springfield, IL: Charles C Thomas.

Mishara, N. L., & Daigle, M. (2001). Helplines and crisis intervention services. In D. Lester (Ed.), *Suicide prevention: Resources for the millennium*, pp. 153–171. Philadelphia: Brunner-Routledge.

Roberts, A. R. (1970). An organizational study of suicide prevention agencies in the United States. *Police, 14* (May-June), 64-72.

Roberts, A. R. (1995). Crisis intervention units and centers in the United States. In A. R. Roberts (Ed.), *Crisis intervention and time-limited cognitive treatment*, pp. 54–70. Thousand Oaks, CA: Sage.

Scott, V. (2001). Befrienders International: Volunteer action in preventing suicide. In D. Lester (Ed.), *Suicide prevention: Resources for the millennium*, pp. 265–273. Philadelphia: Brunner-Routledge.

Part II

CRISIS INTERVENTION AND COUNSELING BY TELEPHONE

Chapter 3

THE UNIQUE CONTRIBUTIONS OF TELEPHONE THERAPY

TIM WILLIAMS AND JOHN DOUDS

Most systems of psychotherapy assume that face-to-face interaction is necessary for effective therapy. This assumption is taken for granted as a *sine qua non* for "genuine" therapy. In agency statistics, a face-to-face interview is called therapy, but a telephone conversation is often given the status of a "contact," as if it does not deserve recognition as equivalent to a genuine therapy session. Although a telephone contact is accepted as better than nothing, it is judged to be depersonalization of true therapy.

The purpose of this chapter is to explore the unique contributions of telephone therapy. Our intent is not to attack the supremacy of face-to-face therapy, but rather to heighten an awareness of the unique value of telephone therapy as a treatment dimension useful for particular client life-styles and problems. We believe that telephone therapy provides an added dimension of therapeutic service and deserves recognition as a special way to link certain people with a helping service. The helping service provided by most agencies reaches individuals who are moderately distressed but excludes others whose problems make it difficult for them to seek help. A telephone counseling service provides greater penetration into the community, for an individual is as close to a helping contact as he is to the nearest telephone.

The telephone has unrealized potential as a therapeutic instrument which can reach many people who might otherwise not receive counseling. It is surprising that a profession whose essential tool is interpersonal communication has for so long ignored the possibilities offered by the telephone. The business world seized upon the invention long ago, using it as an aid in business transactions. (Conference telephone calls, for example, are very common today.) In politics, too, the telephone plays a crucial role. The famous Kremlin White

House hotline exploits to the full the major benefits of the telephone, linking people at all times of crisis, regardless of their geographical distances from each other. This is what McLuhan means when he calls the telephone a "hot" medium.

We shall explore the potential of telephone therapy from two perspectives: first, the unique qualities of telephone therapy, and second, the value of telephone therapy for people with certain life-styles and problems.

The Unique Qualities of Telephone Therapy

Telephone therapy differs from conventional face-to-face therapy in the following ways: (1) the client has more control, (2) the client can remain anonymous, (3) geographic and personal barriers can be bridged, and (4) the therapist can remain anonymous.

Client Control

A person in distress may be so overwhelmed psychologically that he does not have sufficient psychological energy to visit a helping agency. The act of visiting an agency demands certain resources and strengths. To apply for help at a strange agency requires contacting the unknown, a fearful step for most of us. The client has to meet another human being, which can be difficult especially when a person feels an inner helplessness in relation to his problem. Upon entering the agency structure, the person is faced with the fact that the dominance relationship is set so that the agency and the counselor are in command. This compounds the patient's feeling that, to some degree, he is at the mercy of the counselor. The client is often required to give out personal information, information which few of us like to give to someone whom we do not know. Paradoxically, at the beginning of the therapeutic contact, the patient is asked to give more of himself than is the therapist. Furthermore, the client often has no choice of who his helper will be. There are very few of us who would accept these conditions happily.

Our point is this: coming for help may in some instances be positively humiliating. It becomes understandable why many people who need help will not seek it unless driven by desperation. Under these circumstances, the telephone offers a unique advantage as an instrument of help.

In the first place, the client has some power or control over when he contacts the helping person on the telephone. Should the helping person be too threatening to the patient, the latter is in a position to hang up. The knowledge to the patient that he could always cut off the therapist if things become too threatening to him gives him a feeling of freedom that he will not necessarily become a victim to an unknown source. In the office situation, however, we doubt that the patient feels any of this power. If things do not work out well, the patient ends up imprisoned in a strange office with a threatening source whom he must submit to or attack.

Client Anonymity

Experience has affirmed the value of anonymity in the helping process. The advantage of being able to hide one's identity may facilitate greater self-revelation and openness on the part of a patient. Opening oneself up to another is an act of vulnerability and can, in fact, increase one's feelings of inadequacy and helplessness. Anonymity is useful here, for the patient can feel secure, in that he has some control over the potential negative consequences of his self-revelation when his name is not known by the counselor. The value of anonymity in facilitating self-revelation is illustrated by the fact that strangers are often able to reveal themselves to each other on a temporary basis. In a context of anonymity, self-revelation does not threaten normal role functioning. Anonymity reduces the fear of being ridiculed or abused while in a vulnerable position and can reduce the loss in social status involved in presenting oneself as someone in need of help. The reduced threat, therefore, opens the door for help to some clients.

Bridging Geographic and Personal Barriers

Many psychologically distressed people are restricted in their geographic mobility. It may be threatening to leave a place in which they feel secure and rooted. They have established their psychological space within a familiar area. All novel stimuli, whether positive or negative, may initially be experienced as threatening. In order to maintain a very unstable equilibrium, such people have exchanged the possibility of growth and adventure for a form of rigid, closed-in safety. They have locked themselves in to feel safe and secure, but they have paid the price of locking out new creative experiences.

For this type of individual, the telephone may be the one opportunity to begin a new process. From his island, the client can begin to talk with other human beings in a safe way. In the words of one man, "I have lived so much inside myself or the past three years that I believe that I have forgotten even how to approach and talk with other human beings." The telephone represents to this person a safe means by which to begin social interaction. He can do this at a safe distance and on his own terms. There are people who call a telephone counseling service five or six times a day. This could be viewed as too great a dependency. Yet we might note that each of us needs a certain amount of social interaction each day to keep going. Four or five calls each day by an isolated person may be quantitatively no different form the social contact any of us needs. From this perspective, the isolated person is simply focusing the normal need for social interactions onto one agency because it is available to him in his immediate environment. Given this support, the patient may be able to develop confidence that he can eventually begin to seek social interactions in other ways.

Rescue, Inc. in Boston instituted a Life-Line service for the elderly. Once a day the staff of Life-Line called each elderly person on their service. The telephone service was free. Elderly people who wished to become a part of the telephone network simply had to contact Rescue, Inc. and request the service. Life-Line served two purposes. The daily telephone calls served as protection for the elderly when they were ill or when there was an emergency. If the telephone was not answered, a Life-Line volunteer visited the home of the person for a routine check. Second, Life-Line brought the elderly together. All daily telephone calls were made by the elderly to each other. The daily telephone calls started new friendships and often renewed old ones. Many people live alone, and a Life-Line service, therefore, provides a vital service for a community.

Therapist Anonymity: The Power of Positive Transference

Thus far, we have discussed those aspects of telephone therapy which make initial contact easier for the patient. Now, we shall look briefly at another aspect of telephone therapy which can play a significant role, both at the moment of initial contact and at later stages of telephone therapy.

We have already indicated the advantages of the patient remaining anonymous. The other side of that coin is that the therapist may remain anonymous. When a patient contacts a helping agency, he doubtless has some idea of what will happen to him and some notion of what the therapist will be like. (This notion may not, of course, be realistic.) If the client does not know what to expect, he may imagine, consciously or unconsciously, how he would like the therapist to be. Reality may be better than the patient's expectations. He might have expected an impersonal technician but instead been greeted by a warm and sympathetic human being. In face-to-face therapy, the chances are, however, that reality will not match his fantasy, and the psychologically distressed individual cannot, in his present state, withstand the shattering of his illusions. His illusions give him a sense of security.

Of course, the telephone therapist will not be whatever the patient wishes him to be, but he will be far more like the patient's ideal than the face-to-face therapist since the patient is presented with only a part of the reality. On the telephone, we receive none of the visual clues about a person that we receive in a face-to-face contact. We have no idea what the person we are talking with looks like, we cannot see facial expressions, and we get none of the body language clues to his thoughts, feelings, and personality that we generally receive in a face-to-face contact.

The important point is that the telephone contact, much more than the face-to-face interview, permits the patient to make of the therapist what he will. This has the crucial implication that he can make of the therapist what he needs.

For example, one of us had a long series of telephone contacts with a teenage girl trying to break a habit of frequent soft-drug use. She seemed to be making progress and attributed this to the "firm line" that the therapist was taking with her. She thought of the therapist as a well-built, tall, muscular individual. Actually, the therapist did not fit this description at all, and he had done very little in the way of taking a firm line on the drug question. He had, in fact, concentrated more on other areas. It seems, however, the girl had projected onto the therapist the strong, forceful masculine qualities she was seeking in someone who could control her behavior. The medium of the telephone contact provided her with the opportunity to do this.

Of course, there are disadvantages in allowing an individual to dwell too long in a world of fantasy. However, if the therapist is aware of what is happening, he or she can begin to present the patient the reality of the situation when the patient has sufficient strength to accept reality.

In summary, the anonymity of the therapist facilitates the development of transference, which can be used, within limits, to facilitate positive growth on the part of the patient.

The Use of Telephone Therapy as a Treatment Modality with Certain Clients

There are particular kinds of patients for whom telephone therapy provides a particularly useful treatment modality. We have identified four patient or situational categories which appear to respond best to telephone therapy. They are (1) the adolescent, (2) the isolate, (3) the desperate, and (4) the one-shot caller.

The Adolescent

The adolescent needs to spend much time in self-involvement, attempting to master new impulses and experiences. A great deal of energy is tied up in tentatively testing out new roles in an effort to discover a unique identity in a complicated world. It is part of the life process to be perpetually ambivalent about everything and everyone. Adolescents have a pervasive indecisiveness and ambivalence about reality, and thus they find it very difficult to reveal, even to describe, the facets of their inner life. At this point in development, self-revelation becomes very difficult. Adolescents spend a great deal of time trying to create a social image, and do not want to reveal "weaknesses" that threaten their image. A feeling of independence and self-sufficiency is a vital part of the self-image. Those experiences which even suggest dependency, vulnerability, weakness, and lack of self-confidence are all viewed as threats to their self-esteem. The world of appearances is very crucial to the adolescent.

In view of this, therefore, it can be seen that asking for and receiving help can be tremendously threatening to an adolescent. A telephone counseling service provides the possibility of helping adolescents in a way that is less threatening to their self-image, since they can remain anonymous and have a great deal of control.

The Isolate

Telephone therapy is relevant to the needs of the severely distressed person who is simply unable to enter a new situation. A great danger for these individuals is ultimate isolation from the world. Telephone contact with a counselor is perhaps the only step they may be capable of taking in order to obtain help. It is a social input in an otherwise barren existence.

Although the availability in the community of a telephone counseling service may facilitate the isolate's search for help, the great problem with these kinds of individual is that they are unlikely to respond to this passive service. Communities need an active outreach service that can identify and make contact with isolates. The isolate, all too often, has lost the motivation even to call a telephone counseling service. However, a telephone counseling service provides a potential contact with a helping agency for the individual who is falling into greater and greater isolation. If the contact is made, it can, hopefully, prevent complete isolation.

The Desperate

There are many people who need immediate help as a result of a sudden psychological shock which tips their mental balance to a point where they are overwhelmed by feelings of disorientation. A parallel and more dramatic type of situation is actual physical wounding on a field of battle, where the individual is unable to do anything but cry for help. The effects of psychological shock may be similar. For the person who is faced with such a crisis, the presence of a telephone counseling agency becomes a lifeline to reality contact. The very sound of a caring, thoughtful voice can provide emotional support, analogous to the giving of a blood transfusion to the physically wounded.

The One-Shot Crisis Contact

Finally, we believe, that there are many relatively normal people whose sense of pride and integrity is threatened by coming to an agency. Such people may identify coming for help as being sick. A fear of a loss of self-esteem acts as a barrier to seeking help openly. Furthermore, they may perceive their need as quite temporary, in the sense that what they need at the present moment is the presence of someone else so that they can think through their situation better. They do not want to become involved in a longer-term therapeutic relationship. A telephone counseling service is, perhaps, the only means by which such individuals can receive help.

Conclusion: Building Interpersonal Bridges

We have attempted to describe the unique value of telephone therapy in relation to the special needs of patients in crisis situations. Its special usefulness lies in the fact that the therapist can use it to build interpersonal bridges to human beings who, because of their psychological state or external circumstances, simply cannot visit an agency for help.

The telephone serves as a means for a patient to seek help without having to run the gauntlet of bureaucratic procedures (appointments, waiting lists, information disclosure, and so forth) which are necessary for the orderly running of an agency, but which often serve to screen out many of those people most desperately in need of help.

The agency and the patient build psychological barriers which hinder their reaching each other. The telephone can help bypass these barriers. It can enable contact on terms which threaten neither the patient nor the agency. Many people who have been unable to seek help through conventional modalities have been able to receive psychological support and counseling from a telephone counseling service.

Professionals must not underrate the telephone as a therapeutic modality. The telephone counseling service can provide a crucial service for the psychologically distressed individuals in the community. Telephone therapy should not be viewed as a substitute for face-to-face therapy, but rather as a preferred mode of treatment for particular individuals who are in certain kinds of crisis situations.

Chapter 4

CRISIS INTERVENTION

John Kalafat

In the first edition of this book, Brockopp (1973) reviewed the theoretical basis of crisis intervention, including the characteristics and dynamics of crises and their implications for intervention, and detailed an adaptation of the original five-step Los Angeles Suicide Prevention Center model that evolved at the Buffalo Suicide Prevention Center. That chapter presented a rationale and framework for crisis intervention and counseling by telephone that can still provide a solid basis for much work in this field today.

Unlike much psychotherapy that was derived from theories of personality, crisis intervention was developed by practitioners in applied settings who were seeking effective responses to individuals in crisis. The telescoped time frame of crises provides immediate feedback, which fosters the retention of only those interventions that facilitate the effective resolution of crises. Thus, the development of crisis intervention is marked by considerable consensus and relatively few debates among competing schools of thought.

The pioneering staff at the Los Angeles Suicide Prevention Center described five steps in "emergency therapy" by telephone, including (1) establishing a relationship, maintaining contact, and obtaining information; (2) identifying and focusing on the central problem; (3) evaluating the lethality of the threat; (4) assessing and mobilizing the caller's resources; and, (5) formulating and initiating therapeutic or rehabilitative plans.

In this chapter, a variant of that basic strategy is presented that has been informed and affirmed by over 30 years of work by telephone counselors and trainers, and by a body of empirical research in both telephone crisis intervention and general counseling process and outcomes. The strategy serves as a generic framework for responding effectively to the wide variety of callers who present to Telephone Counseling or Crisis Services (TCS).

The Nature of Crises

The characteristics of crises have direct implications for the intentions and interventions of the crisis worker, as follows.

Definition of Crisis

Slaikeu (1990) defined a crisis as a temporary state of upset and disorganization, characterized chiefly by an inability to cope with a particular situation using customary methods of problem solving, and by the potential for positive or negative outcome. Put another way, a crisis is any situation that calls for a response that is at least temporarily outside the repertoire of the individual.

Implications: No one has developed a repertoire that allows them to deal with all situations. Rather, all individuals have repertoires that have strengths and vulnerabilities or gaps. It follows that crises are best approached as *normal, but stressful events*, and not as a sign of pathology or weakness. Even for persons suffering from a chronic mental illness, we must search for a precipitant or hazardous event, coupled with the individual's vulnerable state (Rapoport, 1965) to understand why the person is in crisis. Most people do not understand this – that crises are exacerbated by the fact that persons in crisis are not only upset by the event, but also by their inability to cope or respond effectively. By acknowledging and normalizing the stress and frustration, while avoiding pathologizing, we begin the process of initiating a search for precipitants of the crisis and reducing anxiety that interferes with problem solving.

A second characteristic of the definition of a crisis is that crises are not defined as particular situations or events, or by specific types of persons. No particular event, even the death of a loved one, is universally a crisis. While stressful, such an event is only a crisis if the individual has no internal or external resources for coping with it. Thus, we must look for a current ineffective coping strategy or gap in that person's repertoire, and/or breakdown in external support systems. In this sense, crisis intervention is an ecological approach in which we must look to the individual (internal resources and gaps) and the environment (hazards, demands and supports) to identify both the causes and the possible resolution of the crisis. Thus, for example, a crisis can be resolved by helping the person develop a more effective way of coping and/or mobilizing family or community supports.

Development of a Crisis

Caplan (1964) described a process that most individuals in crisis go through. The first stage is the impact, in which the individual is presented with a particular situation, event, demand, or threat. In response to this, the individual tries his or her usual coping techniques, which, by definition, do not work. This leads to a turning point in which the individual perseverates and is unable to come up with an effective response or, spurred by the unusual demand, mobilizes new internal or external resources to deal with it. One of those new responses can be to seek help, including calling a crisis service. If this stage does not produce an effective response, the individual may proceed to further deterioration and the development of symptomatic behavior such as withdrawal or engaging in destructive behavior such as violence, suicide, or substance abuse. Persons in this stage may call a crisis service in acute crisis or are often the subject of third-party calls.

Implications: It is important to note that each of these stages is marked by increased anxiety and confusion, which creates cognitive constriction or tunnel thinking that interferes with problem solving. Thus, a primary goal of crisis intervention is to reduce anxiety. The antidotes to anxiety and confusion are support and structure. These can be provided in part by conveying an understanding that an inability to cope is naturally stressful, but not abnormal, and by initiating a search for understanding the dynamics of this particular crisis. For example, "It sounds like a lot of things have been happening all at once, any one of which you could handle. But together, I can see how you would be overwhelmed by them."

Also, as we work with a caller at the turning point in crises or when the crises have progressed to the more acute stage, we must look for both maladaptive (e.g., withdrawal) and adaptive (e.g., help seeking) responses, and attenuate the former and promote the latter.

Crises Represent an Opportunity for Growth as Well as Regression

A person in crisis is generally more open to change because his or her usual way of coping has proven to be ineffective. By definition, the successful resolution of a crisis results in some addition to the individual's coping repertoire and enhanced self-esteem or confidence associated with that success.

Implications: It is critical that the crisis worker fosters growth by searching for competence and emphasizing strengths, and by establishing a collaborative relationship as much as possible. The helper should aim for the call to be a success for the caller more than for him/herself. It would be difficult to foster collaboration if the helper does not understand the development of crises as previously described. The helper must understand that he or she is seeing the person at their worst in a temporary state of confusion. Callers may present as less competent and/or more helpless than they are under normal circumstances and, due to the cognitive constriction, may not be in touch with their internal and external resources. The naive helper does not see beyond this presentation and may try to do too much for the caller and thus rob him or her of the opportunity for growth and sense of accomplishment.

Crises Are Time-Limited Events

Crises do not remain static. The situation and the person in crisis either get better or get worse.

Implications: The helper must take an active approach that seeks some positive impact in the space of one contact. The helper must approach the call with the mindset that "I have one contact with this person. What can we realistically accomplish (or what can the caller come away with) that would be most helpful in this particular situation?"

This requires a focus on the now and how more than on the then and why or, as has been put another way, crisis intervention stays on the first level of causation. For example, if a man calls because he is depressed because his wife has taken the kids and moved out, the issues to be explored are the meaning of this event to him and the breadth and depth of his depressed response. Rather than exploring what went wrong in his marriage, the helper must find out how he is currently coping and functioning. Does the loss of his family mean that he has no purpose in life and/or feels so depressed that he has thoughts of killing himself or has started drinking heavily? Is he so immobilized that his work is suffering, which will add to his problems? Has he cut himself off from potential sources of support from other family members or colleagues? What prompted him to call at this time?

In sum, the helper's understanding of the nature of crises enables him or her to convey to callers that:

1. Being in crisis does not mean that the caller is weak or "losing his mind." Rather, the helper accepts the caller as struggling with a genuine concern.

2. She or he will take time to listen and, together with the caller, arrive at a better understanding of what the caller is dealing with.

3. She or he will actively work with the caller to find ways to handle the concern (i.e., identify internal and external resources) that the caller may not have thought about, and to avoid maladaptive responses.

These and other considerations concerning the nature and dynamics of crises come into play during the application of generic intervention approaches. The basic helping model is detailed next, along with examples of its application and supportive findings from crisis and counseling research.

The Helping Model

Table 4-1 depicts a five-phase helping model that, with some variations, is employed in most TCSs. The phases are depicted and will be described separately, although they are not discrete in practice. There is a good deal of overlap among the first three phases, and some information about past coping may also come to light along with the first three phases. Phase five, however, is a distinct phase that cannot occur before the other phases. A common error among novice helpers is to attempt to find solutions before rapport has been established or the problem has been identified. This usually leads to a stalled call or the caller engaging in what trainers have termed "yes-buts" to the helper's suggestions. Follow-up feedback from callers to a suicide center indicates a negative reaction to helpers who tried to identify the problem or move to solutions before allowing the caller some time to feel comfortable talking out their concerns (Lee, 1999).

Table 4-1
BASIC HELPING MODEL

1. Establish Rapport
   Rapidly make contact
   Provide structure
   Reinforce help seeking
   Invite to work

2. Define the Problem
   Precipitant: why calling now?
   Start with the caller's perspective
   Prioritize what to deal with first
   Agree upon a focus

3. Acknowledge Feelings
   Acknowledge
   Accept
   Implications of having these feelings: what does the caller feel like doing?

4. Explore Past Coping
   Inventory of internal and external resources
   Coping style: how has the caller dealt with similar situations

5. Exploring Alternatives
   Generate alternatives
   Explore consequences of each alternative
   Agree on a plan of action

Echterling and Hartsough (1989) conducted a study that provided general support for these phases of helping. The success of outcomes of calls to a crisis center was rated in cognitive, affective, and behavioral dimensions of crisis resolution. Helper responses were placed into categories representing the phases of helping and then related to call outcomes. Results supported the following conclusions about the effective sequencing of helper behaviors.

(1) Their measure of climate setting, which included social conversation, was not effective beyond the minimum necessary to establish rapport. It may be that calls dominated by climate setting behavior are analogous to Carkhuff's (1969) level 1, or lowest level, of helping which consists of reflections that do not go beyond the surface of client's statements. (2) Assessments of the caller's problem in the first two-thirds, but not the final third of the call, lead to success. (3) Active response to a caller's feelings takes place continually but is most effectively done through the middle phase of a call rather than at the end. (4) Some problem-solving may be effective throughout the call but is best done near the end, when both parties focus on specific actions to be taken after the call.

This helping model can provide a framework for a single contact or for ongoing therapy. All five phases can be completed within the space of a half-hour call that concerns a specific problem. The model can also be applied to

Table 4-2
RESPONDING TO ACUTE CRISES

1. Assess Precipitant
   Specific current problem(s)
   Current situation/context
   Current functioning
   Risk
   Who is involved
   Duration of the crisis

2. Cushion the Impact of the Stress
   Provide support and empathy
   Provide cognitive grasp: what is happening and what you are trying to accomplish
   Provide hope: predict targeted outcome & duration

3. Help Mobilize Supports
   External
   Internal

4. Regain Some Control
   Emotional stability: since the start of the contact, has the person noticeably calmed down; or, if they had been immobilized or withdrawn, have they rallied somewhat?
   Cognitive grasp: do they feel less confused or overwhelmed about the situation and its implications; do they have some sense of what to do, i.e,. a concrete plan for the immediate future?

5. Ending the Contact
   Based on the caller's functioning, the helper must decide to end the contact in one of three ways:
   (i) End the contact – the caller is in a position to carry out the agreed upon plan.
   (ii) Refer the caller to another helping agency for follow up assistance.
   (iii) Transport or outreach – the caller is not currently able to carry out a plan and remains at risk; arrangements must be made to get the caller to an emergency screening unit.

special populations such as borderline callers (Shinefield & Kalafat, 1996). Acute crises call for more active, at times directive, helping that places less emphasis on the exploration of feelings (Brockopp, 1973; Lee, 1999). A framework for responding to acute crises is presented in Table 4-2 and will be discussed in the section on acute crises. Also, additional strategies for addressing specific crises, such as suicide and substance use, can be folded into these models. These special issues require additional training and are beyond the scope of this chapter.

Establishing a Relationship

The goals of this phase are to:
1. Create a safe, accepting atmosphere that will encourage and allow the caller to explore his or her concerns openly.
2. Convey a sense of hope for the caller's efforts to at least start to resolve his or her concerns.
3. Establish as collaborative a relationship as possible, given the caller's current level of functioning.

The helper's message is: "I accept you as a person who is experiencing a genuine concern. I see you as a person of worth and capability who is currently struggling. I am willing to work with you to see how you can come through this for the better." The caller's experience should be: "I hear someone who believes my stress is real but does not think less of me. In fact, he or she seems to think that I can work this through. He or she may be able to help me." Table 4-3 provides a list of helper intentions and behaviors that facilitate rapport. Helpers need not explicitly engage in all of these behaviors but may convey some of their intentions by working hard to stay with a caller who presents a confusing or difficult concern or who is reticent or hostile.

While crisis intervention is time-limited, there are several reasons to take some time to establish rapport, including:
1. Sometimes callers won't talk to a helper until they get to know him or her better. So even if callers have a specific concern, they often need some time before they will talk about it.
2. Helpers also need to get to know a caller a little better before they can come up with help that fits for him or her. For example, it may be helpful to know how he or she typically deals with things, what his or her values and beliefs are, etc.
3. Sometimes just talking with someone without trying to solve anything is helpful. Just being someone who listens without judgment or advice is helpful.
4. Sometimes someone will talk about things that don't seem major until they start to trust the helper, and then they will reveal more serious concerns.

Table 4-3
ESTABLISHING A RELATIONSHIP

Helper Intentions	Helper Behaviors
Acceptance	
of the caller	Nonjudgmental
of the problem	Acknowledge caller's concern.
	"I can see how that would bother you."
	"You're going through a lot."
Concern	
Willing to listen	Allowing/encouraging caller to talk.
	"I'd like to hear. . ."
Care what happens to caller	Reinforce help seeking.
	"You've taken an important step."
Support	
Wants to work with caller	Invitation to work.
	"We need to get a clearer sense of what's been going on."
Convey hope	Identify goal.
	"Then we can put our heads together and find some ways of handling this."
Structure	
Helper and caller roles	"I'm here to listen and help you figure out what's going on and how you can deal with it, and I'm hoping you will work with me and not do anything rash in the meantime."
Nature of crises	"It's hard to think straight when something so unexpected happens."
	"I can see how you would be feeling overwhelmed."

This is why all calls, including information calls, must be taken seriously.

The question often arises as to how directive versus collaborative the relationship should be. For example, when are advice or directives appropriate? The main criterion for directives or advice is a clear sense that the situation calls for specific action or decisions because of impending danger or negative consequences, and the caller is at least temporarily unable to make these decisions or is unaware of these consequences – that is, something needs to be done, and the helper believes that the caller cannot do it him or herself. For example, "I understand how your husband feels, but I believe your son is at great risk and you must remove the gun from your house"; or, "You are dealing with a lot right now since your wife's death, but it seems that your drinking is starting to interfere with your work, and that will cause a lot of added problems for you and your kids." Advice or directives given for any other reason probably come from the helper's needs and rob the caller of the opportunity for growth.

TCS studies that obtained follow-up caller feedback as to helpful counselor responses support the importance of relationship variables. Lee (1999) found that callers who were judged to be at low or moderate risk for suicide most frequently mentioned helper characteristics such as availability (let me talk; there when needed), acceptance, concern, and support (easy to talk to; considerate and did not ridicule; tone of voice; understanding). Negative feedback included: tried to get at what's wrong right away, tried to get an address right away, doesn't understand what I'm going through. Callers judged to be at high risk identified more directive responses such as, it was helpful to call my therapist, she gave options to help me; it was helpful keeping me on the telephone, otherwise I would have shot myself; telling me to go to the hospital was helpful, I needed that. Daigle and Mishara's (1995) subjects identified such characteristics as acceptance, approval, and reassurance. Young's (1989) subjects, contacted immediately after the call, most often said understanding and caring, followed by calm and soothing, and nonjudgmental.

Young contrasted his findings with those of Slaikeu and Willis (1978) who contacted callers several days after the call and found that callers identified giving clear and accurate information, helping the caller to organize thoughts, discussing alternative solutions, and providing a new perspective, along with providing an opportunity to talk, and supporting and reassuring. Young hypothesized that, immediately after the call, relationship and anxiety reduction variables were more salient, while after the caller had an opportunity to digest perspectives and try out alternatives generated in the call, the cognitive and strategic aspects of the call were more salient. Thus, as has been found in psychotherapy research, the relationship is a necessary, but not a sufficient aspect of effective helping. Clearly, it is also important for the helper and the caller to focus on identifying and resolving a central problem.

Define the Problem

The goal of this phase is to arrive at an explicit agreement with the caller as to the main concerns that must be addressed. Sometimes this is straightforward, but often it requires some exploration and clarification. At times, the caller is distressed, stuck, or feeling bad, but is unclear what the problem is. At times, the caller is stuck because of the way she or he is framing the problem. For example, Shneidman (1985) has said that "only" is *the* four-letter word in suicide, as in such statements as "I can be happy only if she comes back to me." At times, a crisis is precipitated by the confluence of many events, and the caller needs help in sorting them out and prioritizing which to address and which can be postponed. For example, "It sounds like your plate is pretty full since your husband died, and it is important that you keep your job and find child care. You may not be able to keep up with those classes right now."

It is important to initially understand the problem from the *caller's* perspective: how is this a problem for *them*? The message to the caller must be "I want to understand you – your concerns and your reaction to them – in your terms or from your point of view. I may offer my feedback and perspective later, but right now, I want to promote the flow of your thoughts and feelings, and try to clarify and summarize these for you. I won't diagnose you or try to solve your problem, and I need you to work with me so that we are on the same track."

Four issues to consider here are: (1) breadth – all the implications of the problem (e.g., divorce has economic as well as psychological impacts); (2) meaning (e.g., does this mean, "now I can't pay the rent" or "now life is not worth living"); (3) changeability (e.g., "I'll never get over this" or "I've always been a loser"); and (4) context – who else is involved and what is their role or reaction; and how did this come to a head at this time? For example, a setback with one's child in school that might normally be handled becomes a crisis because the caller has been ill, exhausted, demoralized over other events, has just lost an important support, etc. People often do not make connections between events or situations in their lives and their current crisis.

Basically, within the time limits of the call, it is helpful to think of defining the problem as a funnel in which the helper first engages in a more abroad exploration of the caller's circumstances, thoughts, and feelings, and then begins to arrive at a focus or priority or new frame that can most likely be successfully addressed in this contact.

Common mistakes in this phase include focusing too soon on one aspect of the problem, ignoring or missing important points, making judgments about the problem (e.g., "It's not really a problem if you don't get into your first choice of colleges"), jumping too soon into advice or solutions before the problem has been clearly defined, and failing to choose a focus (i.e., moving from issue to issue without prioritizing, thus duplicating one of the ways the caller has been remaining stuck).

Feedback from callers related to this phase includes "helped me sort things out" and "helped me see things more clearly" (Lee, 1999); "helped me organize my thoughts" and "provided a new perspective" (Daigle & Mishara, 1995).

It is particularly difficult to discuss defining the problem separately from exploring feelings, as these are intertwined. For example, at times the strength of the feelings exacerbates or defines the problem, or the problem does not emerge with any clarity until the caller's feelings have been addressed.

Exploring Feelings

There is a good deal of research that supports the importance of exploring feelings in effective helping (Wiser & Goldfried, 1997; Greenberg & Safran, 1989). In regard to addressing affect in telephone crisis intervention and counseling, it is important to understand why it is done, what it consists of, how to do it, and when to do less of it.

The first reason for dealing with feelings is that feelings are something everyone has in common. Regardless of age, gender, ethnicity, circumstances, or background, humans share a single set of possible feelings. TCS have no selection or eligibility criteria for callers. What, then, does a 20-year-old volunteer have in common with a 50-year-old man who has considerable family responsibilities and has just been laid off from his job? The only way that the volunteer may be able to connect with this caller is if she can get in touch with his sense of impotence and hopelessness. If she cannot do this, she will most likely be unable to help him. This is why one of the selection criteria for helpers is that they have experienced some crises of their own. It is not desirable for a call to represent the first crisis they have dealt with in their lives. It is a much different message to convey, "I hear and understand your sense of hopelessness *and* I want to try to come up with a way of tackling your problems," than to try to convey the second part of that message without the first part.

Acknowledging feelings, then, is an important way of establishing rapport with a caller, and failure to do so can leave the caller with a sense of isolation or even abandonment with their own disturbing feelings. Each of us can relate to the sense of disconnection or isolation associated with experiencing strong feelings – perhaps anger and frustration after a trying day at work – and having these feelings go unacknowledged by someone who is supposed to care. The consequences of this failure of rapport can range from a caller who simply feels that the helper did not understand him or her, as evidenced in the follow-up studies with crisis line callers, to an exacerbation of the isolation and perturbation of the suicidal caller. The message that the suicidal caller can come away with if his feelings are unacknowledged is that these feelings are indeed overwhelming if the helper will not deal with them, or that he is indeed alone and beyond help.

It is also important to address feelings because, paradoxically, they can serve to impede action or they can serve as the basis or engine for action and change. In regard to the former, trainers have said "what you resist, persists," and Shneidman (1985) has said that the first task in dealing with suicidal persons is to reduce their perturbation. Anxious, overwhelmed, or very angry persons cannot engage in problem solving. For many crises, particularly acute crises, the main task of crisis intervention is to reduce anxiety and perturbation. This can be accomplished, not by ignoring or avoiding feelings, but by simply letting the caller tell his or her story and express his or her feelings, and then acknowledging them and conveying that they do not make the caller weak or "bad." This intervention is not an end in itself, but must occur before moving on to problem solving. Many helpers have difficulty dealing with strong feelings, as evidenced by the failure of professionals to inquire about suicide or by crisis line exchanges such as: (caller) "I don't think I can go on much longer;" (helper) "What year are you in at school?"

While certain strong feelings block perspective and problem-solving, at other times, callers are stuck and unable to generate or carry out actions to resolve their situation. Feelings are the basis for action. The decision to take some action, whether it is assertive, supportive, giving up or trying harder, approaching a task or avoiding, depends on whether the caller is feeling angry, caring, scared, incompetent, confident, and so on. Some callers are, at best, only vaguely aware of feelings. For these callers, some effort and persistence is called for to identify their feelings in order to clarify their role in their problem and help them move toward some action. Note, for example, the following interchange:

The caller, a rather passive 27-year-old woman living with her parents, had called complaining about problems with her boss's criticisms at work, and later revealed a home situation in which she had assumed most domestic duties and often tried to mediate her parents' arguments:

Helper (H): You said you would rather stay at home than go to work. How do you feel at home?
Caller (C): OK
H: But emotionally, how do you feel at home?
C: It's OK.
H: Tell me more about "OK."
C: I don't know, it's all right.
H: OK, this might be a bit difficult. Let's try this. You've just had a tough day at work like you described to me earlier. Your supervisor was all over you again. And now you get into your car and start to drive home. What are you feeling as you drive home to your house and your parents? What's it like inside you as you drive home?
C: I don't know, uh, tense.
H: OK, tension. What's that tension like?
C: I don't know, just tension.
H: If you could give it words, what would they be? What would you say to describe or express your tension?
C: I guess I'm just tired.
H: Tired, and now you are facing fixing dinner and maybe refereeing between your parents.

C: Yeah, and I'd just like some relief.
H: Just some relief somewhere. You're feeling some tension as you think about going home. And you want some relief. What do you feel like doing?
C: I don't know.
H: How could you avoid the tension or get some relief?
C: I could not go home.
H: So you could just not go home tonight. Perhaps, call and say "I'll be late, don't wait up." How does that feel as I say that?
C: I don't know. I'm not sure I could do that.
H: So you have doubts that you could pull that off. How do you feel as you think about doing that?
C: I feel really nervous.
H: And that nervous feeling makes it hard to think about doing something different like that?
C: Yeah.
H: Is that how you feel when you think about talking to your supervisor?
C: Yeah, a lot.

The helper had been going in circles with the caller and realized that she needed to try to get at some feelings in order to get some movement. She was supportive, yet persistent, and used scenarios in order to make the situation more immediate in the hope of arousing some feeling in the caller. Perhaps feelings were threatening to this caller. Also, feelings are often strange and unclear to people. Sometimes just identifying a feeling and accepting it is helpful while, at other times, the helper must explore the implications of feelings. Even though the caller may be struggling, as long as he or she is still working with the helper and not becoming more anxious or confused, such persistence is warranted.

In sum, years ago, a group of TCS trainers was asked, "Just what do we mean by dealing with feelings?" After some discussion and reflection on their telephone experiences, they agreed that it consisted of acknowledging the caller's feelings, conveying acceptance of the feelings, and exploring the implications of having those feelings – that is, what did the caller want to do (or not do) based on the feelings.

It is also important to note that there are times when exploration or acceptance of feelings may not be helpful. Caplan (1964) has noted that blame (of self or others) is not helpful. The helper can express that, while it is not unusual for people to be feeling this, it is not productive and will probably distract the person from some constructive action. It is not helpful to explore depressed feelings, as this can lead to a downward spiral for the caller and frustration for the helper. These feelings can be acknowledged and, rather than serving as a basis for action (or inaction), the caller must take some action *in spite of* these feelings. At times the helper may sense feelings in the caller that at present are too threatening for the caller to acknowledge. Often, this is discovered when the helper brings up such an implied feeling and meets with strong resistance from the caller. Examples of this may be a parent's resentment toward their children, or a longing for support or nurturance on the part of a male caller. A telephone contact is not psychotherapy, and the helper must let this go for now and find another route to problem solving. For example, an abused woman may not be ready to acknowledge strong negative feelings toward her spouse, and in fact will defend him if the helper brings these up. Perhaps concern for the safety of her children will serve to motivate her to take some appropriate action.

Brockopp (1973) noted that, the more severe a crisis is, the less necessary it is to focus on emotion and the more desirable it is to focus cognitively on the problem and alternatives. In general, the helper must assess whether the caller is in a high feeling mode that interferes with cognitive functioning or stimulates impulsive behavior, needs their feelings affirmed, or is stuck, obsessing or ruminating and needs to get in touch with their feelings in order to take action. Again, while some callers just need a supportive and empathic listener, the goal of much crisis intervention is problem solving and developing an action plan and addressing feelings is an important part of this process.

Exploring Past Coping

This is a transitional phase as the call moves from an emphasis on the caller's concerns and what has happened *to* the caller to an emphasis on possible resolution of those concerns and the caller as an *actor*. This phase involves taking inventory of the caller's internal (e.g., past successes, self-confidence, motivation) and external (family, friends, organizations, activities) resources, and can be framed as a search for competence. Much information about these resources has often come to fore during the call up to this point, as the helper gains a sense of the caller's coping style and repertoire, experience in dealing with problems, whether the caller is isolated or involved in institutions such as church, workplace or other organizations, and the relationships with and responses of others such as friends and family. A difficulty with telephone work is the lack of collateral information from these sources. The caller may be unaware of or distorting the availability of these supports, or may have progressively withdrawn from them.

In any event, the helper may point out or highlight what he or she has heard – for example, "It sounds like you have dealt with some serious situations in the past," or "You seemed to be effectively managing these demands for some time. What has made it difficult for you now?" Or, the helper may make inquiries such as: Have you dealt with anything like this in the past? Are there friends or family members who can help you with this? Is there someone who can be with you tonight? How is your relationship with your boss?

The caller may identify solutions or responses that she or he has tried to no avail, or she or he may have prematurely rejected or given up on an alternative. For example, the caller may say, "I tried to talk to my (boss, roommate, spouse), but it didn't work," and the helper may explore this attempt, "Tell me what you said. . . and how did they respond. . . ?"

Often, a crisis is precipitated by the withdrawal or unexpected failure of a personal or institutional support. For example, an elderly person may become depressed when a close friend deteriorates and must be placed in a nursing home, or a divorcing parent may experience blame rather than understanding and support from her own parents or her workplace. The helper must deal with the caller's feelings about this and begin a search for alternative supports.

Exploring Alternatives

Once the problem or set of concerns or issues and some of the caller's resources have been identified and explicitly agreed upon with the caller, alternative ways of dealing with the concerns can be explored. Again, depending on how acute the crisis is and the caller's level of functioning, this should be as collaborative as possible. The helper can start with open-ended inquiries such as, "What ways of handling this can you think of?" or "We have identified a number of things going on for you, where would you like to begin?" If the caller seems unable to come up with a response to an open-ended inquiry, the helper may suggest a set of possible alternatives from which the caller can choose. The goal here is to try to get the caller actively involved in problem resolution.

Often the caller is struggling with a variety of concerns, and a decision has to be made as to which to focus on in this call. There are several criteria for choosing a focus. First is the severity of the problem, that is, if *this* problem is not addressed, the consequences will be serious and the crisis will increase in severity or scope. Barring this, the caller can be asked what she or he feels is most pressing. Another consideration is what part of the situation is most amenable to change. Often, this is something that seems well within the caller's current repertoire; an issue the caller has most control over at this time; or requires action only on his or her part, as opposed to requiring some action on the part of someone else as well. This permits the best use of the contact and increases the likelihood of some success that can build the caller's confidence and motivation to tackle remaining concerns. Often, choosing a priority has to be negotiated with the caller, if the helper genuinely believes that one concern should be addressed for one of the above reasons. For example, "I know that your family situation feels pressing to you and I agree that this has to be addressed. I think that we may be able to come up with a resolution to your work situation tonight and then we can find a resource to help you with your family."

It is preferable that solutions that are being considered are within the caller's capabilities, values, or culture. The issue here is, what is the likelihood that the caller can or will do this? For example, if assertion with one's boss is not culturally acceptable to the caller, within the limit of a telephone contact, we may have to explore another alternative. At other times, the situation requires totally new behavior or questioning one's beliefs. This must be explicitly acknowledged and the caller must be helped to adopt these changes. For example, "It seems like your parents are caught up in their own issues and, at least for now, cannot be there for you. And I hear how disappointing that is for you, but it sounds like you are going to have to make some decisions on your own. I'd like to try to help you with that."

Again, in acute situations or when the caller is operating on clear misinformation, the helper may give advice. For example, "Actually, that drug will increase your depression," or "Your suicide would not relieve your family of a burden – it may increase the likelihood that another family member will attempt suicide."

Aside from acute or dangerous situations, the helper may have to accept the caller's decision as to which problem to address or what alternative they will try to carry out. Even in acute situations, we may have to deal with our lack of control over the caller's ultimate choices. Lamb's chapter (Chapter 6) on fallacies in telephone counseling is important reading in this regard. These include the fantasies of omnipotence (we have to do something), omniscience (if only I were or knew. . ., I could. . .), and the ultimate answer (there must be a right answer). An extreme example of this is the belief that if the suicidal caller is calling the crisis line, then deep down he must really want to be rescued; and, if he subsequently kills himself, it is because I did not think of the right thing to do or say. Most suicidal callers are ambivalent, but some who are fully intent on dying call because they feel lonely and want company in their last hour, are angry and want to lash out one more time, want to leave a verbal message, or just want to get their decision off of their chest before they carry it out.

It is important to explore with the caller the consequences of alternatives being considered or planned. This not only helps the caller in choosing the action plan and prepares him or her to carry it out, but also is an important part of the problem-solving strategy that it is hoped the caller will learn as part of the call. Included in this is an exploration of how the caller feels about the plan and the consequences. Many crises involve difficult choices or compromises (recall the four-letter word, "only") that cannot avoid all negative feelings or consequences. It is important that neither the helper nor the caller has a perfect solution as the goal.

Often, callers feel relief near the end of the call because they have been able to discuss their concern and have gained some understanding of their situation and options. That relief can attenuate, and some anxiety can return in the process of carrying out the plan. It is helpful if the helper predicts this and conveys that it is normal and not a sign that the call was futile or the plan should be abandoned.

In sum, the goals of this last phase of telephone crisis intervention are to engage the caller in generating and choosing a plan of action and considering its consequences, and to provide an opportunity for the caller to discuss his or her feelings and concerns about the plan. Again, feedback from crisis service callers (Slaikeu & Willis, 1978; Lee, 1999) and brief therapy clients (Elliot, 1985) identified the provision of new perspectives and the generation of alternate courses of action among the helpful interventions that they experienced.

Acute Crises

The five-step helping model outlines an effective intervention approach for a wide variety of situations. However, when presented with acute crises such as life-threatening situations or callers who are more anxious or perturbed, crisis workers have found that the model presented in Table 4-2 best captures their efforts. This approach involves more activity on the part of the helper, and often more directiveness. Suicidal callers who were considered at high risk in Lee's (1999) follow-up study acknowledged supportiveness and understanding but also identified more directive interventions than callers considered as low or moderate risk. These included several comments to the effect that, without helper directives, they might have acted on their suicidal ideation. Their comments included, "When I talked, they reminded me of things I needed to do to keep safe," "He told me to put away the pills, and that helped," "She kept me on the telephone, otherwise I would have shot myself."

The helper must convey a calm steadiness and a basic acceptance of the caller (e.g., "He didn't put me down"), but must also proceed in an organized way to assess the caller's situation, stressors and reactions, and to provide active feedback and ongoing structure to the caller as to what the helper is doing, what he or she understands about the caller's concerns, and what needs to be done to start to gain some relief and a plan of action. For example, "I hear that you have been struggling with these feelings for some time and right now you don't know if you can handle them any longer. You have taken an important step by calling here, and I'd like the two of us to take however much time we have to in order to put our heads together and see if we can come up with some other ways of handling this. Are you okay with this? OK, first, I'd like to get a better sense of your situation right now by asking you a few questions."

It is important for the helper to be aware that she or he must make a decision to end the call in one of the three ways listed in Table 4-2. The criteria for deciding how to end the call are the emotional stability and cognitive grasp that have been achieved during the call, as well as the degree to which external supports can be mobilized. An example of the latter is the helper may be more inclined to accept the second option if a responsible and supportive second party can be with the caller at the conclusion of the call and perhaps until the caller can follow up on the referral.

While wrapping up a call with a viable plan of action is a goal in crisis intervention, this cannot always be accomplished. Callers may not respond to the best efforts of the helper. They may terminate the call before closure is obtained; and they may, in spite of having placed the call, resist all efforts at closure for a variety of reasons. Sometimes a person may call with a situation that does not call for a specific plan or solution such as an irrevocable loss, a debilitating injury or illness, or the obsessional review that is an important part of grieving. They may need an empathic listener, and would experience any task-oriented interventions as unempathic and a lack of acceptance of where they are at currently. Some callers may get something from the call that is not obvious to the helper, or they may have accomplished as much as they were capable of at this time. Often, such callers will call back or seek out other helpers, if they have experienced the helper as patient and accepting of where they are at. The point is that, while crisis intervention often involves a rewarding sense of immediacy and closure, the helper must be prepared to tolerate ambiguity and lack of closure, as well as callers who accept a resolution to their crisis that is less than satisfying to the helper.

These points are raised because the presentation of a helping model or strategy may imply an inevitably orderly progression in crisis intervention. Even though this is not always the case, it still behooves the crisis worker to understand the nature and dynamics of crises, to keep abreast of effective assessment and intervention strategies, to listen to the feedback from peers and callers, and to draw on these sources to remain an intentional helper.

REFERENCES

Brockopp, G. W. (1973). Crisis intervention: Theory, process, and practice. In D. Lester & G. W. Brockopp (Eds.), *Crisis intervention and counseling by telephone*, pp. 89–104. Springfield, IL: Charles C Thomas.

Caplan, G. (1964). *Principles of preventive psychiatry*. New York: Basic Books.

Carkhuff, R. R. (1969). *Helping & human relations. Vol. II: Practice and research.* New York: Holt, Rinehart, and Winston.

Daigle, M. S., & Mishara, B. L. (1995). Intervention styles with suicidal callers at two suicide prevention centers. *Suicide & Life-Threatening Behavior, 25,* 261–275.

Echterling, L. G., & Hartsough, D. M. (1989). Phases of helping in successful crisis telephone calls. *Journal of Community Psychology, 17,* 249–257.

Elliot, R. (1985). Helpful and nonhelpful events in brief counseling interviews: An empirical taxonomy. *Journal of Counseling Psychology, 32,* 30–322.

Greenberg, L. S., & Safran, J. D. (1989). Emotion in psychotherapy. *American Psychologist, 44,* 19–29.

Lee, K. H. (1999). Experiences of suicidal callers utilizing the crisis and information center: A qualitative and quantitative program evaluation. *Dissertation Abstracts International, 60,* 0834.

Rapoport, L. (1965). The state of crisis: Some theoretical considerations. In H. J. Parad (Ed.), *Crisis intervention: Selected readings,* pp. 2–31. New York: Family Service Association of America.

Shinefield, W., & Kalafat, J. (1996). Effective management of borderline individuals in crisis. *Crisis Intervention & Time-Limited Treatment, 2,* 273–287.

Shneidman, E. (1985). *Definition of suicide.* New York: John Wiley.

Slaikeu, K. A. (1980). *Crisis intervention: A handbook for practice and research.* Boston: Allyn and Bacon.

Slaikeu, K. A., & Willis, M. A. (1978). Caller feedback on counselor performance in telephone crisis intervention: A follow-up study. *Crisis Intervention, 9,* 42–49.

Wiser, S., & Goldfried, M. R. (1988). Therapist interventions and client emotional experiencing in expert psychodynamic-interpersonal and cognitive-behavioral therapies. *Journal of Consulting & Clinical Psychology, 66,* 634–640.

Young, R. (1989). Helpful behaviors in the crisis center call. *Journal of Community Psychology, 17,* 70–77.

Chapter 5

RESPONDING TO SUICIDAL CRISES: THE CRISIS INTERVENTION APPROACH

JAMES R. ROGERS

According to Roberts and Everly (2006), "Crisis intervention has become the most widely used time-limited treatment modality in the world" (p. 6) and Thomas and Leitner (2005) suggest that crisis intervention is "believed to be the most effective model for suicide intervention" (p. 145). However, "crisis intervention" is not a unitary treatment modality in that a number of related but competing models exist (Callahan, 1998). Additionally, despite its apparent universal acceptance, empirical support for the effectiveness of a crisis intervention approach to working with suicidal individuals is lacking (Guo & Harstall, 2004; Rogers & Soyka, 2004; Roberts, 2005). Nevertheless, crisis intervention, as an umbrella conceptualization, is considered the front-line approach worldwide for responding to suicidal crises. The purpose of this chapter is to provide a brief overview of the application of crisis intervention to working with suicidal individuals and to identify some of the controversies surrounding its use in this area.

Although there have been many definitions of crisis in the literature, Slaikeu's (1990) definition provides a synthesis capturing the essence of those various perspectives (Dattilio & Freeman, 1994). Slaikeu defined a crisis as "a temporary state of upset and disorganization, characterized chiefly by an individual's inability to cope with a particular situation using customary methods of problem-solving, and by the potential for a radically positive or negative outcome" (p. 15). Conceptualized from this perspective, suicide can be viewed as the "ultimate coping strategy" that individuals may choose in order to cope with a problem of living when their current repertoire of coping strategies is insufficient for addressing the problem (Shneidman, 1987).

There are a number of models of crisis intervention in the literature including models offered by Gilliland and James (1993), Roberts (1996), and the seminal work by Caplan (1961) which was focused on community psychiatry. However, an integrative model suggested by Callahan (1998) that merges *crisis intervention* with the concept of *emergency intervention* seems most appropriate for describing the application of crisis intervention to working with suicidal individuals. According to Callahan, a patient's consideration of suicidal behavior as a solution to a presenting problem, identified in a crisis intervention session, requires a switch from the traditional crisis intervention model to an emergency intervention protocol. Because of the psychological emergency presented by suicidal ideation, "crisis intervention is temporarily delayed until the emergency is resolved" (p. 34). An overview of this model is provided next.

An Integrative Model

In general, acutely suicidal individuals are conceptualized under the rubric of crisis intervention whereby their *suicidal crisis* is seen as being time-limited and related to difficulties in the domains of *meaning, coping,* and/or *social support*. These three domains are viewed as universal aspects of suicidal crises with the subjective experience of each influenced by culture. Thus, according to Callahan, the primary focus of crisis intervention is assessment and intervention across the three domains of meaning, coping, and social support.

As previously indicated, Callahan's integrative model merges a crisis intervention approach with an emergency intervention component that may or may not come into play depending on the client's level of risk for suicide identified during the initial stages of crisis intervention. According to Callahan, the typical crisis intervention model consists of one to six sessions conducted over a brief period of time to the resolution of the crisis. The first major component of the initial crisis intervention session consists of allowing the patient to tell his or her story. Supported by an empathic clinician using open-ended questions and prompts, this tactic or intervention can allow the person to ventilate and help the clinician identify the underlying message or problem that is related to the crisis (Westefeld et al., 2000).

The second major component of the first crisis intervention interview follows directly from the focal domains of meaning, coping, and social support. The overarching goal is for the clinician to gain an understanding of the meaning that the client ascribes to the events related to the crisis, identify previous coping attempts that the client has made to resolve the crisis, and explore the presence or absence of support systems (Callahan, 1998).

The third major component is the assessment of the presence of a psychological emergency. It is in this third component that an explicit inquiry regarding suicidal ideation must be conducted. In the presence of a psychological emergency exemplified by the identification of suicidality, Callahan suggests that the clinician needs to switch from a crisis intervention strategy or approach to an emergency intervention protocol. The objective of emergency intervention is to determine the level of suicide risk and, subsequently, the appropriateness of continuing to follow a crisis intervention approach. In the absence of a psychological emergency such as a significant risk for suicide, subsequent crisis intervention sessions build on helping the patient develop more adaptive meanings for events, supporting the patient's efforts in learning and applying more adaptive coping behaviors, and working with the patient to identify or strengthen social support systems.

In the presence of suicidal ideation, however, the emergency intervention protocol takes precedence over crisis intervention. Callahan suggests that the emergency intervention consists of three stages including risk assessment, risk reduction intervention, and disposition.

Risk Assessment

The goal of suicide risk assessment is to determine the level of risk for suicide in the short-term. According to Roberts and Ottens (2005), suicide risk assessment focuses on asking specifically about suicidal thoughts, estimating the patient's intent to die, assessing lethality (i.e., extent of a suicide plan, method choice and access, and history of previous behavior), and identifying the presence of additional risk factors. While there is currently no consensus on a set of necessary and sufficient risk factors for assessing suicidality, a number of suicide assessment scales have been developed over the years that have varied in terms of their comprehensiveness. Representative of the more comprehensive risk-factor based scales is the *Suicide Assessment Checklist* (Rogers, Lewis, & Subich, 2002) which prompts for risk assessment on the following empirically identified status and clinical categories.

Status Categories for Suicide Risk Assessment

PREVIOUS PSYCHIATRIC HISTORY. Assessment here includes a general history of psychiatric hospitalization with special attention to psychiatric diagnoses specifically linked to increased suicidal potential such as depression, bipolar disorder, anxiety disorders, schizophrenia, post-traumatic stress disorder, and personality disorders such as borderline personality.

DRUG AND ALCOHOL USE. Whether through their direct pharmacological effects or via their impact on cognitive functioning, the propensity to use drugs and/or alcohol increases the risk for suicide.

PRIOR SUICIDE ATTEMPTS. Prior attempts are viewed both as an indicator of one's willingness to use suicidal behavior as a coping strategy and as potential "suicide rehearsal" behavior, either way indicating an increased risk.

SEX. Males are generally seen as presenting a higher risk for lethal suicidal behavior than females.

AGE. Generally, suicide risk increases with age, although there are deviations from this expectation based on cultural differences.

SUICIDE SURVIVOR STATUS. Individuals who have lost significant others to suicide are often at a greater risk for suicide.

MARITAL STATUS. Divorced, separated, or widowed individuals are potentially at a higher risk for suicide than those who are married.

PRESENCE OF A SUICIDE PLAN. Evaluating the presence of a plan includes determining whether a method has been chosen and the degree of access the patient has to the method. The more thoroughly considered plan, the greater the suicidal risk.

MAKING FINAL PLANS. Making final plans and/or giving away prized possessions are viewed as an indicator of intent to die.

THE PRESENCE OF A SUICIDE NOTE. Although only a fraction of individuals who die by suicide write suicide notes, the presence of a note is seen as an additional indicator of higher risk.

DEPENDENT CHILDREN IN THE HOME. There is some evidence that having dependent children in the home can serve as a protective factor for suicide.

Clinical Risk Factors for Suicide Risk Assessment

In addition to the above status variables, an assessment of suicide risk should include an assessment of the patient on the following clinical factors.

- Sense of worthlessness
- Sense of hopelessness
- Social isolation
- Depression
- Impulsivity
- Hostility
- Intent to die
- Environmental stress
- Lack of a future time perspective

Risk Reduction and Intervention

According to Callahan (1998), if the risk for suicide is judged to be low or moderate on the basis of the risk assessment, the clinician can continue with crisis intervention. Additionally, if the patient's risk for suicide is evaluated as initially high, but can be reduced to moderate or low through interventions such as active listening, providing empathy, helping the patient negotiate interpersonal conflicts, and offering hope, then crisis intervention can continue. However, if suicidal risk continues to be high following attempts at risk reduction, then the third stage of emergency intervention, disposition, is necessary.

Disposition

In the event that suicide risk cannot be reduced and remains high following the assessment and risk reduction and intervention activities, the clinician moves to the disposition component of emergency intervention. The goal of this component of the emergency intervention is to place the patient in a protective environment where efforts can be concentrated on reducing suicide risk. The determination of disposition is often made on a "least restrictive" criterion. This suggests that the clinician determines which of the available options can best provide for the patient's safety while allowing for some degree of freedom of movement and autonomy. In continuing high-risk situations, involuntary hospitalization is often the disposition of choice.

Controversies

Despite its relatively universal acceptance as a brief treatment modality for working with patients in suicidal crises (Roberts & Everly, 2006; Thomas & Leitner, 2005), the application of the model is not without controversy. For example, a central controversy is related to the lack of empirical evidence for its effectiveness in preventing suicide (Roberts & Everly; Rogers & Soyka, 2004; Thomas & Leitner, 2005). In fact, Roberts and Everly suggest that outcome measures or evaluations are rarely a focus in crisis intervention settings, and Guo and Harstall (2004) indicate that the available data on suicide preventive interventions in general do not provide evidence for the effectiveness of the crisis intervention or any other approach to working with suicidal individuals.

Beyond the lack of data in support of the effectiveness of the crisis intervention approach, Rogers and Soyka (2004) have suggested that an application of the model to suicidal individuals might inadvertently exacerbate suicidality for some individuals. Their discussion of the potential problems with the model is especially relevant to the emergency intervention protocol offered by Callahan (1998) and is supported in the work of Thomas and Leitner (2005) who suggest that the typical patient experience of the model is negative and adversarial rather than collaborative and helpful.

Conclusion

Callahan's (1998) model, conceptually and practically integrating crisis and emergency intervention for working with suicidal individuals, provides a helpful outline for clinicians working in this area. Despite the lack of strong supporting empirical evidence, the model represents an important component of standard of care that clinicians need to be aware of when working with suicidal people.

REFERENCES

Callahan, J. (1998). Crisis in theory and crisis intervention in emergencies. In P. M. Kleespies (Ed.), *Emergencies in mental health practice*, pp. 22–40. New York: Guilford Press.

Caplan, G. (1961). *An approach to community mental health*. New York: Grune & Stratton.

Dattilio, F. M., & Freeman, A. (Eds.). (1994). *Cognitive-behavioral strategies in crisis intervention*. New York: Guilford.

Gilliland, B. E., & James, R. K. (1993). *Crisis intervention strategies* (2nd. ed.). Pacific Grove, CA: Brooks & Cole.

Guo, B., & Harstall, C. (2004). *For which strategies of suicide prevention is there evidence of effectiveness?* Copenhagen, Denmark: WHO Regional Office for Europe, Health Evidence Network Report: http://www.euro.who.int/Document/E83583.pdf, accessed 23/12/2006.

Roberts, A. R. (1996). *Crisis management and brief treatment: Theory, technique, and applications*. Chicago: Nelson-Hall.

Roberts, A. R., & Everly, Jr., G. S. (2006). A meta-analysis of 36 crisis intervention studies. *Brief Treatment & Crisis Intervention, 6*, 10–21.

Roberts, A. R., & Ottens, A. J. (2005). The seven-stage crisis intervention model: A road map to goal attainment, problem solving, and crisis resolution. *Brief Treatment & Crisis Intervention, 5*, 329–339.

Rogers, J. R., Lewis, M. M., & Subich, L. M. (2002). Validity of the Suicide Assessment Checklist in an emergency crisis center. *Journal of Counseling & Development, 80*, 493–502.

Rogers, J. R., & Soyka, K. M. (2004). "One size fits all": An existential-constructivist perspective on the crisis intervention approach with suicidal individuals. *Journal of Contemporary Psychotherapy, 34*, 7–22.

Shneidman, E. S. (1987). A psychological approach to suicide. In G. R. VandenBos & B. K. Bryant (Eds.), *Cataclysms, crises, and catastrophes: Psychology in action*, pp. 151–183. Washington, DC: American Psychological Association.

Slaikeu, K. A. (1990). *Crisis Intervention* (2nd ed.). Boston: Allyn & Bacon.

Thomas, J. C., & Leitner, L. M. (2005). Styles of suicide intervention: professionals' responses and clients' preferences. *The Humanistic Psychologist, 33*, 145–165.

Westefeld, J. S., Range, L. M., Rogers, J. R., Maples, M. R., Bromley, J. L., & Alcorn, J. (2000). Suicide: An overview. *The Counseling Psychologist, 28*, 445–510.

Chapter 6

HOW BEST TO HELP SUICIDAL PERSONS OVER THE TELEPHONE AND INTERNET

BRIAN L. MISHARA

This essay discusses a question which is crucial for the establishment and daily functioning of services involved in suicide prevention over the telephone and on the Internet: What is the best approach for helpers to take in order to reduce the risk of a suicide attempt and help suicidal individuals? After a brief review of the history of methods of helping suicidal individuals over the telephone and over the Internet, we review recent research on the effectiveness of intervention techniques and then conclude with a discussion of challenges for choosing the best way to help suicidal persons using these relatively new technologies.

In 1906, the Salvation Army opened their first Suicide Bureau in the Salvation Army building in New York. Suicidal individuals were encouraged to visit day or night to obtain help, and separate services were provided for women and for men. A *New York Times* article (New York Times, 1907) describes their clients and the nature of the help provided. According to the *New York Times*, in one day, six people who had planned to die were rescued, including a woman who survived a morphine overdose the night before and a man who twice jumped into the river but each time was saved. In each instance the suicidal person described a seemingly insurmountable concrete problem: an elder having been swindled out of all his retirement savings, a criminal unable to find honest work, a young man who had lost his job, a destitute "lame" woman unsuccessful in pursuing a singing career. Each suicidal person was dissuaded from suicide by talking about his or her problems and being promised that concrete help would be provided by the organization, often a job at the center, sometimes temporary housing, and free professional services. Their approach essentially involved having a caring individual discuss the nature of the suicidal person's problems and then providing a solution using Salvation Army resources. The solutions almost always involved continued support by becoming involved with the organization and the availability of follow-up discussions with experienced volunteer helpers. This approach was disseminated to Salvation Army branches in other countries, and their suicide prevention model of providing "first aid to depressed people" was adopted by Berlin city officials in 1930 (New York Times, 1930).

An alternative approach was used when the first telephone helpline for suicidal callers was developed, the 1947 helpline at the neuropsychiatry clinic of the University of Vienna (Trowell, 1979). Help was provided by professional therapists who simply transferred their psychotherapy techniques to the telephone setting. Later, when the Reverend Chad Varah founded the Samaritans in 1953, services were provided entirely by volunteers whom he felt had a natural ability to "befriend" suicidal individuals in a manner which helps prevent suicides. Varah, who was trained as a professional psychotherapist, "discovered" that some people have an ability for listening and befriending which can serve to prevent suicides. He said that he originally offered free professional psychotherapy sessions to suicidal individuals. There were far more requests from desperate people for his therapy than he was able to provide. However, he noticed that often his suicidal clients would cancel their appointments after waiting for hours in the waiting room to see him. He observed that the untrained volunteers taking appointments and making the tea, who he described as "ordinary" people, were listening to these suicidal individuals and discussing their problems while they were waiting to see the professional therapist. On the basis of these experiences, he founded the Samaritans, which now exists in over 40 countries and provides telephone, Internet, and face-to-face "befriending" and listening using trained volunteers. Samaritans, like the Salvation Army, listen to callers' problems in a caring and empathic manner. However, they do not provide concrete help or advice about how callers should solve their problems, but rather encourage callers to find their own solutions.

When the Salvation Army began its Suicide Bureau, they applied their existing approach with other troubled individuals, that is, talking with people about their problems and providing them concrete help. When professionals in Vienna offered telephone help, they used their previous training to guide them and simply provided their professional services over the telephone. Samaritans based their methods upon Chad Varah's observations and, to this day, they essentially accept the volunteer approach of nonjudgmental confidential listening which he developed. When these pioneer organizations were founded, there were no scientific studies upon which to determine the best approach with suicidal persons. Furthermore, there were no explicit theoretical models to describe why using a particular approach should be helpful in preventing suicides. If one were to analyze their implicit theories of suicide prevention, the Salvation Army approach can be described as providing emotional support combined with the organization providing concrete solutions to the problems which "caused" the individual to become suicidal. They would probably say that providing concrete solutions to problems which lead to suicide and convincing people to accept those solutions is what saves lives. The implicit theory behind telephone help from professional therapists was that persons who are suicidal suffer from mental health problems, mental health professionals are best-suited providers of help for mental health problems, and that this help, in the form of psychotherapeutic interventions, can be provided over the telephone in the same manner as in face-to-face psychotherapy. Samaritans, on the other hand, believe that carefully selected volunteers, when provided with some training and supervision, can prevent suicides by empathic listening in a nonjudgmental manner. For Samaritans, suicidal callers are able to find solutions to their problems when they are befriended in a respectful and nonjudgmental manner.

When Carl Rodgers developed his theory of psychotherapy, his theory was often used to explain how telephone help for suicidal callers should be provided (Rogers, 1951). The fact that Rogers' nondirective approach was originally developed for use in multi-session face-to-face professional psychotherapy was not of concern to those who used his theory to explain how to best help suicidal callers in a single session over the telephone. Rogers' approach essentially consists of nondirective empathic listening in which the therapist has an unconditional positive regard for the client, and this is expressed using various nondirective techniques. It can describe much of the Samaritan approach, but would not include the Salvation Army practice of actually providing direct concrete help to clients.

In the United-States, many suicide prevention and crisis centers were inspired by the Los Angeles Suicide Prevention Center, established in 1958 "for the evaluation, referral, treatment, follow-up and overall prevention of suicidal behavior" (Suicide Prevention Center of Los Angeles, 1966) using a more directive problem-solving approach. Although the Los Angeles center was established by a professional staff of physicians, psychologists, social workers, and nurses, the Center eventually developed a large voluntary component. Following from their original mandate, their approach is more directive than Samaritans. They pioneered telephone interventions which included direct questioning to assess suicide risk. They encouraged the use of empathic Rogerian methods, but developed a much more active approach in which questions about the nature of the callers' problems are asked, there is an evaluation of the situation and the risk of suicide and referrals to sources of help are made. Unlike the Salvation Army, they did not invite callers to live at the center, nor offer to integrate callers into a work program or provide other direct "solutions" to the person's problems. However, they did refer callers to community resources where they may be able to obtain concrete help for their difficulties.

It was not until the 1970s that researchers began to try to understand the nature of the telephone help which was being provided by suicide prevention centers, crisis centers, and other helplines and to evaluate their effectiveness. Several studies explored clinical aspects of telephone interventions using the same methodologies that were being used in evaluations of professional, face-to-face, longer-term psychotherapy (Bergin & Garfield, 2003; Goodman & Dooley, 1976; Greenberg & Pinsof, 1986; Hill & Corbett, 1993; Kiesler, 1973; Lambert, Christensen, & DeJulio, 1983). Most of these studies started with the implicit assumption that sticking to a Rogerian nondirective approach is an indication of good quality in telephone help. Several studies assessed the presence of "facilitative therapeutic relationships" as described by Rogers (Crocker, 1985; Rogers, 1951; Truax & Carkhuff, 1967), usually measuring empathy, warmth, and genuineness. Whenever studies compared volunteers to professionals, they invariably found that nonprofessionals had higher levels of "facilitative characteristics" (Carkhuff, 1968; Knickerbocker & McGee, 1973; Hirsch, 1981). D'Augelli and colleagues (1978) devised a "helping skills verbal response system" with three categories and eight sub-categories to evaluate the content and affect in responses to callers over the telephone. They concluded that university helpline volunteers were "too directive" and did not use enough open questions. However, there was no scientific evidence that being more or less directive was really any better or worse for callers. These studies of clinical aspects of interventions are all based upon the hypothesis that, if helpers do what they are expected to do according to a preconceived theory, then they should produce good results. However, the models have all been based upon face-to-face psychotherapy involving multiple sessions with the same client. None were developed specifically for telephone crisis intervention with anonymous callers.

In order to better understand the nature of telephone help and to explore the relative merits of different approaches, Mishara and Daigle (1997) conducted a study in which they related process measures on the nature of what helpers do during a call in order to assess outcomes. They listened to 617 telephone calls from suicidal callers at two primarily French-speaking suicide prevention centers in Canada, categorizing each statement by the volunteers according to a reliable 20-Item Helper's Response List, which yielded a total of 66,753 responses. Using cluster analytic techniques, intervention styles could be classified as either directive, which included more investigation and direct questions as well as giving advice and making suggestions, or nondirective "Rogerian" active listening. They found that, within a context where all calls were somewhat directive, having more nondirective Rogerian characteristics was related to a significantly greater decrease in depression, a greater likelihood of making a contract with the caller at the end of the call, and a greater likelihood of the caller keeping the contract. However, analyses on new versus repeated callers indicated that a higher level of use of nondirective Rogerian categories was significantly related to reductions in suicidal urgency only for new callers; with repeated callers, there were significant benefits from using a more directive approach. However, the overall approach in Quebec was generally directive and focused upon problem-solving. Therefore, this study cannot be used to compare Rogerian nondirective techniques with more directive approaches.

After the research findings in the 1970s and 1980s showing that volunteers were "better" than professionals in providing telephone help, volunteer-based centers increased in numbers worldwide. However, the late part of the twentieth century was marked by increasing trends toward using paid staff to answer calls, often requiring advanced university degrees or membership in a professional association.

By the beginning of the twenty-first century, the majority of countries in the world had telephone helplines and thousands of individuals were receiving help over the Internet in response to their e-mails. Helpers were trained in methods for helping callers and Internauts based upon the historical traditions of their centers. Samaritan centers, which are now linked by the international charitable organization, Befrienders Worldwide (www.befrienders.org), generally use a nondirective approach to "befriending" where respect for callers making their own decisions is paramount. In North America, most centers were inspired by the Los Angeles Suicide Prevention Center model of obligatory risk assessment, more directive collaborative problem-solving approaches, and systematic referrals to mental health and other services. Now most United States suicide prevention centers are affiliated with the National Suicide Prevention Lifeline network (www.suicidepreventionlifeline.org), sponsored by the Substance Abuse and Mental Health Services Administration. This network sets standards for best practices and has promoted the use of the more directive collaborative problem-solving approach which is described later in this chapter.

In 2003, researchers at the Centre for Research and Intervention on Suicide and Euthanasia at the Université du Québec à Montréal in Montreal, Quebec (Canada) were contracted to evaluate the nature and short-term effects of telephone help provided by the United States network of telephone helplines which were linked by common national toll-free numbers (originally 1-800-SUICIDE; now also 1-800-237-TALK) (Mishara et al., 2007a; 2007b). Unlike previous research on telephone helplines which had *a priori* notions of what constitute correct and incorrect ways to help suicidal callers, the Montreal researchers first conducted a series of consultations and studies in order to determine what to observe when describing what occurs over calls to the helpline network. They first conducted in-depth interviews with 15 center directors, asking them what they expect helpers to do at different stages of a call, what is most important to do and not to do during a call, what changes they expect in callers and why they think their approach should work. Their responses were transcribed and analyzed, and the synthesis was then mailed to all the centers (N=91 at the time of the study) that were in the 1-800-SUICIDE network. The mailing included descriptions of the two basic models described by different center directors: an active listening model and a more directive collaborative problem-solving model. The 91 center directors were asked to verify if one of the models corresponded to practices in their center. They were also asked for suggestions to complete the model and to validate the lists of qualities that telephone workers should have and things they should and should not do.

Fifty-nine centers completed the questionnaire. Generally, one of the two models proposed was said to be closest to the practices of the centers. These models were compared with our review of scientific and clinical research on the topic, and minor adjustments were made. Finally, the models were sent to five internationally renowned experts in the area of crisis interventions who were asked to validate the final result. Two final adjusted models were used as the basis of determining what to look for when listening to calls. The essential characteristics of helper behavior according to the active listening and collaborative problem-solving models were operationalized in term of items that could be rated while listening to live calls. We also observed behaviors that helpers "should" and "should not" engage in according to the respondents.

Fourteen centers, with 782 crisis intervention workers, who had sufficient daily call volume, and who indicated that they currently identified with one of the two intervention models, participated in this study. Two research assistants independently monitored each call, one coding observations on the helper, and the other coding observations of the caller's behaviors. Research assistants observed calls in real time and identified incoming calls from participating centers over a secure VPN (Virtual Private Network). They could then listen to calls unobtrusively ("silent monitoring") after entering an access code over a separate line. Data were entered during the call using a computer program that stored all coded information and comments, and the time since the start of the call was noted when each data entry was made. For the purpose of this study, we retained 1431 of the 2611 calls monitored (54.8%) which constituted all the crisis calls we could monitor of over three minutes in duration.

We performed an exploratory Factor Analysis of all the observations of helper behaviors. The resulting variables describes what can be called "styles" of intervention as follows:

1. *Supportive approach and good contact:* moral support, good contact, offers call back, reframing, talks about own experience;

2. *Collaborative problem-solving:* fact questions on the problem, questions on resources, suggests ways to solve the problem, questions on the precipitating events, proposes no-harm contract, suggests plan for action, offers referrals;

3. *Active listening:* reformulation, reflection of feelings, questions on emotions, empowers towards resources, empowers to develop plan of action;

4. *Negative style* ("things not to do"): tells caller what to do, reads information, challenges, value judgments.

The only unanticipated result from the factor analysis was that "talks about own experiences," something the center directors agreed helpers should never do, loaded on "Supportive approach and good contact." Qualitative analyses of when this occurred indicate clearly that helpers told of their own experiences to show that they had had similar problems in their own lives but had found solutions. In this context, sharing one's own experience can be seen as having been used to try to increase the confidence of the caller and to develop a better relationship.

We found that positive call outcomes are more likely when the helper expresses empathy and respect for the callers. The ability to be empathic and communicate respect may be qualities of helpers rather than skills that may be easily taught as part of a training program. Chad Varah said this when he founded the Samaritan movement in England over 40 years ago. He felt that some people are natural "befrienders," while others are not. The clear relationships we observed between these qualities and positive effects suggest that these are qualities that centers should screen for in their telephone helpers. The most powerful predictors of positive outcomes were the items in the factor analytically derived scale of Supportive Approach and Good Contact. These behaviors include: validation of emotions, giving moral support, good contact, reframing, talking about own experience, and offers to call back. Training activities exist to teach these behaviors, and our results indicate that they should be encouraged.

The preceding results suggest that some of the characteristics of helpers who use nondirective Rogerian type approaches are desirable attributes for helping callers. Nevertheless, when it comes to overall approaches to telephone help in crisis situations, the Collaborative Problem Solving approach was the only general approach we found to be significantly related to positive outcomes. The nondirective Rogerian approach was simply not related to positive outcomes. The Collaborative Problem-Solving approach involves asking fact questions about the problem, questioning about resources, suggesting ways to solve the problem, questions on precipitating events, proposing a no-harm contract, suggesting a plan of action, and offering referrals. It is important to note that having a Supportive Attitude and establishing a

Good Contact at the beginning of the call explains more of the variance in outcomes than Collaborative Problem Solving. Nevertheless, in the qualitative analyses that involved observer ratings of Directivity, the extent to which helpers follow the caller or lead the conversation, it is the mixed style that combine directive and nondirective techniques that was related to more positive outcomes.

The results of this study imply that, with suicidal callers, the use of a Rogerian nondirective approach alone is simply not warranted. This finding, which questions the practices of many telephone helplines around the world, does not mean that many of the characteristics of nondirective approaches should be abandoned. In fact, the results emphasize the importance of empathy, respect for clients, and establishing a good initial contact. However, the results suggest doing all of that is not sufficient to help reduce the risk in a suicidal caller. In addition to these positive characteristics, it is essential to also ask direct questions to assess risk, identify the full nature of the situation, and to work with the caller to agree upon specific actions to resolve the underlying problems, including suggesting referrals to resources when needed.

Another controversial finding was that sharing personal experiences appears to be helpful to callers in crisis, providing that they are used to convey an understanding of the caller's situation. The prescription of not sharing personal experiences is derived from theories of psychotherapy and may not be relevant to telephone crisis intervention, although this warrants further investigation. Telephone interventions may not need to maintain as strict a boundary between the helper and the caller as in face-to-face psychotherapy, where the client can see the therapist and the helper is identified. Helpers sharing their experiences on the telephone or over the Internet may help compensate for the lack of visual cues in the context of anonymity.

We also observed many instances of clearly undesirable behaviors during the calls we monitored. These findings highlight the need for better quality control of the nature of telephone interventions. One of the most simple and effective means of guaranteeing that callers receive good and appropriate help would be to require that calls to centers be regularly monitored for quality assurance purposes. This is already current practice in most commercial services offered over the telephone.

One of the greatest challenges in future research is to develop means for determining the relationship between short-term proximal effects which one may observe during unobtrusive observations of calls and the long-term impact on callers. Although the methodological challenges may appear daunting, it is important to conduct long-term longitudinal investigations in order to better understand if telephone suicide prevention helplines actually prevent suicidal behavior in the long term and have significant positive effects on people's lives.

A second challenge concerns the increasing use of new media and new technologies in suicide prevention. Samaritan centers around the world now answer thousands of e-mails each week. Crisis centers and helplines are increasingly offering help over the Internet in chats and online self-help programs, and are responding to short SMS text messages from suicidal individuals. However, to date we have no empirical evidence on how to best help suicidal persons when using these new technologies. Satisfaction with services does not mean that suicides are prevented or that people are actually helped by the responses they receive. To date, telephone techniques have been simply transferred to the new media, with compensation for the new limitations. These limitations include the fact that text communications lack the additional emotional content of voice communication, typing a reply can take longer than a vocal reaction, and the fact that tracing a person who has taken a lethal overdose may be impossible. Very often people who reach out for help over the Internet are experienced Internet users who consult multiple sites and may concurrently use different services, some of which may not be legitimate helping organizations.

It is essential to conduct research in order to determine the relative effectiveness of different approaches using new media and to develop empirically-derived models for best practice. Until current practices are scientifically evaluated, it is a question of blind faith and trial-and-error that will determine how we help suicidal individuals over the Internet. In the area of telephone help, it has been found that some practices which seemed logically sound, such as using experienced therapists to answer calls and training based on an exclusively Rogerian nondirective approach, are not the best ways to help suicidal callers. Thus, it is important to take a cautious approach to developing suicide prevention methods using new media and invest early in evaluation studies to confirm that the approaches we take are the most helpful.

REFERENCES

Bergin, A. E., & Garfield, S. L. (2003). *Handbook of psychotherapy and behavior change* (5th ed.). New York: Wiley.

Carkhuff, R. R. (1968). Differential functioning of lay and professional helpers. *Journal of Counseling Psychology, 15*, 117–126.

Crocker, P. J. (1985). *An evaluation of the quality of service at a volunteer-run telephone distress center*. Unpublished Master Thesis, Wilfrid Laurier University.

D'Augelli, A. R., Handis, M. H., Brumbaugh, L., Illig, V., Searer, R., Turner, D. W., & D'Augelli, J. F. (1978). The verbal helping behavior of experienced and novice telephone counselors. *Journal of Community Psychology, 6*, 222–228.

Goodman, G., & Dooley, D. (1976). A framework for help-intended communication. *Psychotherapy: Theory, Research & Practice, 13,* 106–117.

Greenberg, L. S., & Pinsof, W. M. (1986). *The psychotherapeutic process: A research handbook.* New York: Guilford.

Hill, C. E., & Corbett, M. M. (1993). A perspective on the history of process and outcome research in counseling psychology. *Journal of Counseling Psychology, 40,* 3–24.

Hirsch, S. (1981). A critique of volunteer-staffed suicide prevention centres. *Canadian Journal of Psychiatry, 26,* 406–410.

Kiesler, D. J. (1973). *The process of psychotherapy: Empirical foundations and systems of analysis.* Chicago: Aldine.

Knickerbocker, D. A., & McGee, R. K. (1973). Clinical effectiveness of nonprofessional and professional telephone workers in a crisis intervention center. In D. Lester & G. W. Brockopp (Eds.), *Crisis intervention and counseling by telephone,* pp. 298–309. Springfield, IL: Charles C Thomas.

Lambert, M. J., Christensen, E. R., & DeJulio, S. S. (1983). *The assessment of psychotherapy outcome.* New York: Wiley.

New York Times. (1907). Suicide bureau has a busy day. *New York Times,* March 2, 1907. Downloaded from www.nytimes.com.

New York Times. (1930). First aid to depressed people to be organized by Berlin officials. *New York Times,* July 13, 1930. Downloaded from www.nytimes.com.

Mishara, B. L., Chagnon, F., Daigle, M., Balan, B., Raymond, S., Marcoux, I., Bardon, C., Campbell, J. K., & Berman, A. (2007a). Comparing models of helper behavior to actual practice in telephone crisis intervention: A silent monitoring study of calls to the U.S. 1-800-SUICIDE network. *Suicide & Life-Threatening Behavior, 37,* 293–309.

Mishara, B. L., Chagnon, F., Daigle, M., Balan, B., Raymond, S., Marcoux, I., Bardon, C., Campbell, J. K., & Berman, A. (2007b). Which helper behaviors and intervention styles are related to better short-term outcomes in telephone crisis intervention? Results from a silent monitoring study of calls to the U.S. 1-800-SUICIDE Network. *Suicide & Life-Threatening Behavior, 37,* 310–323.

Mishara, B. L., & Daigle, M. (1997). Effects of different telephone intervention styles with suicidal callers at two suicide prevention centers: An empirical investigation. *American Journal of Community Psychology, 25,* 861–895.

Rogers, C. R. (1951). *Client centered therapy.* Boston: Houghton-Mifflin.

Suicide Prevention Center of Los Angeles. (1966). *Brochure describing the center and its activities.* Los Angeles: LASPC.

Trowell, I. (1979). Telephone Services. In D. Hankoff & B. Ensidler (Eds.), *Suicide theory and clinical aspects,* pp. 401–409. Littleton, MA: PSG Pub.

Truax, C. B., & Carkhuff, R. R. (1967). *Toward effective counseling and psychotherapy. Training and practice.* Chicago: Aldine.

Chapter 7

TELEPHONE THERAPY: SOME COMMON ERRORS AND FALLACIES[11]

Charles W. Lamb

This chapter attempts a quasi-facetious summary of some of the common problems encountered in learning and teaching telephone therapy. It is not intended to prevent others from making the same mistakes, which may constitute a kind of initiation to the work. It may, however, aid in early recognition of the afflictions when they strike.

Fantasies

Fantasies of Omnipotence (the "we have to do something" error)

You pick up the telephone and suddenly you are on the spot. There is a crisis, and it seems up to you to provide an instant, expert, final, once-and-for-all answer. Interesting variations to this delusion are the following:

1. *But all I'm doing is listening!*

This may be quite all right. At least it's the first thing to do. Until you've listened, you have no business even trying to be omnipotent! And the caller may not even want an answer. He may want only an ear. Or he may prefer to find his own answers. Your best calls may be those where all you do is let this happen.

---

[11] Reprinted with editing from *Voices*, 1969–1970, 5(4), 42–46, by permission of the author and the American Academy of Psychotherapists.

2. If I talk about it, it may happen (the "power of positive thinking" error).

People in trouble are not nearly as fragile as we make them out to be. In fact, to have survived some of the stresses they have been through, quite the reverse may be true of our callers. If you think the caller might be suicidal, ask him. Don't pussyfoot, and forget all the euphemisms you know about death. If you, the counselor, are too anxious to talk about such matters, how is the caller to deal realistically with them?

3. But he's manipulating me (the "who's in charge here" error).

When dealing with desperate people, it may be all right to be manipulated. Even though your need might be to play the part of the miraculous therapist, the caller's need is what counts. Perhaps all he wants is someone to acknowledge his existence. Perhaps he wants someone to attack. We're here to get him through the crisis. A recent caller said, "Whatever you do, don't call my brother-in-law Henry Smith who lives at 410 Maple Street, because I know if he came down here he'd talk me out of killing myself." Shades of Br'er Rabbit and the briar patch. But we called the brother-in-law. Obviously we were manipulated, but the brother-in-law's visit to the caller that night set in motion a benign cycle and great improvement in the plight of the caller. This does not mean that you should not strive to be aware of being manipulated. Quite the contrary. But in dealing with crisis you don't have time for character analysis. You work to put things back together and start benign cycles.

Fantasies of the Good Mother (the all-loving error)

1. Callers are all lovable human beings (and I am warm, accepting, and tolerant).

One cannot be loving for ten straight hours when dealing with crises. Callers are human and, being human, may often be hateful. They are boring, frustrating, abusive, and often downright nasty. Perhaps, for many of them, one of their biggest problems is that they are not lovable. This leads to a corollary.

2. We are all of us human (counselors as well as callers).

Some of the people who call have tried the patience of every agency in town to the point of rejection, usually well rationalized, but nevertheless rejection. If you find yourself hating a caller and you know yourself fairly well, the chances are good that you hate him because he behaves hatefully. This is not a response for you to eliminate. It is part of the caller's problem and can help you understand his plight. It helps you understand why others reject him. It helps you anticipate what reception he'll get if you make a referral. Awareness of your response helps you avoid getting drawn into the vicious cycle of demand and rejection he may enact with everyone.

Fantasies of Omniscience (the, "if only I knew about . . . , I could help" error)

1. *If only I were a (psychiatrist, psychologist, social worker, medicine man) then I could . . .*

Your therapeutic tool is yourself and the relationship you establish over the telephone. A fancy diploma hanging on the wall is of no use at such moments. Corollaries are

2. *If only I had read. . . ,* or
3. *Why the hell didn't someone tell me . . .*

The key to this is the delusion that there is some specific bit of information which, if delivered properly and with tender loving care, will transform your caller into a paragon of mental health. Forget it. By the same token, watch out for the following traps:

4. *How can they (welfare, VA, private practitioners) be so incompetent?*

Just wait. The caller will demonstrate just how they can, with a deft rendering of "Why don't you, Yes but" or some other carefully polished game.

5. *What if someone asks me for my credentials? (or its corollary, "But I'm only a . . .)*

Look at this question more closely. What is the caller asking? Is he asking "Can you understand me?" or "Can I trust you?" If so, respond to that message. Instead of becoming defensive, respond to the caller's need. For example, "I am an associate here at the center. I think you're wondering if I can understand and help you. Why don't you tell me the problem and we'll see?" Almost any caller who wants to can pick you apart. Don't get caught up in explaining yourself (which, chances are, you cannot do), but turn the conversation with a remark such as "I don't think this is what you called to talk about."

Fantasies of Infallibility/Fallibility (the delusion of fixed alternatives)

1. *If it's all I can think of, it must be the answer.*
2. *If I can't think of one, there must be no answer (and now what do I do?)*
3. *Variant: I'll call the consultant. He'll think of something.*

This kind of thinking stops a conversation dead in its tracks. It implies that, if neither participant knows the answer, there is nothing more to do. Remember that answers are created, not discovered, which leads to the next category involving a failure to use the interpersonal process to solve problems.

Fantasies of the Ultimate Answer (the delusion of wisdom)

1. *There is an answer somewhere out there (the trick is to find it).*

This leads to either an immediate paralysis of the creative apparatus or a frantic search for wisdom of another sort: the fantasy of the perfect referral.

2. *There is an answer somewhere in here (or "let me consult my Muse").*

This response also paralyzes the interpersonal process. It could be referred to as the Fantasy of Soul. It occasionally leads to the phenomenon of preciousness, or "I'm the one with the answers for you, baby" (the "I'll be here on Tuesday night if you need to call me" error). We are all to some degree interchangeable on the telephone. Avoid preciousness. Tell the caller he may call again anytime, and that someone is always here to talk with him.

Fantasies of the Benevolent Caretakers (the "Yes, Virginia, there is a Santa Claus" error)

1. *"The police will help" (or, "Lady, what do you think we're running here, a nursery school?").*

In fact, the police have been most helpful. To make the most of this help, however, you must learn what is an appropriate problem to pose for them. Our early encounters with this reality were embarrassing.

2. *Agencies are set up to help people (the altruism error).*

Being made up of humans, agencies are complexly motivated. They do reject people, often those most in need of help and most difficult to help, but whose problems are not framed in terms which open doors for them. Eventually you will learn what you can expect from various agencies in the city and how to make referrals in such a way as to maximize benefit. Until then, it is best to do all you can on the telephone and refer conservatively. Other agencies are to be used as a valuable and scarce resource, keeping in mind that, if you simply dump the problem, so will they.

On the Positive Side

At this point, the question usually arises, "What can I do, then?" The above is not meant to sound cynical, for there is a tremendous amount that can be done. The above discussion is to suggest that you should keep your expectations realistic. You are limited only by your ingenuity in this kind of work. Within this limit, you can do the following.

You can listen. It may be a rare experience for the caller. He may learn something just from having the opportunity to talk freely. Part of the answer for him may lie in learning to ask a better question.

You can be yourself. You were selected on the assumption that you are a good human being and that relationships with good human beings promote growth. People in a jam need other people.

You can mobilize resources, both in others and for others. The caller often possesses the answer, or the wherewithal to create it, but cannot see it. You can help him find his own answer by helping focus the question to be answered, for example. You can also mobilize resources for him, in the sense of making referrals, making contacts with other agencies, calling a friend or minister to the rescue, sending police, setting up an appointment in the morning, and so on.

You can learn your own limits and know when it is necessary to mobilize resources for yourself – when to yell for help. Always err on the generous side in using your consultants. We'd rather be awakened for nothing than to read of a suicide in the paper the next day. Don't feel that you don't dare call us simply to share your feelings. We know powerful feelings are aroused by this work.

You can provide feedback. You will learn from the telephone work. Share it. Leave notes. Come to the meetings and talk about your experience. Force the agency to take note of its faults. Be involved.

You can:

>empathize,
>question,
>clarify,
>suggest,
>inform,
>just plain be there!

Summary

This chapter has presented some of the recurrent difficulties that I have experienced and observed when training volunteers for telephone therapy with callers to a suicide prevention and crisis service. The therapist is warned against a number of potential traps, such as the pressure for instant answers, the fear of being manipulated, the need to achieve closure and provide ultimate answers, and the tendency to rely too heavily upon referrals. I am convinced that a great deal of truly therapeutic work can be done on the telephone with persons in crisis and that such services are valuable as more than mental health clearinghouses or stop-gap measures.

Chapter 8

THE TELEPHONE CALL: CONVERSATION OR THERAPY

GENE W. BROCKOPP

When working on the telephone at a crisis center, it is important to differentiate sharply between the conversational telephone call and the call that requires therapeutic or crisis intervention procedures. Most training programs emphasize the need for the worker at a suicide prevention center to develop a crisis intervention or problem-solving orientation whereby the worker takes an active, sometimes direct role in responding to the caller. Some centers emphasize a therapeutic orientation, which is usually defined as being a supportive relationship through which we help the caller to organize himself or his life in a more effective way so that he can deal with the problems he is having. However, it is very easy for the worker to move back into his former habit patterns of using the telephone to obtain and maintain a conversation relationship, a relationship based on the interactions of the two personalities. As a result, the therapeutic or crisis intervention process is minimized, distorted, or possibly even entirely eliminated. This is especially true when taking a call from a chronic caller or from an individual with whom the telephone worker has talked previously.

It is my opinion that, in a center which has the designation (defined as such by the client community and the staff) of being a crisis intervention or therapeutic unit, a conversational telephone call with a client is worse than none at all, for it sets up certain expectations on the part of the client regarding his relationship with the telephone worker and defines the relationship and the center in ways that tend to be unproductive and non-helpful. More explicitly, I feel that a conversational telephone call does the following.

1. It virtually eliminates the possibility that the telephone counselor can be objective or therapeutic in his function, for he is cast in the role of a friend

rather than a role of a counselor.

2. It minimizes any confrontation except that which occurs in terms of the personalities of the individuals and their ideas and opinions (which is basically not therapeutic). In contrast, a therapeutic or crisis intervention confrontation takes place when the thought processes and the behaviors of the caller are used as a basis for the interaction.

3. It may reduce the anxiety of the individual caller to the point where he does not feel a need to work on the problem he is having. In this way it may give him a false sense of security, and he may end up *feeling* better but not *being* better.

4. It develops expectations that what is taking place is the process of therapy. Since the caller is calling a place which is designated as being a helping agency, he may feel that the way in which help is provided there is the way help should be given, when in actuality it is only a conversation. If later he moves into a therapeutic situation, he may have the same expectations, thereby making it difficult for a psychotherapist to engage him in a therapeutic or crisis intervention process.

The therapeutic or crisis intervention aspect of a telephone call decreases dramatically if the caller makes subsequent calls to a center. This relationship is formulated more specifically by the statement, "An inverse relationship exists between the number of calls an individual makes to a suicide prevention or crisis center and the amount of therapeutic or crisis intervention process taking place within the call." A corollary to this is that, "When the client requests to talk to one individual and only one individual at a crisis telephone service, the interaction between the two parties has usually moved to a conversational level."

In a short-term intensive training program, emphasis is usually given to helping people become effective crisis interveners, focusing on the problems people have that can be dealt with in a very direct, confrontive way, without a detailed understanding of the personality dynamics involved or the process of therapy as traditionally defined. Telephone counselors are trained to be experts in the process of problem-solving. They are usually not qualified or capable of undertaking and following through with a therapeutic plan in terms of treatment goals relative to the interpersonal functioning of the individual. Therefore, when a chronic caller calls the center, the telephone counselor has very few tools available to work with since the chronic caller usually does not have a problem which can be dealt with in the crisis intervention model (and, in addition, is usually a "yes, but" person). Therefore, the interaction is rarely directed toward a problem-solving goal or toward termination. When the caller requests the same person, the communication that takes place is usually of a personal nature, having little overt therapeutic quality even though the client may rationalize that he wishes to talk to a particular person because he has given this person information on himself and does not want to reiterate the information to another individual. The emotional involvement between the two people, without the corresponding competence on the part of the telephone counselor to deal with this transference or to work with the involved personality dynamics inherent in this situation, results in the helpfulness of the call being limited to a friendly conversation.

This process is very seductive. One of the difficulties in working at a suicide prevention and crisis service as a telephone counselor is that one is constantly responding to individual problems without having much feedback as to results of one's interactions. Therefore, when a client requests to talk to an individual counselor, the amount of reinforcement that this gives to the person is often overwhelming. The result is that the telephone counselor, having a sense of competence and sometimes believing that he is able to work with a client with whom everyone else has failed, develops a relationship in which he is "over his head" and begins to act like a therapist rather than a crisis intervener or a supportive counselor. This relationship usually continues for a period of time until the telephone counselor begins to recognize that he is unable to deal with the problems the client has since he does not have the appropriate tools. His sense of guilt usually overtakes him at this point, and he covertly attempts to "dump" the client without overtly rejecting him. The client often picks up these signals, views the center and the worker as being incompetent and rejects the center and its help before it rejects him. The end result is a frustrated telephone worker.

As I stated previously, to minimize the occurrence of these problems, we need to analyze the interaction in the telephone calls. In a conversational telephone call, the relationship between the two individuals is a social one based on the interactions between the two personalities. In a therapeutic or a crisis intervention orientation, the relationship between the telephone counselor and the client is neither social or antisocial but rather asocial in orientation and content. This permits the telephone counselor to be objective and to view the problem that the caller has in terms of his behavior and his social relationships. The counselor can then engage the client in a discussion of his behavior and problems, with the goal of assisting him to improve his situation or modifying the effect of the problem that he has.

With the relationship being asocial, the telephone counselor is able to relate to the individual emotionally, while at the same time assisting the person to confront his own behavior and make any changes he feels are necessary. The relationship then does not become one of friendly equality or one of dominance and submission, but one in which the primary function of the telephone counselor is to understand the person and the problem which disturbs him (a problem for which the telephone counselor assumes a responsibility to assist the individual) and, through the process of self-confrontation or suggestion, effects a change in the caller's life pattern.

This requires a great deal of finesse and skill on the part of telephone counselors. We must listen very carefully to what is going on in the relationship, not just in terms of the counselor's personal relationship to the client, but in terms of the way the client is relating himself and his ways of interacting with people through his contact with the counselor. Changes in the direction of the conversation, emphasis on aspects of the conversation, changes in mood or omissions, all will be used as a basis for understanding the person. The counselor, through his objective yet emotional involvement with the person, must be able to look past the content into the patterns of behavior through which the person has found himself in difficulty which he is not able to work out for himself.

Within this asocial setting and orientation, the telephone counselor works with the problem the person brings to him in an objective way. By probing into the problem, the emotional reactions the person has to the problem, and the assumptions the person has made about himself relative to the problem, the counselor begins to point out directions by which the individual can marshal his resources, both interpersonally and intrapersonally, into a pattern which will sustain him and hopefully move him to a point of satisfaction or equilibrium.

In summary, I want to emphasize that, in my opinion, a suicide prevention and crisis telephone service is not a social telephone line, nor is its primary purpose that of providing social interaction for individuals. We cannot assume that, if the counselor is doing no harm by being conversational, he can continue being conversational because he may be doing some good. A crisis intervention or therapeutic relationship seldom takes place in a social setting and, when it does, it is achieved only because the counselor is skilled in being able to separate the social elements from the therapeutic ones. It is unlikely that the average telephone counselor has either the insight or the skill to achieve this, nor should he be expected to have this expertise. Therefore, it is necessary that we clearly differentiate between the crisis intervention, supportive, therapeutic relationship and the social, conversational relationship. We must train individuals who work at a telephone service to be involved in the former and not in the latter.

A service which provides social interaction for lonely people may be advantageous and useful. However, when a service which is classified as providing counseling or crisis intervention provides a conversational or social relationship, it is both distorting its purpose and setting up assumptions in the client's mind which often preclude his obtaining therapeutic help. To allow for the advantages of a conversational relationship, it may be necessary for suicide prevention centers to differentiate their telephone services by providing a Care-Ring, call-out, conversational telephone service for the chronic, disabled, isolated individual and a suicide prevention and crisis line for crisis intervention or supportive therapeutic services. To do less would be to confuse both the public and the telephone counselor and result in the fragmentation of a valuable community service.

Chapter 9

ACTIVE LISTENING

David Lester

Active listening is the popular term for the counseling technique based on client-centered therapy which was developed by Carl Rogers. Now referred to as client-centered therapy or person-centered therapy (and formerly as Rogerian therapy or nondirective therapy), Rogers' view of human nature and psychological treatment initially served as a reaction and protest to psychoanalysis and behavior therapy. Rogers advocated a more humanistic perspective which viewed the person as an healthy, integrated organism and focused on the individual's subjective experience as the basis for psychotherapy.

In addition to proposing a technique for conducting psychotherapy, Rogers has also put forward a theory of personality. The most explicit formulation of this theory is found in Rogers (1959), and a brief review of his theory of personality will provide the rationale for his technique of psychotherapy.

Rogers' Theory of Personality

Rogers argued that the infant has an inherent tendency toward actualizing himself, and his behavior is directed toward satisfying this need. If this need is satisfied, he experiences pleasure. Rogers noted that the infant is best conceptualized as an organized whole (a gestalt). Furthermore, his perception of the environment is more critical in affecting his behavior than the environment "as it really is."

Part of the process of actualizing involves differentiation, and soon a portion of the child's experience becomes symbolized in an awareness of being. This awareness can be described, according to Rogers, as self-experience, and eventually this awareness becomes elaborated into a concept of self. About this time of development, the child develops a need for positive regard. This need is universal, pervasive, and persistent, perhaps innate or perhaps learned. When the child interacts with adults, particularly his mother, he comes to search for and be satisfied by love from her. The likelihood of receiving this maternal love eventually becomes more important in affecting his behavior than his need to actualize himself.

Soon the child develops a need for positive self-regard, and whether the child feels this positive self-regard will depend to a large extent on whether his parents give him positive regard. Typically, parents set up *conditions of worth*, that is, they regard the child positively only if certain conditions are met. Their regard for him is said to be conditional. As a result, such a child will have positive self-regard only if he meets these conditions of worth. In contrast, in the healthiest environment, a child would receive *unconditional positive regard*. The child would be prized and valued by his parents no matter what he is or does. In this case, no conditions of worth would be set up. Rogers felt that this case was hypothetically possible, theoretically important, but not found in the real world.

Once conditions of worth are set up, then the child will begin to experience discrepancies between the conditions of worth set up by his parents and his actual experiences. When his experiences are consistent with his conditions of worth, Rogers felt that the child will accurately perceive and symbolize the experiences. When his experiences are not consistent with the conditions of worth, he will feel anxiety and his perception of the experiences may be selective and distorted. This process tends to break down the unity of the organism. Certain experiences tend to threaten his self. To maintain his self-concept, he has to resort to defensive maneuvers. His behavior is regulated sometimes by his self and sometimes by elements of his experience which are not included in his self. The personality becomes divided. He is no longer true to himself. Because of others, he has falsified some of the values he has experienced. Rogers notes that this is not a conscious choice but rather a result of his development in the presence of his parents.

The incongruence between his self and his experience leads to incongruencies in his behavior, some of which are consistent with his self and some with experiences which have not been assimilated into his self. Experiences which are incongruent with the self and with the conditions of worth are perceived as threatening, but Rogers felt that this perception of the threat is not necessarily conscious. The nature of the threat is that, were the experience to be perceived accurately, then the conditions of worth would be violated. Then the need for positive self-regard would be frustrated, and the person would feel anxiety.

This leads to neurosis. Neurosis basically involves selectively perceiving, denying to awareness some aspects of your experience, and distorting your experience in order to keep your total perception of experience consistent with your conditions of worth. Rogers includes in such maneuvers behaviors such as rationalization, compensation, fantasy, projection, compulsions, phobias, paranoid behaviors, and catatonic states.

If the incongruence between an experience and the conditions of worth is large, occurs suddenly, and has a high degree of obviousness, then these neurotic defensive coping mechanisms cannot operate successfully. Anxiety will be experienced, and a state of disorganization will exist. We would see such an individual undergo an acute psychotic breakdown. The behavior will appear to be irrational. Typically, the behavior may be consistent with the denied aspects of experience rather than consistent with the self. For example, if a person has kept his sexual impulses under rigid control, denying them as an aspect of his self, then during his state of disorganization, he may act upon such sexual impulses.

An individual undergoing such a process may take two paths. The denied experiences may stay dominant, and the person will now defend against an awareness of his self. Alternatively, the self may regain dominance but in a greatly altered state. For example, the self will probably contain the idea that it is a crazy, unreliable person with no control over its impulses.

Having briefly reviewed the theory of personality proposed by Rogers, let us now turn to the techniques which he suggested for effective psychotherapy.

The Techniques of Client-Centered Therapy[12]

First, Rogers noted that it is crucial for the therapist to develop an empathic understanding of the client. In empathic understanding, the counselor attempts to understand what the client is saying and feeling and to communicate to the client that he has this understanding. Empathy is not sympathy. Sympathy may require you to feel sad for another person's loss, while empathy requires one simply to understand that the other person is experiencing a loss. Empathy involves the counselor attempting to understand the client's feeling from that person's perspective and to demonstrate, usually verbally, that understanding to the client. In other words, the client-centered counselor is not asking himself "How do I perceive this?" but rather "How does the client perceive this?"

Client-centered counselors do not try to give advice or suggestions, do not direct the conversation, and do not give interpretations of the client's behavior. What do they do? They try to listen and interact with the client in an em-

---

[12] This section was written in collaboration with Michael Braswell.

pathic and genuine manner. They listen to what the client says and reflect back to the client what they think the client is feeling. The counselor listens to the emotion behind the client's words. During the counseling session, the counselor is really trying to understand "Is this what you are saying? Is this what you are feeling? Have I understood you properly? Can I hear what you are feeling?" The following are examples of such interactions:

Example 1

Client: My work supervisor keeps picking on me. He thinks he is better than me. Next time he does it, I'm going to punch him in the nose.

Counselor: You are feeling a lot of anger about the way your work supervisor is treating you.

Example 2

Client: Now my wife wants a divorce. She's all that has kept me going. I don't know if I can take it anymore.

Counselor: You're really feeling depressed about your wife's decision.

Example 3

Client: My parents don't care what I do as long as I don't embarrass them. So what if I do some drugs?

Counselor: Life's hard when you feel alone. You are wondering how much your parents care about you.

Example 4

Client: I'm getting out on parole tomorrow. I've been in the joint for five years. It's a big world out there, but I'm going to make it.

Counselor: I can see that you are really feeling good about getting out. Even with the adjustments you will have to make, you sound ready to give it your best shot.

Second, unconditional positive regard is an important element of Rogers' approach because it attempts to provide the client with a relatively nonjudgmental emotional climate or environment. In such an environment, the client may be able to more freely and accurately express his feelings, attitudes, and values without the fear of being criticized. This core condition might be viewed as an ideal element of counseling that can be approached but never fully realized. As human beings we are all inclined to place conditions on whom we regard positively.

The third condition, genuineness, involves the counselor serving as a role model for the client. If the counselor cannot be open and honest in an appropriate way with the client, it is unlikely that the client will learn to be genuine. The colloquial saying that "Children learn more by what their parents do than by what they say" is also true in the counselor-client relationship. The condition of genuineness requires that the counselor share something of himself with the client. Self-disclosure by the counselor encourages greater openness on the part of the client. The counselor has the opportunity to help the client only to the extent he knows "where the client is really coming from."

Rogers stressed the importance of the philosophical orientation of the counselor. The counselor must respect the client. He must feel a deep respect for the significance and worth of everyone and trust in the capacity of everyone to achieve insight and constructive self-direction (Rogers, 1951). Assuming that he has adopted this orientation, the counselor's role is to concentrate completely on understanding the client as the client seems to himself. If the counselor can do this, then the patient can do the rest. The counselor has to simply understand deeply and accept the conscious attitudes of the client.

Why is this technique effective? If the client can see his attitudes and feelings accurately expressed by the therapist, he can see them objectively, which paves the way toward acceptance of these elements. He then will be able to explore elements which he has hitherto suppressed or denied to himself, especially the negative emotions of guilt and hostility. Faced with an accepting counselor, the client can accept himself.

Rogers noted that, if the counselor maintains the client-centered attitude completely, there will be minimal danger of biasing the client. The distortions of the counselor's perception (which are called countertransference in psychoanalysis) are never completely eliminated, but they are considered reduced in client-centered therapy, for the client-centered counselor is not asking himself "How do I perceive this?" but rather "How does the client perceive this?" Rogers felt that his clients discover that they are responsible for themselves in the therapeutic relationship. They begin to explore their attitudes and feelings, especially those previously denied by them. They then begin to reorganize these thoughts, especially the inconsistencies.

A client-centered therapist does not give advice or suggestions, does not direct the conversation, gives no interpretations of the client's behavior, and rarely answers the client's questions. What does he do? He listens. He may encourage the client to continue, perhaps by saying "mm-hmm," perhaps by being silent. He listens to what the client says and repeats back to the client what he thinks is the essential part of what the client has said. He may listen to the emotion behind the client's words and mention what he has heard to the client. All the time, the therapist is really asking "Is this what you are saying? Is this what you are feeling? Have I understood you properly?"

Rogers (1959) made a very formal statement of his theory of psychotherapy. First, for therapy to occur, the following conditions must be met:

1. the client must be in a state of anxiety;
2. the therapist must be free from anxiety, at least in the therapeutic rela-

tionship;
3. the therapist must experience unconditional positive regard for the client;
4. the therapist must experience an empathic understanding of the client's point of view; and
5. the client must perceive conditions 3 and 4.

Second, if these conditions are met, then therapeutic movement will take place in the following way:

1. the client will express his feelings more freely;
2. these feelings will be more relevant to his true self;
3. he will more accurately perceive his experiences and distort them less;
4. his feelings will pertain more to the discrepancy between his experiences and his self-concept;
5. his self-concept will be reorganized so as to accept those previous experiences which are now accurately perceived;
6. his self-concept will become more congruent with his experiences, and so he will become less defensive;
7. he will perceive the therapist's unconditional positive regard more, and his unconditional positive self-regard will grow; and
8. he will come to experience himself more as the locus of evaluation rather than the conditions of worth.

Rogers does not attempt to explain how this occurs. He is content to state that, if the conditions are met, then the changes will take place.

Carkhuff (1969) has developed a systematic treatment and training model that combines client-centered therapy with behavioral principles. The client-centered therapeutic approach includes: (1) the facilitation stage (building a relationship with the client), and (2) the self-understanding stage (the client gains insight and begins to develop new attitudes regarding himself and others). To these two stages, Carkhuff added (3) the action stage. The action stage involves the counselor acting as a catalyst to help the client gain insight and develop and enact a plan of action that will result in positive behavioral changes.

All forms of psychotherapy these days help patients change by means of the therapist-client interaction, and client-centered techniques are acknowledged by most therapists to be an important component of treatment. Rogers' client-centered therapy, however, goes beyond this and makes the therapeutic relationship the essential core of the therapy. The therapeutic relationship and its quality becomes a goal of the therapist, not merely a technique to be used on the client. The therapeutic relationship is the core of the therapy and the foundation of the whole enterprise.

Active Listening in Crisis Intervention

Client-centered therapy is the crucial first ingredient of the effective crisis counseling. When a client is in crisis, the counselor first must listen. What are the problems, and what is the client's state of mind? Then the crisis counselor must move on to assess the client's resources, and finally the counselor must help the client find a course of action with which to attempt to resolve the problem. Thus, all crisis counselors are trained to be good client-centered therapists.[13]

REFERENCES

Carkhuff, R. R. (1969). *Helping and human relations.* New York: Holt, Rinehart & Winston.

Gordon, T. (1975). *Teacher effectiveness training.* New York: Crown.

Gordon, T. (2000). *Parent effectiveness training.* New York: Three Rivers Press.

Rogers, C. R. (1951). *Client-centered therapy.* Boston: Houghton-Mifflin.

Rogers, C. R. (1959). A theory of therapy, personality, and interpersonal relationships, as developed in the client-centered framework. In S. Koch (Ed.), *Psychology: A study of a science, Volume 3*, pp. 184–256. New York: McGraw-Hill.

---

[13] Gordon (1975, 2000) has advised parents and teachers on the use of active listening, an important first step in problem-solving.

Chapter 10

COGNITIVE THERAPY APPROACHES TO CRISIS INTERVENTION

DAVID LESTER

The cognitive therapies are based on the notion that our negative emotions and disturbing behaviors result, not from the unpleasant events which we experience, but rather from our thoughts about the events which we experience. It is not the fact that we were fired from our job or that our spouse divorced us that makes us anxious or plunges us into despair. Rather, it is what we say to ourselves after these traumatic events which leads to the anxiety and despair.

There have been many systems of psychotherapy based on this premise, but the first and most noteworthy system was called rational-emotive therapy.

Rational-Emotive Therapy

Rational-emotive therapy, devised by Albert Ellis (1962, 1973), is concerned with the emotions which impair our existence. Let us say that the client experiences some unpleasant experience, such as a rejection by a lover. This is the activating experience. In the unhealthy sequence, there follows an irrational belief. "Isn't it awful that she rejected me? I am worthless. No desirable woman will ever accept me. I should have done a better job of getting her to accept me. I deserve to be punished for my ineptness." Finally, particular emotional states result from this irrational belief. The client feels anxiety, depression, worthlessness, or hostility. This is the consequence.

In the healthy sequence, the activating experience is followed by a rational belief. "Isn't it unfortunate, annoying, or a pity that she rejected me," and consequent on this rational belief are the emotional states of regret, disappointment, and annoyance.

Rational beliefs increase happiness and minimize pain. They are related to observable, empirically valid events. Irrational beliefs decrease happiness and maximize pain. They are related to magical, empirically invalid hypotheses for which there is no evidence. They prevent the client from fulfilling his desires in the future. Psychotherapy involves teaching the client that his emotional states are not a result of the activating experiences, but rather the irrational beliefs. The client must be taught to dispute the irrational beliefs. Why is it awful? How am I worthless? Where is the evidence that no one will ever love me? Why should I have done a better job? By what law do I deserve to be punished? Once the client can substitute rational beliefs for his irrational beliefs, he will be much happier and make appropriate choices.

Ellis listed several common irrational beliefs.

1. The idea that it is a necessity for us to be loved or approved by almost every significant other in our lives.
2. The idea that we should be thoroughly competent, adequate, and achieving in all possible respects in order to consider ourselves worthwhile.
3. The idea that human unhappiness is externally caused and that we have little or no ability to control our terrors and disturbances.
4. The idea that our past history is an all important determinant of our present behavior, and that because something once strongly affected our life it should affect it indefinitely.
5. The idea that there is invariably a right, precise, and perfect solution to human problems and that it is catastrophic if this perfect solution is not found.
6. The idea that, if something is or may be dangerous or fearsome, we should be terribly concerned about it and keep dwelling on the possibility of its occurring.
7. The idea that certain people are bad, wicked, and villainous and that they should be severely punished and blamed for their villainy.
8. The idea that it is awful and catastrophic when things are not the way one would like them to be.
9. The idea that it is easier to avoid than to face life's difficulties and responsibilities.
10. The idea that one should become quite upset over other people's problems and disturbances.
11. The idea that we should be dependent on others and need someone stronger than ourselves on whom to rely.

The reader may doubt that he or she ever has such thoughts. Remember that Ellis phrased these thoughts in an extreme way and that they typically occur to us in a much milder form. Consider, for example, what you say to yourself when the line you chose at the drive-in window of the bank moves so slowly. "Why do I always choose the wrong line?" Empirical evidence would probably indicate that you do not always choose the wrong line, but you may remember only the times your line moved slowly. You go out to the parking lot and find that your tire is flat. You curse and say, "This is terrible. I can't stand it" (Irrational thought #8). If you were to give dying from cancer one hundred points, how many points would a flat tire rate? Perhaps five or ten – hardly terrible – and can you stand it? Of course, you can, and you will. It is these sentences that we say to ourselves that lead to our extreme distress.

The Techniques of Rational Emotive Therapy

The rational emotive therapist is active, persuasive, educational, directive, and hard-headed. The therapist teaches the simple basic theory of rational-emotive therapy. He disputes the client's irrational beliefs. There are no "shoulds" or "musts," awful is an indefinable term, and so on. The therapist shows how these irrational beliefs generalize to all aspects of the client's life. The therapist points out that the causes of disturbed behavior are recent and observable. The early experiences of the client affect him now only because he himself perpetuates them. The client must be taught to observe and challenge his own belief system continually. Finally, the client has to *act* in addition to simply understanding.

Rational-emotive therapy does not deal with the client's early history, unconscious thoughts and desires, nonverbal behavior, dreams or any transference that occurs in the therapeutic situation.

The therapist teaches the theory, points out irrational beliefs, and interprets quickly, with no pretense that the interpretation is hard to accept. The therapist is confrontational. He persuades the client to express himself openly and to bring out his real feelings. He reveals and attacks the client's defenses, but he unconditionally accepts the client. The therapist attacks the beliefs, not the client.

The therapist will use any technique that will aid him in this task: role playing, modeling, bibliotherapy, stories, behavior therapy techniques, philosophical discussion, or audiovisual aids. The therapist also stresses homework assignments. The client must be made to act and to experiment. Meet three new people this week. Visit your nagging mother-in-law this week instead of avoiding her. This helps the client take risks, gain new experiences, interrupt dysfunctional habits, and change philosophies.

The client must in the end come to like himself and accept himself. He must accept full responsibility for choosing or not choosing to make himself disturbed. The client *can* make himself undisturbed. The client must get into the habit of questioning himself and finding his own rational answers. Ellis states that the goals of rational-emotive therapy are to leave the client with a minimum of anxiety (self-blame) and hostility (blaming others), and to give him a method of self-observation and self-assessment that will ensure that he will continue to be minimally anxious and hostile. In line with this goal, Ellis has written up his theory and its techniques in popular books, written for the layman. The therapy and techniques are simple enough to enable some people to employ them without visiting a therapist. Rational-emotive therapy requires about one to 20 individual sessions and then 20 to 80 group sessions. It can take as long as two years, but it may require only 10 to 20 sessions.

Cognitive-Behavioral Therapy

Cognitive-behavioral therapy was formulated by Aaron Beck (1976). The goal of the therapy is to modify faulty patterns of thinking, both directly and indirectly. It focuses upon the cognitions (thoughts and attitudes) of the client and the assumptions and premises that underlie these cognitions.

The client is taught to recognize his idiosyncratic cognitions. They are called idiosyncratic because they reflect a faulty appraisal of some aspect of the world. There may be a distortion of what the person perceives, or perhaps he misinterprets what he perceives. Often these faulty cognitions lead to unpleasant emotions. But despite the fact that they are faulty, they seem to the client to be plausible, and they occur involuntarily and automatically. The client is taught to distance himself from his cognitions. He must learn to examine his cognitions objectively, evaluate them critically, and distinguish between his evaluations and reality.

Next, the client must be taught to correct his cognitive distortions. To do this, it helps if the client can specify the particular kind of fallacious thinking that he has. Burns (1981) has provided a list of these types of cognitive distortions and given many examples of each type.

1. In *all-or-nothing thinking*, the person sees things in black and white categories. If your performance is not perfect, you are a failure.
2. In *overgeneralization*, the client makes unjustified generalizations on the basis of one incident. For example, a single failure leads the client to believe that he will never succeed at anything.
3. *Mental filter* involves picking out negative details and dwelling on them exclusively.
4. *Disqualifying the positive* involves rejecting positive experiences because, for some reason, they don't count.
5. When clients *jump to conclusions*, they incorrectly read the mind of others (without checking with those others whether their conclusion is correct or not), and they predict the future incorrectly (usually pessimistically).

6. In *magnification (or catastrophizing)*, the client exaggerates the significance of an event. If you fear dying, you may interpret every unpleasant sensation as a fatal disease.
7. In *emotional reasoning*, clients assume that, because they feel it is, it must be true.
8. *Should statements*, such as "I must," "I ought," and "I should" lead to guilt. They should be replaced with "It would be nice if I . . ."
9. *Labeling* is an extreme form of overgeneralization. Others are rarely as evil as you think they are, and you are not as bad as you think you are. For example, calling others "bastards" or yourself a "loser" leads to stronger negative emotions.
10. In *personalization* you see yourself as the cause of some negative outcome when, in reality, you were not the only, or even the primary, cause.

Similarly, Lazarus and Folkman (1984) noted that people are not simply passive receivers of stressful life events. The experience of stress is mediated by the cognitive appraisal of the stressors made by people. The stressful event is given a personal meaning, and this cognitive appraisal mediates the distress experienced. Events will be perceived as more stressful if they are imbued with personal relevance, that is, if the person feels threatened. They will also be perceived as stressful if the individual feels that he or she has no control over the situation. Stressful events which are chosen by the individual, which are predictable, and over which he or she feels he or she has some control are, in fact, often sought out by people as a source of excitement.

Therapy provides a safe situation in which to test cognitions. The client can be helped to confront them and examine them. This learning process transfers to real-life situations by directly modifying the thoughts and by rehearsing the reality-oriented thoughts. For Beck, then, like Ellis, disturbed behavior and unpleasant emotions are simply a matter of disordered thinking.

Cognitive Therapy in Crisis Intervention

There have been attempts to suggest ways in which cognitive therapy can be used in crisis intervention (e.g., Roberts, 1995). Dattilio and Freeman (1994) noted that cognitive therapy is ideal for crisis intervention because:

1. it invites the client to become an active part of the process,
2. it encourages the counselor to be active and direct in guiding the sessions,
3. it requires the development of a problem list which gives the counseling structure,
4. even as a system of psychotherapy, cognitive therapy tends to be short-term,

5. it requires the counselor and client to collaborate and to work as a team, and
6. it leads to the development of a method of coping with crises in the future so that clients can begin to help themselves without the aid of a counselor.

First, in a cognitive therapy orientation, it is important to assist the client to see that the situation that has brought on the crisis is temporary. From a long-term perspective, it is possible to "wait out" the crisis. Developing the long-term view decreases the perception of the urgency of the crisis situation. Second, it is important to point out to the client that the degree of upset (depression, anger, or anxiety) is partly a result of the client's thoughts and perceptions about the crisis situation and not simply the situation in itself. Third, people in crisis are often confused and disorganized in their thinking. They have a difficult time even seeing clearly what the problem is, and clarifying this can often calm a client. In addition, they typically can think of only one or two coping tactics, whereas many other tactics can usually be identified.

A cognitive therapy approach to crisis intervention has several stages.

1. The counselor must build a relationship with the client and establish rapport, and active listening plays an important role here.
2. The counselor must evaluate the severity of the crisis situation. Is this client in physical danger? Can the client be put on hold if another call comes in to the service?
3. The counselor must develop the "problem list," that is, what are the specific problems that the client is facing?
4. The counselor must then assess and mobilize the client's resources and strengths.
5. Finally, the counselor and client must identify a plan of action through collaborative problem-solving.

Dattilio and Freeman identified five different types of crisis clients.

- *Adolescents* can be of any age and are experiencing a major life change, especially relevant to their self-image. They hesitate to show weakness, vulnerability, or dependency,
- *Isolates* have lost the motivation to make or continue social relationships. They often lack social skills, fear rejection, and are apathetic.
- *Desperate clients* have experienced a sudden psychological shock and are in desperate need of immediate help. They may have only shaky contact with reality, and the counselor's calm and caring manner may reduce the clients' despair and increase their contact with reality.
- *One-shot crisis contact* clients are normal, stable people who seek help to deal with a recent crisis situation. They want some advice or someone to act as a sounding board to advise them on which plan of action to take.

- *Chronic clients* have continual crises and have learned to cope by calling on resources (the telephone crisis service or their therapist) each time. They have not learned to cope by themselves, but rather to rely on others.

From a cognitive therapy perspective, it is important, once a collaborative relationship has been established with the client, to help clients identify the thoughts that they have when confronting crisis. Clients differ in how easy they find this task. Those who talk out loud to themselves (when alone) are usually better at recalling their thoughts because they have given them voice. Clients will often have particular cognitive distortions (or irrational thoughts). Some might be prone to catastrophize ("Yesterday was the worst day of my life!"), while others label themselves in a negative way ("You idiot!").

There is an extensive body of research which indicates that *hopelessness* is the critical mediator of suicidal ideation and behavior. The client who feels hopeless has a set of negative expectations about the future and feels that there is nothing that can be done to change the outcomes. It is important for the counselor to identify and reinforce small gains or improvement in the client for this will improve the client's mood.

Reinecke (1994) noted that it is helpful to acknowledge that suicide is an option if the client is considering suicide. Clients often appreciate that a counselor can understand that. This acknowledgement takes way from the client the tactic of trying to manipulate the counselor by threatening suicide and demonstrates the counselor's candor. The counselor can then lead the discussion to the identification of other alternatives and concrete steps that might be taken. If better alternative options can be identified, then the client may not feel as hopeless.

Examples of Cognitive Crisis Intervention with Suicidal Clients

Ellis (1989) presented an account of one session he had with a suicidal client. Helen was 27 and referred to Ellis by a trainee therapist because she was threatening suicide. She was a chronically depressed resident in obstetrics and gynecology. She had lost three lovers because, she said, they saw her as crazy and as a potentially terrible wife. She had panic attacks and phobias and a strong need to be loved and approved by others. Her younger sister had committed suicide two years previously.

Ellis adopted an encouraging attitude toward Helen. He pointed out to her that she had lots of qualities which make for a good life – intelligence, the ability to work toward long-term goals, a desire to have intimacy with others, and good looks. He pointed out to her that she ignored these qualities because of her perfectionism. If I am not perfect, then I am a failure! He suggested that Martians, if they visited the earth and heard her speak, would die laughing since objectively she was so good. Helen laughed with him, and he congratulated her on her sense of humor.

Ellis disputed her beliefs that she had to be perfect, that she was not permitted to fail at tasks and in love affairs, and that she must be loved by everyone under all conditions. He pointed out that life was uncertain, but that to choose the only certainty – death – would be a Pyrrhic victory. He pointed out that, because she was in emotional pain now, did not mean that she would be in pain for ever. Suicide would, in fact, end the chance of future happiness.

Ellis accepted the client but rejected her irrational thinking and foolish behavior. He encouraged her to accept herself as she was and to stop rating herself globally. Ellis ended the session by giving Helen three homework assignments: (1) to call her therapist or Ellis before she actually tried a suicide attempt; (2) to look for and write down all absolutist and perfectionistic musts and shoulds that preceded her depressions and suicidal thoughts; and (3) to read and sing some of his songs which illustrated his system of therapy. Her therapist informed Ellis several weeks later that Helen was no longer suicidal and that they were working on her long-standing problems of depression.

Emery et al. (1981) presented the case of a married 53-year-old man who, without warning, shot himself. After three weeks of intensive care, he was transferred to a psychiatric unit. His first wife had died of cancer 14 years previously and, when asked about the reasons for his suicide attempt, he mentioned disappointments with his work and worries about his current wife's health. He had been depressed for several months before his suicide attempt. He recalled feeling isolated and alone at work after he had been promoted. He had to tell some men that they were laid off, and he felt that he could not face them. This made him feel like a failure. He saw himself as too weak for his new position, and he expected to be fired.

Emery was able to identify irrational components to the client's statements. He felt he was letting *everyone* down and that *he* was hurting them but, after his suicide attempt, his boss visited him and praised him for his past decisions. This raised his self-esteem and challenged his conclusions about his performance. The therapy focused on the client's view of himself as a boss, his view of himself as a husband, and his interpersonal skills related to anger in others. The client came to perceive and challenge his perfectionist ideas as illustrated by his thought that, if someone became angry with him, it meant that he was incompetent. He was shown how he failed to check his conclusions about himself with others. Role-playing was used to practice his interpersonal skills, and he was taught decision-making strategies.

Emery also presented a case of a suicidally depressed 40-year-old woman who had become depressed after her husband's brother died of leukemia. She had attempted suicide once before, during her college years. When interviewed, she said that she had been useless to her husband. He had wanted her to go with him to the hospital to visit her dying brother-in-law, but she had stayed home to clean the house instead. She had failed her husband. She felt guilty for feeling happy in the months before he died. She was now disgusted with herself and felt that she did not deserve to live. She had taken to drinking heavily, but this further undermined her ability to function effectively. After some additional stressful events (her car breaking down and pain from an intrauterine device), she attempted suicide with antidepressants. She saw suicide both as an escape and as a deserved punishment.

Her irrational thinking included perfectionist goals (to feel good about herself she had to operate always at peak efficiency), evaluating herself in terms of her use to others (so that she had to meet her husband's needs completely), that she should not be happy if others are unhappy, and that if she made a mistake than she was a detestable person. She was worried about her husband's possible negative reaction to her now, so the therapist arranged a joint session so that she could check this out with her husband. Her husband turned out to be caring and supportive. The therapist designed simple tasks for her to complete, such as shopping for groceries with her husband, so that she could successfully complete them and increase her sense of competence. She successfully faced acquaintances without falling apart and managed most of the routine tasks. She was asked to complete a Weekly Activity Schedule in which she rated each activity in terms of the mastery and pleasure it gave her so that she could realistically appraise her accomplishments. The assignment for her was to work in moderation and not at maximum capacity.

The therapist also worked on her all-or-none thinking (either I meet all the demands of others or I am selfish), her shoulds and oughts (I should function perfectly), focusing on the negative and disqualifying the positive, overgeneralizing (she put on a few pounds and saw herself as losing control), and catastrophizing.

Discussion

Although these sessions involved face-to-face counseling, it can be seen how the techniques of cognitive therapy can be used with a suicidal client in crisis during the first session. If a crisis counselor picks up irrational thoughts on the part of the client, it can be useful to point them out and demonstrate that they are increasing the distress experienced by the client. In addition, from the perspective of Transactional Analysis (see Chapter 11), focusing on the irrational thoughts encourages the Adult ego state to take charge of the mind's organization and reduces the influence (temporarily, at least) of the Child and Parent ego states. This will often calm the client.

REFERENCES

Beck, A. T. (1976). *Cognitive therapy and emotional disorders.* New York: International Universities Press.

Burns, D. (1981). *Feeling good.* New York: Signet.

Dattilio, F. M., & Freeman, A. (1994). *Cognitive-behavioral strategies in crisis intervention.* New York: Guilford.

Ellis, A. (1962). *Reason and emotion in psychotherapy.* Secaucus, NJ: Lyle Stuart.

Ellis, A. (1973). *Humanistic psychotherapy.* New York: Julian.

Ellis, A. (1989). Using rational-emotive therapy (RET) as crisis intervention. *Individual Psychology, 45,* 75–81.

Emery, G., Hollon, S. D., & Bedrosian, R. C. (1981). *New directions in cognitive therapy.* New York: Guilford.

Lazarus, R. S., & Folkman, S.(1984). *Stress, appraisal, and coping.* New York: Springer.

Reinecke, M. A. (1994). Suicide and depression. In F. M. Dattilio & A. Freeman. *Cognitive-behavioral strategies in crisis intervention,* pp. 67–103. New York: Guilford.

Roberts, A. R. (Ed.) (1995). *Crisis intervention and time-limited cognitive treatment.* Thousand Oaks, CA: Sage.

Chapter 11

TRANSACTIONAL ANALYSIS AND LEARNED HELPLESSNESS APPROACHES TO CRISIS COUNSELING

DAVID LESTER

The purpose of the present chapter is to suggest how crisis intervention and counseling can use ideas from transactional analysis, a system of psychotherapy, and from a theory of depression known as learned helplessness. First let us examine transactional analysis.

Transactional Analysis

Eric Berne (1961, 1964) proposed a theory of personality, a theory of interpersonal relationships, and a theory of therapy. These theories have come to be known as Transactional Analysis. As a theory of human behavior, transactional analysis consists of a structural description of the mind and an interpersonal description of interactions. The techniques of therapy that stem from these two components are called structural analysis and transactional analysis, respectively.

Berne's initial formulation of the ideas aroused great interest in therapists, and many adopted the ideas as a framework for their therapy. Whereas many therapy systems show very limited receptivity to new ideas, transactional analysis has shown a willingness to listen to and incorporate modifications and additions to basic premises and techniques. This has led to a considerable change in the theory and style of transactional analysis over the years. Initially, transactional analysis had a strong resemblance to the ideas of psychoanalysis from which it stemmed. Since the later additions to the theory and style of transactional analysis have decreased its uniqueness and made it more eclectic, the present section focuses primarily on those ideas that appear in the early formulations of transactional analysis as described by Berne in the 1960s.

Whereas psychoanalytic theory focuses on particular wishes, Berne focused on ego states. An ego state is a coherent set of behavior patterns or a system of feelings that motivates a related set of behavior patterns. Complete ego states can be retained in the memory permanently, and states from earlier years remain preserved in a latent state, with the potential to be rearoused.

Structural analysis is concerned with the analysis of ego states. Berne classified the ego states of the person into three types. The *Parent* ego state is a judgmental ego state, but in an imitative way (primarily, of course, by imitating the person's parental judgments). It seeks to enforce borrowed standards. In psychoanalytic theory, it parallels the superego. The *Adult* ego state is concerned with transforming stimuli into information and with processing that information. It corresponds to the ego in psychoanalytic theory. The *Child* ego state reacts impulsively, using pre-logical thinking and poorly differentiated and distorted perception. It corresponds to the id in psychoanalytic theory.

People are always in some ego state. They can shift from one to another, and these ego states are usually Parent, Adult, or Child states. The state that is predominant is said to be cathected. It has executive power for the moment and is experienced as the real self. Each ego state is an entity in Berne's theory and differentiated from the rest of the psychic contents. It has a boundary which separates it from other ego states. However, the ego boundaries are semipermeable under most conditions. The shift from one ego state to another depends on the forces acting on each ego state, the permeability of the boundaries of each ego state, and the capacity of each ego state to be cathected. Ego states can affect behavior directly by being the predominant ego state of the moment or by influencing other ego states. For example, the Child can function as an independent ego state (free) or under the Parent's influence (adapted).

The analysis of ego states can be made much more complex. Children have three ego states: a Parent ego state, an Adult ego state, and a Child ego state. When a trauma occurs that fixes these ego states, all three are fixed. Thus, a particular Child ego state that an adult has, in fact, contains three components: a primitive Child ego state, a primitive Adult ego state, and a primitive Parent ego state. Similarly, this primitive Child can be subdivided into three states (Parent, Adult, and Child), and so on.

The Parent ego state is an introjection of our parents' demands. But we had two parents. Therefore, our Parent ego state is a dual ego state. Secondly, our parents had parents (our grandparents) and so on. Thus, our Parent ego states contain elements of the ego states of our grandparents and to a lesser extent great-grandparents and so on.

Berne also speculated that the Adult ego state was composed of several components. Adult ego states have an openness that is child-like, which Berne called *pathos*. The Adult ego state also possesses qualities such as sincerity and courage, which Berne called *ethos*. The Adult ego state therefore has child-like and parent-like qualities, not due to influences from the Child and Parent ego states, but on its own.

Berne felt that his three basic conceptual units should be distinguished carefully from the psychoanalytic terms of superego, ego, and id. Ego states are organized states and not merely sets of wishes. For example, the Child ego state has an organization, a unified will, logical processes, and negation, which make it very different from the psychoanalytic conception of the id.

The basic conceptual units that Berne defined gave him a reasonably large armormentarium with which to describe the various psychological disorders. Psychopathology can be looked at in several ways using Berne's structural analysis.

Structural Pathology

Here the pathology is conceptualized in terms of deformities in the structure of the total personality. For example, one ego state may govern exclusively. If the Child ego state governs exclusively, excluding the Adult and Parent ego states completely, we may have a narcissistic impulsive personality (as in a high-class prostitute) or a person with schizophrenia. The Adult and Parent ego states are said, in this case, to be decommissioned. The Child ego state is experienced as the real self.

In mild levels of mania (hypomania), the Child and the Adult ego states exclude the Parent ego state, and the Child dominates the Adult. However, the Adult still has some influence. In mania proper, the Child excludes the Adult as well, but the Parent ego state is still monitoring the person's behaviors and the Child ego state knows that it is being watched. Thus, the Child ego state may have delusions of reference and persecution (such as that people are recording what is taking place). When the Child ego state becomes exhausted, the Parent ego state assumes control and takes revenge, leading to severe depression.

A second structural problem is contamination. One ego state intrudes through another ego state's boundaries. For example, if the Adult ego state contaminates the Child ego state, we may have delusions and hallucinations. In schizophrenia, the predominant ego state is that of the Child, and the hallucinations and the delusions are intrusions from the Parent and Adult ego states respectively. Since it is an intrusion, the Child ego state does not realize that it has been intruded upon. The boundaries are not firm enough to recognize the intrusion for what it is, that is, from a source outside of the Child ego state boundaries.

Processes originating from the predominant ego state plus its contaminated areas are *ego-syntonic*, whereas processes originating from outside the boundary are *ego-dystonic*. Contamination is important in understanding the difference between dissociated thoughts and delusions. If a thought from the Child ego state becomes conscious to the Adult ego state, the Adult ego state experiences it as a strange idea, a dissociated thought. If however, contamination has occurred and the thought from the Child ego state comes from the contaminated area, then the thought is ego-syntonic and may be labelled (by others) as a delusion. The Adult ego state does not realize that it is a thought from outside of its boundary. In neurosis, the Adult ego state is contaminated by the Child and Parent ego states, and the Parent ego state is the prime enemy. In free association, the Child ego state can talk while the Adult and Parent ego states listen. The censorship of the Parent ego state is suspended.

Functional Pathology

Here psychological disorder is described in terms involving the lability of cathexis (that is, the shifting from one ego state to another) and the permeability of ego state boundaries. For example, a person may show a stubborn resistance to shifting ego states, or may shift opportunistically. Ego state boundaries can be firm or soft and, the softer they are, the easier is contamination.

Content Pathology

Berne did not label a third source of pathology, but he implied one. He said that Parent, Adult, and Child ego states can all be syntonic with one another, with no contamination or functional pathology, yet there may be pathology. He gave the example of a happy concentration camp guard. The example suggests that the *content* of the ego states may be sufficient to cause pathology.

What causes pathology? Berne says little about this except that trauma during childhood is responsible, a conventional psychoanalytic view. Since trauma is responsible, however, and since a child may experience several trauma, there is no reason why a person may not grow up with several Child ego states, each with its organization and characteristics.

Berne's theory is obviously derivative from psychoanalytic theory. His definition of ego states parallels the tripartite division of the psychic structure proposed by Freud. Yet his focus on the complexity and organization of ego states encourages us to view them more like holistic systems.

As a system of psychotherapy, transactional analysis first helps clients recognize and label their ego states. The therapist then helps the clients make the boundaries between the ego states firm so that ego states do not intrude upon one another. In longer-term psychotherapy, the therapist then explores how these ego states operate in interpersonal relationships, in the games that people play, and in the scripts that they develop for their life. Only the structural analysis has relevance for crisis intervention.

The goal of a structural analysis is to teach clients this language for description of their psychological processes and to help them identify the source of each of their wishes, impulses, thoughts, and feelings. Clients must be led to discover the areas of contamination between ego states and helped to clean up this contamination. We want them to develop three separate and distinct ego states with firm boundaries. We want them to switch from ego state to ego state easily and appropriately. If one ego state is governing their behavior too exclusively, then we try to increase the influence of the other ego states on their behavior.

Suicidal Behavior in Transactional Analysis

Suicide in transactional analysis is seen as deriving from an injunction given to the child (Woollams et al., 1977). Infants need permission to exist and belong in the world. From the moment of birth, infants receive messages, both verbal and nonverbal, from parents and significant others about whether they really want him around. The infant or child can receive a "Don't exist" message at any age and in various ways. Perhaps the infant is handled stiffly or with distaste. Perhaps a parent actually says, "I wish you'd never been born." These "Don't exist" injunctions can come from the mother's or father's Parent ego state (You are bad! Go away!) or from their Child ego state (I hate you! You are a nuisance). If several significant others make such "Don't exist" injunctions, then the injunction will be stronger than when only one significant other makes the injunction.

This injunction becomes part of the individual's *script*. Since these injunctions are made to the child, they become part of the Child ego state. Thus, in later life, even though the individual's Adult ego state may make a decision not to commit suicide, the individual's Child ego state must also accept this decision for the individual to be free of suicidal impulses. Furthermore, even when a client's five-year-old Child ego state may decide not to kill himself, his two-year-old Child ego state may not be listening (Woollams & Brown, 1978).

Scripts can be classified into four types based on two decisions: "I'm ok" versus "I'm not ok" and "You're ok" versus "You're not ok" (Harris, 1967). Berne (1972) labeled suicidal people who have decided "I'm not ok and they're not ok" *futility suicides*. Suicidal people who believe that "I'm not ok but everybody else is ok" are *melancholic suicides*. It is unlikely that anyone in the "I'm ok" position would be suicidal.

Goulding and Goulding (1978) have argued that, since it is the child who makes decisions on the basis of the information available to him, then it is the Child ego state which can make new decisions. The Gouldings try to create a situation in which the client can make a *redecision* for himself. At first, this redecision may have to come from the Adult ego state, but eventually, for complete transformation, it must come from the Child ego state.

Drye et al. (1973) described an initial approach to this problem. They argued that an evaluation of suicidal risk should involve the client. The client knows how intense his suicidal urge is and how strong his controls are. He knows how long and under what circumstances he trusts himself not to commit suicide. If a client has suicidal impulses, Drye suggested having the patient make a no-suicide contract for a specific period – an hour, a week, six months, or however long the client can sincerely agree to. This decision by the client's Adult ego state frees the client from the suicidal ruminations which have often diverted him from dealing with the interpersonal or intrapsychic problems which are confronting him. However, not all therapists think that no-suicide contracts are useful in preventing the client from killing himself (Goldblatt, 1994), and they warn that therapists should remain alert to the possibility of suicide in their clients after they have signed such contracts.

Stewart and Joines (1987) noted that the "Don't exist" injunctions probably came from the Child ego states of the parents. The father may be jealous of the attention his wife gives to the newborn. The mother may resent having the family pressure of raising children. It is the Child of these parents that covertly or overtly conveys the "Don't exist" injunction to their infant. Children may also perceive "Don't exist" injunctions where there are in fact none. Hearing that his birth was a difficult one may lead the child to think "Just by being born, I hurt Mommy. Therefore, I am dangerous, and so I deserve to be hurt or killed." Children defend against the "Don't exist" injunction by making *compound decisions*. For example, a child may decide that it is all right to go on existing as long as he. . ., and complete this thought with various possibilities – as long as I work hard or as long as I do not get close to people.

English (1969) has described a phenomenon which she called *episcript*. In this, a parent conveys an injunction to the child and adds to it the non-verbal message "I hope this happens to you so that it won't happen to me." For example, a mother with a "Don't exist" injunction in her own Child ego state may pass it on to her child, hoping that, if the child commits suicide, then maybe she will not have to. The injunction is like a hot potato, passed on from generation to generation.

Transaction Analysis in Crisis Counseling

Orten (1974) has applied the transactional analysis perspective to the crisis counseling of the suicidal individual. Noting that it is the client's Child ego state which is feeling the despair and hopelessness, Orten suggested that the counselor must seek to get the client's Adult ego state in control. Responses from the counselor's nurturing Parent ego state will not accomplish this. Messages which convey "Somebody loves you," "Oh, promise me you won't kill yourself," or "I won't let you do it" simply reinforce the client's Child ego state as executive.

Asking questions designed to elicit information is the most effective method of getting the client's Adult ego state to take over control. The questions should be non-threatening, that is, unrelated at first to the problems causing the depression. A premature rush into considering the client's problems strengthens his Child position. Once clients are firmly established in the Adult ego state, they may immediately feel relief for, in this ego state, they see the world differently and feel more capable of dealing with it.

The counselor can then decide whether it would be useful to now begin discussing the problems confronting the client or to postpone such a discussion to the next contact. If the counselor begins an exploration of the personal problems, he must be alert for signs that the client is slipping back into a Child ego state. If this happens, the counselor should recontact the Adult ego state by moving away from the topics which have elicited the Child ego state.

Learned Helplessness

Seligman (1974) argued that depression was a manifestation of a phenomenon that he called learned helplessness. Seligman exposed dogs to inescapable electric shock. When he then permitted these dogs to escape the painful electric shocks, they did not learn to do so. In contrast, dogs not previously exposed to the inescapable electric shock soon learned to escape the electric shocks. Seligman suggested that the dogs who were forced to endure inescapable electric shock had learned to be helpless, that is, they had learned that the shock was *always* inescapable. The experience of previous failure caused them to make little effort in the future.

For human depression, therefore, it has been argued that, in psychologically painful situations, the person tried to escape the pain but failed. He then generalized from this experience and learned (or decided) that he could never escape the pain. Seligman noted that depressed people typically decide that the cause of their failure is stable and that it will persist into the future. Thus, they see their depressed state as permanent rather than transient. They may label themselves as stupid or the task as too difficult (an internal and an external factor respectively). Both of these causes are stable. Finally, depressed people generalize from their failures. Rather than seeing their failure as specific to that particular task in that situation at that time, they anticipate a continued progression of failures in all kinds of situations in the future.

Rosenthal (1986) has given several examples of suicide in the context of learned helplessness. A 17-year-old girl could get no positive reinforcement from her father. She noticed that he liked football, so she enrolled in a football league for women and excelled. Her father still refused to praise her even after impressive performances on the field, and she took an overdose of medication. A second case involved a woman who was physically abused by her husband, a local politician whom the police refused to believe capable of physical abuse. When she failed to persuade the police to take action, she attempted suicide.

Rosenthal outlined steps which can help the client who is suicidal within the context of a learned helplessness syndrome. First, Rosenthal suggested having the client sign a written contract to call the therapist if he feels suicidal. This shows the client that his behavior has had an effect on one person, the therapist.[14] Second, it helps if the therapist intervenes in the client's environment. For example, perhaps the therapist can talk to a suicidal teenager's parents? This shows the client that the therapist is on his side and that he does not have to tackle his problems alone. It demonstrates that the situation, though undesirable, is not catastrophic and can be approached rationally.

Third, Rosenthal suggested having the client keep a log of self-defeating thoughts and feelings. Unlike cognitive therapists, Rosenthal did not advocate challenging these thoughts and changing them. Simply tabulating the thoughts lessens their frequency and impact. Fourth, the therapist can work on anger. Rosenthal believes that anger and suicide are closely related. Shy and timid people need to be taught assertive skills and then to express anger in socially acceptable ways. Aggressive clients need to be given homework assignments in which they practice more empathic ways of expressing their feelings.

Finally, Rosenthal suggested that it is important that the therapist hold out hope that solutions are possible. A teenager ignored by her parents can be told that the therapist will talk to them or teach her ways of dealing with them. A physically abused wife can be told that tomorrow the therapist will take her to court to get a police protection order and then to a women's shelter.

---

[14] Range (2005) provides a good analysis of the pros and cons of no-suicide contracts.

REFERENCES

Berne, E. (1961). *Transactional analysis in psychotherapy.* New York: Grove Press.
Berne, E. (1964). *Games people play.* New York: Grove.
Berne, E. (1972). *What do you say after you say hello?* New York: Grove.
Drye, R. C., Goulding, R. L., & Goulding, M. E. (1973). No-suicide decisions. *American Journal of Psychiatry, 130,* 171–174.
English, F. (1969). Episcript and the 'hot potato' game. *Transactional Analysis Bulletin, 8*(32), 77–82.
Goldblatt, M. J. (1994). Hospitalization of the suicidal patient. In A. A. Leenaars, J. T. Maltsberger & R. A. Neimeyer (Eds.), *Treatment of suicidal people,* pp. 153–165. Washington, DC: Taylor & Francis.
Goulding, R. L., & Goulding, M. E. (1979). *Changing lives through redecision therapy.* New York: Brunner/Mazel.
Harris, T. (1967). *I'm ok – you're ok.* New York: Avon.
Orten, J. D. (1974). A transactional approach to suicide prevention. *Clinical Social Work Journal, 2,* 57–63.
Range, L. M. (2005). No-suicide contracts. In R. I. Yufit & D. Lester (Eds.), *Assessment, treatment, and prevention of suicidal behavior,* pp. 181–203. Hoboken, NJ: Wiley & Sons.
Rosenthal, H. (1986). The learned helplessness syndrome. *Emotional First Aid, 3*(2), 5–8.
Seligman, M. (1974). Depression and learned helplessness. In R. J. Friedman & M. M. Katz (Eds.), *The psychology of depression,* pp. 83–113. New York: Halstead.
Stewart, I., & Joines, V. (1987). *TA today.* Chapel Hill, NC: Lifespace.
Woollams, S., & Brown, M. (1978). *Transactional analysis.* Dexter, MI: Huron Valley Institute Press.
Woollams, S., Brown, M., & Huige, K. (1977). What transactional analysts want their clients to know. In G. Barnes (Ed.), *Transactional analysis after Eric Berne,* pp. 487–525. New York: Harper's College Press.

Chapter 12

GESTALT THERAPY APPROACHES TO CRISIS INTERVENTION WITH SUICIDAL CLIENTS[15]

Lin Young and David Lester

As we have seen in previous chapters, the major influence in the development of crisis intervention techniques has been client-centered therapy (Lester & Brockopp, 1973) and, more recently, cognitive-behavioral therapy (Dattilio & Freeman, 1994; Roberts, 1995). Suggestions have also been made for orienting crisis intervention using the concepts of transactional analysis (Orten, 1974) and learned helplessness (Rosenthal, 1986). Nevertheless, Roger's client-centered approach to crisis intervention remains the predominant technique taught to crisis interveners working in suicide prevention centers. However, a client-centered approach is not suitable for every client in crisis, and it is important to provide additional tactics for crisis interveners to utilize for clients who do not respond well to a client-centered approach.

Gestalt therapy, developed by Perls, Hefferline, and Goodman (1951), has enjoyed a modest popularity since its description, and it offers some guidelines for counselors engaging in crisis intervention which may be suitable for *some* clients. For example, O'Connell (1970) provided a general orientation for the crisis intervener from a Gestalt perspective, but he did not develop specific techniques or suggest issues which must be addressed.[16]

---

[15] Adapted from Young and Lester (2001).
[16] Additional works on Gestalt therapy, aside from those cited in the text, include Polster and Polster (1973), Korb, Gorrell, and Van De Riet (1989) and Wheeler (1991).

Gestalt Theory

Perls (Perls et al., 1951) focused upon the interaction between the organism and the environment. Organisms live by maintaining the difference between themselves and the environment. They assimilate parts of the environment and reject others and, therefore, grow, sometimes but not necessarily at the expense of the environment. The parts that are assimilated are always novel, and so assimilation involves creative adjustments by the organism. Whenever the person and the environment interact, there is *contact*. Perls refers to the contact boundary as foreground, the immediate environment as the field, and the contact as a mutual interaction.

Gestalt therapy is concerned with analyzing the structure of the actual experience of the contact and providing the client with awareness of both the foreground and the field. The counselor is not only concerned with what is being experienced, but on how it is being experienced; not on what the person says, but how he says it. The goal is to heighten the contact and brighten the awareness of both the experience of contact and the boundary disturbances experienced by the person within the contact. This translates into a fuller experience and appreciation of the contact and an awareness of how individuals disturb their contact boundaries.

As people grow and assimilate new experiences, they have to make creative integrations of this new material with the old material. This often involves destroying the status quo, the former ways of perceiving the world. The person needs to aim for a better integration of all the material, not a mere reshuffling of the components. This process may easily arouse fear and anxiety, for it is scary to change our set habits when the new material demands that we must. The psychologically healthy person does not shrink from that task, whereas neurotics avoid restructuring their perceptions and habits and hold to their old perceptions of reality which are likely to be distorted by the unfinished traumatic experiences of the past.[17] When neurotic people do enter new experiences, these experiences are unlikely to be perceived accurately in the new context, and the neurotics fail to recognize their distortions.

The *self* is your system of contacts with the environment at any time. Healthy people identify with their *self* and are able to perceive choices within their contact. Unhealthy people are alienated from their self. Unhealthy people try to conquer their own spontaneity, believe they are restricted and without choices, and limit their assimilation of new experiences. The set of identifications and alienations one has is called one's *ego*.

---

17 Perls uses the term "neurotic" as defined in the older versions of the Diagnostic and Statistical Manual of the American Psychiatric Association.

Since Gestalt therapy aims to increase the contact and the awareness of the contact between the person and the environment, therapy works on the ego. The goal is to train the ego by inviting and encouraging it to experiment with awareness, to make it more aware of the environment and of physical responses within the body of the person. Once the ego has its senses revived and is making better contact, therapy is finished, and the client can take over from the counselor.

The role of the therapeutic situation is to provide clients with safe opportunities to experiment by opening up their awareness. Perls is aware that the major difficulty is to release the clients' healthy power of creative adjustments, without having them mimic the counselor's conception of reality. The aim is growth, not correction. Can society tolerate people regulating themselves with less regard for societal norms and values? Perls felt that society can tolerate more self-regulation than occurs at present.

The therapeutic situation is safe. It allows clients to experiment with mild levels of anxiety since there is a clear invitation to do so without judgment and recrimination. Clients do not flee from anxiety but remain aware of both their anxiety and their responses to it. The role of the counselor is to increase awareness of the client's responses, while providing enough support for the client to continue.

Perls believes that the organism can be trusted to self-regulate. For example, if the client has some inner conflicts, the counselor should not try to reduce or remove these conflicts. Conflict is a means of growth. The counselor's task is to heighten the client's awareness of both sides of his conflict so that they may feed on the environmental material and come to a crisis point within the safety of the therapeutic environment. The sharper a conflict, the greater the struggle, and the more likely the outcome will be positive for the client. Working through conflicts enables people to grow. Neurotics have become neurotic partly by attempting to resolve conflicts prematurely, leaving a great deal of material outside of their awareness and employing elaborate defense mechanisms to avoid intense experiences.

Many conflicts stem from early situations left unfinished and unresolved. They affect present behavior because the client repeatedly tries to finish current situations which are not accurately differentiated from the past. Energy is diverted from growth-producing activity as a result of confusion and raised levels of anxiety. One of the tasks of therapy is to uncover these unfinished situations and support the person in resolving them. To complete therapy, clients need to become aware of how the unfinished situations affect their decisions and behaviors in the present context. Once the unfinished situation is completed, the trauma is lessened and is less likely to repeat in new situations outside of the client's awareness.

When we experience conflict, we need to recognize that both opposing forces are within us. People typically do not tolerate their ambivalence (awareness of polarities), and they project one aspect of their conflict onto the environment. Both aspects of the conflict need to be integrated into the whole, with awareness. When self-regulation is not in place, individuals are likely to project their major life conflicts onto the perceived regulatory bodies (parents, spouses, society, etc). This projection creates a reliance on the projected party to provide resolution and removes from the individuals the power to resolve their own conflicts.

For Perls, the way to psychological health lies in the harmonious integration of all aspects of one's self. Therapy aims to increase awareness and to teach the client to trust in organismic self-regulation. Awareness will assist in resolving issues. The body is wise and, left to itself, will heal itself. The counselor does not try to direct clients, but rather to free them for growth that is self-directed. This is central to the development of an internalized and powerful locus of control. Thus, the implication is that people will self-regulate, be responsible for their own behaviors, and seek constructive relationships within their environment. Seligman's (1974) work on learned helplessness indicates that people, even when they have an internal locus of control, can perceive themselves as powerless or without choice in important situations. The responsibility and potency gained from self-regulation places an enormous responsibility and freedom upon the individual. External regulation removes responsibility and choice, and individuals are, in a sense, victims of their immature ability to achieve self-regulation. They may, therefore, perceive their lives as limited by enforced or limited choices.

Gestalt Approaches to Crisis Intervention

Acknowledgement of Suicidal Ideation

Clients need to talk openly about their thoughts and feelings regarding suicide while feeling safe and accepted. Many clients will give mild clues or hints in order to check whether the counselor has the courage and alertness to discuss these issues. Some clients need only this – time with someone who is present, receptive, and respectful with whom they can talk openly about their suicidal thoughts and despair. However, individuals who are suffering from a high level of perturbation and have a history of maladaptive behaviors and unsatisfying relationships do not feel relief quickly from discussing their situation and need more intense therapy.

Exploration of the Suicidal Plan

Discussing the client's plan for suicide is typically used as an assessment tool, but it has far more important aspects. If the counselor can provide acceptance and support as clients talk about their plans, this is likely to build a trusting relationship, establish a stronger sense of connection, and bring invaluable awareness to the clients. Clients will have a greater understanding of the gravity of their situation and become more willing to engage in a therapeutic relationship. Clients will be able to discover a largely dissociated part of the self and begin to integrate rather than simply suffer. Exploration of death and funeral fantasies can assist them to integrate death concepts, reduce the romantic aspects of suicide (when it is discussed in a down-to-earth manner), and facilitate awareness of revenge (and other) aspects involved in their suicidal desires. An opportunity to gain insight into the unconscious forces that are motivating them toward suicide is often uncovered in their death and funeral fantasies.

Exploring Anger

The act of suicide can be viewed from a psychoanalytic perspective as an expression of anger directed inward onto the self. Yet many suicidal clients are often unaware of this aspect of themselves. When they are able to fantasize the pain and anguish that their parents, partner and children will go through after their suicide, they can be encouraged to explore and own their anger (or sadness). It is useful for them to gain a sense of their power and their anger so that they no longer perceive themselves as merely victims. On the other hand, clients who are openly acting-out anger are likely to discover their more vulnerable emotions and feel some compassion toward themselves.

Angry thoughts need to be explored with care since outbursts of rage can fuel angry thinking. Anger is a "mover emotion," designed to help people protect themselves. Angry thoughts can be employed as a means to avoid other emotions. When people are hurt or threatened, anger is often their first response, and to avoid the vulnerability and pain associated with sadness they can continue on a circular treadmill of angry thinking and blaming. Talking over the reasons for anger usually does little to dispel it, even though venting these thoughts may be temporarily satisfying. A good strategy is to encourage the client to not repress anger, but neither to act upon it prematurely. A workable strategy is to locate the sensations of anger and stay in touch physically with the sensations until the energy dissipates. Differentiating between angry thoughts and the experience of anger is important when working with suicidal clients since their angry thoughts without the experience of the emotion will easily recycle without any new insight. Their angry feelings can then prematurely move into unsafe actions turned inward onto the self and possibly others.

When they can experience their anger physically and express some of that to the counselor, clients will frequently discover their grief and sadness. Motivating and activating clients' anger can seem very useful and energizing although, when they are not able to allow their sadness to arise and be experienced, they become trapped with their anger and are unable to let go of damaging relationships and situations. In other words, anger is an agent of change but, when change is initiated, grief for the loss of the relationship must be able to be tolerated by the clients. When this is not possible, their risk factors escalate, and they are forced by their unresolved pain to return to the situation or to harm themselves.

Awareness of Ambivalence

Many suicidal clients are quite intolerant of the conflicting forces within them. They are confused, and they mistrust and cannot tolerate their own ambivalence toward living and dying. Recognition that it is possible, and indeed normal, to hold opposing thoughts can reduce their cognitive dissonance. It can also provide time and initiate the process of integration. They do not have to make a decision right now, and they can take the time they need to establish resources, support and skills to integrate their polarities. An exploration of the opposing forces assists them to explore whether they want to die or whether they wish to escape their turmoil, pressure, or confusion. When the counselor inquires about their motivation for suicide, the responses conform to Shneidman's (1996) commonalties of suicide – the purpose of suicide is to escape unbearable psychological pain. This one issue – the wish to escape pain and confusion – is vital and needs clarifying. A clear direction for the counselor and client can become the foreground – to address the unbearable pain.

If they could radically diminish their incessant thoughts and tensions, they would most likely choose life. If they do reach their crisis in this conflict during therapy, they will be in a safe and supportive place with the counselor, and this is most likely to occur when the client is very close to suicide. Working with polarities and holding the awareness of both polarities (as well as the motivations behind the opposing polarities) will create integration and awareness of the choices between these polarities. It can also facilitate awareness of repressed memories of important events which have propelled the client toward suicide. During the exploration of these polarities, clients will often express despair. To be fully present, listen and support despair when clients are in despair without reducing or minimizing their despair is vital.

Acknowledgement of Their Psychological Struggle

Many suicidal clients describe incessant thoughts that pervade their waking hours and interrupt their sleeping. They seem trapped, and we must not add more elements to their trap. Rather we can facilitate awareness of their entrapment. An opportunity to stand outside their struggle, and observe how circular and self-defeating the process is, can facilitate understanding and awareness. Some time to be still and operate fully in the present moment can bring much needed relief.

Some clients are keenly interested in a confluent relationship (bonding) with the counselor. Suicidal clients are so desperately lonely and rudderless that their desire to seduce a potent individual into their problems is powerful. Counselors must remain aware of this process, and the processes here are most frequently the clients' avoidance of emotional experiences by distracting with talk about problems and suffering. The counselor needs to be interested in what it is like for clients to be trapped in their problem, but only empathically. Empathy must not change into confluence. An urge to give in to confluence will eventually give rise to despair on the part of the counselor when he or she tries to escape the confluent relationship and when clients manipulate the counselor with suicidal threats or actions.

Understanding the Major Issues

Individuals can become stuck on constricted or circular thinking, and this circumvents their awareness of their primary or deepest needs and concerns. Intense listening on the part of the counselor is necessary to assist the client to uncover these concerns. In Gestalt therapy, the counselor is alert to deflection – the process where clients speak of a major issue or event and minimize their responses to that event (in particular, existential issues that include lack of meaning, loneliness, fear of death and dying, fear of freedom and making choices). Frequently, clients have unresolved grief or intensely shameful issues that they are unable to acknowledge – to themselves or to the counselor. In the case of existential issues, they may not have the words to express these deep concerns, or they may have accepted them as insignificant since everybody experiences them. Although Gestalt therapy does not focus primarily on the content of what is said by clients, listening to clients in their terms, with their content, will often reveal the issues. Some individuals fall into despair when faced with the freedom of making life choices; others wish to die in order to join deceased loved ones; yet others are bored and frustrated with their deadness and see no hope for release from their despair. Many suicidal people consider themselves victims, blaming their past experience of abuse or their parents or partners. These people are more likely to seek a confluent relationship. Others are so very interpersonally isolated that they seek help in order to decide calmly to commit suicide, without wanting any connection at all.

For suicidal clients, particularly those whose suicidality has been chronic and who have seen many counselors, it is important to help them become aware of where they are and how they stand to gain from being there. This is a sensitive issue for suicidal clients, particularly if they have the fantasy that the counselor can do something to take their despair away and alleviate their lonely struggle. If clients have seen health care workers who let them down, they may have a considerable investment in holding on to their despair and struggle. However, when they realize that they have been holding on to the feelings, and that consistent talking about feelings is quite different from experiencing them, they have the beginnings of awareness.

Framing the major issues, their impact, and their time frame with the client, and checking that this is accurate, will assist in forming a picture of the whole, set the scene for what needs to be addressed, and define what is foreground for the client. For example, if the client believes that the issue is that his wife has to come home or he will commit suicide, it is imperative to help him differentiate between his inability to cope with the emotions involved in losing his wife and his desire to commit suicide.

Addressing the Underlying Loneliness

The majority of suicidal clients experience loneliness as a central issue. Their loneliness may not be apparent to them, particularly when they have many superficial relationships or when they consider loneliness to be a natural state – in these cases, they may not raise the issue. Acknowledging their loneliness can make them vulnerable since they need a counselor to connect with them. In order for lonely people to receive attention, they need to present problems to the counselor, preferably problems with no solution in sight. This is likely to be how they look for attention from any friend. It is important to establish how lonely they are on an interpersonal and intrapersonal level, and help them recognize how they withdraw, psychologically or behaviorally. Acknowledgement of the pain and suffering in their loneliness can assist in developing a strong and clear connection. It will also alert the counselor to possible dependency issues. In some instances, clients have relationships where the people involved are very willing to provide support but are met with rejection or do not know what to do to be effective. This may be near to the clients' awareness, yet not acknowledged. Their loneliness is significant in terms of the therapeutic relationship, and it is invaluable to check the parallel process – whether they are lonely now, with the counselor, and whether they are aware of their resistance to contact with the counselor. It is likely that what they do with significant others is repeated with the counselor if they are chronically suicidal and, if they do not feel lonely with the counselor, he or she needs to check whether there is a degree of confluence already established.

Clarity in Their Responses to Feeling Questions

When suicidal clients are asked "How do you feel?" they frequently respond with a thought or a state mistakenly believed to be a feeling. This creates confusion, and the clients' tendency to repress emotions is reinforced. An acknowledgement of their response as a thought and a return to a focus on their feeling is essential.[18] There is also the issue of "trained" clients who can label their emotion without experiencing it. Finding out how their emotional energy is impacting on them is imperative in Gestalt therapy, and the accurate labeling is merely a side issue. Many who are trapped in chronically maladaptive behaviors will display resistance to experiencing emotions.

Working with their resistance, exploring what their resistance is, and the purpose of their resistance (usually reported by clients as fears of disintegration, going crazy or not knowing how to stop their crying) are empowering and provide greater self-awareness and will further enhance the quality of the therapeutic relationship. The understanding that they are not expected to do what is too difficult for them and the willingness on the part of the counselor to be patient and respectful toward their difficulty will enhance their self-respect and enable more trust to enter the relationship.

Awareness of How the Client Is Repressing Emotions

It is useful for clients to become aware of how they repress emotions. Such awareness allows them to make choices on when and where they will be able to express their emotions. It can also bring awareness that they are active in repressing emotions when they are not aware that they are doing so. This increases the clients' personal awareness and power. A focus on their bodily sensations such as muscular tension in the throat, neck, shoulders, chest, fist, or jaw, or an awareness of how they regulate their breathing in order to block their emotional experience, will assist them in gaining awareness of how they

---

[18] Feelings are sensed physically – emotion is the feeling in action, moving the energy through the body and out to the environment to make contact.

block emotions and provide them with the opportunity to choose to get in touch with their emotions and eventually express them. When clients become afraid of being overwhelmed by their emotions, they can be reminded of the process they employ to block emotion. This process is an asset that can now be employed by choice rather than as an automatic, out of awareness, function. Even when clients choose not to allow their emotions to be released, they have begun to experience another way out of their suffering. For clients to perceive another way through their struggle which is within their own control provides hope and a reason to "hang in there." They will, in addition, have a new experience – one of being seen, respected, and acknowledged. It can be very useful to assist clients to explore and acknowledge the energy and confusion that it cost them to repress their feelings. Working with clients, rather than against their choices, is imperative.

Experiencing Repressed Emotion

Feelings are the physical sensations which allow us to touch and express our emotions. The tension and numbness that results from repressing emotion, and the confused circular thoughts that provide distraction from our emotional experience are known as suffering. This suffering can become unbearable in suicidal clients. They want their suffering to cease. Ventilation of emotion can reduce the impetus to suicide. Rather than experiencing their life in the moment, suicidal clients talk about their life in a past or future context and remain detached from their emotions. The release that comes from releasing repressed emotion will allow organismic self-regulation, and trusting the self will provide the freedom to choose life or death with clarity. When clients can contact some repressed emotion and feel supported and accepted by the counselor, they may realize their pain is bearable, and they can achieve closure. They have survived the crisis and gained new experience and skills.

Grounding

When they have experienced some of their repressed emotion and taken risks with the counselor, they may need a sense of groundedness and connectedness to their environment. Counselors need to be able to provide clients with a sense of potency when the clients feel "out of control" and to be able to ground and soothe the clients when intense experiences have occurred. The clients need to acknowledge that some of their tension has been relieved and that they can relax. They are able to center or, in other words, establish an internal locus of control, and they need to acknowledge this.

Acknowledgement of Their Relief

When clients acknowledge the relief they have experienced by ventilating safely whilst in the presence of another, they have learned something new, and they can relearn how to trust others. We need to acknowledge that they have taken risks and chosen to let go a little (or a lot). This is invaluable for self-efficacy – the belief that one has mastery over the events of one's life and can meet challenges. Belief about one's ability has a profound effect on that ability. This is also a good check of the efficacy of the therapeutic intervention. A client who feels calmer and less anxious and who is not troubled by incessant thoughts is likely to have experienced an effective intervention.

Self-Acceptance and Understanding

Self-acceptance and understanding are essential. When clients gain perspective into their situation and are able to feel compassion for themselves, rather than condemnation, they are less likely to self-harm. Instead, they can begin to hope. When they have experienced receiving empathy at the very depth of their being, they will be more able to be empathic toward others. Empathy is crucial for constructive intimate relationships.

Exploring Options

This is a good time to enquire what it is that clients need right now and what they would like to do. They may well be quite clear on what they can do to get through, how they can soothe themselves, where they can go for support, what they will and won't be able to cope with, and what is tenable for them. Follow-up appointments are crucial. When individuals indicate that they do not have anyone in whom they can confide, apart from you, a 24-hour hotline is essential. Always provide one to your clients.

Commitment to Treatment

Near the close of the intervention, the individuals' suicidal intentions must be reassessed. Simple questions on how safe they feel with themselves right now and which supports they have available to them should they feel suicidal in the future are useful. A "No Suicide or Self-Harm" contract (Drye, Goulding, & Goulding, 1973) until their next appointment (and in the event of cancellation) is useful only *if the client is fully involved in the negotiation.* This needs to include an agreement to use the 24-hour service in an emergency or if something unforeseen occurs with their appointment. "No Suicide Contracts" are never watertight. They do serve to place responsibility for initiating help onto the client. The validity of such a contract hinges on the relationship between the counselor and the client.[19]

Discussion

The major difference between the approach suggested here and the traditional client-centered approach is that the client-centered counselor simply listens to what the client is saying and reflects back the verbal and nonverbal component of the communication. In the approach suggested here, the counselor establishes particular areas which need to be explored by the client and is alert to exploring these areas in depth when the client hints or raises the surrounding issues. Thus, the counselor using the present approach would be more active and interventionist than the traditional "passive" crisis counselor.

The approach, based as it is on Gestalt therapy, assumes that the counselor remains sensitive to the emotional and cognitive state of the client and can make clinical decisions on whether the client is able to integrate the material discussed and whether the experience and ventilation of emotions will dissipate them. The approach places a great deal of emphasis on the integration of polarities, ventilation and awareness of emotion, and attention to loneliness, ambivalence, lack of constructive intimacy, and unbearable psychological suffering, all of which are major factors in suicide.

Since clients differ in their ego strength, counselors should initiate interventions with caution, listening for cues as to how well the clients are dealing with the material which is being discussed. Issues can always be flagged and put aside temporarily, to be returned to if and when the counselor decides that the clients can handle them more adaptively. When the issue is directly related to the clients' motivation to commit suicide, and if suicidal behavior seems imminent, it is recommended that the focus is on how the counselor can provide enough support to the client and on exploring major blocks in dealing with this issue, rather than putting it aside. The assumption is that people who have long histories of being suicidal move away from the major issues that motivate them to commit suicide because of their inability to negotiate these issues.

As with Gestalt therapy in general, crisis intervention using a Gestalt therapy approach is not suitable for those with severe psychiatric disturbance (Greenberg & Johnson, 1988). Some therapists would hesitate also to use

---

[19] Range (2005) provides a good analysis of the pros and cons of no-suicide contracts.

Gestalt therapy approaches for suicidal clients, but a Gestalt orientation may prove useful for *some* suicidal clients, and some Gestalt tactics may be effective for *some* suicidal clients.

Finally, it should be noted that a Gestalt therapy approach to crisis intervention may work better with clients in face-to-face counseling and for clients with whom the counselor has already established a therapeutic relationship. It may not be as useful as a guide for crisis counselors working for the first time with a caller to a telephone crisis intervention service.

REFERENCES

Dattilio, F. M., & Freeman, A. (1994). *Cognitive-behavioral strategies in crisis intervention.* New York: Guilford.

Drye, R. C., Goulding, R. L., & Goulding, M. E. (1973). No-suicide decisions: patient monitoring of suicidal risk. *American Journal of Psychiatry, 130,* 171–174.

Greenberg, L. S., & Johnson, S. M. (1988). *Emotionally focused therapy for couples.* New York: Guilford.

Korb, M. P., Gorrell, J., & Van De Riet, V. (1989). *Gestalt therapy: Practice and theory.* New York: Pergamon.

Lester, D., & Brockopp, G. W. (Eds.). (1973). *Crisis intervention and counseling by telephone.* Springfield, IL: Charles C Thomas.

O'Connell, V. F. (1970). Crisis psychotherapy. In J. Fagan & I. L. Shepherd (Eds.), *Gestalt therapy now,* pp. 243–256. Palo Alto, CA: Science & Behavior Books.

Orten, J. D. (1974). A transactional approach to suicide prevention. *Clinical Social Work Journal, 2,* 57–63.

Perls, F. S., Hefferline, R. F., & Goodman, P. (1951). *Gestalt therapy.* New York: Julian.

Polster, E., & Polster, M. (1973). *Gestalt therapy integrated.* New York: Brunner/Mazel.

Range, L. M. (2005). No-suicide contracts. In R. I. Yufit & D. Lester (Eds.), *Assessment, treatment, and prevention of suicidal behavior,* pp. 181–203. Hoboken, NJ: Wiley & Sons.

Roberts, A. R. (Ed.). (1995). *Crisis intervention and time-limited cognitive treatment.* Thousand Oaks, CA: Sage.

Rosenthal, H. (1986). The learned helplessness syndrome. *Emotional First Aid, 3*(2), 5–8.

Seligman, M. (1974). Depression and learned helplessness. In R. J. Friedman & M. M. Katz (Eds.), *The psychology of depression,* pp. 83–113. New York: Halstead.

Shneidman, E. S. (1996). *The suicidal mind.* New York: Oxford University Press.

Wheeler, G. (1991). *Gestalt reconsidered: A new approach to contact and resistance.* New York: Gardner Press.

Young, L., & Lester, D. (2001). Gestalt therapy approaches to crisis intervention with suicidal clients. *Brief Treatment & Crisis Intervention, 1,* 65–74.

Part III

PROBLEM CALLERS

Chapter 13

THE OBSCENE CALLER

Gene W. Brockopp and David Lester

RESPONDING TO THE MASTURBATOR

After a few days of working at a suicide prevention and crisis service, answering calls from people in various types of difficulties and crises, the telephone counselor learns to respond to most problems with a type of "concerned objectivity." Yet some problems seem to tap a system of responses which generally is not therapeutic and leaves the counselor with a feeling of hurt, anger, or uselessness. One of the situations which probably does this more than any other is a call from a male who seems to use the services of the center for the sole purpose of masturbating to the voice of a female. For example, a few months ago, the following note was entered into our case file:

> A man masturbating while saying: "Talk to me. Don't leave me." I was not able to locate the file but felt he had called before. As he became more excited he became more verbal with remarks like "Open your legs." I terminated the call by suggesting he call back when he had finished to discuss why he needs a stranger rather than a friend at this time.

In checking our case file we noted that over the past few months, this type of telephone call had been received about three times a week.

The problems associated with this type of call can be divided into three categories: (1) how to develop an appropriate treatment plan for this type of caller; (2) how to deal with the feelings of the telephone counselor who receives the call; and (3) the effect of this type of call on the task the agency is to perform in the community at large. It should be noted that these problems are not unique to calls from masturbators, but are associated with any type of difficult call that a telephone service receives. For example, females may call the center and act seductively to a male counselor, callers may arouse hostility and anger in counselors by the difficult problems they present, or callers may, by their unwillingness to work with the telephone counselor, evoke feelings of inadequacy in the counselor. Certainly the call from a person who is actively suicidal will raise the anxiety of the telephone counselor and may make it more difficult for him to react appropriately to the crisis situation.

Yet the masturbator does, perhaps, require special attention because his calls have a very disrupting effect on counselors by arousing very strong negative emotions in them which may result in their inadequate handling of the call. They also have a "fall out" which affects the effectiveness of the counselor with calls made by individuals with other types of problems.

From our analysis of the calls received at the center, there appear to be two types of masturbating callers. One type will discuss a problem which may or may not be fictional, and either the counselor may suspect that the caller is masturbating and confront him with this, or the client himself will state that he is masturbating. In working with this type of person, the counselors have reported feeling "useless" or "ineffectual" and "furious at putting in hard work to no end."[20] The second type of caller merely breathes heavily and says words like, "Talk to Me," "Don't leave me," "Please let me finish," and so on. He frequently may hang up and then call back immediately.[21] To this type of person, who does not allow the counselor to establish a relationship that can be seen by her as possibly therapeutic, the counselor reports feeling used, sexually exploited, angry, uptight, or disgusted. These feelings are intensified if the counselor is alone at the center and if the call comes in at night. Often the counselor feels that she can handle the situation intellectually, but not emotionally.

Without question, the counselor's feelings of anger, hostility, or disgust interfere with the appropriate handling of this type of call. In most cases, the counselor is responding to her own feelings rather than to the client's problem. It appears that this may be a result of the counselor's attitudes toward deviant sexual behavior, her inability to know what a therapeutic response would be, or a combination of both. If the problem is the result of the counselor's attitude toward this type of behavior, it should be dealt with on an individual basis between her and her supervisor. The discussion would, of course, extend beyond the particular case of the masturbator to cover such issues as the counselor's attitudes towards sexual behavior in general and the feelings aroused when the counselor feels inadequate in handling any client

---

[20] These are the responses of female telephone counselors. Our experience with this type of caller is that he will hang up whenever a male answers the phone.
[21] On one occasion as many as twenty calls have been received from such an individual in the space of two hours.

call. From our discussion with the telephone counselors, it appears that their inability to respond therapeutically to the masturbator is a result of a lack of specific knowledge on the handling of this type of call, combined with the intense emotional feelings of being used inappropriately by the caller. It is to these issues that we would like to address ourselves.

Before discussing the possible methods of working with the masturbator, it might be well to discuss the philosophy of the telephone service. The unique feature of telephone therapy is its ability to respond immediately to individuals in difficulty, on their own terms, with anonymity, and with the control remaining with the client. In this type of therapy situation more than any other, counselors are at a distinct disadvantage in that they do not have personal face-to-face knowledge of the client. They have minimal clues with which to work, and they must accept the fact that the client has as much (possibly more) control of the situation as they do. It is, therefore, necessary for them to move into the problem situation on the client's basis, and only on the client's basis.[22] If they do not do this, they may lose the client, probably irretrievably, since in many cases they have no knowledge of the person's name, address, or telephone number. It would, therefore, seem imperative that the axiom of meeting clients "where they are" would become the basic guideline for working with all types of difficult calls.

With this as a background we would like to list five possible approaches to responding to the masturbator in the hope that these suggestions would aid the counselor in a practical way when receiving such a call by making alternative behaviors available to her so that she may feel more adequate in handling this type of caller.

1. The counselor can respond by saying nothing or with controlled silence.

2. The counselor can communicate her disgust to the caller and/or hang up.

3. The counselor can try to be accepting, point out that the caller has a problem and that he could benefit from seeing someone in a therapeutic relationship, and then hang up.

4. The counselor can establish a minimal relationship with the masturbator, refuse to stay on the telephone while he is masturbating, but urge him to call her back after he has finished masturbating.

5. The counselor can stay with the caller, allow herself to be used if necessary, with the hope that the relationship can move from this level to one in which she can be more therapeutic to the person calling.

---

[22] We would like to emphasize that we are speaking here about the development of a relationship and not about the subsequent therapeutic movements.

It appears to us that the first two approaches are at odds with the concept of a telephone service devoted to rendering therapeutic assistance to individuals in the community. Both of them either reject the client overtly or communicate non-acceptance of the client by the counselor. Without acceptance of the client, regardless of his behavior or feelings, a therapeutic relationship is most difficult, if not impossible, to establish. It could be argued, however, that a strong negative response on the part of the counselor might negatively reinforce the behavior and cause it to extinguish. This may take place in a controlled therapy situation. On the telephone, however, a more likely occurrence would be the calling of another person by the masturbator until he had obtained the verbal assistance of a female to satisfy his need. Mere rejection of the behavior by the counselor would appear to be of value only in allaying some of the counselor's feelings.

Response 3 is better, but since many of the callers do not see masturbation as a problem, they may not see any reason for coming in for a face-to-face discussion. Indeed, it is most unlikely that this type of exchange will take place, for this person is unlikely to make himself known to the counselor. Also, this approach rejects, but to a lesser extent, the use of a telephone as a means of aiding the individual. However, if the counselor has personal concerns in handling such a call, this approach is probably the best for her to take.

Response 4 requires more acceptance of the client by the counselor, but the chances of the person calling back after he has finished masturbating are probably slight. An extension of this approach would be for the counselor to suggest other stimuli for the masturbator to use to achieve sexual gratification in a more private manner, such as the Internet, television, radio, or records. This may reduce the negative social aspects of the client's behavior, but it is also likely to decrease the possibility of his receiving appropriate help.

Response 5 is clearly the best, in that the counselor is responding in a way that will maximize the chances for developing a relationship with the client which may be used later for therapeutic purposes. It should be emphasized here that acceptance of the person does not imply the reinforcing of the behavior or the condoning of it. It means tolerating the condition while attempting to develop a more honest, trusting relationship with the client to achieve this balance. The counselor, of course, must be careful not to be too seductive or encouraging.

Conversely, she also must not be too confrontive with the client. To ask the person why he is masturbating may be too difficult a question for him to answer and impose too much distance between him, the counselor, and his present behavior. The focus of the counselor should be on the affective relationship and the value of it for the client. Perhaps the client is lonely and depressed or is having difficulty in developing socially desirable relationships. Focusing on these areas may facilitate establishment of a more sustained and positive therapeutic relationship and may facilitate the client's visit to a counselor if the relationship moves to a point where trust can be established between the client and the counselor. Also, focusing on the purpose or goal of the behavior seems to be more appropriate and less threatening than an attempt to discover the underlying genesis of the behavior. The client can be asked what he feels his behavior is achieving for him, how he feels that calling achieves this end for him, and how he sees his own behavior.

To use this last approach, the counselor must be aware of her own feelings in responding to this type of client but keep them in the background. She must recognize that her approach to him must be one that meets him at the level of his needs, with the covert intent that, if a relationship of trust can be established, the client may look at his behavior in a more therapeutic manner. Recognition must be given to the fact that this may never be achieved — the client may simply use the counselor for his own end without any therapeutic movement on his part. Even though this may take place, and the therapeutic relationship misused, we feel that the counselor on the telephone cannot set demands which might be appropriate when counseling a person on a face-to-face basis. Therefore, we feel that, if a person can only relate on the telephone through masturbating, it is necessary to meet the person at this level, not to demand that he change his behavior, and hope that, in the process of being used by him in this way in the present, a therapeutic movement can be made in the future.

THE OBSCENE CALLER: A LOOK AT THE RESEARCH AND ITS IMPLICATIONS

DAVID LESTER

In the previous section, we discussed the problems associated with the caller to a 24-hour telephone service whose purpose in calling is to masturbate while being stimulated by a female voice. We discussed the emotional reactions of counselors handling this kind of caller and possible approaches that they can take in dealing therapeutically with him. There is some research and clinical opinion about obscene telephone callers, and I will review this material in this section and discuss the implications.

There have been several surveys of people in the community that inquire about their experiences of obscene telephone calls, and Katz (1994) has provided an excellent review of these surveys. The results of such surveys usually have little relevance for crisis intervention centers, but Katz himself carried out a national survey in the United States which does have some interesting implications.

Katz found that about 16% of women had received an obscene call in the prior six months and, in addition, 39% in the more distant past. Receiving an obscene call was not related to age, urban/rural location, or occupational status. Divorced and separated women, full-time employed women, and African-American women were more likely to receive obscene calls.

Katz saw the high incidence for employed women as supporting an "opportunity" theory, since such women have contact with a wider variety of men, some of whom may exploit their contact to target them. The high incidence of obscene calls received by divorced and separated women also fits this theory, since such women can be assumed to live alone and be "available," at least in the men's fantasies. There was no support for a theory that men target socio-economically powerful women since the occupational status of the women was unrelated to receiving obscene calls. The "displacement" theory, that men attack women whom they perceive as having less power, received some support from the high incidence of calls received by African American women. Katz also noted that the profile of the woman who is most likely to receive an obscene call closely resembled the profile of the woman most likely to be raped.

The results of such surveys may differ by country. For example, Pease (1985) in England and Wales found that obscene telephone calls were received more by women who were younger, living in inner cities and who were separated or divorced. No association was found with unemployment or living alone. Only the association with marital status replicated the results from the United States. In a national survey in Canada, Smith and Morra (1994) found that 67% of women had received an obscene or threatening telephone call lifetime and 24% in the prior year. Similar proportions reported receiving "silent" telephone calls. Women who were divorced or separated, young, living in Ontario and living in a major metropolitan area were more like to report receive such calls. The modal call was received after dark, when alone, and at home. About 7% of the women knew the caller, while 19% were not sure if they knew the caller.

Reactions

Several studies have asked women how they felt after the call. In the study of Canadian women (Smith & Morra, 1994), 75% reported some degree of fear. Sheffield (1989), in a study of American women, found responses ranging from humorous and pathetic to anger, disgust, degradation, and paranoia. When those receiving the calls are children, the reactions of the victim are, of course, more severe (Larsen et al., 2000).

Types of Obscene Calls[23]

Murray (1967) interviewed 34 female undergraduates who reported receiving obscene telephone calls and classified the calls they had received into five kinds:

1. The prank, nuisance call which is made by teenagers of either sex to either friends or people selected randomly from the telephone directory. An example is, "Is your refrigerator running? Then you'd better catch it before it gets away."

2. One kind of obscene call has implicit sexual propositions. There is no lewd or foul language in these calls, but they have reference to sexual behavior. The caller often seems to know the daily routine of the victim. An example is, "How about going with me to some place dark and quiet and we'll really make love?"

3. Another kind of obscene call has explicit sexual propositions and employs lewd and foul language. The caller may know the victim. For example, the calls are often received immediately after the victim arrives home from a social engagement. Many obscene callers, however, select names at random from the telephone directory or from the news media.

4. The vicious or threatening call may consist merely of silence and breathing but be received frequently. One victim received about 18 a day over a six-month period. An example of a spoken vicious call is, "Is this . . .? I am going to kill you because your father cheated me."

5. Other nuisance calls use particular ruses such as surveys or quizzes: "A friend recommended you . . .," and so on.

Mead (1975) described three types of obscene calls made to women in the community: (1) crude, typically made by adolescents; (2) ingratiating, in which the caller presents themselves as a friend of a friend; and (3) tricks in which the caller pretends to be taking a survey.

Leising (1985) classified the obscene calls received by crisis intervention centers as: (1) chronic masturbators who openly admit what they are doing; (2) men who present a possibly valid sexual problem and gradually turn the call into vulgar, sexually explicit call; and (3) men who are cold and detached or angry and who talk about raping and torturing women.

Are Obscene Callers Exhibitionists?

It is commonly asserted that obscene telephone callers also show other sexual deviations, in particular exhibitionism. Is this true?

---

[23] Pakhomou (2006) noted that other terms for this behavior include telephone scatolgia, telephone icophilia, acoustic voyeurism, and verbal exhibitionism.

Dalby (1988) reported four cases of obscene callers who showed no other sexual deviations, while Saunders and Awad (1991) reported on two cases of adolescent obscene telephone callers, one of whom was also an exhibitionist. In two cases of obscene telephone callers treated with covert sensitization (Alford et al., 1980; Moergen et al., 1991), one was also an exhibitionist. Freund et al. (1983) found that, of the clients referred to their Forensic Department for evaluation, one of the seven voyeurs (14%) also made obscene calls, 11 of the 86 exhibitionists (13%), two of the 22 touchers/frotteurs (9%), and one of the 23 rapists (4%). Thus, voyeurism and exhibitionism were more often associated with obscene telephone calling than other sexual deviations.

Lang et al. (1987) found that 32% of a sample of exhibitionists had made obscene telephone calls as compared to only 5% of nonviolent nonsexual offenders. The exhibitionists had also often showed voyeurism (70%), toucherism (26%), frotteurism (38%), and rape (17%).

Who Are the Obscene Callers?

A survey of almost 2,000 Canadian women (Smith & Morra, 1994) indicated that the majority of obscene telephone callers are male, adults, and unknown to the victim, but occasional callers are female, children, and known to the victim.

Abel et al. (1987) surveyed 561 sex offenders in psychiatric treatment, of whom 19 were obscene telephone callers. The median number of victims of the obscene telephone caller was 30 (with a mean of 103, indicating that a few of the men had made very large numbers of obscene calls, thereby skewing the distribution), and they admitted to calling each victim an average of 1.3 times.

Stone (1992) reported data from a survey of 114 obscene telephone callers after a hotline was set up for them following a television program on the problem aired on the BBC in the United Kingdom. The mean age was 27 with a range of 19 to 46. About one-third (32%) were married, less than the general population of males, another third (30%) single, and 17% divorced. Of those who disclosed their occupation, 42% were white-collar, 30% in the trades, and 8% unemployed, a lower rate of unemployment than in the general population. Almost half (46%) made one call per week, 31% three to four calls per week, and 23% more than ten calls per week. Only 18% admitted to their calls being extremely obscene.

Half of the callers (46%) chose names from the telephone directory, 22% from advertisements in the newspapers, and 13% dialed randomly. Nineteen percent called women about whom they knew casual details (such as those obtained from hairdressing salons or friends) so that the woman knew that they were aware of their appearance or whereabouts. The majority did not call back women if they thought that they were frightened by the call, but 6% pursued the same woman especially if she sounded upset. The majority (87%) made the call from home or their office, when alone.

They typically reported a build-up of tension prior to making a call, and they developed a single-mindedness and erotic anticipation for the call. Over half (58%) masturbated during the call. Half (48%) thought that their behavior was problematic, but only 8 percent of these experienced guilt. Most of them saw their behavior as problematic because they were often frustrated by the response of the woman or because of their fear of being apprehended. Although some of the men said that they were motivated to receive treatment, none followed up the referrals they were given. When asked why they engaged in the behavior, the men mentioned loneliness, low self-esteem, poor interpersonal skills, boredom, and alienation from and hostility toward women. Thus, the men showed some self-insight since their motives agreed with those proposed by the researchers.

Hribersek et al. (1987) found that more calls from masturbators were received by a telephone support system on days with good weather, perhaps because the men used outdoor telephones for their calls.

Pakhomou (2006) noted that there is no conclusive data on the question of whether men who make obscene telephone calls are potentially violent, but he noted that this behavior is "safer" than exhibitionism and voyeurism where the man is in close spatial proximity to the female victim.

The Modern Era

Most of the papers on obscene telephone callers are from an era before the advent of the Internet. Before the advent of computers, legal telephone sex lines opened up where, for a fee charged to a credit card, people can call and engage in lewd talk with a woman. The Internet has provided channels for open sexual conversation for a fee via a personal computer with a partner. The fee-paying pornographic websites have now been replaced by free pornographic websites. All of these channels provide anonymity, closeness (but distance), and easy access, and they permit the involvement of fantasy and imagery which are important for the obscene telephone caller.

The one thing that these channels do not provide is the negative reaction of the women receiving the call – the disgust, shock and fear. For this, the obscene caller stills needs to call an unsuspecting woman. However, in the context of telephone crisis counseling services, for many male callers, the negative reactions from the female counselor were *not* the goal. Occasional counselors stayed with the masturbator and spoke what the caller wanted to hear on condition that he stay to talk with her later. Although such callers often hung up without talking to the counselor, their behavior indicates that their desires could be satisfied by Internet chat services.

Counselor Reactions

Clark et al. (1986) found that male and female counselor volunteers had similar reactions to sexually abusive callers. They categorized the responses of counselors to such callers as empathic/helpful, sympathetic/bored, uncomfortable/frustrated and abused/manipulated. On the other hand, Walfish (1983) found that female counselors were made more uncomfortable than were male counselors to obscene calls.

Leising (1985) noted that counselors react with self-criticism for not handling the call better, anger over being used, genuine fear, competitiveness with other counselors over who can help the men best, and overgeneralizing and assuming that all male callers are going to be sexually abusive.

Deterring Obscene Calls

Two community studies have shown that obscene calls can be deterred by the technological advances. Clarke (1990) showed that Called ID and Caller Trace in communities in New Jersey resulted in a 25% decrease in annoyance and obscene telephone calls, more than in control communities Buck et al. (1995) found that a publicized call tracing program in Hull, England, led to a drop in obscene and threatening calls, more than in a control city. In two cases, geographic profiling has pinpointed the rough location of a caller who made calls to many women in one case and to children in another case (Cantor, 2003; Ebberline, 2008).

Case Studies

Dalby (1988) presented four cases of obscene telephone callers who showed no other sexual deviations. (1) A divorced man caring for his two-year-old son, dressed in women's clothes before calling and discussed clothing with the women while masturbating. (2) An unmarried man who had lived with a woman for five years, began by calling sex hotlines, then random women and finally a woman who worked in the same firm as he did. (3) A married man, with one child, had a long history of making obscene telephone calls (and had been expelled from the military for this behavior) and, if he found a woman who responded as he wished to his calls, he would call the woman repeatedly. (4) A man who had never married made obscene and threatening calls to women (telling them he had planted a bomb or kidnapped a family member) and claimed to have a multiple personality. Two of the men had completely normal profiles on the MMPI, one had only an elevated scale 4 (Psychopathic Deviate) score, while case (4) had three elevated scale scores – defensiveness and scales 1 (Hypochondriasis) and 3 (Hysteria).

Dalby felt that none of the four men showed any other psychiatric disorder aside from their sexually deviant behavior, and none engaged in exhibitionism or other sexual deviations. All of the men had successfully developed relationships with women, and two were married, but their obscene telephone calls indicated dissatisfaction with their partners.

Goldberg and Wise (1985) presented the case of a 25-year-old married businessman who made obscene calls. He was depressed, under stress from work (where his employers had changed), and under stress from efforts to obtain money from his father. He began to drink and smoke marijuana. He called random women and men while his wife slept nearby, but he denied having an erection or masturbating. His psychoanalyst saw the psychodynamics involved as identification with his mother and gaining satisfaction for his needs for power and dependency, combined with a masochistic need to be punished for his bad thoughts and desires directed toward his parents.

Weich (1989) presented a case of a 23-year-old graduate student who made obscene calls when stoned. Weich suggested that the psychodynamics involved a fear of viewing the female genitals and castration anxiety. Murgatroyd's (1993) case was a married 29-year-old man who made random obscene calls to women. He felt good during the calls because he was in control, masturbating and breaking the rules of society. However, he felt bad afterwards. The psychodynamics appeared to involve, in part, a lack of sexual gratification from his wife who felt uneasy indulging in the acts he desired (such as anal sex).

Matek (1988) reported a case of the 23-year-old man who began making calls when he was 14 and who, in therapy, felt that he was motivated in part by anger and getting even with his mother and stepmother for their poor treatment of him. His girlfriend knew about his calling and was deeply puzzled by it. Another case was married man, a successful advertising writer, who was both an exhibitionist and an obscene telephone caller. His wife was a court reporter who met him when he was in court on trial for his exhibitionism. His behavior began in high school where he was an outcast and seems to have been a reaction to his mother who wanted a daughter and who oscillated between ignoring him and criticizing him.

Pakhomou (2006) reported the case of 39-year-old man, divorced and working in the warehouse of a department store, who was indicted for 188 incidents of harassment by communication. His prior criminal record included theft-related offense such as burglary and retail theft, and a previous arrest for making sexually explicit calls to juveniles. For his calls, he pretended to be a female calling for advice, either as a mother whose son was masturbating wearing her panties or as an athletic coach with sexual feelings toward her female athletes. He masturbated after successful calls.

Nadler (1968) presented three case reports of men who had made obscene calls.

1. A 16-year-old white male started making obscene calls to his friends and moved to calling at random. His calls became more threatening with time. His need to call ebbed at times – when he had a job, when he was in camp, and when he was hospitalized. His frequency of calling increased when he was tense or fearful about his adequacy or performance in almost any area. He would become increasingly tense until eventually he telephoned. After the call, the tension went away without any genital activity. While telephoning, he was fearful and felt as though he had no control over what he might say. He was not close to his parents or his sister and did not fraternize much with boys of his own age.

2. A white graduate student in his mid-twenties came into therapy for impotence. Whenever he felt particularly unworthy because of schoolwork or after an argument with his mother he would try to demean a woman in a sexual way. For example, he would pick up a black prostitute while dressed impeccably himself and would insult her with lewd phrases. Occasionally he would engage in sexual activity with her. He then began masturbating (while not exposed) in subways, seeking to contrast the crudity of his action with his appearance. Finally, he began making obscene calls. He had always been a lonely youngster, unable to get close to anyone, and seemed to be defending against a sense of inferiority.

3. A 25-year-old white male was referred by a court for exhibitionism. He began making obscene calls to telephone operators after his release from military service when other sexual activity became less easy to obtain.

Nadler noted the low self-esteem and the dependence upon others for reassurance in these men. In each case there was evidence of anger toward women which perhaps stemmed from their relationships with the mother. Their mothers were described as bossy, overprotective, and dominating. The fathers tended to be meek with regard to the mother and uninterested in the sons. From a psychopathological point of view, Nadler noted schizoid and depressive tendencies. Nadler noted that the use of the telephone for exhibitionism eliminated the anxiety felt in face-to-face confrontation. The man feels safer from retribution, and he is less likely to be laughed at. It prevents him from getting too involved with the person and protects him from the danger of physically acting out his rage and murderous fantasies.

The use of telephone calls in order to gain a sense of mastery and power through the reactions of others was seen by Nadler as similar to the behavior of the exhibitionist. It is likely, however, that the obscene caller is more timid and scared than the exhibitionist since he lacks the "courage" to physically confront another but would prefer to interpose the telephone.

Kisker (1964) also saw the obscene caller as similar psychodynamically to the exhibitionist, but a case report of a 16-year-old boy describes a boy with gross sexual confusion and lack of awareness of appropriateness. This boy was apprehended for patting coeds on the rear in a park, and he had formerly made sexual advances to his teacher and an older friend's wife. Kisker diagnosed the boy as having strong, but latent homosexual inclinations. Although Kisker does not report on the boy's social relationships, it appears that they were poor and minimal. Again, we have a relatively lonely and isolated individual, perhaps with feelings of inferiority, trying to find a sexual outlet and to master his feelings of inadequacy.

Myers (1991) presented the case of a man who came into psychotherapy for physically abusing his wife when drunk, but who revealed that he made obscene telephone calls and rubbed up against women in subway cars, both to the point of ejaculation. He made his telephone calls to women when his wife was away or drunk nearby. He started the calls by taking a survey and moved the questions to the woman's sexual practices. As he masturbated and got close to orgasm, he would verbalize aloud his desire to "fuck the woman into oblivion" and other desires. The analysis indicated that he felt anger toward his mother after his younger brother was born and "dethroned" him, his wife (for having had other lovers before marrying him), and his psychoanalyst (for going on vacation). Although motivated in part by anger, the telephone served to place distance between him and his "love" object, so that he could not act out his murderous rage. It was also possible that the telephone calls and his heavy breathing recalled the childhood memories of sleeping in the same bedroom as his parents and overhearing their sexual activity. His frotteurism had similar motivations.

Perspectives

Steley (1990) viewed the obscene telephone callers from three perspectives.

1. Behaviorist

From a behaviorist perspective, the female recipient of the calls reinforces the man's behavior each time he calls. He becomes sexually aroused, may masturbate to orgasm and is satisfied by the woman's response. Thus, a behaviorist approach would recommend that crisis workers not reward the behavior and terminate the call quickly, perhaps after allowing ten seconds for the caller to discuss real, nonsexual problems. With repeated termination, the behavior should extinguish. An alternative is to transfer such calls to male counselors. This approach protects the staff of crisis centers from exploitation, although some counselors may experience guilt because they departed from their usual caring role. This approach also does not tie up lines, thereby allowing urgent calls from getting through.

Also from a behaviorist point of view, Haywood (1980) argued that there was no point in reinforcing masturbators who call crisis services and that they do not accept referrals. Haywood recommended training counselors to recognize the cues that a male caller is masturbating and, if this is likely, to ask:

> Are you masturbating during this call? If so, I am required to point out to you that our telephone calls are taped and that obscene calls and callers using this service to masturbate are illegal according to law. We want to help, but our lines must be kept open for crises and emergencies. Please call back later if you wish to something to help with your problems.

Then the counselor can hang up. Alternatively, the female counselor can transfer the call to a male counselor if one is available.

Payne (1980) suggested a similar approach, that is, having the counselor offer to discuss a real problem, yet keeping the offer to a minimum of time so as to prevent her voice from reinforcing the masturbator. The counselor can offer to deal with a real problem and say that, if the caller chooses not to, she will hang up in ten seconds.

Leising (1985), noting that obscene telephone callers are not amenable to treatment, recommended that counselors terminate the call as soon as they realize that the caller is masturbating. Clark and Borders (1984) too, while urging caution before hastily terminating a call, argue that it is pointless to continue the call after the counselor determines that she is being used for sexual gratification.[24]

2. Psychodynamic

Stone (1992) noted that the masturbator has been viewed both as an exhibitionist and a voyeur with the motive of trying to overcome his fear of his own sexual inadequacy. These callers have low self-esteem, a conflict between self-aggrandizement and self-deprecation, with schizoid and depressive features. They have difficulties with close interpersonal relationships, tending to show infantile dependence and antagonism toward women. Calling women

---

[24] Incidentally, Moergen et al. (1990) report "curing" an obscene telephone caller, using behavior therapy, by means of covert sensitization (that is, pairing the behavior of making obscene telephone calls with very unpleasant imagery) and social skills training.

on the telephone lessens their anxiety by giving them more control in the "relationship" and lessening the psychological consequences of rejection.

Rosen (1996) noted that the men are poorly integrated and need recognition from others. The responses of the women help them feel grandiose and compensate for their feelings of nothingness. The men fear and are angry at women, partly because they see women as frustrating and emasculating, yet they also want to unite with them symbiotically. They make when the calls when their self-esteem is threatened.

Leising (1983) and Wark (1981) hypothesized that the caller's mother was probably overprotective and infantilizing, and the father disengaged. The mother was dominant in the family, and the father strong but aloof. The callers probably never felt that their mothers loved them, and the men may be starved of affection. Almansi (1979), based on his case of a voyeur who also made obscene telephone calls, suggested that viewing the "primal scene," that is, observing one's parents having sexual intercourse, perhaps by having one's crib placed in the parent's bedroom for several years, was a possible childhood trauma that increased the likelihood of obscene telephone calling later in life.

From this perspective, crisis counselors should try to desexualize the call and confront the caller in a caring manner about his real problems. For example, Matek (1980) thought that counseling obscene telephone callers might be possible by making interpretations concerning the psychodynamics of the behavior. However, this may require a higher level of counseling skill than most nonprofessional crisis counselors possess.

3. Humanistic

In this perspective, the caller is obviously not coping well with the typical problems that life presents, especially those which are stressful. From this perspective, the counselor can sometimes create the conditions for growth and change by adopting a caring and accepting attitude. Although the humanistic perspective would recommend a non-confrontational style of counseling, perhaps it is possible to point out the unacceptable and exploitative nature of the call.

Wark (1982) handled calls from many sex callers over a five-month period and found two types. The first openly admits to masturbating and pleads for the counselor to stay with him until he finishes. The second presents a plausible sexual problem and masturbates while discussing the problem or after the call. Wark found that the first type of caller was not amenable to counseling. For the second type, the most effective response was to try to accept the caller while rejecting the behavior. It was important to desexualize the call.

Wark persuaded nine of the approximately 60 callers to drop their fantasies and speak to her.

Wark found that these nine men typically spoke to her with a flat voice during the sexualized part of the call but sounded depressed once the call was desexualized. The men expressed relief at being discovered and welcomed the opportunity to discuss their problem. They admitted to feeling guilt after their calls and making vows to stop such calling. They were quite isolated, their self-esteem was low, and they had difficulty reaching out to others and forming interpersonal relationships. They described their fathers as "supermen" and as unemotional and cold, and they also felt that their mothers had never loved them. They had reacted by denying their need for affection.

They were not clear about the causes of their behavior. They admitted to fantasizing that the counselor was also masturbating, and Wark saw this as reinforcing her advice to counselors to desexualize the call so as to end such fantasizing. Wark gave a list of clues to the possibility that a man is masturbating during the call:

1. voice tone has no emotion
2. hesitant speaking
3. seems boyishly innocent about sexual matters
4. gives a first name immediately and asks for the counselor's first name
5. will not speak with a male counselor
6. states his "problem" briefly and waits for the counselor to respond
7. asks the counselor personal questions (age, marital status, hair and eye color, etc.)
8. asks the counselor her opinion about his "sexual problem"
9. shows resistance toward any resolution of the problem
10. is often silent

The "problem" presented often involved sex with a female member of his family (immediate or extended), lending his partner to another man, and enjoying sex with young girls or boys. He will ask for information but refuse referrals to organizations that can provide such information. Typical opening lines include: I want to talk, Can I talk about anything here? I have an embarrassing problem, and Are you understanding?

Therapy for the Obscene Caller

We have seen how the obscene caller is frequently seen as similar to the exhibitionist. Ideas for the therapeutic handling of the obscene caller may be obtained, therefore, from experience with the therapy of exhibitionists. Mathis and Collins (1970) have reported upon their experiences with group therapy with exhibitionists, and their conclusions have some relevance for the obscene caller. Their group work was with exhibitionists forced into a therapy situation by legal authorities. All had been arrested as least once. Of the 45 men treated, 15 were able to escape the legal pressure, and all but two of these quit treatment. It appears, therefore, that legal pressure is essential initially to keep the men in treatment.

In the course of the group therapy, Mathis and Collins noted six distinct phases.

1. Initially, the men used denial extensively. They usually felt remorse, shame and guilt after the first few exhibiting episodes, but these uncomfortable feelings were quickly denied access to awareness. The men remained convinced that treatment was unnecessary since the problem no longer existed. Occasionally, the abnormality of the act is denied. This use of denial permeated the whole life style of the exhibitionist. They had low tolerance for anxiety and little awareness of emotional aspects of life, which in turn led to a poverty of relationships. They frequently denied the need for the group. Mathis and Collins felt that it takes up to six months for this pattern of behavior to break down and for the exhibitionist to face reality and to continue treatment voluntarily. The presence of confrontations from exhibitionists who have passed through this phase is necessary to break through the denial. Interpretations and explanations by the group leaders have little effect here.

2. There follows a period of acceptance that he is emotionally immature, and the exhibitionist begins to talk and recognize emotions. The group is now over-idealized by him.

3. Anger is most frightening to the exhibitionist, probably because he fears being overwhelmed by his infantile-like rage if he allows it expression (rather than fearing retaliation). Eventually, anger begins to be expressed in the group and in other situations.

4. There follows a phase of disappointment resulting from the overidealization in the second phase and fright encountered during the phase of anger. He becomes disappointed at his lack of progress and improvement.

5. After about a year of group participation, the clients, who are usually underachievers, begin to make changes that promote upward mobility and promote feelings of mastery. For example, one of the clients in Mathis and Collins' group returned to college while maintaining his job as a laborer and managing to stay independent from his parents.

6. Finally, the phase of separation must be faced.

Mathis and Collins noted that these phases may not be unique to the exhibitionist and may be characteristic of many kinds of groups. Furthermore, the phases are rarely as distinct as implied by a formal presentation and description. However, their findings have many implications for the treatment of the obscene caller.

If the obscene caller is motivated by psychodynamics similar to those of the exhibitionist, then there are several clear implications. First, the obscene caller is very likely to use denial as a defense mechanism. He may deny that he has a problem or that he needs treatment. He may resist ordinary counseling because of his avoidance of talk and consideration of his emotions. It is notable that no obscene caller to our center in Buffalo (New York) was ever been successfully referred in for therapy. This may mean that, if we want to treat the obscene caller meaningfully, we must identify him and have him forced into therapy by legal pressure. To generalize from the experience with exhibitionists, this pressure must be maintained for a long period of time (up to six months or more) or he will terminate treatment. This entails tracing the obscene caller and instituting legal procedures to commit him to treatment. Clearly, this may conflict with the values and policies of crisis intervention services and their counselors. However, not to do so may mean that successful therapy with the obscene caller is impossible. The necessity for legal pressure in the case of the obscene caller is perhaps even greater due to the fact that he is possibly even more timid and anxious than the exhibitionist, who can at least face open confrontation with his "viewer."

It may not be feasible for such calls to be traced and for the callers to be referred in for therapy by a court unless a center feels that it is ethical for such callers to be traced and threatened with legal action. However, if there is no reason to suppose that telephone counseling can assist the obscene caller therapeutically, then perhaps centers should give up trying to be therapeutic toward these callers. Trying to be therapeutic may result only in the telephone counselors providing sexual stimulation for such callers with no therapeutic movement and, thus, they may be merely reinforcing the behavior of these men. It may be more appropriate to discourage such callers from using the telephone service for sexual stimulation. To discourage callers is against the policy of many crisis centers, and many counselors might feel that to do so is inappropriate for a telephone crisis intervention service where the aim is to help people with any kind of problem. Occasionally, however, when a crisis service realizes that it is ineffective in dealing with particular types of callers, it may be legitimate to discourage such callers from using the service.

Secondly, Mathis and Collins argue for the use of group therapy for such men. They note that other men who are in a later stage of therapy are more useful in building up the ability of the client to face reality and admit his problems than is the counselor. However, since exhibitionists are more common than obscene callers, it may prove difficult to form a group of obscene callers for therapy. One possibility is, therefore, to integrate the obscene caller into a group of exhibitionists.

REFERENCES

Abel, G. G., Becker, J. V., Mittelman, M. S., Cunningham-Rathner, J., Rouleau, J. L., & Murphy, W. D. (1987). Self-reported sex crimes of nonincarcerated paraphiliacs. *Journal of Interpersonal Violence, 2,* 3–25.

Alford, G. S., Webster, J. S., & Sanders, S. H. (1980). Covert aversion of two interrelated deviant sexual practices. *Behavior Therapy, 11,* 15–25.

Almansi, R. J. (1979). Scopophilia and object loss. *Psychoanalytic Quarterly, 48,* 601–619.

Buck, W., Chatterton, M., & Pease, K. (1995). The prevention of obscene, threatening and other troublesome telephone calls. *Security Journal, 6,* 171–175.

Cantor, D. (2003). *Mapping murder.* London, UK: Virgin Books.

Clark, S. P., & Borders, L. D. (1984). Approaches to sexual and sexually abusive callers. *Crisis Intervention, 13*(1), 14–24.

Clark, S. P., Borders, L. D., & Knudson, M. L. (1986). Survey of telephone counselors' responses to sexual and sexually abusive callers. *American Mental Health Counselors Association Journal, 8*(2), 73–79.

Clarke, R. V. (1990). Deterring obscene phone callers. *Security Journal, 1,* 143–148.

Dalby, J. T. (1988). Is telephone scatologia a variant of exhibitionism? *International Journal of Offender Therapy, 32,* 45–49.

Ebberline, J. (2008). Geographic profiling obscene phone calls. *Journal of Investigative Psychology & Offender Profiling, 5,* 93–105.

Freund, K., Scher, H., & Hucker, S. (1983). The courtship disorders. *Archives of Sexual Behavior, 12,* 369–379.

Goldberg, R. L., & Wise, T. N. (1985). Psychodynamic treatment for telephone scatalogia. *American Journal of Psychoanalysis, 45,* 291–297.

Haywood, C. H. (1980). Guidelines, purpose and design in counseling chronic callers. *Crisis Intervention, 11,* 148–170.

Hribersek, E., van de Voorde, H., Poppe, H., & Casselman, J. (1987). Influence of the day of the week and the weather on people using a telephone support system. *British Journal of Psychiatry, 150,* 189–192.

Katz, J. E. (1994). Empirical and theoretical dimensions of obscene phone calls to women in the United States. *Human Communication Research, 21,* 155–182.

Kisker, G. W. (1964). *The disorganized personality.* New York: McGraw-Hill.

Lang, R. A., Langevin, R., Checkley, K. L., & Pugh, G. (1987). Genital exhibitionism. *Canadian Journal of Behavioural Science, 19,* 216–232.

Larsen, H. B., Leth, I., & Maher, B. A. (2000). Obscene telephone calls to children. *Journal of Clinical Child Psychology, 29,* 626–632.

Leising, P. (1983). The negative effects of the obscene telephone call upon crisis intervention services. *Crisis Intervention, 14,* 84–92.

Matek, O. (1980). Teaching volunteers of a crisis phone service to respond therapeutically to callers with sex problems. *Journal of Sex Education & Therapy, 6*(2), 24–28.

Matek, O. (1988). Obscene telephone callers. *Journal of Social Work & Human Sexuality, 7*(1), 113–130.

Mathis, J. L., & Collins, M. (1970). Progressive phases in the group therapy of exhibitionists. *International Journal of Group Psychotherapy, 20*, 163–169.

Mead, B. T. (1975). Coping with obscene telephone calls. *Medical Aspects of Human Sexuality, 9*(June), 127–128.

Moergen, S. A., Merkel, W. T., & Brown, S. (1990). The use of covert sensitization and social skills training in the treatment of an obscene telephone caller. *Journal of Behavior Therapy & Experimental Psychiatry, 21*, 269–275.

Murgatroyd, S. (1993). Metamotivation complexity. In J. H. Kerr, S. Murgatroyd & M. J. Apter (Eds.), *Advances in reversal theory*, pp. 283–294. Amsterdam: Swets & Zeitlinger.

Murray, F. S. (1967). A preliminary investigation of anonymous nuisance telephone calls to females. *Psychological Record, 17*, 395–400.

Myers, W. A. (1991). A case history of a man who made obscene telephone calls and practiced frotteurism. In G. I. Fogel & W. A. Myers (Eds.), *Perversions and near-perversions in clinical practice*, pp. 109–123. New Haven, CT: Yale University Press.

Nadler, R. P. (1968). Approach to psychodynamics of obscene telephone calls. *New York State Journal of Medicine, 68*, 521–526.

Pakhomou, S. M. (2006). Methodological aspects of telephone scatologia. *International Journal of Law & Psychiatry, 29*, 178–185.

Payne, D. S. (1980). The behavioral analysis of the obscene phone call. *Crisis Intervention, 11*, 111–120.

Pease, K. (1985). Obscene telephone calls to women in England and Wales. *Howard Journal, 24*, 275–281.

Rosen, I. (1996). Exhibitionism, scopophilia, and voyeurism. In I. Rosen (Ed.), *Sexual deviation*, pp. 174–215. New York: Oxford University Press.

Saunders, E. B., & Awad, G. A. (1991). Male adolescent sexual offenders. *Child Psychiatry & Human Development, 21*, 169–178.

Sheffield, C. J. (1989). The invisible intruder. *Gender & Society, 3*, 483–488.

Smith, M. D., & Morra, N. N. (1994). Obscene and threatening telephone calls to women. *Gender & Society, 8*, 584–596.

Steley, J. R. (1990). Sexually abusive callers in the context of crisis agencies. *Australian Journal of Marriage & Family, 11*(1), 19–27.

Stone, C. R. (1992). Who's speaking? *Journal of Social Behavior & Personality, 7*, 639–648.

Walfish, S. (1983). Crisis telephone counselors' views of clinical interaction. *Community Mental Health Journal, 19*, 219–226.

Wark, V. (1981). Working with the sex caller. *Crisis Intervention, 12*(1), 13–23.

Weich, M. J. (1989). The fetishistic use of speech. *International Journal of Psychoanalysis, 70*, 245–253.

WORKING WITH THE OBSCENE CALLER

Gene W. Brockopp

In a previous section on working with the person who masturbates while making a call to an emergency telephone service, we stated that, when a caller uses any verbal aspect of sexuality in his relationship with the telephone counselor, he usually puts the helping person at a distinct disadvantage. This is, in part, due to the usual "up-tightness" one has when confronted in this area and also by the lack of experience the average telephone counselor has in working with this type of problem. The tendency to blame, moralize or punish the caller by hanging up the telephone is almost automatic and the superego pat-on-the-back that we receive when we do these things helps to assuage any feelings of guilt that we may not have helped the caller by our actions.

Some of the information in the previous section by Lester can be very useful in dealing with this type of caller. However, to transpose the concepts and therapeutic approaches that he develops to this type of caller would result in a grave error. To place the information he reports on in the context of emergency telephone service, I feel three points must be emphasized:

1. There is very little basis for assuming that the motivational pattern and personality structure of the obscene caller and the exhibitionist are similar enough to assume that a treatment program which works for one will work for the other.

2. It is much easier to obtain legal sanctions against and treatment for the exhibitionist than for the obscene caller.

3. It is important to recognize that the obscene call to a telephone counseling service differs form an obscene call to the general public, for the standards of "acceptable" behavior are much broader at such a center and the level of tolerance should be much greater. Also, the purpose of the center is to be responsive to individuals with all types of difficulties, even those who use the ticket of obscenity.

I believe it follows from the above statements that a telephone counseling service must differ both from the way the public would respond to this type of individual and from the way that this individual would be responded to in a normal psychiatric or clinical setting. If, for example, the center attempted to trace every obscene caller and obtain legal sanctions against them, it is questionable whether they could remain an effective agent in the community, for word would quickly spread throughout the area that a call to the telephone counseling service, which was not made in a way that was appropriate to the center's standards of behavior in the community, would result in the individual's incarceration. Generalizations would automatically take place on the part of the individual who has any type of paranoid personality streak.

Certainly calls from drug users would begin to decline. In no way can the center service as a policeman or an arm of the legal agencies in the community if it is to maintain an open-door policy for individuals in crisis or problem situations. Nor can the center simply be an arm of the mental health agencies in the community. If necessary, even at the price of not getting a person into counseling or not getting a person who has violated the law into the courts, the integrity of the telephone service as a place where any person can call with any type of problem and receive interested, concerned, and therapeutically appropriate responses must be maintained.

Even with this philosophical concept in mind, what is a therapeutically appropriate response to the obscene caller at a telephone counseling service? It would appear to me that it is necessary to make an arbitrary grouping of the obscene caller into two categories: (1) the one-time or occasional obscene caller, and (2) the chronic obscene caller. Each of these types of callers will be dealt with separately.

The One-Time or Occasional Obscene Caller

From a theoretical point of view, the individual who calls a telephone counseling service and uses obscene language or other overt sexual material should be dealt with in a similar way to the person who calls the center and masturbates while on the telephone – that is, the telephone counselor should respond to both the overt and covert messages in the telephone call and not merely to the words or the content of the telephone call. Usually the covert message is, "I am very angry" or, "Can you accept me as I really feel I am" or, "Can I embarrass, unnerve, or frustrate you with my language (and my problems)." By responding to both messages, the telephone counseling service gives the individual a chance to use the service to meet his own needs in the hope that, through the accepting attitude of the telephone counselor, he will develop a trusting relationship with the center and move past the overt sexual aspects of this call into the problems or areas or concerns that he is covering up through his aggressive approach. The telephone counselor must clearly keep in mind the concept that she is and must be a transitional, social object for this type of caller and recognize that, in order to be a pipeline for this individual to a resource in the community that is more appropriate for his treatment, she will need to accept his frustration, irritation, and obscene language. If this can be done, then either through a continuous telephone contact with the center or by taking a referral to an appropriate mental health agency, the caller may move past the overt, obscene language into an appropriate therapeutic relationship.

For this type of caller no trace should be initiated nor should any threat of police or legal action be used. To do so is to help him achieve his covert goal of being rejected and thereby confirm his feelings about himself and about other people in his environment. This caller is usually ambivalent about dealing directly with his problem and, therefore, uses a method that has typically resulted in his being rejected in the past, in order to assure himself that nobody really cares about helping him. By threatening to trace his call or initiate police or legal action, the telephone counselor is dealing with only the overt behavior. By refusing to do this, she is passing his test for acceptance. Only by getting past this test of self-rejection can the telephone counselor or any other counselor give him the help he is asking for in his ambivalent yet aggressive way.

The Chronic Obscene Caller

The chronic obscene caller must be handled in a different type of way, for the dynamics behind his call are usually quite different. Even though anger at a world may be an essential part of his personality structure, the intensity of the anger is much greater. By flaunting his problem at the telephone service, he may be asking for direct assistance with this problem which he cannot consciously control, even though he would be the first to deny either that it is a problem or that he is asking for help. Yet through his continual calling (of an obscene nature) to a telephone counseling service that advertises itself as a helping agency in the community, he is covertly asking for this assistance. If this were not so, he could be making these types of calls to any other person or agency in the community. This type of call requires a different method of approach.

Initially, the response of a telephone service to this type of caller would be the same as to the occasional obscene caller. Only after the pattern is clearly established (that this person can only relate in an obscene way) should a more intensive method be approached. The following steps would be recommended in developing that approach. First, a conference should be called for individuals who have worked with this obscene caller, along with a consultant who has dealt with people having this type of problem. In the conference, a case history, including a summary of the client's contacts with the center, should be presented. If they are available, tape recordings of his calls might be appropriately used to clarify whether the obscene calls are made in response to some of the latent, nonverbal messages of the staff or as a result of the pathology of the individual.

The staff should then explore what type of help he is requesting through his continued obscene calls to the center and develop some recommendations regarding what type of treatment program would be most appropriate for him. If it is felt that an appropriate treatment program can be developed for him either at the center or at any agency in the community, a decision may be made at this point to trace the call so as to obtain the person's name and address so that a legal sanction can be obtained against this individual. Before this is done, however, the center should clearly examine the probable legal results of this action. If the individual is apprehended for placing obscene calls, will he be given an opportunity for treatment or will he be turned loose because of lack of evidence or because the telephone company, police agencies, or legal community do not wish to deal with this type of problem situation. In some communities, it is also important to know whether or not this individual will be simply placed on probation or incarcerated for a period of time rather than given appropriate psychiatric attention.

If it is determined that he would be given the opportunity for therapeutic treatment, it is necessary to determine whether or not this type of therapy is available in the community. As was emphasized in the previous section by Lester, at least one year of intensive therapy is necessary in order to effectively treat a person with this type of problem. If the center is going to attempt to get help for the individual by using the legal sanctions of the community, we must be willing to completely and thoroughly follow this recommendation so that the individual who is placing the obscene call can obtain the type of help which will assist him in overcoming the problem that he has. If this does not occur, tracing the call can simply result in his going to jail for period of time, being given a fine, or placed on probation. This type of treatment would simply reaffirm to him that the community really does not care about him or about assisting him with the problems that he has.

It is necessary to emphasize that for most obscene callers, tracing the call and the use of legal sanctions will be the exception rather than the rule for a telephone counseling service. The results of having individuals of this type in therapy are not sufficiently clear that this method can be unequivocally recommended. It is my feeling that a trusting, accepting, understanding relationship with this person which deals both with the covert and the overt messages he is giving would result in a better final outcome. To achieve this goal is extremely difficult, for in any encounter, the telephone counselor will find that this type of caller is one of the most difficult to relate to for he stimulates our fantasies while at the same time affronts our sense of modesty and our moral standards. The telephone counselor who can work with this type of caller without being seduced through the titillations of his sexual fantasies, or conversely responding with anger because of the negative countertransference, is an unusual person. Yet it is within these two bounds that probably the most effective work with this type of person can be accomplished.

Chapter 14

THE CHRONIC CALLER

David Lester, Gene W. Brockopp, and Diane Blum

CHRONIC-CALLERS TO A SUICIDE PREVENTION CENTER[25]

The opening of 24-hour telephone counseling services by suicide prevention centers has made available to the communities served by them a means to obtain help and support during times of crisis. Only a small proportion of calls to suicide prevention centers are from people who are suicidal. (At our center in Buffalo, New York, the proportion was about 20%.) The majority of calls come from people who are lonely, depressed, or in conflict with a significant other, but who do not claim to be suicidal.

One group of people who do make use of 24-hour telephone services is characterized by the fact that they make numerous calls to the center. Our center received 3,910 calls from 2,128 separate clients in its first year of operation. In this population of callers, there were 24 individuals who called more than 10 times each. The number of calls made by these 24 individuals is shown in Table 14.1. As can be seen, the most frequent caller had called the center on 173 occasions by the time the data were analyzed.

It is frequently thought that these chronic callers are not suicidal risks and that they merely tie up the staff operating the suicide prevention centers. One consequence of this point of view is the suggestion that chronic callers should be discouraged from using the center. An alternative viewpoint is that a suicide prevention center can help these individuals lead an adequate life out in society by providing them with periodic help and support. To do this costs very little (both in expense and time) compared to the cost of long-term treat-

---

[25] Adapted from Lester and Brockopp (1970).

ment and custodial care.

The aim of the present chapter is to describe these chronic callers, to investigate the types of problems that they have and to explore the ways in which a suicide prevention service can help them.

Table 14-1
CHARACTERISTICS OF 24 CHRONIC CALLERS TO THE SUICIDE PREVENTION & CRISIS INTERVENTION SERVICE IN BUFFALO

Age	Sex	Marital Status	Treatment Status	Number of Calls
25	male	divorced	seeking treatment	10
29	female	married	seeking treatment	10
37	female	married	seeing psychiatrist	10
44	female	married	former patient	11
54	female	widowed	no indication	12
43	male	single	seeing psychiatrist	12
41	female	married	former patient	12
23	male	single	seeking treatment	13
39	female	married	no indication	13
20	male	single	former patient	14
55	male	widowed	no indication	15
56	male	married	former patient	15
?	female	?	no indication	17[26]
25	female	single	no indication	18
37	female	married	no indication	18
42	female	widowed	former patient	18
35	female	single	former patient	18
55	female	single	former patient	19
25	female	single	former patient	21
30-40	female	married	seeing psychiatrist	42
23	female	single	seeing psychiatrist	42
36	male	single	seeing psychiatrist	47
44	male	single	former patient	69
52	female	married	seeing psychiatrist	173

[26] This client claimed to be a 33 or 21-year-old married female, but the staff believed her to be a young girl aged 10 to 15.

General Characteristics of Chronic Callers

The 24 chronic callers were compared with a sample of 378 callers to the Suicide Prevention and Crisis Intervention Service of Buffalo who called only once. The chronic callers did not differ from the one-time callers in sex, age, marital status, presence versus absence of children, number of children, race, living arrangements (alone versus with others), suicidal history, rated suicidal risk on the first call, or the presenting problem. The chronic callers were significantly less often anonymous callers, but this was probably a result of the fact that, after many calls, chronic callers were more likely to identify themselves than the individual who called only once. It appears, therefore, that the chronic caller did not differ in general characteristics from the individual who called only once.

Some Categories of Chronic Callers

The chronic callers fell into four categories with regard to their aims in calling the center. These categories were defined in terms of the treatment status of the callers.

1. Seven of the chronic callers were seeing an additional therapist during the time that they were calling the center. They often used the center to voice anxieties about therapy and criticisms of their present therapist. In a few cases, it appeared that the visits to the therapist were not felt to be sufficient by the caller, and the center was used as an additional source of support.

Case (12 calls): A depressed, lonely man, aged 43 and single. After being healthy all his life, he was now suffering from several illnesses. He came to our center for short-term treatment, but his therapist suggested that the treatment plan should be to urge him to use his therapist rather than the center. He continued to call and express hostility toward the therapist and to claim that our center was more useful. He attempted suicide and subsequently obtained a different therapist.

2. Two callers were seeking treatment of some kind and used the center to help them.

Case (13 calls): A 23-year-old single male. His family had been killed in a car accident, and he appeared to feel guilty. He was temporarily employed through the use of labor pools. He was hostile and looking for someone to take care of him. He tried to get himself admitted to several psychiatric hospitals but was not admitted. He came to the center once and demanded that the center negotiate with his landlady for the sale of a television to him.

3. Six callers gave no indication of having received psychiatric treatment in the past or of being in therapy at the present time. They called the center merely to "ventilate" their feelings.

Case (12 calls): A 54-year-old female who had survived two husbands. She had been alone now for 12 years. She had two children who had left home, and she had stopped working. She would not leave the house, and she drank and smoked a lot. She tried to cover her loneliness with jokes, but she had broken down once and cried. She was understanding if the counselor was busy and had to hang up. She thanked the center for allowing her to call and talk.

4. Nine callers had been in treatment in the past and appeared to be disturbed people who called to ventilate their emotions and pursue their delusions.

Case (18 calls): A 35-year-old single female living with her parents. She was paranoid and delusional and had been hospitalized three times. She called to ventilate, especially when her customary listeners got irritated with her. She was concerned with body deformations and her revelations from God.

Reactions of the Staff to Chronic Callers

The staff at the center responded to chronic callers in a way that depended upon the characteristics of the callers and those of the staff member. The staff became quite concerned about many of the callers and were often fond of them. The callers were discussed, and their continued calling was followed by most of the counseling staff. This reaction was shown in the extreme by their reactions to the 52-year-old married female who called 173 times. This woman was seeing a psychiatrist, and she called both him and the center about once a day. She rarely talked for more than a few minutes. She was depressed but was always interrupted, supposedly by her employer or her husband. She appeared to find no help in being questioned by the counselor or by discussing her problem. All she appeared to want was to reiterate her problem. At one point, she was hospitalized for shock treatment for a few weeks and did not call. When she finally called again, the counselor who answered the telephone expressed her pleasure that she had called again and how the staff had missed her. Eventually, she and her husband moved to another state. In her last few calls, she said how much better she felt and how much she had appreciated the staff and the center. Her departure coincided with the departure of one of the counselors who had been at the center since its opening, and much was made of this coincidence. She wrote from her new home to express her gratitude and to tell of her activities. In a sense, by virtue of her frequent calls, this chronic caller had become as much a part of the center as the staff.

How Suicidal Are the Chronic Callers?

Of the 24 chronic callers, 11 gave no indication of current or past suicidal ideation. Four of them threatened suicide, and one of these claimed to have attempted suicide but called back later to say that she had only tried to scare her husband. Five of the callers reported having attempted suicide in the past, and three attempted suicide during the period that they were in contact with the center. Thus, these chronic callers were equally as likely to be suicidal as those who were not chronic callers. Furthermore, since they called the center frequently, there was more opportunity for the staff to intervene and to prevent their suicidal actions.

Discussion

With some chronic callers, there is no problem in deciding how the center is going to deal with them. They call with specific problems, will accept referrals to other community resources, and will visit the center so that more adequate evaluation and diagnosis can be made. There is a feeling on the part of the staff that some improvement is possible for such a caller.

In other cases, where the caller is already in treatment, the center can coordinate with the psychiatrist of therapist with whom the caller is in treatment. In some cases, this can mean simply urging the caller to use her present therapist rather than the center. In other cases, this can entail providing support for the caller in addition to that received from the therapist.

Problems arise mainly with those chronic callers who call the center frequently, who avoid questions put to them by the counselor, who refuse to focus upon and to discuss their problems, and who seem to want someone to merely listen to them talk. These callers often arouse a great deal of resentment on the part of the staff. The staff feels ineffective and frustrated in their attempts to help the caller. They feel that their time is being wasted by these callers when there are more important things to do.

Four approaches are possible with such callers, two of which seem to be useful.

1. The callers could be discouraged from calling the center. This approach seems unacceptable because it goes against the whole concept of a 24-hour telephone service. A center that provides such a telephone service is obligated to accept calls. The image of a center might be seriously impaired if calls were refused. From a clinical point of view, it may well be argued that repetitive and unfocused support can serve only to reinforce maladaptive behavior when no valid treatment is operating as a corrective. Even if this were the case, the center's position is a difficult one if it proposes to take all calls. In a therapeutic relationship, within a longer-term and face-to-face situation, one may choose to allow dependency, seductiveness, demands, projections and so forth in the beginning months of treatment with a plan to help the client in the course of time to understand and then relinquish those aspects of his personality and behavior. Perhaps the very nature of telephone contacts acts as a limit in this regard and also limits effective treatment with chronic callers, short of real help, to merely listening.

2. A second approach is simply to listen to the caller. The counselor can listen to chronic callers for as long as there is time and there are not other individuals calling the center. Perhaps this is not harmful to the caller, but it may lead to hostility on the part of the counselor and a feeling that her time is being wasted. Thus, the counselor's functioning may be impaired.

3. One constructive approach is for the counselor to limit the call of the chronic caller from the outset. The counselor can say that it is a very busy time and that she can spend only ten minutes with the caller. Many chronic callers understand this and will offer to hang up when they hear another line ring. Those who do not respond appropriately have at least been warned at the beginning of their call that their conversation may be terminated. They can also be told to call back in a few hours.

4. The most constructive approach is to keep a list of chronic callers and to have the professional staff formulate a plan, however limited in scope, for dealing with the caller. For example, it may be decided for a client that the counselors should try to encourage self-disclosure. Thus, the counselors have a plan of action when dealing with the caller and can feel that therapeutic intervention has not been abandoned for this particular caller. If, to pursue our example, a particular chronic caller begins to make more self-disclosures, then the professional staff can reformulate their plan. The next stage may require the counselors to reinforce self-disclosures of a particular type, and so on. In this way, over the course of many calls, a caller may be helped to some small extent along a path that is recognizable to the counselors as focused, therapeutic and useful. Not only does this approach fit in with the concept of a 24-hour telephone service available to all, but it also serves to reduce the feelings of hostility on the part of the counselors and gives them a sense of task involvement.

REFERENCE

Lester, D., & Brockopp, G. W. (1970). Chronic callers to a suicide prevention center. *Community Mental Health Journal, 6,* 246–250.

THE THERAPEUTIC MANAGEMENT OF THE CHRONIC CALLER

GENE W. BROCKOPP

With the chronic caller, the emergency telephone service is faced with an usual problem. As the number of calls the individual makes to the center increases, factual data about the person (personal history, background, home and life experiences) develop into an impressive case history. With this amount of material, it would seem that it would be easier to develop an effective treatment program for this caller than for most other callers. This, however, is not the case. Here is a caller who very likely has been to most of the social agencies in the community and has not received desired the assistance. But he still may continue to contact them, possibly out of the remote possibility that someone, somewhere, may have the magic answer to solve his problem. So, in most instances, the chronic caller is being heard, not only by the center, but also by many other agencies and organizations in the community. The center, because it is limited to verbal contact with the chronic caller and often has little influence over the range of the person's therapeutic and personal experiences. Therefore, it has little basis to assume that any behavior change on the part of the individual is a result of the contact with the center. Often these individuals call regardless of the nature of their most recent relationship with the center. This may indicate that they are receiving some therapeutic aid from the counselors, or it may indicate that they are calling to maintain contact in case one of the other sources of help begins to fail.

With the chronic caller, it is therefore very difficult to know which treatment method is therapeutic and almost impossible to isolate a single, most effective treatment approach for them. From an analysis of this type of caller at the Erie County Suicide Prevention Center, certain principles appear to be appropriate for use as guidelines when dealing with this type of caller.

1. The center must develop a consistent method of responding to this type of caller. This is quite difficult to achieve since most telephone emergency services use a large number of volunteers, each of whom has his own particular approach and therapeutic style in working with individuals in crisis situations.[27] In working with this type of caller the individualism of the counselor must be minimized and the patterned response of the center maximized in order to formulate and implement a reasoned, consistent, therapeutic response.

---

[27] The male pronoun is used throughout this section, as opposed to using a "his or her" format, for readability.

Every effort must be made by the volunteers to keep their response to the chronic caller in agreement with the approved program, for differences between the telephone counselors will often be taken by the chronic caller as signs of weakness or lack of knowledge. Consistency in telephone work allows for the person-to-person concern to come through by minimizing the hostility and frustration that the counselor may feel when working with the client who has called the center many times. The therapeutic plan also helps counselors develop more of a sense of sureness which is transmitted to the client in the noncognitive aspects of the communication.

2. Determine the scope of the reaching out behavior. With the chronic caller it is important to be aware that the individual may be seeing a therapist and calling other mental health services in the community and is possibly a client of one or more physicians. An attempt should be made by the staff to determine what organizations and groups in the community the chronic caller is contacting. If the person is seeing a therapist on a regular basis, it is important that the center obtain permission from the client to talk with this therapist and together with him develop a consistent approach of working with this individual. If it is determined that other agencies and organizations are also being contacted by this person, it is necessary to work with them to determine the appropriate area of help each of the agencies will provide. Sometimes it is useful to call the members of the agencies together with the chronic caller to work out a plan how each of them will work with the problems the person is presenting.

3. Suicidal risk must be continually evaluated. Chronic callers, especially if they have had any suicidal ideation in the past or have engaged in suicidal behavior, are very prone to make suicide attempts to underline the critical nature of their chronic condition and to "prove" their need for help. As a result, they may (accidentally or intentionally) kill themselves. With the natural habituation that a telephone emergency service undergoes after the continual threats of the chronic caller, unless it is very alert, it will miss the cues that this caller will give out before making a serious suicide attempt. These missed cues, covert as they may be, are often seen by the chronic caller as a direct rejection of their being. Care must be taken, therefore, not to underestimate the seriousness of any life-threatening behavior mentioned by the chronic caller. Many times mentioning this behavior is a test by them to determine whether or not the center still cares. Although the chronic caller is a low risk at any particular time, and even though he makes many suicide threats (since this person tends to live in a continual upset state), he is a high suicidal risk over a lifetime and may end his life through suicide.

4. Telephone therapy with the chronic caller should emphasize the person-to-person relationship. The chronic caller is usually operating at a very basic level in his relationship with other individuals. Often he is lonely, has a sense

of separation and isolation from other beings, and feels that no one cares for him or is willing to take him seriously. Unsureness, both in his interaction with people and in his feeling of self-worth, results in his being convinced that no one is interested enough in him to make a caring response. The focus of the telephone therapy should, therefore, emphasize trust, support, and confidence. Confrontation should be used sparingly, and no attempt should be made to develop insight on the part of the caller regarding the basis for his problems. If confrontation with the individual is necessary in order to develop and maintain an appropriate treatment program, the confrontation should be made on the content of the telephone conversation rather than on an emotional aspect of the relationship. Even if the confrontation is used in this way, it is difficult for the chronic client not to seize on the confrontation as evidence of their rejection by the telephone counselor. When confrontations are used, they are best stated in terms of open-ended, nonpejorative statements, which allow the caller to accept and define the confrontations at a level which is not too threatening to his psychological integrity. This will give the counselor a good idea of whether or not it is appropriate to move ahead with any further confrontation.

5. Develop neighborhood support systems for the chronic caller. While it is necessary to allow the chronic caller to maintain some dependency on the center and on persons at the center, the emphasis in all the contacts should be to direct the person back to those systems in his home or neighborhood which would give him support. Help must be given so that he will see the center and its personnel as a transitional social object which he can use, but one which must be supplanted by relationships that are more fixed and permanent in his environment. The direction of all the contacts should be on assisting the individual to make better use of himself and of his own environment and on developing embracing systems in the environment rather than focusing on the center and the telephone contact for sustenance and support. It is important to note in this regard that, with some chronic callers, the telephone counselor gives the caller clues which imply that he or the center has a desire to maintain contact with the caller and to continue the dependency relationship. This is especially true if the chronic caller is a young person and presents a seductive set of problems or involves the counselor in a personal way.

6. Focus on specific reality-oriented problems. The chronic caller usually presents a plethora of problems, each one more involved than the last, and each one adding to the difficulty in understanding the condition that the individual is in and in developing a solution for the condition. With each additional problem that the caller elucidates, his anxiety increases and his ability to cope decreases. Our experience with the chronic caller indicates that, when we help the client focus on specific life problem situations, we not only reduce the length of the calls and his anxiety, but we also maximize his ability to

work with his problems and develop appropriate solutions. To achieve this, it is necessary for the telephone counselor to become quite selective and direct with the material the client presents. Statements summarizing the problem that the client has are important. Through this type of teaching approach to the chronic client we are helping to develop a method of approaching and solving problems which he can use on his own. By refusing to focus on the emotional aspects of the call and emphasizing the content or rational aspects of the client's life, we are helping him to become more objective about his concerns and to feel a sense of being able to deal with his life problems in a more appropriate way than simply emoting about the hardness of his life and the many difficulties with which he is burdened.

Chronic callers are extremely taxing on the emotional energies of staff of an emergency telephone service. In an attempt to work with them more effectively and to utilize our time more efficiently, we have formulated a number of new methods for working with them which may improve their basic condition and minimize the negative effect they have on the center and its personnel.

1. Arrange a liaison between the chronic caller and other lonely people in the community who may desire a relationship or who may wish a human contact but be unable to obtain it. As was mentioned previously, the chronic caller is usually a person who is very lonely and who uses his contact with the center to obtain and maintain a relationship with someone who cares. Through a careful analysis of the telephone calls received by the center, a number of people can usually be found who also need a human contact and who could profit from listening to the hurts and problems of another person and responding to them on a feeling level. Although the chronic caller may call throughout the day, he usually makes his calls at night and in early hours of the morning when the loneliness of his existence is compounded by his inability to sleep. To develop relationships that may be useful to him at these times, the center may need to enlist the help of people who tend to be awake at night or who for one reason or another do not go to sleep until early in the morning, such as the wives of men who work on a swing shift. The center can sometimes enlist their help and support to take telephone calls at night. Of course, the center must maintain a liaison with people who take these calls and must provide them with the needed backup services of consultation, counseling, and referral.

2. Enlist the assistance of former telephone counselors. Every center has a list of individuals who have volunteered their time at the center and who have dropped out of active volunteer service. Some of these maintain a high interest in the work of the center and recognize the value of the service the center is performing in the community. Although they may not be willing to continue to work a regular shift at the center, they might be willing to have their

name and their telephone number given out to some chronic callers. The chronic callers could then call them for support and friendship rather than calling the center. The use of former telephone counselors, of course, would help to assure the center that appropriate types of decisions would be made regarding the problems that the chronic caller is bringing up.

3. Use community groups for support relationships. Since the chronic callers tend to be older individuals or individuals who demand a great deal of support and succorance, groups of individuals in the community who can give time can sometimes be tapped to work with the chronic caller. For example, Golden Age Club members could talk with these individuals either by telephone or in person. Even individuals who are bedridden (for example, individuals in nursing homes) could be utilized for this purpose and, while giving help, could be obtaining desirable outside contacts for themselves.

4. Group therapy for chronic callers. By bringing together a group of individuals who are chronic callers at the center for a period of time each week and allowing them to interact with each other, the amount of time they spend calling the center could be substantially reduced. At the same time, this approach could help them develop additional personal contacts in the community, see the way other people are handling their problems, and provide a support base for them when they try out new behaviors. During the group therapy period, discussions could be initiated as to the value of the telephone service for them and the ways in which they could make more effective use of this service.

5. Use writing therapy. We have found it is sometimes useful to have a chronic caller write to a center rather than calling the center. Some individuals communicate their difficulties much more precisely and carefully through the written word rather than through the telephone, and the real needs, which they cover up through a large amount of verbiage, may become clear when they are asked to put them in writing. This process also allows the center to give a more thoughtful type of response to the chronic caller and, thereby, deal with the problem in a less demanding and time-consuming method. Letter writing also effectively moves the person into a more objective relationship which may allow the client caller to deal more with the reality-oriented aspects of his problem and less with his feelings.

6. Call the chronic caller. Sometimes the center can best help the chronic caller by showing interest and concern for them through calling them rather than waiting for them to call the center. In this way, the telephone counselor can help them to "set their day" in a more positive framework and can help them plan the activities of their day. It also allows the counselor to have more control over the conversation, directing it and terminating it without the caller feeling hurt. The call also gives the client the assurance that the center is interested and concerned about him and often makes it less necessary for him

to call the center and be reassured that the agency is still there and available to him.[28]

The usual, often nonverbal reactions of telephone counselors to another call from a "crock" interfere with the appropriate handling of the caller and destroy any therapeutic relationship which the counselor may have with the caller. To effectively deal with this type of caller, the center must formulate and implement a reasoned and consistent policy of working with this type of client and develop new and innovative methods of responding to them. If this is not done, the chronic caller will eventually be rejected, either covertly or overtly, by a frustrated telephone counselor.

REPORT OF A CASE

Diane Blum and David Lester

In the previous sections, we discussed the individual who makes a large number of calls to a suicide prevention center. We described the characteristics of these chronic callers, presented some case illustrations, and discussed possible policies that a center might adopt for the chronic caller.

The present section examines one chronic caller in greater detail and explores some of the approaches that the counselors have taken with her, their reactions to her, and how these reactions affected the counseling process.

Mrs. A was a 40-year-old divorced woman who called the center at least once a day (and often as many as three or four times a day) for over six months. She usually discussed her feelings of loneliness, depression, and rejection, and she expressed hostility toward all the people who have been unwilling to establish relationships with her. Much of her concern centered on why her 15-year-old daughter chose to live in a foster home rather than with her. Mrs. A was often hostile and angry, but occasionally she was happy and talked to the counselors about cheerful topics.

The problem facing a suicide prevention center in trying to help such a client is increased by the fact that a caller who calls frequently may speak to any one of about two or three dozen counselors. Therefore, not only is it difficult to formulate a therapeutic plan that might prove useful in helping the caller, but it is also difficult to implement such a plan. Consequently, the caller experiences a variety of therapeutic approaches. The counselors were able to identify a number of different approaches that they had taken with Mrs. A.

---

[28] This is one form of the care-ring service which has been extremely effective in some parts of the country as a means of dealing with lonely people.

1. Many of the counselors tried to demonstrate their acceptance of Mrs. A and convey warmth and support. This approach was used especially after she had been released from a state hospital and felt very insecure living alone. Counselors employed this approach to encourage Mrs. A to find a job and to support her efforts to succeed in it. The counselors using this approach assured Mrs. A that they realized how difficult working was for her and they acknowledged her loneliness.

This approach was helpful since Mrs. A had few interpersonal contacts and received very little support from any person in her life. The continued support she received may have helped her find a job and maintain it. The disadvantage of continually expressing acceptance to Mrs. A lay in the reactions of the counselor. When the counselors told Mrs. A that they knew how difficult things were for her, she often replied, "How do you know how hard it is? You've never been alone like I am." The counselors felt frustrated when Mrs. A reacted in this way to them.

2. The counselors sometimes focused on particular problems Mrs. A presented and offered interpretations to her as to why she was feeling a certain way. Concentrating on a particular problem helped to focus Mrs. A's often disorganized conversation. However, interpretations such as, "Are you feeling bad today because your daughter did not call?" and discussing Mrs. A's feelings about her daughter often resulted in her generalizing her feelings about her daughter to everyone else. Her conversation again became a statement of her overwhelming loneliness and unhappiness. Consequently, focusing Mrs. A's thoughts was extremely difficult.

3. The counselors also reacted with hostility to Mrs. A and told her that they were tired of listening to her problems. This approach was used when a particular counselor had had several long conversations with Mrs. A during which Mrs. A had been especially angry.

The counselors all said that at times their only reaction to Mrs. A had been one of hostility. However, usually they controlled their anger, but they felt that Mrs. A had sensed their hostile feelings. Anger is an understandable feeling here, but it may result in guilt on the part of the counselor as it is at odds with their idealized aim of communicating acceptance. It is also very likely that Mrs. A recognized, at some level, the hostility in the counselor and reacted to it. Expression of anger by a counselor to a client is not necessarily unwise or damaging. However, for a counselor to use such a response to a client usefully, the counselor should, in general, be aware of these feelings and be in control of them (as opposed to being controlled by them).

4. The counselors limited Mrs. A's time to ten or 15 minutes and permitted her to control the conversation during this time. This response to Mrs. A often occurred inadvertently as the counselor had to terminate her call to take another call. A time-limited conversation did not seem to upset Mrs. A since

she believed that the counselors at the center would talk to her again when she called later.

5. The counselors confronted Mrs. A with the fact that she was not accepting any of their suggestions and demonstrated to her that this was a pattern of behavior for her. The counselors indicated that, if she treated her friends and relatives the way she treated the counselors, then it was not surprising that people rebuffed her attempts at friendship.

Confronting Mrs. A with her patterns of behavior might be a valid treatment method if it was utilized consistently by all counselors. On the other hand, the counselors' lack of patience weakened the usefulness of this approach. Several of the counselors expressed the feeling that when they confronted Mrs. A, she merely turned their statement back to them and said they had no idea of what she was going through. This made them frustrated and angry.

6. The counselors concentrated on specific suggestions such as going to Recovery, bingo, or church. It seems as if Mrs. A usually initiated the possibility of some activity and then questioned various counselors about their opinion of it.

This approach was utilized frequently. However, there was no combined effort on the part of the counselors to develop particular plans of activity for Mrs. A, and no one was able to determine who initiated a certain suggestion. One counselor suggested that it was Mrs. A who first mentioned an activity and then each counselor reacted to it personally. The danger in this stems from the fact that Mrs. A could have received conflicting opinions from the various counselors with whom she spoke. However, she did receive consistent advice and support for the idea of going to Recovery and bingo, and she expressed satisfaction from participating in these activities. Several of the counselors focused on the importance of her medication since Mrs. A was refusing to take her medicine.

It is the general impression of the counselors that Mrs. A improved during the time she called the center. Initially, she appeared unable to leave her house alone, whereas later she appeared to have sought and found employment. It is difficult to estimate to what extent her contact with the center was responsible for this change. It is impossible, therefore, to try to evaluate the usefulness of the different approaches utilized by counselors.

Two general points are worth emphasizing here. First, the reactions of counselors to particular types of callers may on occasion interfere with the effective development of the therapeutic relationship that the counselor must establish with the caller. Second, since a suicide prevention center uses a large number of counselors, attempts must be made to formulate and implement a reasoned and consistent policy for particular clients. Both of these problems can be dealt with by means of case conferences centered around particular clients. In such meetings the feelings of the counselors can be expressed and dealt with, and a therapeutic intervention policy can be formulated.

WHEN PLANS GO WRONG

David Lester

In a book such as this, it is common to present only effective interventions and cases that illustrate our successes. However, we can learn as much from our failures as from our successes, and so this section of the chapter presents two examples of how a center can "mishandle" problems callers, in this case, chronic callers.

Joan

Joan was a teenager who called the center over a period of four months, building up in frequency until she was calling five times each day. She preferred to talk to male counselors and was hostile if women answered the telephone. She was able to deduce the schedule of the counselors from monitoring who answered the telephone so that she soon would learn who was working the different shifts. She also managed to elicit information about the counselors from others (full name, profession, and so on) even though this breach of confidentiality on the part of the counselors was forbidden by the staff of the center.

Joan's aim in calling seemed to be to engage in teenage chit chat. Although she was unhappy with various aspects of her life, most notably her relationship with her parents who tended to be somewhat restrictive with her, she resisted strongly any attempts to investigate these areas. At one point, she stated that she did not want to deal with her problems since, were she to improve, she would no longer have an excuse to call the center. The lack of focusing by counselors with her was indicated by the fact that no counselor could ever inform the professional staff of the center what exactly her problem was.

Joan became increasingly enamored with particular counselors, and the fantasy aspects of her calling became increasingly evident. She began to write to the counselors and send them poems which indicated a great deal of romantic attachment to them. Because the counselors had to handle other calls, most of which were more serious than Joan's, they often had to tell her to call back or to put her "on hold." In time, this became an excuse, and counselors pretended that they had to handle other calls. Some also were made anxious by Joan's increasing attachment to them, and Joan, on her part, resented being put off. She reported that to be put on hold and left there for five, ten or 15 minutes was unpleasant, frustrating, and rejecting.

At this point, one of the center's professional staff members decided to take over. He took the next call from Joan and told her of the staff's concern. He suggested that she call only him, that conversation was no longer permissible, that they would discuss any problems that she had, and that the counselors had been told to limit her calls and to tell her to call him. She was, understandably, very angry at this turn of events. She did eventually call the staff member a couple of times, but she complained about him afterwards to the telephone counselors. She continued to refuse to focus on problems. Eventually, this staff member decided that, because she was so angry with him, another staff member should take over the case.

Accordingly, a new staff member was assigned to talk to Joan, and he limited her to three calls of 15 minutes each in each week. Despite this, she continued to call at other times to talk with the volunteer counselors. Again, it was difficult to get her to focus on her problems and to deal with her manipulative behavior. This staff member was about to leave the center, and this had been known when Joan was assigned to him. Thus, his imminent departure, combined with Joan's refusal to limit herself to talking with one staff member, led to the quick dissolution of this relationship.

A few weeks later, her case came up for discussion again, and she was assigned to a third staff member. This staff member instituted several procedures. First, he tried to limit her calls to the center. Second, he tried to be more accepting and understanding of her situation. At this point, she was still angry and hurt by the new policy of the center toward her. Third, he persuaded her to visit the center and meet the staff and the volunteer counselors in order to introduce some reality into the fantasy world which everyone (Joan and the counselors) had created. This particular staff member was able to deal with her hostility and to get across to her that the staff wanted to help her, but the dependency continued. Joan began visiting the center just to sit in the waiting room, talking to the receptionist and the staff and counselors as they passed to and fro. Eventually, the relationship between Joan and the staff member assigned to her became less intense, and there was little contact between them.

A year after Joan began calling the center, she was still a "problem."

Jean

Jean was divorced and living alone. She did not work and lived off her alimony. She went out of the house only to shop and for necessities. She was lonely, depressed, and eventually was calling the center for about 35 hours each week. The counselors noted that her behavior remained consistent. Even certain phrases, such as, "How am I going to care again?" continued to recur, delivered in exactly the same tone of voice, month after month.

When the situation with Jean came to the attention of the professional staff, one staff member was assigned to handle her case. He tried to persuade Jean to visit the center, but she refused. It was decided to send a second staff member to visit Jean at home, a very unusual response for the center to undertake. The staff member learned very little that was new but concluded that the center was providing a useful service for Jean. It appeared that everyone, including the center's counselors, her priest, her doctor, and other agencies, had failed to get her to change her life-style. There seemed to be no prospect that her loneliness would end, and so her use of the center's telephone service helped her survive in the community. The staff member did learn that Jean had drunk quite heavily before she started calling the center and that she had stopped since. Thus, the center was helping her to lower her intake of alcohol.

The professional staff decided to instruct the telephone counselors to limit the calls from Jean to 20 minutes and to make her focus on specific plans to deal a particular problem. The time limit was applied successfully, but focusing proved difficult. Jean's attitude was described by one counselor as "Please help me, but I defy you to."

The reactions of the counselors to Jean varied considerably. Those beginning to work at the center felt sorry for her and thought that the center was being cruel in limiting her calls. Eventually, they began to feel frustrated in talking to her and to become hostile.

Discussion

It is clear that insufficient training and the administrative complexities involved in supervising counselors can lead to problems for a telephone counseling service. Many chronic callers follow the pattern described here: the problem develops, the staff eventually learns of the case, and then the staff takes corrective measures which typically fail.

In handling these cases, the staff at the center displayed some ambivalence. For example, Joan was shuttled from one staff member to another and treated in a way that was bound to alienate her. It became clear to her that she had become a "nuisance." If at this point, she had become so alienated that she never called the center again, the problem would have been "solved." Since the center had no way of contacting her (her name and telephone number were not known), the center would have been in the position of building up dependency in an individual only to reject that individual when she became a nuisance!

In handling these two cases, different measures are called for. Joan was young and had many potential outlets for her emotional needs. She had siblings, parents, girl-friends, a boy-friend, and worked as a volunteer during her vacations. Essentially, the center should have found some way to wean her from her attachment to the counselors at the center, a way that was gradual and nonrejecting.

Jean, on the other hand, was elderly, and there was little prospect of her changing. Attempts to get her to restructure her life had failed. The center had two alternatives. It could accept that, by talking to Jean for several hours each week, they could help alleviate her loneliness, keep her drinking under control, and perhaps help her function in the community rather than allowing her to disintegrate to the point where institutionalization became necessary. If the center were to decide to do this, then instruction and supervision of the counselors would be necessary to ensure that the therapeutic plan was adhered to.

Alternatively, the center could attempt to create a service for people like Jean, a service in which volunteers call or visit particular individuals regularly. Using a small number of volunteers, each volunteer could be assigned to one or two individuals to counsel on a regular basis, preferably via the telephone, again with close supervision from the professional staff.

Chapter 15

CHRONIC CALLS PLACED TO SUICIDE AND CRISIS INTERVENTION HOTLINES: CASE STRATEGIES FOR THE PERSISTENT MENTALLY ILL AND VULNERABLE

LORIE L. SICAFUSE, WILLIAM P. EVANS, AND LAURA A. DAVIDSON

Chronic callers are of significant concern to agencies providing telephone crisis counseling, suicide prevention, and related services (MacKinnon, 1998). According to MacKinnon, "The most stressful dilemma facing a crisis line is the repeat or regular caller" (p. 21). Though many individuals repeatedly call centers during periods of emotional distress, a "chronic caller" may contact a particular hotline on hundreds of occasions throughout the year (see Chapter 14), and may or may not be experiencing crisis. Such calls often are lengthy and occur during especially busy times at centers (e.g., late-night hours; Hall & Schlosar, 1995; Kinzel & Nanson, 2000). Chronic callers tax the limited resources of crisis call centers and may prevent others in crisis from getting the help they need. In addition, chronic callers cause stress in many hotline counselors and volunteers, who often feel manipulated by the chronic caller or experience anger and frustration when chronic callers repeatedly ignore their suggestions (MacKinnon, 1998). This sense of inefficacy among hotline workers has been associated with increased counselor burnout and turnover (Ingram et al., 2008).

Both the first and second editions of this volume highlighted the challenges presented by chronic callers and strategies for managing chronic calls. Yet, decades later, chronic callers remain an understudied population. Data obtained from a sample of chronic callers were presented in the first edition of this volume (Chapter 14) but, since then, few empirical studies have focused on chronic callers (e.g., Hall & Schlosar, 2005; Ingram et al., 2008; Mishara

& Daigle, 1997). Scholars and mental health professionals have repeatedly acknowledged the potential negative effects of chronic callers on crisis center staff and on crisis center clients in general (Kehoe & Grant, 1997; Kinzel & Nanson, 2000; MacKinnon, 1998; Mishara & Giroux, 1993). However, in-depth discussions of tactics designed to minimize chronic calls are less common (but see Hall & Schlosar, 1995; MacKinnon, 1998; Mishara & Daigle, 1997).

As crisis call centers and the number of clients in distress continue to expand throughout the nation (SAMHSA, 2009), there is an urgent need for an enhanced understanding of chronic callers' characteristics (e.g., patterns, motivations, and presenting issues). Such an understanding may further inform the development of strategies aimed at managing this population and addressing their needs. This chapter builds on the discussion of issues surrounding chronic callers presented in the first two editions of this volume (see Chapter 14). First, it provides an update on current knowledge of chronic callers' characteristics, motivations, and use of crisis center resources. Recent data collected from chronic calls placed to a large crisis center in the western United States are presented to further elucidate the nature of such calls and the specific needs of chronic callers. Next, it discusses means of reducing chronic callers' reliance on crisis call centers, highlighting technological advancements and other recent approaches to addressing the needs of persistent mentally ill and vulnerable populations. Finally, it presents avenues for additional research in this area related to understanding chronic callers' issues and assessing the impacts of management strategies.

Current Knowledge of Chronic Callers: Resource Utilization, Patterns, and Characteristics

Several researchers have documented the frequency of chronic calls placed to crisis centers throughout the United States, Canada, and Australia. There is a general consensus that between 25% and 33% of calls received by crisis centers are placed by individuals who contact the center on a routine basis (Brunet, Lemay, & Belliveau; 1994; MacKinnon, 1998; Mishara & Daigle, 1997; Watson, McDonald, & Pearce, 2006). Fewer efforts, however, have been made to explore the characteristics and patterns of chronic callers and to determine the extent to which chronic callers may differ from first-time or "acute" callers. Many studies describing the users of crisis call centers fail to identify cases representing chronic callers or exclude chronic calls from analysis (e.g., Kalafat, Gould, Munfakh, & Kleinman, 2007).

Chronic callers have posed significant challenges to crisis centers since their inception. Lester and colleagues (Chapter 14) provided initial data regarding the characteristics of chronic callers contacting the Suicide Prevention and Crisis Service of Erie County. This particular crisis center had received a total of 3,910 calls from October 1968 to June 1969; 1,728 (44.2%) of these calls were placed by repeat contacts (those who had called the center on more than one occasion). Many of these repeat callers may have contacted the center for follow-up purposes or occasional advice. Yet, Lester and colleagues isolated 24 individuals who had contacted the crisis center in excess of ten times during this eight-month time period, and these clients comprised the population of "chronic callers" for their analyses. A comparison of the characteristics of these chronic callers with those of first time or acute callers revealed minimal differences. Chronic callers were highly similar to acute callers in terms of demographics (e.g., gender, age, ethnicity and marital status), presenting problems, and assessed suicide risk.

More recent (albeit limited) findings illuminate differences between acute and chronic callers to crisis centers. Data collected from American and Canadian crisis call centers suggest that chronic callers are disproportionately female, single, unemployed, and in their 30s or 40s (Hall & Schlosar, 1995; Ingram et al., 2008). These characteristics are shared by the majority of acute callers to crisis hotlines (de Anda & Smith, 1993; Gould, Kalafat, Munfakh, & Kleinman, 2007). However, Hall and Schlosar's data obtained from the Canadian Samaritan crisis hotline suggest that an overwhelming (rather than a simple "majority" as observed in prior research) number of chronic calls are placed by females. These researchers analyzed a series of chronic calls to the Samaritan hotline over an unspecified time period. Among the 1351 chronic calls included in the sample, 82.2% ($n = 1110$) were placed by females. Gender differences were further noted in the issues that chronic callers presented to Samaritan hotline counselors. Although both female and male callers primarily cited "general" issues during their calls, women were more inclined to discuss emotional issues (e.g., depression, loneliness, and anger) than were men, whereas men were more likely than women to discuss substance abuse problems. This study did not include a comparison group of acute calls. It was noted, however, that suicide risk assessed in the overall sample of chronic calls was relatively low, with approximately 2% of both male and female callers discussing plans to commit suicide.[29]

Ingram et al. (2008) conducted a limited comparison of acute and chronic calls placed to the Girls and Boys Town National Hotline from 2001 to 2005. Nearly half (47%) of the 349,464 calls received during this time period were placed by individuals who had previously contacted the hotline. No signifi-

---

[29] An additional comparison of acute and chronic callers focuses on their responses to different types of therapeutic interventions (Mishara & Daigle, 1997). These findings will be included in the later discussion of strategies aimed at managing chronic callers.

cant age and gender differences emerged between acute and chronic callers. With respect to presenting issues, chronic callers were most likely to identify mental health concerns as the primary reason for their call (cited in 27% of chronic calls), whereas acute callers were most inclined to discuss "parent/adult issues." Although no other comparisons between these two groups were reported, this finding is consistent with anecdotal evidence of severe and persistent mental illness among chronic callers (Kehoe & Grant, 1997; MacKinnon, 1998; Seeley, 1993). As Lester and colleagues (Chapter 14) noted, many chronic callers likely have already sought help from multiple social and mental health community resources, with little improvement. Thus, crisis hotlines may provide a sense of certainty or comfort to chronic callers who have exhausted community resources. Crisis center counselors often are unable to help chronic callers address their issues due to lack of client cooperation and focus, but they are, by the nature and purpose of their organization, available to listen to their clients' concerns.

Other literature focusing on chronic callers primarily discusses anecdotal evidence of the extent and nature of the problem (e.g., Brunet, Lemay, & Belliveau, 1994; Kehoe & Grant, 1997; Kinzel & Nanson, 2000; Seeley, 1993). Such accounts provide further insight into the motivations of chronic callers, ultimately suggesting that these clients experience extreme loneliness and lack of social support. They often contact crisis counselors "just to chat" or to discuss daily "crises" (presumably magnified by mental illness) such as what groceries to buy (Brunet et al., 1994; Hall & Schlosar, 1995). Specific emphasis is placed on the stress and frustration chronic callers elicit in crisis counselors, who report that they are unable to motivate chronic callers to focus on a particular problem and its underlying causes, and that they struggle to maintain control over such calls (Kehoe & Grant, 1997; MacKinnon, 1998). Counselor testimonials further suggest that many chronic callers respond to recommendations and advice with defensiveness and anger, and tend not to follow through with action plans or utilize referral services (Kinzel & Nanson, 2000; MacKinnon, 1998). "Setting boundaries" is one of the most frequent difficulties counselors face when dealing with chronic callers (Kehoe & Grant, 1997).

As this brief review illustrates, the problem of chronic callers has not subsided since examined in the first edition of this volume, and may be increasing in magnitude. Considerable literature has documented chronic callers' excessive use of crisis center resources and their negative effects on counseling staff (Brunet et al., 1994; Hall & Schlosar; 1995; Kehoe & Grant, 1997; Watson et al., 2006). A general description of "typical" chronic callers has emerged from call center staff testimonials and limited empirical research. Such individuals appear to be predominantly female, middle-aged, and have few or no meaningful social relationships and connections to the community. This is not a significant departure from the characteristics of acute or crisis callers in general. Chronic callers, however, may be more likely to suffer from severe and persistent mental illness than acute callers. They also may be less amenable to treatment and common methods of crisis intervention.

Despite these accounts, research has yielded only basic insights (at best) into chronic callers' characteristics and issues. Little is known about the specific problems chronic callers face and report, and how these may differ from problems presented by acute callers. Suicidality among chronic callers is also not well understood. Though Hall and Schlosar (1995) reported minimal suicide risk in their sample of chronic callers, others have found no difference in suicidal ideation among chronic and acute callers (e.g., Lester & Brockopp, 1970) or a slightly *increased* risk among chronic callers (Mishara & Daigle, 1997).[30] A more thorough understanding of these topics is critical in determining the best means of addressing chronic callers' needs and in minimizing the burden this population places on crisis center resources.

An Examination of Chronic Calls Placed to the Crisis Call Center of Northern Nevada

The Crisis Call Center of Northern Nevada (CCC) provides 24-hour emergency telephone crisis intervention, support, information, and referral services throughout Nevada. In addition to suicide prevention, the center also addresses a wide range of crisis situations such as addiction, mental health and relationship issues, sexual assault, and domestic violence. As in other large crisis centers, managing chronic calls is a significant concern at the CCC. The center received 95,023 crisis calls between January 2005 and February 2009; approximately 23,884 (25.1%) of these calls were attributed to individuals who had contacted the center on multiple occasions. We examined this sample of 23,884 chronic calls to better understand the nature of these calls and the individuals who place them. In particular, we sought to provide a more detailed picture of the problems chronic callers may face, differences between this population and "acute" callers, and their use of call center resources.

The data reported here were obtained from a comprehensive database maintained by the CCC including information on all calls placed to the center between January 2005 and February 2009. CCC counselors systematically record details for all calls on paper data collection forms. These data are subsequently transferred to an electronic database. The data forms are organized into multiple topic categories followed by a series of response options,

---

[30] It should be noted that this sample consisted of chronic and acute callers contacting a suicide hotline rather than an overarching crisis hotline (dealing with suicidal ideation as well as multiple other types of crises). Thus, this specific finding may be unique to individuals already contemplating suicide and not reflective of the general population of chronic callers.

and are designed to collect information regarding caller demographics, suicide risk and lethality assessments, presenting issues, referrals, and call resolution. It should be noted that some categories are not mutually exclusive. For instance, counselors identify all issues presented by each caller. Further, each issue category contains additional descriptive response options to obtain more specific information about the type and nature of the issue.

Criteria used to differentiate chronic callers from general or acute callers are highly subjective. Such individuals typically contact the center multiple times per day, exhibit signs of severe mental illness, discuss the same problem repeatedly without following up on counselors' suggestions, or present routine activities of daily living as "crises." Ultimately, any individual who overutilizes call center resources and does not respond to traditional methods of crisis intervention is classified as a chronic caller. Once chronic callers are identified, they are placed on a "case management program," and informed that they may only make one five-minute telephone call to the center per day. This guideline is subject to the counselors' discretion and may be waived for chronic callers experiencing severe emotional distress or a genuine crisis. Similar policies have been adopted at many other large crisis call centers.

The current subset of 23,884 calls placed by chronic callers was extracted from the sample of 95,023 calls included in the database. Counselors were asked to indicate whether each call was placed by a chronic caller on the data form, and this information was entered into the database along with the caller's first name or alias. Data corresponding to callers with unique names were then combined to determine the extent to which each caller contacted the center. Though this technique likely excluded some unidentified chronic callers and may have erroneously combined data from a few chronic callers, it provides an estimate of the degree to which chronic callers utilize crisis hotline resources and the issues they report.

Missing data are a problem in crisis center research (Fakhoury, 2002), and the present analysis is no exception. As all calls are anonymous, clients are not required to provide any particular type of information. In striving to develop a positive and trusting relationship with callers, many counselors may refrain from interrupting with questions for the purposes of data collection. Further, such probes may be perceived as inappropriate or insensitive by some crisis callers. Thus, some variables in the current analysis (namely demographics) are characterized by a large proportion of missing cases.

Findings

The findings are consistent with the notion that a substantial portion of crisis call center resources are expended upon a relatively small group of individuals. Approximately 298 unique individuals accounted for all 23,884 calls. The majority of these 298 chronic callers (65.1%) contacted the center on ten separate occasions or less; 6.4% contacted the center 11-20 times, 11.4% called 21-50 times; 6.4% called 51-100 times; 8.3% called the center 101-1000 times, and 2.3% of these individuals placed more than 1,000 calls to the crisis hotline. Overall, seven unique individuals accounted for over half (51%; $n = 12,175$) of all chronic calls and for 12.8% of all calls placed to the center within the five-year time frame.

Primary chronic caller cases (representing the first instance in which a chronic caller was identified) were isolated and analyzed in an effort to obtain a demographic profile of chronic callers. No gender differences emerged in the current sample of chronic callers: 50% of the 298 callers were male and 49.3% were female. (Gender was "unknown" for 0.7% of the sample.) This is consistent with Lester and colleagues' analysis (Chapter 14), but not with more recent findings suggesting that chronic callers are predominantly female. Additional demographic characteristics of chronic callers were similar to those documented in studies focusing on chronic callers and on crisis callers in general. The majority were Caucasian, between the ages of 31 and 54, unemployed, and lacked primary means of social support (e.g., children, spouses, and close friends). The demographic characteristics of acute callers contacting the CCC were generally similar to those of chronic callers with the exception of gender. Most acute callers were female (65.8%).

PRESENTING ISSUES. The high frequency of calls placed by unique clients and the nature of the data did not permit an analysis of the specific issues discussed by each individual caller during all contacts with the crisis center. Consequently, issues were examined in terms of their presence or absence in the total number of chronic calls placed to the center ($n = 23,884$) rather than in the collapsed sample representing 298 unique chronic callers. Frequencies of issues presented in acute calls ($n = 71,139$) also were calculated for comparative purposes. (See Table 15-1 for a comparison of issues reported in chronic and acute calls.) Two major themes emerged from this analysis. First, chronic callers were less inclined to report specific problems or issues as recorded by crisis counselors than were acute callers, with the exception of mental health-related issues. Second, a small proportion of unique chronic callers accounted for the majority of issues reported in chronic calls.

Consistent with Hall and Schlosar's (1995) findings, very few chronic calls involved concerns over suicide. Lethality assessments were completed in less than 1% of all chronic calls. Current plans to commit suicide and prior attempts also were rare (reported in 0.4% of chronic calls). Further analysis of these variables within the sample of chronic calls indicated that five unique callers accounted for over half of all lethality assessments, and three unique callers accounted for nearly half of all reports of current plans to commit sui-

Table 15-1
FREQUENCIES OF ISSUES PRESENTED IN CHRONIC AND ACUTE CALLS

Issue	Chronic Calls (N = 23884)	Acute Calls (N = 71139)
Lethality assessment conducted	0.9%	6.0%
Current plans to commit suicide	0.4%	3.0%
Prior suicide attempt	0.4%	2.6%
Relationship issues	19.6%	30.0%
Substance-related issues	2.7%	12.6%
General mental health concerns	19.5%	17.3%
Diagnosed psychiatric disorder	14.7%	5.8%
Mental health assessment/treatment needed	6.3%	9.3%
General medical concerns	6.0%	6.7%
Financial concerns	4.0%	13.9%

cide. Lethality assessments were completed at a substantially higher rate in acute calls. In addition, a larger (though still minimal) proportion of acute calls concerned prior suicide attempts and current plans to commit suicide (see Table 15-1).

General relationship issues were reported in 19.6% of all chronic calls, whereas relationship issues were cited in nearly one-third (30.0%) of acute calls. Specific relationship issues discussed in chronic calls included conflicts with family of origin and/or significant other, concerns about others' relationships, work-related conflicts, and loss of a loved one. Seven unique callers accounted for over half of all reports of relationship issues in chronic calls. One unique caller reported a relationship issue in 755 different calls to the center, and another reported a relationship issue in 514 separate calls.

Less than 3% of all chronic calls focused on substance-related issues, which were reported in 12.6% of acute calls. Reports of a current addiction, however were similarly low in both chronic (0.9%) and acute (0.4%) calls. The majority of the 206 chronic calls made by current substance users focused on alcohol addiction, followed by drug addiction and gambling addiction. Again, chronic callers reporting addiction issues were likely to do so over the course of many separate calls. Five callers accounted for over half of all reports of general addiction issues.

General mental health concerns were slightly more common in chronic (19.5%) than in acute calls (17.3%). In addition, reports of a diagnosed psychiatric disorder were more prevalent in chronic calls. However, it should be noted that many chronic calls involving mental health issues were placed by the same caller (nine individuals were responsible for over half of such calls), whereas acute callers were represented only once in analyses. The proportion of general medical complaints did not differ among chronic and acute calls.

Finally, finance-related issues were reported in 13.9% of acute calls but only in 4% of all chronic calls. Common financial concerns discussed in chronic calls included unemployment and lack of money for food, lodging, and transportation. As observed in other issue categories, a very small group of three chronic callers placed over half of all calls involving finance-related issues.

CALL RESOLUTION. Counselors provided information or support in the majority of chronic calls (81.5%) and made referrals in nearly one-third (32.6%) of chronic calls. A welfare check or trace was initiated in only 0.1% of chronic calls. Acute calls were similarly resolved, with 1.4% involving a welfare check-trace and 31.4% leading to referrals. Many chronic callers received referrals on multiple occasions, suggesting that they may have failed to "follow through" or utilize the referrals. For example, referrals were made for the same caller on 82 separate occasions, and another caller received referrals in 69 different calls to the center.

Summary

The current findings mostly support previous research and anecdotal evidence regarding the characteristics of chronic callers (Brunet et al., 1994; Michara & Daigle, 1997; Watson et al., 2006). Our data indicate that chronic callers make disproportionate use of call center services. A small subset of individuals were responsible for all chronic calls, and less than 10 people accounted for nearly half of all chronic calls. Further, many of these individuals discussed the same problem repeatedly with counselors, appeared reluctant to follow up on suggestions or referrals, and often suffered from severe mental illness. Demographic characteristics of chronic callers were similar to those observed in other samples of both chronic and acute callers with the exception of gender. Interestingly, women and men were equally likely to be chronic callers. This is inconsistent with prior research that reported that both chronic and acute callers are predominantly female (de Anda & Smith, 1993; Hall & Schlosar, 1995; Ingram et al., 2008; Watson et al., 2006). Further examinations of the profiles of chronic callers contacting other crisis centers are warranted to confirm these gender differences and identify factors that may account for them.

Chronic callers were less likely than other callers to identify common sources of crisis that may be addressed through referrals or more traditional problem solving approaches. For example, they were less inclined to report problems with relationships or substance abuse, and the vast majority was not at risk for suicide or self-harm. Reports of such experiences among chronic callers were dominated by a few select individuals, who apparently continued to contact the crisis center after receiving multiple referrals for outside assistance. This suggests that the issues underlying many chronic calls (e.g., mental illness and paranoia, and severe loneliness and isolation) are complex and not easily managed via telephone counseling. Although reports of diagnosed mental disorders were indeed higher among chronic callers, this is likely an underestimate of the true incidence of mental illness in this population. According to CCC staff, nearly all of the chronic callers exhibited signs of severe mental illness but may never have sought treatment or received an official diagnosis.

Though accompanied by methodological limitations (e.g., missing data issues and likely overestimations of reported issues among chronic callers), the current results, in conjunction with prior research, may inform the development and implementation of measures aimed at managing chronic callers. In particular, a specific focus on managing chronic callers may dramatically decrease the frequency of chronic calls and reduce counselor stress and workload, helping them to target callers' issues more effectively. Multiple strategies designed to minimize chronic callers' use of crisis center resources and address their needs are discussed next.

Effective Management of Chronic Callers

Many researchers and practitioners have discussed the challenges presented by chronic callers and their effects on crisis center resources and staff (Brunet et al., 1994; Kehoe & Grant, 1997; Kinzel & Nanson, 2000; Mishara & Giroux, 1993; Seeley, 1993). Potential strategies for managing this population, however, have been less forthcoming. Lester and colleagues (Chapter 14) described multiple means of handling chronic callers, many of which are still relevant today. Since then, only a handful of studies have proposed and evaluated strategies targeting chronic callers. This section reviews the literature in this area and proposes more recent technologically-based measures that may prove useful in minimizing chronic calls placed to crisis hotlines.

Anecdotal evidence suggests that chronic callers do not respond well to common crisis intervention methods. The analysis of the chronic calls described in this chapter seems to support this contention, as it indicates that the most frequent callers failed to utilize referrals and follow action plans. Only one published study (to our knowledge) has empirically examined the impact of crisis intervention styles on chronic callers. Mishara and Daigle (1997) compared the effects of the "Rogerian" method (characterized by empathy, acceptance, approval, and "active listening") and the "Directive" problem-solving approach (involving orientation, information, suggestions, advice, and reflection) on the outcomes of both acute and chronic calls placed to a suicide hotline. The Rogerian method was more effective overall then the Directive approach, significantly reducing levels of depression (assessed at the beginning and end of each call) among both types of callers. Counselors employing the Rogerian method also documented a decrease in suicidal urgency and an increased likelihood of reaching a contract among acute but not chronic callers, who were similarly unaffected by Directive approaches.

In spite of these findings, neither traditional problem-solving nor "helping" intervention styles are likely to be successful in addressing the issues of chronic callers or in reducing the volume of repeat calls to crisis hotlines. Such methods have been applied dozens or even hundreds of times by experienced hotline volunteers and counselors to address the issues of unique chronic callers, who continue to contact the crisis center while discounting counselors' recommendations. Although counselors are trained to be patient and adapt to callers' needs, crisis intervention styles require some structure and often elaborate multiple "steps" for the counselor and client to follow in order to arrive at a solution (Chapter 4). This may be unrealistic considering the difficulties counselors experience in controlling chronic calls and in encouraging these clients to focus on the most relevant concrete issues. Furthermore, both helping and more directive approaches aim to mobilize the callers' internal and external resources to cope with crisis (Kalafat et al., 2007), yet chronic callers are often socially isolated and suffer from pervasive mental illness.

Recognizing that most chronic calls are likely driven by severe mental illness, Lester and colleagues (Chapter 14) recommended that crisis counselors coordinate their efforts with chronic callers' therapists and other community agencies providing treatment for them. Although this approach may be valuable, it is only feasible if: (1) clients are currently in treatment; (2) clients volunteer such information; and (3) clients grant permission to contact and coordinate with these outside sources. Instances in which all three criteria are present are likely to be rare, and counselors today must be especially cognizant of recent policies (e.g., HIPPA laws) designed to protect patients' privacy. In the absence of full client permission and cooperation, crisis center counselors cannot ensure that mentally ill chronic callers receive treatment. Combining crisis call centers with larger mental health clinics may facilitate efforts to address chronic callers' issues, but such integrations are not always feasible and may require extensive community funding. Until these barriers can be overcome, suicide prevention and crisis call centers will likely need to rely on more practical means of reducing the volume of chronic calls.

Crisis hotlines generally receive the highest volume of both acute and chronic calls during the evening and late night hours (Albers & Foster, 1995; Hall & Schlosar, 1995). This may be attributable partially to the decreased accessibility of mental health and other crisis services at these times. Contracting with mental health facilities/providers to provide after-hours care (e.g., telephone assessment and support services) for their mentally ill clients may help provide a funding stream that could mitigate the resource burden that chronic callers place on crisis call centers. This is a potential win-win strategy since many mental health service providers now routinely give call center contact information to their clients as an after-hour resource.

"Warm Lines" established throughout the United States may offer another strategy for supporting callers with persistent mental health issues. These services are typically affiliated with mental health facilities and staffed by trained peer volunteers who also have struggled with mental illness. Counselors may engage in problem solving or active listening, and generally provide social support and encouragement for callers (often repeat contacts) who are distressed or just need someone to talk to (Pudlinski, 2001, 2004). Suicidal callers or callers in a state of acute crisis are transferred to suicide prevention or crisis intervention hotlines. Because they are staffed entirely by volunteers, most Warm Lines have limited hours, and such services are not available in many areas. Some Warm Lines may lack adequate resources or office space. Volunteers may simply be "on call" in their own homes and receive forwarded calls or pages to contact a client in need. Moreover, it is unknown whether Warm Lines are effective in promoting well-being among clients and volunteers. Nevertheless, Warm Lines may significantly reduce the volume of chronic calls placed to overburdened crisis centers and address the issues (such as mental illness) underlying chronic calls rather than providing a "quick fix" solution.

A "case management" strategy for handling chronic callers was described in the first edition of this volume (Chapter 14). This approach limits both the number and length of calls placed by identified chronic callers each day (e.g., one call per day lasting 5-10 minutes), and relies on effective communication between call center staff. Crisis centers maintain records of chronic call patterns and individual profiles for each caller, including individualized management strategies. These strategies should be continuously updated and modified based on client progress (or lack thereof), and counselors should strive to maintain consistency in their responses to individual chronic callers. Importantly, suicide and self-harm risk should still be assessed at the beginning of each call, and limitations on call frequency must be relaxed if a counselor determines that the caller is experiencing significant problems or in a state of actual crisis. This policy has numerous potential benefits: It can reduce stress and frustration among call center staff, make counselors available for others in crisis who may be suicidal, and encourage chronic callers to address their issues more independently. As one call center administrator noted, allowing individuals to contact the center repeatedly is not always healthy or beneficial for the caller. They must learn to handle everyday situations without counselors' advice.

Despite these advantages, practical case management interventions targeting chronic callers have seldom been discussed in recent crisis and suicide prevention literature. Yet, it appears that many crisis centers have implemented case management strategies, including the crisis center described in this chapter. Case management led to a 20% reduction in chronic calls placed by females to the Canadian Samaritan crisis hotline (who accounted for the majority of such calls), although no changes were observed in chronic calls placed by males (Hall & Schlosar, 1995). Importantly, comparisons of suicide and self harm risk assessments completed before and after the implementation of the policy indicated that limiting the number and length of chronic calls did not exacerbate suicide risk (Hall & Schlosar, 1995).

Lester and colleagues (Chapter 14) proposed writing therapy as a means of reducing the volume of chronic calls to crisis centers and helping repeat clients to focus on their issues. Specifically, chronic callers could participate in a letter-writing program with counselors or community volunteers. Through written communication, clients may be able to express themselves more clearly and their actual issues may emerge. This process also allows for more thoughtful responses to the chronic caller. Brunet, Lemay, and Belliveau (1994) conducted a small case study assessing the outcomes of a letter-writing program in which five chronic callers discussed their problems in mail correspondence with community volunteers. Calls from these participants to the hotline dropped dramatically after the first three months of correspondence with the volunteers, and follow-up surveys revealed that four out of five participants were very satisfied with the program and had taken measures to address their problems (e.g., journaling and beginning psychotherapy).

Much of the literature outlining strategies for managing chronic callers was published before technological advancements made cellular phones and Internet use a routine part of daily living for most Americans. Such technologies may help address the problem of chronic calls more efficiently. For instance, volunteers could correspond with chronic callers via e-mail in addition to or instead of through letters. Crisis centers also can create electronic databases to help organize and update chronic caller information profiles. This may increase staff awareness of chronic callers' issues and the most effective communication method to use with each caller, as well as ensuring consistency in counselors' responses.

The call center described in this study has recently implemented a text messaging program (the first of its kind in the United States) targeting adolescents and hearing impaired populations. Clients simply send a text with a "keyword" (e.g., "Listen") to the number provided by the crisis center, and counselors are able to respond to these texts almost immediately via computer. Counselors then proceed to communicate and discuss the client's issues through text messages unless the client wishes to have a telephone conversation or requires emergency services. Although this program is still in its early stages, preliminary evaluations have yielded promising findings (see Chapter

25 in this volume), and this also may be valuable in communicating with chronic callers. Counselors responding to text messages via computer may assist more than one caller at a time, and using text messages may help chronic callers focus on the most pertinent issues rather than simply "chatting" with the counselor at the end of a telephone line. Texting also may allow counselors to demonstrate concern and provide support for chronic callers without subjecting them to a lengthy and redundant telephone conversation. Case management strategies could be applied to text messages if such contacts become excessive (e.g., chronic callers may be limited to a few texts per day).

In sum, there are a variety of strategies available for managing chronic callers. Some require relatively extensive collaborations between crisis call centers and community agencies, whereas others involve intra-organizational changes in crisis call center policy and practice. Crisis call centers also may seek help from community volunteers (and perhaps from former crisis line volunteers/counselors) in executing letter-writing or e-mail programs for chronic callers. Improved means of handling chronic callers would not only benefit crisis center staff, but also may increase the quality of services extended to both acute and chronic crisis callers. It should be noted that some of the strategies described above (e.g., case management) have already been implemented by many North American and international crisis call centers. Yet, there has been little discourse regarding these measures in the crisis and suicide prevention literature, and more empirical evidence is needed to help determine their effectiveness.

Future Directions

The existing crisis and suicide prevention literature, along with the analysis presented in this chapter, provide a foundation for understanding chronic callers' characteristics, patterns, and issues. Additional research is needed, however, in order to verify and expand the current knowledge of chronic callers. Studies have yielded inconsistent findings regarding chronic caller demographics (e.g., gender) and their suicide risk as compared to acute callers (Hall & Schlosar, 1995; Mishara & Daigle, 1997). Researchers and crisis center staff tend to agree that most chronic callers suffer from severe and persistent mental illness, but little is known about the nature of such illnesses and the factors inhibiting effective treatment. To our knowledge, the incidence of specific types of mental illness (e.g., depression, bi-polar disorder, anxiety disorders, and schizophrenia) in samples of chronic callers has not yet been empirically examined. Furthermore, it is unknown if chronic callers are simply less amenable to treatment than acute callers, or if they have not received the appropriate type of treatment. (It is also possible that chronic callers may be less willing to seek treatment or adhere to treatment plans.) Finally, additional studies are necessary to support prior research findings and testimonials regarding chronic callers' presenting issues and how these may differ from acute callers' issues. Data collection regarding such topics may be challenging given privacy concerns and the counselors' primary objectives of establishing positive client relationships and attenuating crisis situations. Yet, to the extent possible, we encourage researchers and crisis call centers to collaborate in exploring these more elusive aspects of chronic callers. Ultimately, more extensive knowledge of chronic callers' characteristics and motivations should foster the development, implementation, and refinement of measures aimed at addressing the needs of this complex population.

This chapter has reviewed several strategies for chronic caller management. Some are primarily focused on minimizing chronic callers' disproportionate use of crisis center resources (e.g., case management), whereas others target chronic callers' mental illness or maladaptive coping behaviors (e.g., collaborating with outside mental health professionals and community organizations, and therapeutic writing). A few of these strategies, namely case management, have received anecdotal support. In addition, Hall and Schlosar (1995) demonstrated the effectiveness of case management techniques in managing a large sample of chronic calls placed by women. Although a letter-writing program also was determined to be an effective means helping chronic callers articulate their underlying issues and minimizing their contacts with the center, this case study was limited to only five clients (Brunet et al., 1994). Future research should evaluate both the processes and outcomes of these common strategies targeting chronic callers. Evaluations of more recently advanced strategies (e.g., text-messaging programs) also need to be conducted.

Despite the promise of advancing technologies in minimizing chronic callers' disproportionate use of crisis center resources, management of this population will always be a component of crisis line work. Furthermore, many crisis centers have likely experienced an increased volume of chronic calls in recent years due to dramatic cuts in community mental health services. The pervasiveness of this issue highlights the need for collaboration among researchers, practitioners, crisis centers, and other mental health organizations in addressing the chronic caller problem. Researchers must continue to work with crisis center staff to yield a more comprehensive understanding of chronic callers' characteristics, issues and needs, as well as in evaluating management strategies. Information sharing also is critical in assisting crisis centers with chronic caller management. Many crisis centers have implemented measures designed to decrease the volume of chronic calls. However, these measures are seldom discussed in the crisis and suicide prevention literature. Research exploring chronic caller management typically focuses on a single strategy implemented in one individual crisis center. Although such research is useful, crisis centers would benefit from increased sharing of research, evaluation results, management strategies, and experiences with chronic callers. This would facilitate the implementation of new management strategies, as well as illuminating the strategies best-suited for particular types of crisis services (e.g., suicide hotlines vs. overarching crisis centers) with varying resources. Finally, to the extent possible, crisis centers should consult with practitioners and community organizations in maintaining a balance of resources expended on chronic callers and in efforts to increase accessibility and adherence to appropriate treatment.

REFERENCES

Albers, E. C., & Foster, S. L. (1995). A profile of 97,100 crisis intervention contacts over a six year period. *Crisis Intervention, 2,* 23–29.

Brunet, A. F., Lemay, L., & Belliveau, G. (1994). Correspondence as adjunct to crisisline intervention in a suicide prevention center. *Crisis, 15,* 65–38, 76.

de Anda, D., & Smith, M. A. (1993). Differences among adolescent, young adult, and adult callers of suicide help lines. *Social Work, 38,* 421–428.

Fakhoury, W. K. H. (2002). Suicidal callers to a national helpline in the UK: A comparison of depressive and psychotic sufferers. *Archives of Suicide Research, 6,* 363–371.

Gould, M. S., Kalafat, J., Munfakh, J. L. H., & Kleinman, M. (2007). An evaluation of crisis hotline outcomes: Part 2: Suicidal callers. *Suicide & Life-Threatening Behavior, 37,* 338–352.

Hall, B., & Schlosar, H. (1995). Repeat callers and the Samaritan telephone crisis line: a Canadian experience. *Crisis, 16,* 66–71.

Ingram, S., Ringle, J. L., Hallstrom, K., Schill, D. E., Gohr, V. M., & Thompson, R. W. (2008). Coping with crisis across the lifespan: The role of a telephone hotline. *Journal of Child & Family Studies, 17,* 663–674.

Kalafat, J., Gould, M. S., Munfakh, J. L. H., & Kleinman, M. (2007). An evaluation of crisis hotline outcomes: Part 1: Nonsuicidal crisis callers. *Suicide & Life-Threatening Behavior, 37,* 322–337.

Kehoe, S., & Grant, P. R. (1997). *A needs assessment of the volunteer program at the Saskatoon Sexual Assault Centre.* Saskatoon, Canada: University of Saskatchewan.

Kinzel, A., & Nanson, J. (2000). Education and debriefing: Strategies for preventing crises in crisis-line volunteers. *Crisis, 21,* 126–134.

Lester, D., & Brockopp, G. W. (1970). Chronic callers to a suicide prevention center. *Community Mental Health Journal, 6,* 246–250.

MacKinnon, C. (1998). Empowered consumers and telephone hotlines. *Crisis, 19,* 21–23.

Mishara, B. L., & Daigle, M. C. (1997). Effects of different telephone intervention styles with suicidal callers at two suicide prevention centers: An empirical investigation. *American Journal of Community Psychology, 25,* 861–885.

Mishara, B. L., & Giroux, G. (1993). The relationship between coping strategies and perceived stress in telephone intervention volunteers. *Suicide & Life Threatening Behavior, 23*, 221–229.

Pudlinski, C. (2001). Contrary themes on three peer-run warm lines. *Psychiatric Rehabilitation Journal, 24*, 397–400.

Pudlinski, C. (2004). The pros and cons of different warm line settings. *Psychiatric Rehabilitation Journal, 28*, 72–74.

SAMHSA (2009). SAMSHA announces additional funding to bolster increasingly strained national suicide prevention lifeline crisis centers [press release]. Retrieved from http://www.samhsa.gov/newsroom/advisories/0908030709.aspx.

Seeley, M. F. (1993). Hotlines: A case study. *Crisis, 14*, 59–60

Watson, R. J., McDonald, J., & Pearce, D. C. (2006). An exploration of national calls to Lifeline Australia: Social support or urgent suicide intervention? *British Journal of Guidance & Counseling, 34*, 471–482.

Chapter 16

THE COVERT CRY FOR HELP

Gene W. Brockopp

The cry for help takes many different forms in a crisis telephone service. When most individuals are in a crisis, they make it quite clear that they are at the end of their resources and in need of assistance. They call for help in a direct and unmistakable way and in so doing obtain the aid of counselors who have the understanding, background, and skills necessary to help them with their problems.

For other individuals, the call for help is initially a covert one. To express overtly that they need help is not possible for them for a number of reasons. Some people feel that to call for help is a sign of weakness; others fear the possibility of rejection if it is announced to the world that they are in the vulnerable position of needing help. Some have been rebuffed before by their direct cry for help and are uncertain whether they should try to obtain help in a direct way. Any of the above individuals may use a covert cry for help as a test to see if the service is willing to reach out to them, even though they have not committed themselves to accept the help if it is offered to them. The covert cry for help is often a method by which they hope to make a determination whether or not they can trust the unseen helper with the problems that are upsetting them and putting them in crisis.

Because of its very nature, a telephone counseling service must be very careful not to define too precisely the modes and ways it will become involved with people in difficulty. It must be alert to the nuances that individuals use in making a call for help and respond to them with openness and honesty, listening for the covert message while responding to the overt questions or concerns that the individual is raising on the telephone. Each call to a crisis center, no matter what the overt purpose of the call may be, is potentially a call from an individual in crisis.

Probably the most common covert call for help is the call that is made ostensibly for another individual who is in difficulty – one whom the caller has a close association. At the Buffalo suicide prevention center, 20% of the calls were made out of concern for a third party. It is difficult to tell, of course, when the call is really about a third party or when it is about the callers themselves. The rules at our center were: (1) to always make the assumption that the call is about the person who is on the telephone, and (2) never attempt to force individuals to prove that the call is about someone else, but rather take the call as they overtly state it to be. The initial focus with this type of call is to get the callers involved with the person that is supposedly in crisis, by helping them to organize the resources in their neighborhood that the person in crisis can call on for assistance. A secondary focus (which is usually used) is to give the callers some additional resources that they can use in the community. Often we use our center as one of these resources and tell the callers that their friend can come to the center at any time he or she wishes and can come anonymously, if he or she so desires. This type of statement, I feel, indicates to the callers that we are more interested in working with them, and their problem, than in personal information which they are often reluctant to give.

Another set of covert cries come in terms of what I call "checking out the service" calls. These fall into four categories. The most common probably is the call where the individual dials the service, reaches the crisis counselor, and then hangs up the telephone before making verbal contact. Irritating as this may be to the crisis counselor, I believe that this is also a test. The person may be sensing acceptance or rejection, consciously or unconsciously, from such things as whether a male or female voice answers the telephone or whether the tonal qualities or other cues that are present in the voice of the crisis counselor indicate acceptance of and concern for the caller. When speaking to individuals who have told us that they have called the service a number of times and have hung up immediately after the telephone has been answered, they speak about not having enough courage to go on, of being afraid, or feeling that the problem was not one that they should bother someone else with. Until they found someone who could successfully pass their test, they continued to hang up the telephone.

Another variation on this theme is the person who calls the center and then responds by saying, "I have the wrong number." At a suicide center, it should be axiomatic that there are no wrong numbers. This response on the part of the caller should be greeted with, "May I help you? What number were you calling?" and then followed with a clear statement as to the type of service that they are connected with. We have found that some people will say something like, "Oh, since I have you on the telephone, I may as well talk about – ," and then go on talking about a problem they have. Others hang up the telephone, possibly evaluate their reception at the center and then decide to either dial again (if they were actually calling the service) or dial the number they want.

A third type of "checking out the service" is seen in the person who calls and then does not talk, but rather waits for the crisis counselor to make the correct statement or connection before making any comment. More than likely, this individual will eventually hang up the telephone before making a comment, yet the way that the telephone is answered by the crisis counselor is critical, in that it will often determine if this person will call back a second time and begin to talk about the problem.

The last variation on this theme is the person who calls up and then makes a statement in a semi-surprised voice: "Oh, is someone really there? I thought it was probably an answering service, or a recorded message." Again, if the question is answered only on the surface level, the person is not likely to bring up any problem. In all of these cases, the telephone counselor must make himself or herself readily available to the individual calling and facilitate that person's movement into a discussion of the problems he is having.

Often people who call asking for information are setting themselves up to be rejected by the telephone service. The counselor may simply answer their question and not respond to the problems that they are having at this particular period of time. To only give the specific information requested is to not respond to the emotion that is usually present in these callers. These emotions usually convey a message such as the fear of going to a social or mental health agency, the possibility of rejection, the sense of unsureness about oneself, or the need to deal with the problem immediately. Crisis counselors must be very careful that they are not unknowingly rejecting these callers by simply giving the person the information they are asking for and nothing more. The information call is often a call covertly designed to keep the level of conversation on an intellectual plane. With this type of call, the ability to deal with the affective needs of the caller, while giving the information desired, is the crucial test of effectiveness for the crisis counselor.

Sometimes the covert cry for help comes in a humorous cloak. The caller is likely to say something like, "You mean there really is a service like that?" or, "I'll bet you hear some real good ones from people who call there," or, "You must be crazy to work in a place like that." Regardless of its form, this type of call usually has a very serious purpose to it, and these callers are often using these phrases as a test to determine how their feelings will be handled by a telephone service. We find it best to handle this type of call in a very direct and factual way, not responding at all to the humor that may be implied in the message. To respond to the humor is to play directly into the hands of this individual and to fail the test being made of the telephone service, which is, "Will you handle my call in a humorous way, or will you be serious about what I want to talk to you about?"

A covert call for help that is handled in exactly the opposite way is the one from a person who cries for help in a hostile, abusive manner. This individual is usually trying to test the service through a direct and assaultive manner. Generally, the best way to respond to this type of individual is through a cool, intellectual response in which the abuse that the individual is giving is accepted or tolerated and at the same time met with the controlled anger and personal stability of the telephone counselor. This gives these callers a chance to vent their wrath within a stabilized setting and helps them obtain the clear message that the service is not going to be ruffled by belligerent and loudmouthed behavior, but rather is able to tolerate this and still respond in a direct and helpful and unemotional way.

Intellectual callers are difficult people to work with. Usually these callers are very cool, calculating and precise in manner, knowledgeable in the field, and capable of "unnerving" most telephone counselors. As they are likely to know more about the subject that they are speaking about than the counselor does and since they are usually very capable, argumentative individuals, they are able to win whenever they are challenged on their own grounds. The key to working with these callers is not to challenge them. Under the cool, calculating exterior is often an individual who is quite concerned and somewhat unsure of himself. To remain on an intellectual level with these callers is to assist them in their process of covering over their unsureness with intellectualizations. Since one of the important factors involved with these individuals is the question of control, I have found that one of the best ways to work with them is to allow them to "defeat" me by telling them directly that I will not fight with them and then to talk about the feelings that they have when they have succeeded in controlling the situation. The conversation usually moves into the problems that they have been trying to cover up through the process of intellectualization. These callers can then begin to deal with their problems on an emotional level.

Another type of the covert call for help is the "yes – but" caller. This individual is extremely exasperating to the telephone counselor for it seems that no matter what type of answer one gives to the problem that the individual is presenting, the caller responds with "yes – but" and then proceeds to move to another facet of the problem or to predict the impossibilities of working with the solution as it has been developed in conjunction with the telephone counselor. A variation of this type of caller is the person who continually asks the question, "What would you do if I – ?" then completes the statement with a behavior that usually has dire consequences. For both of these types of callers, the best approach is generally one which brings them back to the realities of the situation, that is, one which focuses on the specific problem that they are having at this particular time and gives them reasonable directions for handling the problems that they are presenting. Usually with the "yes –

but" caller, a summarization by the telephone counselor of the concerns that the individual has presented along with directions that the person may take to ameliorate the problem moves the person into an action stage. Getting the "what would you do" callers involved with the solution to their own problems will often help eliminate in moving toward closure with the caller.

The exasperated caller, the wrong number, the calls for a third party, the person who is hostile and abusive, the individual who uses humor or intellectualizations, or the person who calls for information are often callers who are making covert cries for help. They are all calls in which individual callers may speak on one level, while indirectly hoping to receive help and understanding of their problems at another level. If telephone counselors listen to only the overt level of the conversation, they are certain to miss the real message and likely to turn the callers away from the source of help they are actually seeking.

Chapter 17

THE SILENT CALLER

Vanda Scott, David Lester, and Gene W. Brockopp

LISTENING TO SILENCE[31]

Silence between client and counselor can occur in the course of crisis intervention, counseling, or psychotherapy. It can occur over the telephone, in face-to-face sessions, or during group therapy. Silence often provokes anxiety in both counselor and client. As the silence grows in length, there is sometimes a compulsion to break it with some utterance – but also a fear of doing so. Yet, is silence always bad, and must it always provoke anxiety? Can it not serve a useful and therapeutic function?

Silence can indicate pleasure, joy, or peace; or it can indicate anger, contempt, or disinterest (Liegner, 1974). It can radiate warmth or a chill (Zeligs, 1961). This dual view of silence was noted also by Caruth (1987) who observed that silence can be threatening, perhaps reminding an individual of those times in infancy when the mother had (albeit temporarily) abandoned the infant. Yet it can also lead to a merger experience with the silent other person at times when the spoken word would intrude, annihilate, and take over. Caruth felt that viewing speech as an intrusion was especially common in borderline personality disorder and schizophrenic patients, for whom speech can mean loss of control. These clients can maintain an illusion of autonomy when silent.

Silence can be useful once a sound therapeutic alliance has been established (Ladany et al., 2004). Silence can be useful for enriching and strengthening the self (Elson, 2001), a source of quiet growth during which the client

---
[31] Modified from Scott and Lester (1998).

can reflect on distortions of the self and transform the self. Clients can communicate emotional and relational messages of need and meaning through their silence, while counselors can communicate safety, understanding and containment (Lane et al., 2002). However, if a sound therapeutic alliance does not exist, silence on the part of the counselor can be viewed by the client as distance, disinterest and disengagement, resulting in a breach of trust and safety in the therapeutic alliance (Lane et al., 2002). Silence is rarely useful with clients who are psychotic, highly anxious, or angry (Ladany et al., 2004).

Silence on the part of the client can be obstructive, moments when they detach themselves from the therapeutic process (Levitt, 2001). In psychoanalysis, silence is usually seen as resistance, either to transference or to remembering, perhaps derived from the negativism of children, as in their occasional refusal to go to the toilet. Although it is easy to find cases in which silence in a client undergoing psychoanalysis is a sign of resistance (Liegner, 1974), psychoanalysts are also prepared to use silence in a positive way. For example, Liegner (1974) once had as a client, a six-year-old boy who had been operated upon at seven months and whose mother had come close to suffocating him when he was only three months old. He maintained a silence for five sessions. During the fifth session, Liegner showed him the toy cupboard, and he played with toys for several weeks. Then one day he opened a checker board, and Liegner joined him to play checkers. Eventually he responded to Liegner, but he still did not initiate conversation. Soon the conversation became richer, with discussions of emotions which Liegner verbalized for him while he acted them out. After one year of treatment, his mother removed him from therapy even though Liegner had not had an opportunity to begin psychoanalysis proper.

Can Counselors Tolerate Silence?

Counselors often become anxious during periods of silence in the counseling sessions, and Broadbar (2010) noted that, early in her career, she felt the need to fill the silences. She learned to control her anxiety so that her clients could have the space that they needed to establish their own pace.

Ward (1974) reported on a group she had led, composed of individuals with schizophrenia in a day-treatment program who had not spoken in the regular group. The first meeting began with her introductory remarks and then 50 minutes of silence. She felt that the group members learned that their leader would wait until they were ready to talk and that it was all right for them to be silent. The experience also taught them that they were responsible for what occurred in the sessions. Although the group had periods of silence thereafter, they never again lasted the whole session. Ward began to ask the members how they felt about the silence and to interpret it by recalling previous silences and what lay behind them. Her patients reported reasons such as a fear of disappointing the leader, not being a good patient, or boring the others – fears that they had learned from childhood experiences. One period of silence occurred after the suicide of a patient at the center, a silence of sorrow and contemplation.

In psychoanalytic psychotherapy, Liegner (1974) had a patient who simply did not know how to talk; she had become used to being a listener. Liegner had to train her to talk, by modeling and by asking questions, until she eventually learned to talk spontaneously. Morgenstern (1980) reported on a 30-session psychotherapy with a client who eventually fell into silence for most of the sessions. Morgenstern realized that this enabled the patient to recapitulate both adolescent experiences with her father, when they often read together in the same room in silence, and the time when she nursed him as he lay dying. When Morgenstern made this interpretation during the 26th session, it freed the patient to talk more spontaneously in the final sessions. Morgenstern quoted Weisman (1955, p. 258): "The basic need is to understand silence, not merely to get the patient to talk."

Murphy and Lamb (1973) compared the responses to clients of counselors in training with those of untrained staff and found that the training led to an increase in the percentage of time spent in client-counselor silence, whereas this percentage decreased over time in the untrained staff. Murphy and Lamb suggested that silence was possibly a measure of effectiveness in counseling rather than an indication of anxiety.

Silent Callers to Crisis Intervention Centers

When crisis intervention and suicide prevention centers first began operating, using the telephone as a primary mode for counseling, several "problem" callers were identified, and special training of the crisis counselors became necessary. Among such callers was the "silent caller" who called and said nothing. Brockopp (p. 205) has addressed this problem. He stressed that there were no "problem" callers; there were only callers with problems. No call should be seen as a nuisance. Rather, all calls should be regarded as coming from clients in distress or clients who may call again later and speak. If the counselor stays with these clients, speaks sympathetically and encourages them, they may eventually overcome their fear of embarrassment.

Why might a caller remain silent? Perhaps because previous contacts with mental health personnel have been unpleasant and unhelpful; perhaps because they are anxious; or perhaps they are afraid of intimacy. The counselor can, therefore, try to interpret the silence to the caller with an initial response such as, "You know, sometimes it is difficult to begin talking about things that trouble you. I'm here to talk to you when you are ready." After a pause, the counselor can again make reassuring, supportive statements. Eventually the counselor may decide that he or she has to end the call, but the counselor can explain that the center is busy and that she will have to hang up. She can tell the caller that the staff are there 24 hours a day, and that perhaps the caller can try again later. Such clients can also be encouraged to write to the center if they find talking difficult. Brockopp found that some clients went through a ritual of calling and saying nothing several times before finally talking.

Two Cases

Susan

Susan was 16 years old when she first contacted the center and in the midst of a year of important exams. She was well-liked at school by her teachers and friends. Life appeared to be good for her, except for her health, for she kept visiting her family doctor with minor ailments, until one day the doctor had to visit her in the hospital. On the previous evening she had "had a dreadful headache" and had taken some of her mother's sleeping pills. This was the first attempt that Susan made on her life. She made a further attempt a few weeks later which was also unsuccessful.

Susan's life had become unbearable. Her mother was drunk by lunch-time every day, and her father was trying to keep his job and his life from falling apart. Studying for exams was becoming impossible. The house would be a wreck each day when she returned from school, and her mother would be unconscious. The doctor suggested to Susan that she should telephone the local Befrienders Center, and with her permission, he contacted the Director to advise him of Susan's vulnerable state. The volunteers were alerted, but she did not contact the Center – or did she?

A number of weeks later the volunteers noted that silent calls were occurring more frequently between 11:00 p.m. and 3:00 a.m. in the morning. The calls varied in length – sometimes a few minutes, on one occasion 18 minutes and finally 47 minutes. It was thought that the calls were made by one person; the sound of silence was the same.

Twenty years later she wrote to the center! "To dial the number (I can still remember it: 327-0000) and hear a voice was all that I needed. I was locked into my mind, my thoughts, my whole body. Words would not come – I felt strangled, voiceless, yet theories and pain in my world were excruciatingly loud and painful.

"For weeks I telephoned the Center, and always someone answered – the comfort of listening to a person! Once or twice I felt the volunteer was frustrated with me and put the telephone down. Many times I felt guilty. I couldn't say anything and would only want to hear the volunteer say 'Hello' before putting down the telephone, fast. Then I would cry and cry – almost uncontrollably until I was exhausted and could sleep.

"I was sorry to be nuisance, but I needed someone to care for me, to worry about me, to listen to me. Then after getting through on the call, I could not talk. It was all very confusing, yet I knew it stopped me hurting myself; well, I mean killing myself. I made these calls late at night. Always after my parents had finished fighting and screaming and killing each other. The noise was tremendous, yet they loved each other. I don't think they loved me – I was never noticed. Early one morning, after a long period of silence, I suddenly found my voice and said something. I remember it sounded stupid – but I started to talk. Only a few words, but it was a start. I kept saying to myself, 'It is a stranger. They cannot hurt me.' And I talked.

"I have wondered over the years whether the talking helped more than being silent for all those weeks. And I don't know the answer. All I do know is the enormous relief I felt every time I dialed that number and found a real person who was there for me, waiting for me.

"Twenty years ago this happened; all I can say is that each year I send a card to that Center to say 'Thank you'."

Frank

Frank telephoned at 1:00 a.m., a man of few words, hesitant and uncertain whether to make the connection. He sounded depressed. He asked if he could talk just for a few minutes, as others would need us more than he did. Frank talked of his grief, of his despair, and of his failure in life, even of his failure in trying to kill himself a few months ago. "I am a living failure" was his statement.

It was almost three years since a long-term relationship with his girlfriend had to come to an end, a mutual decision, but one that took some major adjustment. Only four months later his mother died. He had been very close to her, and the death, although not unexpected because of her age, came as a shock to him. He began to withdraw from his friends, and he had no close family. Eventually, he lost his job and his car and moved into a one-room apartment. Frank realized that he was not coping well, and he became depressed.

Eventually Frank visited a doctor. He described his visit as "Five minutes of answering questions in which all I saw was the top of the doctor's bald head." The doctor prescribed sleeping pills and antidepressants and asked Frank to return in two weeks' time. The following weekend Frank intentionally took an overdose. He had not taken an adequate amount to kill himself. He called an emergency service and survived the attempt. His life lacked quality, and he saw no future or reason for living. He was acutely depressed and had decided to throw himself in front of a train. He occasionally called the local Befrienders when he was feeling particularly agitated, isolated, and distressed.

There was silence for two or three minutes while Frank and the Befriender both absorbed the pain, and then Frank spoke again, quietly. He asked tentatively if he could tell the Befriender something. He hesitated, then he said that he was wearing ladies' silk underclothes. He talked of the emotional relief and peace he found when, from time to time, he dressed in these beautiful garments. It helped him to reconcile himself to some of the grief he felt and to the isolation of his world.

It was some time later, when the call was coming to an end, that the Befriender found the courage to ask Frank a question. What caused his hesitation in telling of his desire, or need, to wear these ladies' clothes? His response was gentle and uncritical. When he does telephone the center and broaches his subject, he can sometimes hear the tension build up in the volunteer's voice. On a few occasions he has been rebuked for "talking dirty." He retreats and hangs up. He already feels rejected by his doctor and does not want to embarrass volunteers. Sometimes Frank did not have the courage to talk on the telephone as he was unsure of the reception he would get. He had been a silent caller.

Discussion

A psychiatrist told us the sad story of one of the first patients he counseled just after qualifying as a psychiatrist. A young woman in her early twenties had been referred to him by her family doctor for eight sessions of psychotherapy. During the first five weekly sessions, she would not talk; she sat in silence. As a newly qualified psychiatrist, he was perturbed by this behavior and was uncertain of the value of the sessions. At the end of the fifth session he suggested to the patient that she was wasting her time, and also his, by sitting in complete silence, and that she should only make the next appointment with his secretary when she was ready to talk. On the following day, she took her life. Now, fifteen years later, he continues to feel the discomfort of failing his patient by not listening to her silence.

Listening to the silence is an essential role for counselors who are helping clients in crisis. Much of the pain, the suicidal feelings, and the turmoil are often shrouded in silence both for the individual and for society as a whole. Communication is the focus of crisis intervention and befriending, and counselors are sometimes very uncomfortable at sharing the silence of their callers. But silence is an important aspect of human interaction for, after all, verbal communication consists only of words strung together on a background of silence. Silence can have different meanings. It is not simply an absence of words; it can be an active presence.

There is a need for individuals, for society, to listen to silence. We, as counselors, as Befrienders, must listen to it and, in doing so, strengthen the acceptance of silent callers and the turmoil of their internal world.

REFERENCES

Broadbar, D. (2010). Beyond silence and survival. *Women & Therapy, 33*, 235–244.
Caruth, E. G. (1987). Language in intimacy and isolation. *Journal of the American Academy of Psychoanalysis, 15*, 39–49.
Elson, M. (2001). Silence, its use and abuse. *Clinical Social Work Journal, 29*, 351–360.
Ladany, N., Hill, C. E., Thompson, B. J., & O'Brien, K. M. (2004). Therapist perspectives on using silence in therapy. *Counselling & Psychotherapy Research, 4*, 80–89.
Lane, R. C., Koetting, M. G., & Bishop, J. (2002). Silence as communication in psychodynamic psychotherapy. *Clinical Psychology Review, 22*, 1091–1104.
Levitt, H. M. (2001). Clients' experience of obstructive silence. *Journal of Contemporary Psychotherapy, 31*, 221–244.
Liegner, E. (1976). The silent patient. *Psychoanalytic Review, 61*, 229–245.
Morgenstern, A. (1980). Reliving the last goodbye. *Psychiatry, 43*, 251–258.
Murphy, W. A., & Lamb, D. H. (1973). The effects of training in psychotherapy on therapists' responses to client hostility. *Journal of Community Psychology, 1*, 327–330.
Scott, V., & Lester, D. (1998). Listening to silence. *Crisis, 19*, 105–108.
Ward, J. T. (1974). The sounds of silence. *Perspectives in Psychiatric Care, 12*(1), 13–19.
Weisman, A. D. (1955). Silence and psychotherapy. *Psychiatry, 5*, 241–260.
Zeligs, M. A. (1961). The psychology of silence. *Journal of the American Psychoanalytic Association, 9*, 8–11.

WORKING WITH THE SILENT CALLER

Gene W. Brockopp

One of the most frustrating persons to work with, either in a face-to-face therapeutic interview or over the telephone, is the person who chooses not to engage in a verbal interaction with a therapist. In a face-to-face interview, other nonverbal means of communication can be elicited and utilized by the therapist to engage the client. When the telephone is used as the medium for communication, the therapist is at a distinct disadvantage because most of the usual avenues of nonverbal communication are not available.

In silent callers, we have an excellent example of ambivalence. Here are people who deliberately make the effort to call a center designed to assist people who have personal problems. When they reach the source of assistance, for any number of reasons, they choose not to engage in verbal communication which may be necessary to ameliorate their problems. This behavior, which appears inconsistent, usually has a basis either in their psychological makeup or in their previous experiences with helping agencies. Many callers to a suicide prevention center have been rejected by other agencies and organizations, or by their families and friends, and therefore are unsure whether or not they will be accepted and listened to at the suicide prevention center. As a result, they may call in a reluctant manner in order to reduce the psychological effect of the potential rejection.[32]

One of the apparent advantages of a telephone conversation is that the caller, from a psychological point of view, is intimately close to the person he is talking to regardless of the physical distance. To the silent caller this may be a disadvantage. With his concern about being accepted by the telephone therapist, the immediacy of this intimate relationship with another individual may be too frightening for him. While he utilizes the telephone in order to gain psychological mobility without a change in his physical environment, the rapidity of the change and the impact of the closeness may frighten him away from beginning a conversation unless the person on the other end of the telephone is aware of his concern and does something to facilitate his talking with a statement that says, "You can trust me," or "I'm here to listen."[33]

But what does one do when the caller makes no verbal response, yet remains on the line, making his presence known? Faced with this type of caller, telephone therapists must first overcome their initial tendency (which may be appropriate in other nontherapeutic situations) to hang up the telephone on the assumption that it is a so-called prank or nuisance call. They must remember that their first task as a telephone therapist is to meet the caller at his

---

[32] This behavior is quite normal for, in every type of therapeutic situation, the patient presents a test to the therapist whereby he, the patient, ascertains whether or not the person he is talking to is one who will understand him or one who is worthy of the trust which he, the patient, has to give. The only real difference is that, for this type of caller, the test is more ambiguous.

[33] This type of caller is also one who may use the ploy after the telephone is answered of saying, "Oh, I'm sorry, I must have the wrong number." It is for this reason that the telephone therapist must respond with a helpful comment such as "What number were you calling?" or "May I be of assistance to you?" Even though this usually will not engage the person in a conversation at that time, it does indicate to him that the people at the center are real, human, and interested in helping him if he needs help. It will be easier for the caller to place his call and to complete it next time.

level of acceptance and to try to remove any impediment which may keep the person from communicating his problem or difficulty.

At our center, we have developed the following procedure for working with this type of caller. If upon answering the telephone with "Suicide Prevention and Crisis Service, may I help you?" therapists receive no response from the caller, they are to respond to any of the nonverbal cues which they feel may be used at that time. If there are any sighs or heavy breathing, they may say, "Sometimes it's very hard to begin talking about things that trouble you" or, if they feel that the person may have hurt himself or be in pain and is unwilling to verbalize this, they may say, "Have you hurt yourself? Is there any way in which I can help you?"

If there is no response and if counselors are convinced, based on the minimal cues they have, that the person is not in any desperate situation, the telephone therapist will repeat, "This is the Suicide Prevention Center, may I help you?" and continue to sound reassuring, interested, and willing to wait until the caller is ready to talk. They may, after a few moments of silence, say "I'm here willing to talk with you as soon as you're ready." Again, after a silent period, they may respond with "I would like to talk with you. Maybe together we can work out the problem that's bothering you." After a few moments they may say "It's very hard for me to know what's happening to you and what kinds of things are taking place that make you feel you can't talk to me about your problems. If you like, maybe we can talk about something else for a few minutes." If there is still no response they may, after a period of silence, say "I'm here to listen and talk with you as soon as you're ready." If a minute or so has gone by without any response on the part of the caller (and assuming that the telephone therapist feels that the individual is in no physical danger), the telephone therapist may say, "I'd like to talk to you, but I guess you find it very difficult to talk right now, I'll stay on the line for about another minute. If you want to talk I'll be here to listen to you." Again following a period of silence they may say, "I'd like to talk to you, but I'll have to hang up the telephone in about another half-a-minute, unless we can begin a conversation. I want you to know that I'm interested in talking with you about any problems that you may have and that there is someone here 24 hours a day." After a few moments of silence the telephone therapist will terminate the call with a statement like, "I'm sorry you found it difficult to talk at this time. Sometimes it's hard to talk about problems that one feels very deeply. There is someone here at 854-1966, 24 hours a day. If you feel we can be of any help to you, please call us. If you would rather talk to someone in person, you can come to the center at 560 Main Street any time between nine in the morning and nine at night. I have to hang up the telephone now. Thank you for calling. Good-bye." They then hang up the telephone, terminating the call.

For some callers the silent call has the special significance of a ritual. We find that a very small number of callers must go through this process before they are willing to engage in a verbal relationship with the telephone therapist. These callers force the center to go through the above routine, wait for the telephone to be hung up and then immediately call back and begin talking, sometimes to the same telephone therapist.

We also have noted that some individuals are unable or unwilling to talk over the telephone about things that disturb them or problems that they have. In some cases, we have engaged in a therapeutic relationship with these individuals by asking them to write to us at the center (which is an effective way of removing one's self one more step from the intimacy of the telephone relationship). Other individuals want a closer relationship, in which they can see the therapist, and will accept the invitation to come into the center and be seen on a face-to-face basis. That a person has accepted the invitation is, of course, only known after the patient has been seen at the center and, in the course of therapy, identifies himself as a person who did not just "walk-in" to the center, but one to whom it was suggested to come into the center and talk because he was unwilling to converse over the telephone.

Silent callers present the center with a problem and a challenge. By refusing to engage with us on a verbal level, they hit the telephone therapy service at its most vulnerable spot. Expecting anger, rejection, or hurt as a response to this "low blow," they wait for the telephone therapist to hang up. By accepting their feelings and concerns and exploring with them the kind of relationship which is acceptable to them, the center can reinforce its role as an accepting, therapeutic service.

THE CALLER WHO REMAINS SILENT: REPORT OF AN UNUSUAL CASE

David Lester

As noted above, suicide prevention centers and crisis services occasionally receive calls in which the caller remains silent. The aim of this section is to describe an unusual solution to this problem.

It is important to note that counselors frequently classify these kinds of calls as nuisance calls or pranks. To do this runs the danger that people in crisis will not be aided by the service. Gene Brockopp discusses the so-called nuisance call in Chapter 18 and notes that no call to a center should be viewed as a nuisance call. The telephone counselor cannot reliably judge a call to be a prank call. As Brockopp notes, to classify a call as a prank call is to set up an arbitrary standard as to the type of problem or situation with which the counselor will work.

If the counselor stays with the person, speaks sympathetically to him, and encourages him, he may eventually overcome his fear or embarrassment. If the caller hangs up without talking, this may reflect upon the counselor's competence rather than the seriousness of the caller.

If the caller initially remains silent, it may later prove to be difficult for him to begin talking to the counselor, to break the silence. In that case, the counselor has several alternatives. He can stay with the caller and continue to encourage him to talk. He can suggest that the caller hang up and call back at another time. He can suggest that the caller write to the center rather than call. The following case report describes another possibility. In this the counselor suggested to the caller that she answer yes or no by code. A sigh represented yes and silence represented no. In this way he was able to elicit a great deal of information from the caller.[34]

In order to best illustrate how this call proceeded, some extracts from the call are reproduced below.

(1) . . . OK. So here's what I know. I know that you are 15. I know that you're a girl. I know that you broke up with your boyfriend on Tuesday, and you've been thinking about it. You felt really bad and depressed, and you have cried a lot since then. You haven't talked with anybody about it, and you cut yourself. You cut your wrists tonight, and they bled a little. Did you call us before you cut your wrists or after?

Did you call after? Sigh.

Did you call before?

You called after. OK. So I know that about you. That's when I stopped being able to find out things about you. I know that you haven't talked to your parents about it. I know you haven't talked to your girl friends about it or anybody else. And I know you say you want to talk to me and I know you can talk. But you won't. And I don't know why.

Do you know why?

You don't know why.

(2) . . . Do you want to use words to talk with me? Sigh.

You do.

Have you started to talk to me but never been able to begin?

Sigh.

---

[34] To those readers who feel that the patient here was playing games, I would again point out that it is not really essential for the counselor to decide whether the patient is playing a game. A patient may equally well play games during a verbal conversation with a counselor. To prejudge and accuse a caller of playing games may serve to reject the caller and render therapeutic intervention impossible.

(3) . . . I don't know how you feel when you can't talk with me. I know you feel bad and depressed. You feel like it's the end of the world, and you can't live without your boyfriend. I know you feel all that but I don't know what it is that won't let you talk.

(4) . . . I'm interested in what you do when you're silent – when I don't say anything and you never say anything, when I don't say anything and you don't sigh and everything's just kinda pretty quiet.

Are you thinking? Sigh.
Are you thinking about talking with me? Sigh.
A little bit. Are you thinking about your boyfriend? Sigh.
Are you thinking about yourself? Sigh.
A lot? Sigh.
Are you going to hurt yourself tonight? Sigh.
(5) Have you told me the truth tonight? Sigh.
Yes? Sigh.
All of it?
Was all of it the truth?
Did you lie to me tonight? Sigh.[35]

It is clear that the counselor here was able to learn a lot about the patient. Although having to ask questions that could be answered "yes" or "no" restricted him, he was able to discuss feelings, events, and assess the lethality of the caller. He was also able to present himself as a sympathetic and understanding person. In doing so, he increased the likelihood that this patient would call back and make use of the service. It is possible that on subsequent calls, her reluctance to talk was less and that this first contact served to reduce her inhibitions about talking to a counselor.

---

[35] Further questioning revealed that she had lied about the area of the city in which she lived.

Chapter 18

THE NUISANCE CALLER

GENE W. BROCKOPP

One of the concerns of a crisis center is how to respond to the nuisance, prank, fake, or hang-up call. A nuisance call may be defined as a call about a trivial or inappropriate situation or condition. It implies that certain calls can, on the basis of their substance or length, be defined as noncritical, noncrisis, or nonproblem calls, and that there is some standard by which we can designate some calls as being nuisance calls, whereas other calls of a similar nature will be designated as being "real" problem calls.

I feel that it is questionable whether we can categorize calls into real calls and nuisance calls. To define a call as a nuisance call is to set up an arbitrary standard as to the type of problem or situation which an emergency telephone center will accept. It involves making a judgment and setting criteria which individuals must meet before they make a call to the center. As such it forces individuals to make a decision about the validity or severity of their problem before they attempt to seek help. I feel it is inappropriate to require this of a caller. To do so will eventually be detrimental to the telephone counseling service.

Just as a face-to-face psychotherapist needs some kind of communication before he can work on a problem that a client presents (and these communications may come in a variety of ways, many of them nonverbal), telephone counselors need calls before they can begin to work on a problem. Any impediment placed in the callers' way, which may keep them from making a call, or any movement to force them to predefine the validity of their call before they make it, would seem to be an unnecessary hurdle for callers and would place the crisis service in the same category as many other helping agencies, that is, a problem of a client is considered to be a real problem only when the agency defines it as such.

Some agencies work only with 16-year-olds and above, or children, or marriage problems, or psychotics, or individuals with neurotic disorders. The crisis telephone service, in contrast to these predefined types of agencies, should be a source of help which is open to all individuals, regardless of their age, orientation, background, or difficulty. It should be a place where anyone can have a therapeutic relationship with a counselor by means of a telephone contact.

Most people who have a personal or emotional problem feel uncertain whether or not they should attempt to get help for themselves or whether they should be "strong" and live with the problem, hoping it will work itself out. Stated another way, people in crisis are often unsure about the validity of their seeking help with their problem and whether they will be accepted by a counselor. The center should not force these individuals into a situation where they have to decide whether or not their problem is severe enough before they can call. This will mean that the center must be open to all types of calls, many of which may appear to be trivial and many of which may appear on the surface to be of a nuisance nature. As a result of this orientation, the center may receive a number of calls that might be better described as being incomplete, that is, calls in which substantial interaction with the counselor is not allowed to take place because the caller decides not to allow the conversation to develop.

Acceptance of all calls is consistent with the goals of telephone counseling services for it lets callers define their problem in their own way, while the counselor assumes that the callers are being honest. In essence, it places all the responsibility on the individuals calling, for it does not allow the callers to manipulate the telephone counselor into making a decision as to whether or not the call is "real."

We found in our center that even the most obvious type of nuisance call, that of a call from teenagers at a party, often can begin to focus on a problem if handled correctly. We have found that individuals who make a nuisance or incomplete call to a crisis intervention center may not be completely aware of why they are doing this. They may give the impression of being nonserious callers and in so doing unconsciously set themselves up to be rejected by the center as they have been by other agencies. Therefore, it seems to be imperative that the center not make decisions on which calls are real and which are not. It must accept all calls, allow itself on occasion to be manipulated by a caller and accept this as part of the price it has to pay to be available to all individuals.

Another point is also important. People who make a call classified as either a nuisance call or as an incomplete call should be considered to have a problem, even though they may not recognize it at the time. To cut such people off by making a statement such as, "One should only call when one has a problem to talk about," would seem to reinforce them not calling because of the possibility of rejection. Conversely, accepting any call as a call from an individual with a problem, regardless of what takes place or how short the call is, will indicate to the individual that a call to the center will be handled in a direct way, with full acceptance of the individual and the problem. Stated another way, people may not be consciously aware that they have a problem at the time they are making the nuisance call, but they will be left with the attitude that the center does not play games, and that it will respond to any call in a direct and honest manner. When the anxiety of callers increases because of the undefined problem they have, the possibility of them making a call to the center is greatly enhanced.

Based on the foregoing considerations, I would like to make the following conclusions and suggestions.

1. There is no such thing as a nuisance call at a 24-hour telephone crisis intervention service. No call taken at the center should be designated as such, since to do so is to prejudice the telephone counselor against the caller and to preclude, if not eliminate, the possibility of assistance being given to the caller. Labeling a call as a nuisance call gives the telephone counselor the feeling that she can handle the call in a less serious, less considerate, less concerned manner.

2. Calls coming in to the center should be designated as complete or incomplete calls. Complete calls are those in which the termination of the call is made through the mutual agreement of both parties. Incomplete calls are those in which the termination of the call is determined by one of the parties without consideration for the other individual.

3. The telephone counselor should assume that there is no such thing as a wrong number or a mistake in dialing a number. Every effort should be made to engage the person who places this type of call in a conversation by being helpful and concerned about giving assistance to the individual. Persons who make these calls are often testing the telephone counselor to determine whether or not they will be accepted before they reveal that they intended to place the call to the suicide prevention and crisis service.

4. The telephone service must allow itself to be used or manipulated (if necessary) by answering all calls in a straight-forward, direct, and honest way. After a period of time, it is possible for a telephone counselor to begin to hear the "ring" of an honest call or of a dishonest manipulative call. But to make this type of judgment incorrectly can have negative consequences for the care or treatment of the caller and may result in the telephone counselor losing a real emergency call. We have found that when we play a call out, even though we may suspect it may be a crank, manipulative, or fake call, individuals will sometimes call back after they hang up the telephone and tell us that they are not in danger, and that they are sorry they have placed the call.

5. Each time a person calls the center and obtains a response which is positive and facilitative, regardless of whether the person calling is calling with a real problem, the center is developing the concept in the community that individuals at the center will not "play games" with people on the telephone, but that they will listen to them honestly and directly and respond to them in this manner.

Rather than being detrimental, the number of incomplete calls the center receives can be looked on as being a positive measure of the interest that a community has in the center and a measure of the increased number of individuals in the community who know about the center and are calling it to see if it is really there.

Chapter 19

THE "ONE COUNSELOR" CALLER

GENE W. BROCKOPP

Every telephone emergency service, like any service system which deals with a large number of people and has a large diverse staff, eventually must deal with the problem of the client who wishes to relate with only one person on the staff. Unlike large service agencies, for example, welfare or Medicare, which divide clients among various full-time case workers who maintain contact with the client and assume responsibility for helping them obtain the service they need, suicide prevention centers are usually staffed by volunteers who have limited training and only part-time contact with the agency. The kind of client who wants to relate to only one person usually has insistent needs for "distant intimacy" (such as a telephone might permit), a history of rejections by various social and mental health agencies, and some feeling of concern that now he is calling a suicide or crisis service. The reason a client states why he wants to talk to the same person as spoken to before may be one of the following:

1. This person has helped me before. Most clients will automatically return to those individuals who have helped them previously or those with whom they have developed a sense of trust. Their advice, assistance or thoughtful listening has proven useful in reducing the anxiety of the individual or in working through the problem which they had. However, the line between obtaining assistance and developing a dependency relationship is very close. Although I am not opposed to the development of the dependency relationship when it is appropriate or needed by the individual for maintaining himself or his life, I do feel that the person who continues to call a telephone service usually is not in this state but rather is a chronic caller who is usually not too lethal. If the person were seriously self-destructive, it is certainly hoped that there would be encouragement by the telephone counselor for professional

intervention on a face-to-face basis rather than on the telephone service.

2. This person understands me. Again, although this is an important characteristic of a counseling relationship and necessary if help is to be given to the individual, the implicit assumption is that no one else can understand her or give her the help she needs. This attitude often closes off many other areas of help for the individual and makes a referral to an agency improbable and unlikely to be taken by the person.

3. I won't have to repeat myself or begin at the beginning once again. Although some callers delight in telling their story of grief and trouble to various individuals, most individuals would prefer not to go through the details of the problems with another individual unless this is absolutely necessary or unless they are trying to rationalize their feelings or reinforce the correctness of their actions.

4. I like talking to this person. Requests or demands for the same counselor which fall into this category usually imply that the relationship between the counselor and the client is one of conversation and friendship rather than one of counseling. In this kind of relationship, there is little chance of confronting the individual with his problems or making a movement toward a solution of these problems.

5. I can't or won't talk to anyone else. In this situation, the caller is setting demands on the service or on the counselor which, if granted, will overtly and covertly place him a controlling position – one in which the relationship is much more important than the solving of a problem or the working through the difficulty. The person who sets up this condition generally is not hurting very much and usually has more of a friendship relationship than a counseling one with the counselor.

These five reasons, or variations of them, are commonly used by callers to request talking to the same counselor with whom they have spoken before. I feel that the only ones that are justified are the first and third. The other three indicate that the client has reduced the therapeutic relationship to one of a conversation, thereby making the emergency telephone service into an old-fashioned party-line type of operation.

I feel there are decided disadvantages to allowing this type of relationship to develop from the point of view of the service itself.

1. The counselor may not be there or able to take the call from the client at that particular time. If there is a stated or implied agreement that the counselor is going to take calls from this particular individual, the counselor must be available to the individual at all times or deal with the feelings of rejection that the individual may feel as a result of her lack of availability to the client. In addition, since the person working on the telephone must be available to any individual regardless of his previous relationship with a specific client, to develop a relationship with one client makes this task difficult and distorts the

purpose of the telephone service.

2. Calls of this type tend to become conversational rather than remaining therapeutic partly because of the type of training the telephone counselor has had. In most cases, the volunteer telephone counselor is able to deal with crisis calls quite well and to work through crisis situations. However, dealing with individuals on a long-term basis is a different task and requires a different type of competency. This skill is usually not available to the telephone counselor, and so the telephone call from the one person caller generally deteriorates into a conversational one. Although talking may give some support to the individual who is calling the center, the function of the telephone counselor is often then limited to merely listening. In a sense he prostitutes his counseling function by becoming a conversationalist. This service may be very useful, but it does not appear to me to be a desirable one for a telephone operation.

3. Pressure by the client on the counselor may result in covert rejection. Extending the idea expressed above, since the counselor is usually not able to handle this type of call over a long period of time in an appropriately therapeutic way, what often occurs is an initial sense of importance on being requested by the client to work with him with his problems. As the telephone call deteriorates into a conversational relationship, a sense of inadequacy often develops on the part of the counselor. In a short time, a sense of frustration and covert wishing to get rid of the problem caller develops because nothing seems to work with him. In either case, whether the person is covertly rejected or maintained at a conversational level because of the inadequacy of the telephone counselor, change is unlikely to occur in the caller and eventually neither the caller nor the counselor find the relationship satisfactory.

4. Calls of this type move toward an "owning" of callers by specific counselors. The feeling of importance that each of us has about ourselves and wishes to maintain and enhance is tapped by the single-person caller. What results is that rather than functioning in a cooperative way, a competition develops between telephone workers regarding specific callers and each person, in essence, sets up a private practice within the center.

5. The one-person caller may develop more out of the need of the counselor than the needs of the client. Extending point (4) above, we find that some individuals who work in a telephone answering service do so to fulfill deep needs in themselves for developing close personal relationships with other individuals. They use the one person caller to achieve these ends. Consequently, a symbiotic type of relationship develops in which each person is fulfilling his or her own pathological needs, and the problem of the client is ignored.

6. Manipulation by the caller is much easier. With a dependency relationship developing between the counselor and the client, which taps some of the

needs of the counselor for consistency, importance, and value, the one-person caller (who is often a past master at using the environment to maintain a level of functioning which is neither healthy nor sick) is usually able to keep his pathological "hooks" into the counselor, controlling and manipulating him to his own ends.

At the same time as there are disadvantages to the center in allowing the one-person caller, I feel that there are important advantages that need to be considered in determining whether a telephone service should allow the one-person caller.

1. Consistency in the counseling approach is enhanced. Clearly, consistency in working with an individual is enhanced when only one counselor maintains the counseling relationship. Each person in the dyad develops some sense of the style of the other individual and is able to work within that style, although as pointed out above, the handling of the call may not be appropriate. It is, however, consistent, and this is an important value to consider with certain types of callers.

2. Calls from the chronic caller can be limited, focused, and evaluated. Chronic callers pose a number of severe problems for the telephone emergency service. Since their life-style is usually self-destructive from a long-range perspective, it is critical that an evaluation be made of each caller to find out where the individual is at that particular time so that an appropriate response without manipulation can be made. If one person handles the calls from a chronic caller, this can be achieved.

3. The one-person caller gives the counselor a sense of continuity. Probably one of the most difficult aspects of working at a telephone emergency service is the sense of discontinuity in working with people. Each time the telephone rings, a crisis is occurring in someone's life, and the individual who answers the telephone must be able to respond to that crisis without, in many cases, knowing the disposition of the previous problem to which he has responded. We have found that the professional staff members in a suicide and crisis service need a few long-term patients to maintain a balance for themselves, to see outcomes and maintain a perspective on the work they are doing with crisis clients. The same may be true of the person who works on the telephone service.

4. The client does not need to repeat himself. I emphasized this point previously and would merely like to add here that the need for an adequate record system is evident if the calls are to be handled properly.

5. The client has an increased sense of belonging and value. Through the one-person contact, the client takes on an identity as a person rather than losing his identity and becoming a number or a file folder in the center. Since the individuals who call a telephone service are often on the periphery of society, the sense of belongingness may be important to them and may give

them a base from which they can move into more involved areas of social life.

6. With the one-person caller, both the level and the extent of the communication may be enhanced if the telephone counselor is adequately trained to respond to this type of caller. For example, the insecure individual, who may trust only one person or be able to relate to only one individual, may, through this relationship, develop sufficient trust to move out into the community. Also, the problem which the individual has (which may be embarrassing because of its severity or because of the area of concern) may be more easily brought out as the depth of relationship with one person increases and positive transference develops.

Reviewing the advantages and disadvantages of this problem within the context of an emergency telephone service, I feel that the following guidelines are appropriate in working with this type of caller.

1. The one-person caller should not be encouraged. The emphasis should be placed upon calling the agency for assistance rather than calling an individual person. I feel that an analogous situation would be for an individual who is being robbed to call the police station and request to talk to a specific policeman or call a fire department and request that a certain fireman come to put out the fire. If a telephone service is to maintain its integrity as an emergency service, it must be responsive as a unit to individuals in crisis. At the same time, I recognize the importance and value of the conversational-friend relationship that each individual appears to need. This, however, is not the area of responsibility of a crisis telephone service. Rather than providing this service to individuals, the service should help them develop it within their circle of friends or community. By focusing individuals on their home environment for conversation and friendship relationships, we are decreasing the possibility that a dependent relationship will develop and, with it, a distortion of the emergency telephone service.

2. If a person calls requesting a particular counselor, everything should be done by the counselor who takes the call to develop a relationship with this individual rather than giving in to the caller's wish to talk to a specific person.

3. During each telephone call, the counselor should make references to the agency and to calling the agency for assistance rather than calling a specific person at the agency. In addition, at the end of the telephone call, a statement should be made to callers regarding the fact that, if they wish, they can again call the agency, not the person, for assistance and that there are a number of individuals at the service who are able to take their calls and to work with them in any crisis situation they may encounter. In addition, telephone counselors should not fall into the trap of giving out personal information about themselves to callers, for this will enhance the conversational aspect of the call. To do so gives callers de facto permission to develop a friendship relationship with counselors.

4. The process of selecting counselors to work at a telephone service should include looking at the needs of the counselors who are applying for this position. An attempt should be made to obtain individuals who are secure themselves and who do not need dependent relationships with other individuals to maintain their integrity, value, or importance.

5. During the call, the interaction with clients must be continually focused on the problem that they are having and in assisting them in working toward a solution or amelioration of the condition. Telephone counselors must be alert to the test that callers will give them to determine whether or not they (the callers) can move the telephone relationship into a conversational area. If telephone counselors are alert, and secure in themselves, they will move toward terminating the call when individuals go beyond the problem and into a conversation relationship.

6. Each counselor must be constantly on guard so that personal information, such as the names, addresses, or telephone numbers of individual counselors working at the center, is not given out to people who call the center. In addition, in no case should the time when any specific counselor is working at the center be given out to a caller, either by the counselor himself or by other counselors who work at the center.

7. Finally, recognizing that there may be times when a one-person relationship is desirable for a caller, I feel that, before a counselor is allowed to develop this type of relationship with a client, the decision as to its value and need should be made at a consultant or clinical director level. It appears to me that this should be done only when the caller requires the consistency in working with a specific person or when the tenuousness of the relationship requires contact with one individual. When it is decided that this approach is to be used, a careful study should first be made of the individual who is calling, his or her specific needs, and the type of person who would be most appropriate for handling this type of caller. Then a clinical plan for obtaining the appropriate therapeutic relationship should be developed with the selected counselor to insure that it will be carried out. The rest of the telephone counselors should then be apprised of the treatment plan. It should be emphasized that this procedure should be the exception and not the rule. Only a few callers require this type of approach.

In summary, it does not appear to me to be appropriate that a crisis telephone service should allow its emergency responding ability to degenerate to a mere conversational, supportive relationship. By permitting this type of relationship to develop, the telephone service is reducing the effectiveness of its function and in many cases enhancing the pathology of the individual who is calling or feeding the psychological needs of the counselor working on the telephone.

Part IV

SPECIAL TOPICS

Chapter 20

ADOLESCENTS

Sarah C. Westen

An adolescent in crisis could be experiencing a variety of acute issues or behaviors, such as trauma, neglect, substance addiction, psychosis, pregnancy, identity crises, or violence. While the use of the telephone and the Internet as means of crisis counseling and intervention apply to these and other youth crises, this chapter focuses on suicidal ideation and behavior among adolescents within this context.

Suicide is the third leading cause of death among youth (Mathews et al., 2011), and is associated with other mental health conditions and high-risk behaviors (Waldvogel et al., 2008). Warning signs and risk factors for suicide have been identified specific to youth (Taliaferro & Borowsky, 2011). However, research has shown appropriate suicide risk assessment to be one of the most challenging tasks facing crisis hotline staff (Mishara et al., 2007), as well as among other mental health professionals (Coombs et al., 1992; Ozer et al., 2009; Lake, 2008; Frankenfield et al., 2000). With a growing usage of telephone and Internet devices by teenagers (Lenhart, 2010), and technology increasing the portable nature of such devices, these modes of communication are becoming increasingly accessible to adolescents in crisis situations. Although the establishment of standards for the assessment of suicidal callers is in place (Joiner et al., 2007), a discussion of suicide crisis counseling specific to adolescents is critical to guide professionals, paraprofessionals, and non-mental health workers (e.g., website moderators) in an increasing world of connectivity within this special population.

The first section of this chapter defines adolescence and describes recent research on the adolescent brain and adolescent high-risk behavior. Second, this chapter reviews known warning signs and risk factors associated with youth suicidality. Third, the chapter discusses the assessment of youth suicide, the adolescent's understanding of the concept of suicide, and cognitively-appropriate counseling of the adolescent via the telephone and the Internet. In the fourth section, adolescent help-seeking behavior via the telephone and Internet is discussed. At the end of the chapter, select resources for youth crisis hotlines and youth networking websites are listed.

The Adolescent

An introduction to the period of adolescence and adolescent brain development is essential to guide counseling and intervention strategies. The goal of this section is to familiarize crisis counselors with the adolescent population through a cognitive-developmental point of view. Risk factors for suicide are noted within this section.

What Is Adolescence?

Adolescence is characterized as the period of psychological, biological, and social transition between childhood and adulthood, typically thought to begin at puberty and end at around age 20. However, because adolescence is also a cultural phenomenon, its endpoints are not necessarily age-specific and depend on social context and psychological maturation. Erik Erikson's theory of psychosocial development defines adolescence as a stage of identity formation versus role confusion. Adolescents practice different identity roles in their relationships and experience the stressors of cultural shifts in expectation and responsibility (Erikson, 1950). Radzik et al. (2002) describe three psychosocial developmental phases: early adolescence (10–13 years), middle adolescence (14–17 years), and late adolescence (17–21 years). These ages are approximate, and it is important to note that adolescents display a wide variability in developmental growth, both physically and psychologically. These stages, therefore, may overlap. Adolescents respond to life's struggles and transitions in unique ways. They must learn to cope with the consequences of their own high-risk behaviors as well as the high-risk behaviors of their peers (Galambos & Leadbeater, 2000; Lerner & Galambos, 1998). Silbereisen and Todt (1994) describe adolescence as a context-driven period of transition, noting that even biological processes cannot be fully understood without examining the interplay of family, school, and peers, as well as the effects of societal norms and living conditions.

The Adolescent Brain

Cross-sectional and longitudinal studies using brain magnetic resonance imaging (MRI) have shown that brain maturation continues during adolescence and young adulthood, dismantling the old belief that development ends in childhood (Giedd et al., 1999; Paus et al., 1999; Sowell et al., 1999; Thompson et al., 2000). Most major neuropsychiatric disorders are now thought to be the result of deviations from normal brain development, which could explain why many psychiatric disorders first present in late adolescence and young adulthood. Gogtay and Thompson (2010) provide a detailed review of recent developmental brain imaging research and implications for vulnerability to psychopathology.

With the advent of dynamic imaging models, which can show detailed 3D and 4D images in "time-lapse" movies, scientists have been able to visualize cortical brain development. Gogtay et al. (2004) found that the order in which the brain matures corresponds to cognitive and functional development sequences. Areas associated with more basic development mature early. These include areas responsible for sensory reception and motor activity. Regions responsible for instinctual reactions, including fear and aggressive behavior, are among the early-developing regions. Brain areas involved in executive function mature later. Planning, problem-solving, inhibition, and monitoring of one's actions are among the cognitive processes involved in this level of functioning. The frontal cortex, which controls reasoning and impulsive behavior, continues to mature well into adulthood (American Academy of Child and Adolescent Psychiatry, 2008a).

Lebel and Beaulieu (2011) reported that growth continues into the mid-twenties and, in some subjects, continues into the early thirties. This diversity could be suggestive of the role of brain development in various mental disorders and requires future study. The authors note that, since structural brain changes can be induced by learned behaviors, brain development in young adults may be influenced by life experiences such as advanced education, employment, independence, and new social or family relationships. Adolescent brains are therefore continuously reshaping and growing to adapt to experiences. Crisis counselors should have basic knowledge of how adolescent brain development contributes to risk-taking and may create a particularly vulnerable environment for adolescents in distress.

High-Risk Behavior

Brain changes during adolescence may result in vulnerability to high-risk behaviors, including behaviors that contribute to injuries and violence (Society for Neuroscience, 2011; CDC, 2010). King et al. (2003a) describe a connection between suicide and the "continuum of adolescent self-destructiveness" (Holinger, 1979). On this continuum, high-risk behavior ranges from the covert (e.g., reckless driving) to the overt (e.g., suicide attempts). The authors review shared antecedents between risk factors for problem behaviors and adolescent suicide, such as the traits of impulsivity, recklessness, and aggression, and family and social risk factors. The authors discuss the consideration of suicidality as part of the continuum of teenage problem behavior. Although efforts to link prevention and treatment require additional research and comprehensive approaches, it is important for the crisis worker to be aware of an evolving adolescent brain in the context of other developmental issues when working with an adolescent who exhibits suicide ideation or behavior. It is also important for the counselor to know that, while adolescents are known to experience periods of psychological turmoil, most adolescents are able to cope adequately with life stressors and transitions. About 80% of adolescents cope well with the developmental process, and 70% of these adolescents experience what are considered to be normal periods of stress mixed with periods of calm (Radzik et al., 2002). The crisis counselor should be wary, however, of dismissing high-risk behaviors as simple teenage tendencies, and they should treat every case with caution.

The research of the developmental psychologist Laurence Steinberg suggests that adolescents take greater risks than adults, not because they do not understand the risks, but because adolescents weigh risk versus reward differently. Using functional magnetic resonance imaging (fMRI), Steinberg's team measured brain activity in adolescents and adults as they made decisions in a simulated driving experiment called the "Stoplight Task." The goal of the task was to drive from one point to another as quickly as possible. At each intersection, participants had to decide (by pressing a button) whether or not to brake as the simulated vehicle approached a traffic signal changing from green to yellow to red. Risk-taking (not braking) saved time and resulted in greater incentives. However, if the light turned red and the simulated vehicle did not make it through the intersection, more time would be lost than if the individual had waited at the traffic stop. The study found that adolescents take the same number of risks as adults when alone in the room. However, in the presence of a peer, adolescents took twice as many risks. During peer observation, adolescent brains showed greater activation in reward-related brain regions, suggesting that the presence of peers increases adolescent risk-taking through heightened reward sensitivity (Chein et al., 2011). An epidemiological study by Simons-Morton et al. (2011), which examined the real-life driving of newly-licensed adolescents, showed a higher rate of risky driving behavior among adolescents when in the presence of friends versus adults. This evidence suggests that social influence is a powerful factor in influencing high-risk behaviors in teenagers.

The neural coordinates of reward and social interactions overlap. The adolescent brain experiences higher levels of dopamine, a hormone responsible for feelings of pleasure, in the frontal cortex, but decreasing levels in the brain's reward center. This suggests higher levels of excitement are needed to achieve the same level of pleasure from an activity than an adult would experience (Spear, 2000). Dopamine is also secreted during high-risk behaviors, such as substance use. This is combined with a surge in oxytocin and vasopressin during adolescence, hormones that function to increase a feeling of reward via social connections. Oxytocin, for example, acts to bond a female to her mate during sexual activity. Limited parental connections may influence an adolescent's biological drive to seek this sense of bonding elsewhere. Adolescent brain development may also explain why adolescents react to rejection by peers as an existential threat. Brain regions activated in adolescents who experience social exclusion have been shown to correlate positively with symptoms of depression (Masten et al., 2009) and correlate negatively with resistance to the influence of peers (Sebastian et al., 2011). Studies suggest that emotional brain responses are activated by social exclusion in early adolescence, but brain regions responsible for emotional regulation may not develop until late adolescence, suggesting a vulnerability to social rejection in adolescents (Bolling et al., 2011). Since disruption of a romantic attachment is often a precursor of suicidal ideation and behavior in teenagers, knowledge of the biological underpinnings of the teenage reaction may help crisis counselors sympathize with what the adolescent is feeling (Brent et al., 1993).

Of additional clinical relevance is new research which suggests that the neuroanatomical expression of intelligence in children and adolescents is dynamic. The level of intelligence is associated with the trajectory of cortical development. This is true primarily in the frontal cortex, involved in planning and impulse control (Shaw et al., 2006). Ramsden et al. (2011) report that verbal and nonverbal intelligence quotient (IQ) scores can rise or fall during the teenage years; that is, a person's intelligence relative to their peers may change during their adolescence. This means that an adept 10-year-old may not grow to be a highly adept 20-year-old. The implications for social well-being could include marked increases or decreases in self-esteem and may contribute to identity shifts, especially if areas a teenager considered to be strengths before may no longer be strengths. Of additional clinical relevance is the finding that self-reported exposure to childhood maltreatment (e.g., physical abuse, physical neglect, and emotional neglect) is associated with reductions in corticostriatal-limbic gray matter in the adolescent brain. In females, this was found in regions controlling emotion regulation, whereas in males, this was found in regions associated with impulse control (Edmiston et al., 2011). Because childhood abuse is a familial risk factor for adolescent suicide (Weller et al., 2001; Popenhagen & Qualley, 1998), these findings could help explain how abuse impacts brain development and leads to suicidal tendencies.

Overall, research supports a relationship between adolescent brain development, high-risk behaviors, and risk factors for suicide. The National Longitudinal Study on Adolescent Health interviewed 13,491 adolescents in grades seven through 11 in 1995 and again one year later and found early high-risk behaviors (e.g., sexual activity and drug use) to be linked to depression. However, depression did not *cause* the high-risk behavior (Hallfors et al., 2005). In a separate analysis of the same population, teenagers who had been involved in substance use or sexual activity were found to be significantly more likely to suffer from suicidal ideation and suicide attempts (Hallfors et al. 2004). Known risk factors for suicide include substance abuse (Beautrais, 2003; Gould & Kramer, 2001; Pompili et al., 2005), disruptive relationships, parental conflict and impaired parent-child relationships (Gould et al., 2003; Gould & Kramer, 2001; Pfeffer, 2001), and dissolution of romantic relationships (Beautrais, 2003; Brent et al., 1993). The aforementioned vulnerability in the adolescent brain to such behaviors and stressors could lead to psychological crisis in the absence of coping mechanisms (Wilson et al., 1995).

Evidence-based research on adolescent brain development shows that adolescent years are a time of rapid brain development and increased vulnerability. Although risk behavior can pose danger, risk behavior can also be adaptive. Increased sensation seeking and liking novel experiences leads to an urge to meet new people, develop new social connections, gain independence, and experience new realms of life. These traits are crucial to healthy adolescent development and eventual functioning as independent adults. However, when vulnerability surpasses adaptability, these traits can be detrimental. Psychopathologies may develop, and psychological crises may occur. For those adolescents who are unable to cope alone with life stressors, crisis counselors may provide a pivotal role in ensuring youth safety. Because suicide is associated with high-risk behaviors and because the cognitive development of adolescents creates a vulnerable state for suicidality, the youth crisis counselor should be trained to identify warning signs and risk factors for suicide in adolescents. The next section of this chapter provides an overview of warning signs and risk factors associated with youth suicide.

Warning Signs and Risk Factors Associated with Youth Suicide

According to the latest data from the Youth Risk Behavior Surveillance of the CDC, 13.8% of high school students have seriously considered suicide, 10.9% have made a plan about how they would attempt suicide, 6.3% report making at least one suicide attempt, and 1.9% have made a suicide attempt that resulted in an injury, poisoning, or an overdose that required medical attention (CDC, 2010). The suicide rate among adolescents has been on the rise in recent years despite stability among other populations (Cash & Bridge, 2009; Beautrais, 2003). In the 1990s, one in five adolescents reported knowing a friend who had attempted suicide in the past year (Resnick et al., 1997), while three in five adolescents reported knowing a teenager who had attempted to take his or her own life (Ackerman, 1993). With the growing advance of social networking and increasing communication between teenage groups, these numbers are likely to be much higher a decade after the turn of the millennium. The broader impact of this high prevalence is worth noting. Not only is the death of a friend who has completed suicide a risk factor for suicidality in teenagers (Bearman & Moody, 2004), but also exposure to the suicidal behavior of others and media coverage of suicidality are known risk factors (Gould & Kramer, 2001; Gould et al., 2003).

Warning Signs

Adolescent hotline callers or social network users may not readily state how they are feeling. In adolescents, feelings may manifest as vague somatic symptoms or behavior that is atypical (Taliaferro & Borowsky, 2011). Because teenagers are in the process of identity formation and focus on peer image development, teenagers may not want to relay a sense of weakness to others. The adolescent may, therefore, express suicidal ideation indirectly, through art drawings or verbal hints in journaling and Internet blog entries. Other changes may include unusual neglect of physical appearance, persistent boredom, difficulty concentrating, loss of interest in activities the adolescent once enjoyed, frequent somatic complaints such as head or stomach aches, and changes in sleeping or eating habits (see Table 20-1).

Mood changes, marked personality changes, substance use and increased aggression are also warning signs of potential risk of suicide (American Academy of Child and Adolescent Psychiatry, 2008b; Taliaferro & Borowsky, 2011). Crisis hotline operators or other professionals monitoring adolescent behavior should be aware of the warning signs of suicide and know that many adolescents will be wary of verbalizing their vulnerabilities directly. The list in Table 20-1 summarizes the warning signs of adolescent suicidality.

Risk Factors

A primary prevention strategy for youth suicide is the identification of risk factors. Depending on the level of imminent risk, a crisis counselor may or may not be in the position to inquire about risk factors for suicide. However, if the counselor is in need of additional information to determine an adoles-

Table 20-1
WARNING SIGNS OF ADOLESCENT SUICIDALITY[36]

- Verbal or written expression of suicidal hints (e.g., "I won't be a problem for you much longer")
- Feelings of guilt (e.g., complaints of feeling like a "bad person")
- Frequent complaints about physical symptoms such as headaches, stomachaches, or fatigue that are often related to emotions
- Violent actions or rebellious behavior, such as running away
- Drug and alcohol use
- Unusual neglect of physical appearance
- Personality change
- Persistent boredom, difficulty concentrating, or decline in the quality of schoolwork
- Loss of interest in once pleasurable activities
- Not tolerating praise or rewards
- Change in sleep patterns
- Putting his or her affairs in order (e.g., giving away favorite possessions)
- Signs of psychosis (e.g., hallucinations)
- Sudden cheerfulness after a period of depression (this could be a sign of relief at the decision to end one's life)

[36] Sources: American Academy of Child and Adolescent Psychiatry (2008b); Taliaferro & Borowsky (2011).

cent's risk level, a working knowledge of individual, family and socio-environmental risk factors can aid in the formulation of a treatment approach. The list in Table 20-2 summarizes risk factors for adolescent suicide and cites relevant evidence-based research.

Crisis counselors should also be aware of gender differences in high-risk factors for suicide in adolescents. Similar risk factors have been shown for both sexes (Brent et al., 1999), particularly the presence of a mood disorder or a previous suicide attempt (Shaffer et al., 1996). However, the degree of risk factor importance in completed suicide has been shown to vary (Shaffer et al., 1996). The presence of major depression has been shown to increase the risk of suicide 20-fold in girls (Shaffer et al., 1996), and a previous attempt to increase the risk of suicide more than 30-fold in boys (Brent et al., 1999; Shaffer & Craft, 1999). In boys, depression, substance abuse and disruptive behavior followed a previous suicide attempt (Brent et al. 1993b; Shaffer et al. 1996). Although similar risk factors have been shown for nonfatal suicide attempts among male and female youth, Thompson and Light (2011) found younger age and presence of somatic symptoms were reported to be additional risk factors in females. Although knowledge of gender differences may inform suicide prevention strategies, counselors should treat the presence of any risk factor seriously.

Table 20-2
RISK FACTORS OF ADOLESCENT SUICIDALITY[37]

- History of mental disorders (mood disorders, substance use disorders)[1, 3, 6, 10, 11, 12]
- Prior suicidal behavior or attempt[2, 3, 6, 7, 10, 11, 12]
- Impulsivity or risk taking[1, 2, 5, 9, 11]
- Past sexual or physical abuse[2, 5, 7, 10, 12]
- Parental psychopathology[1, 2, 3, 5, 12]
- Poor family cohesion or family discord[1, 2, 3, 5, 6, 7, 9, 10, 11, 12]
- Poor parent-child communication or neglectful parenting style[1, 2, 3, 5, 9]
- Socio-demographic disadvantages[1, 2, 12]
- Contagion (i.e., media coverage of suicidal behavior)[2, 3, 12]
- Sexuality issues (i.e., homosexuality or bisexuality)[3, 5, 10]
- Difficulties in school[2, 3, 4, 6, 10, 12]
- Interpersonal losses (i.e., break up of a romantic relationship)[1, 2, 3, 7, 10]
- Legal or disciplinary crisis[1, 2, 3, 5, 12]
- Death of a peer or loved one[5, 7]
- Teen pregnancy[12]

[1] Beautrais (2003)
[2] Gould et al. (2003)
[3] Gould & Kramer (2001)
[4] Huff (1999)
[5] Pfeffer (2001)
[6] Pompili et al 2005
[7] Popenhagen & Qualley (1998)
[8] Rutter & Behrendt (2004)
[9] Seibel & Murray (1988)
[10] "Suicide and Suicide Attempts in Adolescents" (2000)
[11] Toumbourou & Gregg (2002)
[12] Weller et al. (2001)

[37] Source: Adapted from Waldvogel, Rueter, & Oberg (2008).

Assessment of Youth Suicide Risk

Crisis center youth suicide risk assessment should follow the National Suicide Prevention Lifeline Suicide Risk Assessment Standards (Joiner et al., 2007), in which risk assessment follows four core principles: suicidal desire, suicidal capability, suicidal intent, and buffers/connectedness. Differences in assessment techniques between youth hotline and Internet users versus adult users will vary between states and crisis centers, as each state's law governing child welfare will vary regarding the duties of responders to notify parents or others. Rather than reviewing specific scales that are useful in the assessment of suicidal behaviors and risk factors among adolescents (crisis centers typically have procedures in place), this section discusses crisis counseling with the adolescent from a developmental point of view. For a helpful review of assessment measures for suicide in children and adolescents, see Goldston

(2004), a report prepared under funding from NIMH's Developmental Psychopathology and Prevention Research Branch.

The Concept of Suicide

Pfeffer (2003) defines suicidal behavior as any self-destructive act in which a person *intends* to kill him or herself. As described previously, adolescents often exhibit high-risk behavior which, when maladaptive, may be detrimental to their health or well-being. Pfeffer notes that destructive behaviors, such as self-cutting or reckless driving, may be considered suicidal behavior if the intent to die is present. However, adolescents may have difficulty verbalizing intent to die or may deny intentionality (Pfeffer, 1986). Therefore, it is essential that the crisis counselor obtain all information possible concerning the adolescent's current situation, feelings and behaviors in order to make an informed judgment on whether the adolescent has any intent to die.

Pfeffer notes that the assumption that children should not be considered suicidal if they do not understand the finality of death is final is incorrect. "Such concepts may be immature but if a child wants to achieve the state they believe to be death, the child can carry out a self-destructive act to achieve this aim" (Pfeffer, 2003, p. 213). Piaget (1952) noted that most adolescents, from the age of eleven, have developed operational concepts and the ability to think in abstract terms. However, as described above, cognitive growth varies by individual, and it is important for the crisis counselor to be aware that, even if a teenager does not appear to understand the concept of death, this does not mean that the teenager is not suicidal. Furthermore, it is important to understand that teenagers may not be cognitively aware of the true lethality of suicidal methods. A youth crisis counselor, therefore, needs to take every method of self-harm seriously. Indeed, if a 13-year-old in crisis plans to ingest four acetaminophen tablets in attempt to end his or her own life, this situation should be regarded as a suicide plan despite its actual nonlethality. The thought process of this teenager needs to be addressed with consideration and deemed a potential opportunity to intervene through empathic conversation and identification of coping strategies and persons from whom further help may be sought. As Pfeffer notes, the careful consideration and assessment of teenagers takes time, but the crisis counselor is in a position to establish an immediate degree of safety and provide a plan of action to help prevent future danger.

In a study designed to investigate the relationship between death concept and suicidal behavior in adolescents, Gothelf et al. (1998) found that adolescents do perceive death as a final state, as do adults. Suicidal inpatients were more preoccupied with death than nonsuicidal inpatients or normal controls. However, a surprising finding was that emergency room suicidal subjects were the least preoccupied with death of all study groups. No correlation was found between suicidality and intelligence level. These findings suggest that adolescents do understand lethality and indicate that, while suicidal adolescents do tend to have a preoccupation with death, a crisis counselor should be wary of dismissing nonpreoccupation with death as indicating no intent to die.

A Note on the Iatrogenic Risk Myth of Youth Suicide Screening

There has been concern that asking about suicide will induce feelings or thoughts about suicide in individuals that otherwise would not have been present. However, there is no evidence to suggest any potential harm from suicide screening in youth. Gould et al. (2005) conducted a randomized controlled study of 2,342 high school students and found no evidence of iatrogenic effects of suicide screening. Similar results have been found in an adult population (Crawford et al., 2011). In a recent study in the emergency department, Ballard et al. (in press) found 149 of 156 (96%) patients aged 10 to 21 years old supported the idea that nurses should ask youth about suicide. The patients reported identification of who was at risk, a desire to feel understood, the connection with help and resources, prevention of youth suicidal behavior, and a lack of other individuals to speak with about these issues as reasons why they supported being asked direct questions about suicide. Thus, there is no evidence to suggest asking about suicide will harm youth. Instead, asking will provide the crisis counselor with information on whether the adolescent in crisis has had thoughts or developed plans to kill himself or herself and, therefore, aid in suicide prevention strategy.

Talking to the Adolescent in Crisis

In crisis situations, counselors cannot always provide a significant amount of time for assessing the multiple factors associated with suicidal behavior. In these instances, counselors should first and foremost address the risk of danger. Whenever possible, it is essential for adolescents to know that the counselor is able to help, and the purpose of the telephone or Internet conversation is to help the adolescent without punishing the individual for his or her beliefs, thoughts, or actions. In cases where the counselor has time to develop rapport, casual questions about the individual's current life difficulties may be discussed. A nonthreatening, hierarchical approach to asking about suicidal behavior is useful with an adolescent population. Establishment of the importance of treatment is essential. Questions about the adolescent's suicidal ideation or acts should be direct (American Academy of Child and Adolescent Psychiatry, 2001; Jacobsen et al., 1994; Pfeffer, 2003). Pfeffer (2003) suggests a progression from a discussion of thoughts (Did you ever think that you wanted to hurt yourself?) to behavior (Did you ever try to hurt yourself?) to direct questions about suicidal intent (Did you ever plan to kill yourself?) and, finally, to direct behavior (Did you ever try to commit suicide? When did you do this?). Identification of the context in which the suicidal ideation or behavior occurred (time, place, and triggers) are important factors that may aid the counselor in distinguishing such things as similarity to the present instance, major cause of distress, or identification of surrounding safe environments. Identification of any possibilities for future rescue should be made, for example, by asking the adolescent whether they have plans to notify someone prior to attempted suicide or whether they plan to take preparations prior to the act (i.e., borrowing a parent's firearm).

Pfeffer (1986) reports that adolescents use the same self-destructive methods as adults in their suicidal acts. Methods include the use of firearms, overdosing, self-cutting, jumping in front of a moving vehicle, jumping from heights, and hanging. The American Academy of Child and Adolescent Psychiatry (2001) notes that the methods used to commit suicide by adolescents vary by geographic region, which may reflect availability. For example, firearms are used more often in rural areas where they may be more available for sporting purposes; jumping is more common in urban areas where tall buildings are more prevalent; and asphyxiation by carbon monoxide exhaust is more prevalent in suburban neighborhoods, areas where adolescents have access to cars and garages.

Crisis workers can make observations using active listening and empathic inquiry, keeping in mind the adolescent's stage of cognitive development. As Berman et al. (2006) explain, suicidal adolescents have often experienced a decrease in self-esteem, sense of self and ability to cope because of years of conflicting states, stressors and traumatic life experiences. The authors note that taking a family history is essential for an adequate assessment of suicide risk. Not only can genetic contributions of psychopathology come into play, but early experiences can affect future coping ability.

Additionally, certain adolescent diagnostic groups are considered to be more at risk for suicidal behavior than others. These include: (1) the depressed adolescent; (2) the substance-abusing adolescent; (3) the borderline or schizotypal adolescent; (4) the antisocial, acting-out, or conduct-disordered adolescent; (5) the marginal, isolated loner; (6) the rigid, unifocal perfectionist; (7) the psychotic adolescent; and (8) the in-crisis adolescent. The in-crisis adolescent does not necessarily fall into one of the other seven categories but is presented with stressors which creates a tendency for impulsive and irrational stress-provoked behavior (Berman et al., 2006). When talking to an adolescent in a suicidal crisis, gathering information which could assist the crisis counselor in identifying into which diagnostic group the adolescent falls may enhance the counselor's ability to talk to that adolescent.

Kids under Twenty-One (KUTO): A Peer-Staffed Hotline's Experience with Youth Callers[38]

Kids Under Twenty One (KUTO) is an agency which provides peer-facilitated crisis prevention, suicide intervention, and postvention support to youth in the St. Louis metropolitan area. Implementing the "teenagers helping teenagers help themselves" philosophy, trained youth crisis workers assist callers in working through their difficulties and developing plans to manage stress and mediate conflict. Most volunteers are high-school-aged students. Utilizing the critical elements and components of the National Suicide Prevention Lifeline's assessment guidelines, KUTO conducts a lethality assessment of all youth callers. The hotline uses a script which volunteers use to ask if callers are having suicidal thoughts. Approximately 5% to 10% of callers answer affirmatively and receive a follow-up call either during the next shift or the following day. The follow-up call serves a dual purpose of asking the caller if they need additional resources and also letting adolescent callers know that they are not alone. Crisis workers obtain demographic information from callers and brainstorm with callers to identify other trusted adults. KUTO has the ability to facilitate three-way calling to connect callers with these resources. Crisis workers suggest talking with parents, ask the youths if someone is home with them, and try in whatever way to connect the adolescent to a person in real time.

An important feature of KUTO is the emphasis on peers assisting peers. Speaking to a peer makes the situation feel more normal. Peer volunteers are able to build rapport and empathize with the caller. Elizabeth Makulec, KUTO's Executive Director, notes that connecting with a peer may give the callers a greater sense of relief. All youth volunteers are debriefed after calls which allows for de-escalation of the crisis workers' stress and makes sure the workers are in a safe place, as well as recognizing their own boundaries.

According to Makulec, young callers use the word suicide because it is often the only word they know to encompass feelings of hardship. It is one word that stresses the degree of life difficulties an adolescent may be facing. At KUTO, crisis workers try to identify coping mechanisms that perhaps the youths did not know they used in the past. Parents are not automatically notified because callers often state that parents are part of the problem. KUTO's primary concern is to ensure the safety of the caller. Makulec notes a tendency for teenagers to express fear. Teenagers are fearful because they do not understand what is happening and fearful they will get in trouble for their thoughts

---

[38] This section was written via information from personal correspondence with Elizabeth Makulec, Executive Director of Kids Under Twenty One (KUTO), December 20, 2011.

or actions. Often, teenage-parent communication is poor to begin with, and families may be underresourced. Teenagers may perceive parental worry for their safety as anger, and teenagers may be concerned that their mental health issues could create a financial burden for the family.

Makulec notes that teenagers tend to understand "safety" over "life and death" words and, therefore, recommend an emphasis on safety terminology. If the youth caller has access to lethal means, KUTO volunteers do what they can to increase safety, such as asking the youth to put down a weapon and go into another room while on the phone. KUTO believes in honesty with peer callers and will have a conversation with the callers if there are feelings the caller is not safe. Adolescents are, therefore, told if the police have been called.

KUTO's strategy provides an example of how crisis hotlines can incorporate knowledge of the cognitive development of adolescents into counseling procedures in order to obtain positive outcomes.

Why Use Telephone and Internet Resources for Adolescent Crisis Intervention?

Crisis hotlines and Internet resources can provide adolescents with anonymity, comfort, and familiar technology. Teenagers can use them quickly and without significant financial burden. As described above, poor parent-child communication and sociodemographic disadvantages are risk factors for suicide in adolescents. Adolescents who are not familiar with speaking to their parents on a regular basis would not feel comfortable initiating a conversation with those parents when in a crisis. Adolescents may not have insurance, likely need to go through parents to obtain insurance information, or may be unaware of in-person services available to help them cope with mental health difficulties. Because social inclusion and a sense of belonging is a major factor in adolescent cognitive development, crisis hotlines and Internet resources can aid in either of two ways: (1) to be a protective factor for anonymity (i.e., parents and peers may not be aware the youth is seeking help), and (2) to stimulate peer-to-peer communication in an effort to gain a sense of belonging and intimacy with the peer group (i.e., through social media sites and blogging with peers [friends or strangers], or through peer-to-peer counseling on youth lines).

The results of a Student Needs Assessment Survey (Dolan, 1991) found that most youths prefer to talk to someone their own age regarding interpersonal, school, or relationship issues before approaching a trusted adult, such as a teacher, counselor, coach, or parent. Berman et al. (2006) note that the typical nonprofessional staffing of youth crisis centers and telephone hotline services "theoretically make this form of entry to the help-giving system more acceptable than direct, face-to-face contact with an office-based professional (p. 310). The authors note that crises may either be resolved in this fashion or referrals to clinical care can be made when needed. In either case, the use of telephone or Internet resources has the ability to provide immediate assistance in emergency situations, which may be vital to saving lives, particularly in an adolescent group where impulsivity is more common.

Adolescent Help-Seeking Behavior via the Telephone and the Internet

Adolescent Media Technology Usage

The Pew Internet and American Life Project conducted 800 interviews in a nationally-representative sample of 800 parent-child pairs in 2009, 700 parent-child interviews in 2007, and 935 parent-child interviews in 2006 (Lenhart, 2010; Lenhart et al., 2007). The project's 2009 data revealed that 93% of teenagers go online and 63% of online teenagers go online daily; 75% of teenagers own a cell phone, and 69% own a desktop or laptop computer; 73% of teenagers use an online social network site (up from 55% in the 2007 data); 7% of social networking site users send messages through the social networks daily. Fifty percent of teenagers with telephones talk to friends daily; 54% of teenagers send text messages daily; 27% use their phone to go online; and 80% of teenagers own a game console, while 51% of teenagers have a portable gaming device (teenagers can connect and interact with others through online games).

David-Ferson and Hertz (2007) noted that the growing use of technology by adolescents has potential benefits, including ease of regular communication with family and peers, which may translate to a stronger sense of connectedness, opportunities for adolescents who have difficulty making friends (such as home schooled or socially anxious youth) to make social connections, and quick and easy access to Internet resources which may increase adolescent knowledge and education. The authors additionally noted the risks of this new media technology usage in teenagers, including opportunities for aggressive behavior, such as cyberbullying and violence perpetrated through online e-mail or instant messaging. However, the use of media technology can also be used to convey health related information and provide assistance in the case of a crisis. For youths who exhibit suicidal ideation or behavior, the telephone and Internet have the potential to provide immediately-needed resources.

Adolescent Help-Seeking Behavior via the Telephone

Few studies have examined the use of crisis hotline services in adolescent populations. Data that do exist are derived from either call volume reports from hotlines or from surveys of adolescent. Gould et al. (2006) note that hotlines which answer calls from all ages record teenagers' calls as a proportion of total calls but do not conventionally perform a demographic intake for all callers on the basis of age. Even with peer-exclusive hotlines, usage is difficult to ascertain because the number of nonrepeat callers and the originating geographic location of calls is not known (Gould et al., 2006). The studies that do exist suggest that adolescents access hotlines infrequently (King, 1977; Slem & Cotler, 1973). In 1985, Franklin et al. (1989) found that adolescents account for 8% of suicide-related crisis telephone contacts per year in a survey of nearly 400 suicide prevention and intervention services in the United States. A study by Boehm and Campbell (1995) of 11,152 calls to an adolescent peer listening phone service received between May of 1987 through December of 1992 found 441 calls to be about suicide. Callers were more likely to be female (57%), particularly when the calls concerned suicide (65%). Calls about suicide were more likely to be made by adolescents aged 15-16 years. Teenagers calling about suicide were less likely to call "just to talk" and more likely to call about issues related to self-esteem, family problems, drugs and alcohol, abuse, pregnancy, mental illness, death, spirituality, school problems, legal issues, and eating disorders; all of which are known to be risk factors for suicidality.

Research suggests that gender differences in adolescent suicide callers resemble the research that finds that women threaten and attempt suicide more frequently than men (Frederick, 1985). In a study examining differences among adolescent, young adult and adult callers of suicide help lines, de Anda and Smith (1993) report that nearly two-thirds of helpline callers were female across all age groups and, within the adolescent group, 70% of callers were female. The authors suggest that differences in help-seeking behavior may account for the gender difference in callers. Suicide ideation in women tends to lead to greater help-seeking behavior than does suicide ideation in men, with gender differences decreasing with age. The authors note that male adolescents may be a particularly at-risk population. Therefore, development of crisis prevention and intervention strategies which are perceived as welcoming, particularly to the adolescent male, are needed.

Evidence suggests that teenagers who use hotlines benefit from their call. King et al. (2003) found that crisis hotlines yield significant decreases in suicidality and improve the mental state of teenagers throughout the call. In an effort to determine the reasons behind infrequent adolescent usage of suicide hotlines despite reported benefits, Gould et al. (2006) studied the attitudes that adolescents have toward the use of crisis hotlines. In a study of 519 adolescents in ninth through twelfth grade in six high schools in New York State, the authors found that only 2.1% of adolescents had ever used a hotline, and negative attitudes toward hotlines were stronger than toward other formal sources of help. Objections to hotlines were strongest among students most in need of help – those with feelings of hopelessness or impaired functioning. Females were more likely than males to call a hotline, yet endorsed reasons for nonuse more than males. Males, therefore, did not require as negative of an attitude toward hotlines as a reason for not to call. Adolescents reported feelings of shame (i.e., "I was concerned about what my family might think or say"), self-reliance (i.e., I wanted to solve the problem by myself"), and structure (i.e., "I did not know where to call") as reasons for not using crisis hotlines. The authors note that outreach efforts are needed for teenagers, and state services must operate in a manner compatible with a teenager's lifestyle in order to increase utilization among adolescents. The Internet is one avenue to enhance crisis services for adolescents.

Adolescent Help-Seeking Behavior via the Internet

In the population of 519 high school students described above, Gould et al. (2002) reported that nearly one in five adolescents (18%) sought help on the Internet for emotional problems, substantially more than who sought help via crisis hotlines in the year prior (1.7%). There were no significant differences in the proportions of males and females seeking Internet help. The study found that Internet help-seekers were more likely to score above the clinical threshold on the Columbia Impairment Scale or the Beck Depression Inventory than were non-help-seekers. However, only 14% of adolescent Internet help-seekers felt that Internet resources helped them "very much," and more than 20% of Internet help-seekers were dissatisfied with the help they received. These findings suggest a need for Internet resources to be improved in order to best help teenagers and promote prevention strategies (Gould et al., 2002).

Recent research suggests that the online behavior of teenagers may provide clues for preventive intervention. Ybarra et al. (2005) investigated the online communications and self-disclosure practices of teenagers reporting depressive symptomatology via the Youth Internet Safety Survey, a nationally representative telephone survey of 1501 Internet-using teenagers between the ages of 10 and 17 years, and one caregiver in their household, conducted between 1999 and 2000. The authors found that talking with strangers online, using the Internet most frequently for e-mailing others, and intensity of Internet use differentiated youths reporting depressive symptoms from asymptomatic peers. Mitchell and Ybarra (2007) examined data from the Second

Youth Internet Safety Survey conducted in 2005, and found that teenagers reporting deliberate self-harm in the past six months (3%) were significantly more likely to have a close relationship with someone they met online than nonself-harm engaging peers (38% versus 10%). At least three in four (76%) teenagers reporting self-harm used instant messaging via the Internet. Together, these findings suggest that teenagers with depressive symptomatology and youths who self-harm may be more likely to place themselves in risky situations online, but also they suggest that the use of instant messaging or e-mail may be useful for adolescents as means of crisis intervention.

With the advent of social media websites, youth forums, and blogging, the Internet presents both advantages and drawbacks for vulnerable youths. Advantages include immediate access to health information, such as mental health disorder definitions, symptoms, and prevalence, and knowledge that conditions can be treated; information for self-help; access to both community and national resources; e-mail or messaging contact with both peers and adults which offer anonymous (when desired) and self-directed support; and information on crisis management. These advantages can prove life-saving for adolescents who often seek interconnectedness while protecting their own anonymity. Teenagers who feel they cannot express their feelings to parents and teenagers who are dependent, insecure, or frightened may look for guidance online, and these same teenagers may be more at-risk for self-harm. On the one hand, the presence of the Internet may help these teenagers develop support and find resources. On the other hand, without thoughtfully-developed online resources designed for teenagers, these teenagers may end up learning misinformation or obtaining misguided advice. Websites may potentially trigger suicidal behavior in adolescents, particularly suicide forums or sites which discuss means of completing suicide. It is essential that guidelines on suicidality continue to be developed in the realm of social media and for websites and youth forums to provide informed resources for teenagers in crisis. Overall, the ability of the Internet to facilitate a sense of interconnectedness among teenagers and to provide resources in the event of a crisis make use of the Internet pivotal in modern suicide prevention endeavors.

Summary

Adolescent brain development and high-risk behavior have been discussed as they pertain to crisis counseling. This chapter reviewed known warning signs and risk factors associated with youth suicidality which may aid the crisis counselor in better recognizing at-risk teenagers. The adolescent's perception of the concept of suicide has been discussed in the context of adolescent suicide assessment. Crisis counseling in an adolescent population has been reviewed from a cognitive-developmental point of view, and a case has been made to support the use of the telephone and the Internet as means for adolescent crisis intervention. Media technology usage among adolescents has been reviewed and research concerning adolescent help-seeking behavior via the telephone and the Internet has been outlined.

Crisis counseling in adolescents is most effective when based on an understanding of the biological, developmental and cognitive contexts contributing to suicide ideation and behavior. With the advent of media technology and the growing usage of new media among teenagers, adolescents have more access than ever before to phone and Internet resources geared toward suicide prevention and intervention. In general, teenagers who use these resources find benefit from using them. The telephone and Internet allow for anonymity and have the potential to create an atmosphere of interconnectedness, trust, and empathy among youth users.

Resources

Hotlines and Internet Chat Resources

Childhelp
http://www.childhelpusa.org/
1-800-4-A-Child (2-24453)
Hours: 24-hour support
National child abuse hotline.

Girls & Boys Town National Hotline
www.boystown.org/nation-hotline
1-800-448-3000
Hours: 24-hour support
Accredited by the American Association of Suicidiology (AAS). Parents, teenagers, and families can find help from trained counselors. The hotline now offers instant messaging or "online chat" to teenagers at yourlifeyourvoice.org.

Kids Under Twenty One (KUTO)
www.kuto.org
1-888-644-5886
Hours: Sunday-Thursday 4:00pm-10:00pm; Friday and Saturday 4:00pm-midnight.
Offers counseling via trained teenage volunteers via the phone.

Teen 2 Teen Hotline
http://www.teenline.org/
(714) New-Teen (639-8336)
Hours: 5:00pm-9:00pm
Offers counseling via trained teenage volunteers via the phone or live Internet chat counseling at http://www.newhopenow.org/counseling/liveperson.html.

TeenHelp.org
www.teenhelp.org
Trained volunteers provide support. Live Help allows users to talk to counselors one-on-one online.

Teen Relationships
http://www.teenrelationships.org/
800-300-1080
A site for teenagers about dating violence, recognizing warning signs of an abusive relationship, and understanding what a healthy relationship is, and resources for teenagers in abusive relationships.

The Trevor Project: Lifeline & Trevor Chat
www.thetrevorproject.org
1-866-488-7386
Hours: 24-hour support
Trained counselors support youths who are in crisis, feeling suicidal, or in need of a safe and judgment-free place to talk for lesbian, gay, bisexual, transgender, and questioning youths.
TrevorChat is available Friday's between 1:00pm and 7:00pm Pacific at http://www.thetrevorproject.org/chat.

National Hopeline Network
http://www.hopeline.com/
800-SUICIDE
Hours: 24-hour support
Crisis hotline which automatically routes calls to the nearest crisis center.

National Runaway Switchboard
http://www.1800runaway.org/
800-621-4000
National crisis intervention system for runaway and homeless youth.

NINELINE: Crisis Counseling for Homeless and At-Risk Kids
http://www.covenanthouse.org/youth-homeless-programs/crisis-hotline
1-800-999-9999
Hours: 4:00pm-8:00pm, 365 days a year
Sponsored by Covenant House, NINELINE seeks to help young people in need gain immediate access to crisis and counseling services.
NINELINE is also available on the Internet at www.NINELINE.org. Young people can ask questions via e-mail or participate in forum conversations monitored by NINELINE counselors.

Rape, Abuse & Incest National Network (RAINN)
http://www.rainn.org/
800-656-HOPE (4673)
Hours: 24-hour support
Network for survivors of rape, abuse, and incest.

REACHOUT.com
http://us.reachout.com/
ReachOut.com is a safe, supportive place where teenagers and young adults can find resources and share real stores about how they got through a tough time.

Suicide.org: Suicide Hotlines
http://www.suicide.org/suicide-hotlines.html
Provides a list of suicide hotline phone numbers by state.

Youth America Hotline
www.youthline.us
1-877-YOUTHLINE (968-8454)
Hours: 24-hour support.

REFERENCES

Ackerman, G. L. (1993). A congressional view of youth suicide. *American Psychologist, 48*, 183–184.

American Academy of Child and Adolescent Psychiatry. (2001). Practice parameter for the assessment and treatment of children and adolescents with suicidal behavior. *Journal of the American Academy of Child & Adolescent Psychiatry, 40*(7 Supplement), 24S–51S.

American Academy of Child and Adolescent Psychiatry. (2008a). *Facts for families: The teen brain: Behavior, problem solving, and decision making.* Retrieved December 8, 2011, from http://www.aacap.org/cs/root/facts_for_families/facts_for_families.

American Academy of Child and Adolescent Psychiatry. (2008b). *Facts for families: Teen suicide.* Retrieved December 8, 2011, from http://www.aacap.org/cs/root/facts_for_families/facts_for_families.

Ballard, E. D., Bosk, A., Snyder, D., Pao, M., Bridge, J. A., Wharff, E. A., Teach, S. J., & Horowitz, L. (in press). Patients' opinions about suicide screening in a pediatric emergency department. *Pediatric Emergency Care.*

Bearman, P. S., & Moody, J. (2004). Suicide and friendships among American adolescents. *American Journal of Public Health, 94*, 89–95.

Beautrais, A. (2003). Life course factors associated with suicidal behaviors in young people. *American Behavioral Scientist, 46*, 1137–1156.

Berman, A. L., Jobes, D. A., & Silverman, M. M. (2006). *Adolescent suicide: Assessment and intervention* (2nd ed.). Washington, DC: American Psychological Association.

Boehm, K. E., & Campbell, N. B. (1995). Suicide: A review of calls to an adolescent peer listening phone service. *Child Psychiatry & Human Development, 26*, 61–66.

Bolling, D. Z., Pitskel, N. B., Deen, B., Crowley, M. J., Mayes, L. C., & Pelphrey, K. A. (2011). Development of neural systems for processing social exclusion from childhood to adolescence. *Developmental Science, 14*, 1431–1444.

Brent, D. A., Baugher, M., Bridge, J., Chen, T., & Chiappetta, L. (1999). Age- and sex-related risk factors for adolescent suicide. *Journal of the American Academy of Child & Adolescent Psychiatry, 38*, 1497–1505.

Brent, D. A., Perper, J., Moritz, G., Baugher, M., & Allman, C. (1993). Suicide in adolescents with no apparent psychopathology. *Journal of the American Academy of Child & Adolescent Psychiatry, 32*, 494–500.

Brent, D. A., Perper, J. A., Moritz, G., Baugher, M., Roth, C., Balach, L., & Schweers J. (1993). Stressful life events, psychopathology, and adolescent suicide: A case control study. *Suicide & Life-Threatening Behavior, 23*, 179–187.

Cash, S. K., & Bridge, J. A. (2009). Epidemiology of youth suicide and suicidal behavior. *Current Opinion in Pediatrics, 21*, 613–619.

Centers for Disease Control and Prevention (CDC). (2010). Youth Risk Behavior Surveillance – United States, 2009. *Morbidity and Mortality Weekly Report: Surveillance Summaries, 59*(No. SS-5), 1–148.

Chein, J., Albert, D., O'Brien, L., Uckert, K., & Steinberg, L. (2011). Peers increase adolescent risk taking by enhancing activity in the brain's reward circuitry. *Developmental Science, 14*(2), F1–F10.

Committee on Adolescents: American Academy of Pediatrics. (2000). Suicide and suicide attempts in adolescents. *Pediatrics, 105*(4 Pt 1), 871–874.

Coombs, D. W., Miller, H. L., Alarcon, R. D., Herlihy, C., Lee, J. M., & Morrison, D. P. (1992). Presuicide attempt communications between parasuicides and consulted caregivers. *Suicide & Life-Threatening Behavior, 22*, 289–302.

Crawford, M. J., Thana, L., Methuen, C., Ghosh, P., Stanle, S. V., Ross, J., Gordon, F., Blair, G., & Bajaj, P. (2011). Impact of screening for risk of suicide: Randomized controlled trial. *British Journal of Psychiatry, 198*, 379–384.

David-Ferdon, C., & Hertz, M. F. (2007). Electronic media, violence, and adolescents: An emerging public health problem. *Journal of Adolescent Health, 41*(6 Suppl 1), S1–S5.

de Anda, D., & Smith, M. A. (1993). Differences among adolescent, young adult, and adult callers of suicide help lines. *Social Work, 38*, 421–428.

Dolan, F. B. (1991). A student needs assessment survey: Discovering what students want from their school counselor. *Guidance & Counselling, 7*, 56–60.

Edmiston, E. E., Wang, F., Mazure, C. M., Guiney, J., Sinha, R., Mayes, L. C., & Blumberg, H. P. (2011). Corticostriatal-limbic gray matter morphology in adolescents with self-reported exposure to childhood maltreatment. *Archives of Pediatrics & Adolescent Medicine, 165*, 1069–1077.

Erikson, E. (1950). *Childhood and society.* New York: Norton.

Frankenfield, D., Keyl, P., Gielen, A., Wissow, L., Werthamer, L., & Baker, S. (2000). Adolescent patients – healthy or hurting: Missed opportunities to screen for suicide risk in the primary care setting. *Archives of Pediatrics & Adolescent Medicine, 154*, 162–168.

Franklin, J. L., Comstock, B. S., Simmons, J. T., & Mason, M. (1989). Characteristics of suicide prevention/intervention programs: Analysis of a survey. In *Alcohol, Drug Abuse, and Mental Health Administration, Report of the Secretary's Task Force on Youth Suicide: Vol. 3. Prevention and interventions in youth suicide* (DHHS Publication No. ADM 89-1623, pp. 93–102). Washington, DC: U.S. Government Printing Office.

Frederick, C. J. (1985). An introduction and overview of youth suicide. In M. L. Peck, N. L. Farberow, & R. E. Litman (Eds.), *Youth suicide*, pp. 1–16. New York: Springer.

Galambos, N. L., & Leadbeater, B. J. (2000). Trends in adolescent research for the new millennium. *International Journal of Behavioral Development, 24*, 289–294.

Giedd, J. N., Blumenthal, J., Jeffries, N. O., Castellanos, F. X., Liu, H., Zijdenbos, A., Paus, T., Evans, A. C., & Rapoport, J. L. (1999). Brain development during childhood and adolescence: A longitudinal MRI study. *Nature Neuroscience 2*, 861–863.

Gogtay, N., Giedd, J. N., Lusk, L., Hayashi, K. M., Greenstein, D., Vaituzis, A. C., Nugent III, T. F., Herman, D. H., Clasen, L. S., Toga, A. W., Rapoport, J. L., & Thompson, P. M. (2004). Dynamic mapping of human cortical development during childhood through early adulthood. *Proceedings of the National Academy of Sciences, 101*, 8174–8179.

Gogtay, N., & Thompson, P. M. (2010). Mapping gray matter development: Implications for typical development and vulnerability to psychopathology. *Brain & Cognition, 72*, 6–15.

Goldston, D. B. (2000). *Assessment of suicidal behaviors and risk among children and adolescents.* Technical report submitted to NIMH under Contract No. 263-MD-909995. Retrieved December 1, 2011 from http://www.suicidology.org/c/document_library/get_file?folderId=235&name=DLFE-141.pdf.

Gothelf, D., Apter, A., Brand Gothelf, A., Offer N., Ofek, H., Tyano, S., & Pfeffer, C. R. (1998). Death concepts in suicidal adolescents. *Journal of the American Academy of Child & Adolescent Psychiatry, 37*, 1279–1286.

Gould, M. S., Greenberg, T., Munfakh, J. L. H., Kleinman, M., & Lubell, K. (2006). Teenagers' attitudes about seeking help from telephone crisis services (hotlines). *Suicide & Life-Threatening Behavior, 36*, 601–613.

Gould, M. S., Greenberg, T., Velting, D. M., & Shaffer, D. (2003). Youth suicide risk and preventive interventions: A review of the past 10 years. *Journal of the American Academy of Child & Adolescent Psychiatry, 42*, 386–405.

Gould, M. S., & Kramer, R. A. (2001). Youth suicide prevention. *Suicide & Life-Threatening Behavior, 31*(Suppl), 6–31.

Gould, M. S., Marrocco, F. A., Kleinman, M., Thomas, J. G., Mostkoff, K., Cote, J., & Davies, M. (2005). Evaluating iatrogenic risk of youth suicide screening programs: A randomized controlled trial. *Journal of the American Medical Association, 293*, 1635–1643.

Gould, M. S., Munfakh, J. L., Lubell, K., Kleinman, M., & Parker, S. (2002). Seeking help from the Internet during adolescence. *Journal of the American Academy of Child & Adolescent Psychiatry, 41*, 1182–1189.

Hallfors, D. D., Waller, M. W., Bauer, D., Ford, C. A., & Halpern, C. T. (2005). Which comes first in adolescence – sex and drugs or depression? *American Journal of Preventive Medicine, 29*, 163–170.

Hallfors, D. D., Waller, M. W., Ford, C. A., Halpern, C. T., Brodish, P. H., & Iritani, B. (2004). Adolescent depression and suicide risk: Association with sex and drug behavior. *American Journal of Preventive Medicine, 27*, 224–231.

Holinger, P. C. (1979). Violent deaths among the young: Recent trends in suicide, homicide, and accidents. *American Journal of Psychiatry, 136*, 1144–1147.

Huff, C. O. (1999). Source, recency, and degree of stress in adolescence and suicide ideation. *Adolescence, 34*, 81–89.

Jacobsen, L. K., Rabinowitz, I., Popper, M., Solomon, R. J., Sokol, M. S., & Pfeffer, C. R. (1994). Interviewing prepubertal children about suicidal ideation and behavior. *Journal of the American Academy of Child & Adolescent Psychiatry, 33*, 439–452.

Joiner, T., Kalafat, J., Draper, J., Stokes, H., Knudson, M., Berman, A. L., & McKeon, R. (2007). Establishing standards for the assessment of suicide risk among callers to the National Suicide Prevention Lifeline. *Suicide & Life-Threatening Behavior, 37*, 353–365.

King, G. D. (1977). An evaluation of the effectiveness of a telephone counseling center. *American Journal of Community Psychology, 5*, 75–83.

King, R., Nurcombe, B., Bickman, L., Hides, L., & Reid, W. (2003). Telephone counseling for adolescent suicide prevention: Changes in suicidality and mental state from beginning to end of a counseling session. *Suicide & Life-Threatening Behavior, 33*, 400–411.

King, R. A., Ruchkin, V. V., & Schwab-Stone, M. E. (2003a). Suicide and the "continuum of adolescent self-destructiveness:" Is there a connection? In R. A. King & A. Apter (Eds.), *Suicide in children and adolescents*, pp. 41–62. Cambridge, UK: Cambridge University Press.

Lake, C. (2008). How academic psychiatry can better prepare students for their future patients. Part I: The failure to recognize depression and risk for suicide in primary care: Problem identification, responsibility, and solutions. *Behavioral Medicine, 34*, 95–100.

Lebel, C., & Beaulieu, C. (2011). Longitudinal development of human brain wiring continues from childhood into adulthood. *Journal of Neuroscience, 31*, 10937–10947.

Lenhart, A. (2010). *Cyberbullying: What the research is telling us.* Washington, DC: PEW Internet & American Life Project Youth Online Safety Working Group. Retrieved December 1, 2011, from http://www.slideshare.net/PewInternet/cyberbullying-2010-what-the-research-tells-us-4009451.

Lenhart, A., Hitlin, P., & Madden, M. (2007). *Teenagers and technology: Youth are leading the transition to a fully wired and mobile nation.* Washington, DC: Pew Internet & American Life Project. Retrieved December 1, 2011 from http://www.pewinternet.org/PPF/r/162/report_display.asp.

Lerner, R. M., & Galambos, N. L. (1998). Adolescent development: Challenges and opportunities for research, programs, and policies. *Annual Review of Psychology, 49*, 413–446.

Masten, C. L., Eisenberger, N. I., Borofsky, L. A., Pfeifer, J. H., McNealy, K., Mazziotta, J. C., & Dapretto, M. (2009). Neural correlates of social exclusion during adolescence: Understanding the distress of peer rejection. *Social Cognitive & Affective Neuroscience, 4*, 143–157.

Mathews, T. J., Miniño, A. M., Osterman, M. J., Strobino, D. M., & Guyer, B. (2011). Annual summary of vital statistics: 2008. *Pediatrics, 127*, 146–157.

Mitchell, K. J., & Ybarra, M. L. (2007). Online behavior of youth who engage in self-harm provides clues for preventive intervention. *Preventive Medicine, 45*, 392–396.

Mishara, B. L., Chagnon, F., Daigle, M., Balan, B., Raymond, S., Marcoux, I., Bardon, C., Campbell, J. K., & Berman, A. (2007). Comparing models of helper behavior to actual practice in telephone crisis intervention: A silent monitoring study of calls to the U.S. 1-800-SUICIDE network. *Suicide & Life-Threatening Behavior, 37*, 291–307.

Ozer, E., Zahnd, E., Adams, S., Husting, S. R., Wibbelsman, C. J., Norman, K. P., & Smiga, S. M. (2009). Are adolescents being screened for emotional distress in primary care? *Journal of Adolescent Health, 44*, 520–527.

Paus, T., Zijdenbos, A., Worsley, K., Collins, D. L., Blumenthal, J., Giedd, J. N., Rapoport, J. L., & Evans, A. C. (1999). Structural maturation of neural pathways in children and adolescents: In vivo study. *Science, 283*, 1908–1911.

Pfeffer, C. R. (2003). Assessing suicidal behavior in children and adolescents. In R. A. King & A. Apter (Eds.), *Suicide in children and adolescents*, pp. 211–226. Cambridge, UK: Cambridge University Press.

Pfeffer, C. R. (2001). Diagnosis of childhood and adolescent suicidal behavior: Unmet needs for suicide prevention. *Biological Psychiatry, 49*, 1055–1061.

Pfeffer, C. R. (1986). *The suicidal child.* New York: Guilford.

Piaget, J. (1952). *The origins of intelligence in children.* New York: International University Press.

Pompili, M., Mancinelli, I., Girardi, P., Ruberto, A., & Tatarelli, R. (2005). Childhood suicide: A major issue in pediatric health care. *Issues in Comprehensive Pediatric Nursing, 28*(1), 63–68.

Popenhagen, M. P., & Qualley, R. M. (1998). Adolescent suicide: Detection, intervention, and prevention. *Professional School Counseling, 1*(4), 30–36.

Radzik, M., Sherer, S., & Neinstein, L. S. (2002). Psychosocial development in normal adolescents. In L. S. Neinstein (Ed.), *Adolescent health care: A practical guide* (4th ed.), pp. 52–58. Philadelphia. Lippincott Williams & Wilkins.

Ramsden, S., Richardson, F. M., Josse, G., Thomas, M. S. C., Ellis, C., Shakeshaft, C., Seghier, M. L., & Price, C. J. (2011). Verbal and non-verbal intelligence changes in the teenage brain. *Nature, 479*, 113–116.

Resnick, M. D., Bearman, P. S., Blum, R. W., Bauman, K. E., Harris, K. M., Jones, J., Tabor, J., Beuhring, T., Sieving, R. E., Shew, M., Ireland, M., Bearinger, L. H., & Udry, J. R. (1997). Protecting adolescents from harm: Findings from the National Longitudinal Study on Adolescent Health. *Journal of the American Medical Association, 278*, 823–832.

Rutter, P. A., & Behrendt, A. E. (2004). Adolescent suicide risk: Four psychosocial factors. *Adolescence, 39*, 295–302.

Sebastian, C. L., Tan, G. C. Y., Roiser, J. P., Viding, E., Dumontheil, I., & Blakemore, S. J. (2011). Developmental influences on the neural bases of responses to social rejection: Implications of social neuroscience for education. *NeuroImage, 57*, 686–694.

Seibel, M., & Murray, J. N. (1988). Early prevention of adolescent suicide. *Educational Leadership, 45*(6), 48–50.

Shaffer, D., & Craft, L. (1999). Methods of adolescent suicide prevention. *Journal of Clinical Psychiatry, 60*(Suppl 2), 70–74.

Shaffer, D., Gould, M. S., Fisher, P., Trautman, P., Moreau, D., Kleinman, M., & Flory, M. (1996). Psychiatric diagnosis in child and adolescent suicide. *Archives of General Psychiatry, 53*, 339–348.

Shaw, P., Greenstein, D., Lerch, J., Clasen, L., Lenroot, R., Gogtay, N., Evans, A., Rapoport, J., & Giedd, J. (2006). Intellectual ability and cortical development in children and adolescents. *Nature, 440*, 676–679.

Silbereisen, R. K., & Todt, E. (1994). Adolescence: A matter of context. In R. K. Silbereisen & E. Todt (Eds.), *Adolescence in context: The interplay of family, school, peers, and work in adjustment*, pp. 3–21. New York: Springer-Verlag.

Simons-Morton, B. G., Ouimet, M. C., Zhang, Z., Klauer, S. E., Lee, S. E., Wang, J., Chen, R., Albert, P., & Dingus, T. A. (2011). The effect of passengers and risk-taking friends on risky driving and crashes/near crashes among novice teenagers. *Journal of Adolescent Health, 49*, 587–593.

Slem, C. M., & Cotler, S. (1973). Crisis phone services: evaluation of a hotline program. *American Journal of Community Psychology, 1*, 219–227.

Society for Neuroscience: Advancing the Understanding of the Brain and Nervous Systems. (2011). *Brain briefings: The adolescent brain*. Retrieved December 8, 2011, from http://www.sfn.org/index.aspx?pagename=brainBriefings_Adolescent_brain.

Sowell, E. R., Thompson, P. M., Holmes, C. J., Jernigan, T. L., & Toga, A. W. (1999). In vivo evidence for post-adolescent brain maturation in frontal and striatal regions. *Nature Neuroscience, 2*, 859–861.

Spear, L. P. (2000). Neurobehavioral changes in adolescence. *Current Directions in Psychological Science, 9*(4), 111–114.

Taliaferro, L. A., & Borowsky, W. (2011). Physician education: A promising strategy to prevent adolescent suicide. *Academic Medicine, 86*, 342–347.

Thompson, P. M., Giedd, J. N., Woods, R. P., MacDonald, D., Evans, A. C., & Toga, A. W. (2000). Growth patterns in the developing brain detected by using continuum mechanical tensor maps. *Nature, 404*, 190–193.

Thompson, M. P., & Light, L. S. (2011). Examining gender differences in risk factors for suicide attempts made 1 and 7 years later in a nationally representative sample. *Journal of Adolescent Health, 48*, 391–397.

Toumbourou, J. W., & Gregg, M. E. (2002). Impact of an empowerment-based parent education program on the reduction of youth suicide risk factors. *Journal of Adolescent Health, 31*, 277–285.

Waldvogel, J. L., Rueter, M., & Oberg, C. N. (2008). Adolescent suicide: Risk factors and prevention strategies. *Current Problems in Pediatric & Adolescent Health Care, 38*(4), 110–125.

Weller, E. B., Young, K. M., Rohrbaugh, A. H., & Weller, R. A. (2001). Overview and assessment of the suicidal child. *Depression & Anxiety, 14*, 157–163.

Wilson, K. G., Stelzer, J., Bergman, J. N., Kral, M. J., Inayatullah, M., & Elliot, C. A. (1995). Problem solving, stress, and coping in adolescent suicide attempts. *Suicide & Life-Threatening Behavior, 25*, 241–252.

Ybarra, M. L., Alexander, C., & Mitchell, K. J. (2005). Depressive symptomatology, youth Internet use, and online interactions: A national survey. *Journal of Adolescent Health, 36*, 9–18.

Chapter 21

WAR VETERANS

Karolina Krysinska and Karl Andriessen

The experience of war leaves no one unchanged, and active duty military members, war veterans and their families have to cope with serious stressors. Paradoxically, a soldier who is well trained for active duty and effective functioning in the war zone is often unprepared for homecoming. In the words of Friedman (2006), "military returnees face several psychological challenges, including the shift away from an adaptive, continuous, combat-ready, hypervigilent state. After many months of deployment to a war zone in which the threat to life and limb is continually reinforced by surprise attacks, direct assaults, deaths of colleagues, inadvertent civilian casualties, and narrow escapes, it can be quite difficult to settle quickly into quiet domesticity" (p. 587).

A homecoming veteran might face additional challenges. For example, a soldier trained to be strong and courageous, and who has managed to survive in a war zone, may experience emotional and psychological problems after returning home. In such situations, recognizing the need for help and seeking it may be easily interpreted as a sign of weakness, a serious barrier to seeking support and help. This chapter presents the common mental health problems and challenges faced by returning veterans, with a special focus on the returnees of two latest military operations: Operation Enduring Freedom (OEF) in Afghanistan and Operation Iraqi Freedom (OIF). It presents also an overview of online mental health resources available for veterans and their families.

The United States War Veteran Population

At the end of September 2011, there were 22.2 million total living veterans in the United States (US GAO, 2011). This number includes veterans of the

World War II (1.7 million), Korea (2.3 million), Vietnam (7.4 million), the Persian Gulf War (3.3 million), OEF/OIF (2.6 million), and peacetime operations (5.7 million). Although veterans of all eras share the war trauma experience, the United States troops deployed as part of the OEF/OIF operations since October 2001 comprise a special population (Tanielian et al., 2008; US GAO, 2011). They typically have intense and long deployments, frequent redeployments, and infrequent breaks between deployments. There is evidence showing that repeated deployments can have serious negative effect on the physical and mental health of the troops. A survey of National Guard members deployed to Iraq in 2008 showed that previously deployed soldiers were more likely to score below the general population norm on physical functioning and were more than twice as likely to report chronic pain (Kline et al., 2010). In comparison with soldiers never deployed before, they were more than three times as likely to show symptoms of post-traumatic stress disorder (PTSD) and major depression.

The troops engaged in OEF/OIF also experience war zone stressors relatively unknown in earlier armed conflicts, such as roadside bombs and other improvised explosive devices, including bombs attached to a moving vehicle, and suicide bombers. Table 21-1 presents the detailed rates of war trauma exposure among the Afghanistan and Iraq veterans (Schell & Marshall, 2008). In addition, advances in both body armor and medical technology have resulted in lower casualty rates than in earlier prolonged wars, such as in Korea and Vietnam, and the current ratio of 7:1 of wounded to killed is the lowest in history (Tanielian et al., 2008). The price for this high survival rate, however, is the high prevalence of physical and "invisible" psychological wounds, such as traumatic brain injury (TBI), PTSD, major depression, substance abuse, and high suicide risk (Schnurr et al., 2009). "Wounded soldiers who would have likely died in previous conflicts are instead saved, but with sig-

Table 21-1
RATES OF TRAUMA EXPOSURE IN SOLDIERS DEPLOYED TO OEF/OIF (SCHELL & MARSHALL, 2008)

Having a friend who was seriously wounded or killed	50%
Seeing dead or seriously injured noncombatants	45%
Witnessing an incident resulting in serious injury or death	45%
Smelling decomposing bodies	37%
Being physically moved or knocked over by an explosion	23%
Being injured, not requiring hospitalization	23%
Having a blow to the head from an incident or injury	18%
Being injured, requiring hospitalization	11%
Engaging in hand to hand combat	10%
Witnessing brutality towards detainees/prisoners	5%
Being responsible for the death of a civilian	5%

nificant physical, emotional, and cognitive injuries. Thus, caring for these wounded often requires an intensive mental-health component in addition to traditional rehabilitation services" (Tanielian et al., 2008; p. 6).

Veterans' Mental Health Problems and Mental Health Care

Between 2006 and 2010 about 2.1 million veterans received mental health care from VA in specialty mental health care, primary care clinics, and other settings employing mental health providers (US GAO, 2011). Given the intense and frequent deployments and high survival rates among the OEF/OIF veterans, it is not surprising that they account for a growing proportion of the recipients of VA mental health care. While in 2006 they comprised 4% of veterans receiving help, in 2010 this number increased to 12%. This rise can be related to both the high number of veterans with psychological "invisible wounds" and to changes in the VA mental health screening protocols, such as obligatory screening for a number of mental health conditions, such as PTSD, depression, substance abuse disorders, and military sexual trauma, in primary health care settings.

Adjustment reactions (including PTDS), depressive disorder, episodic mood disorder, neurotic disorder, and substance abuse disorder were the five most common diagnostic categories for veterans receiving mental health care in the VA in 2010 (US GAO, 2011). In general, veterans of all wars have similar diagnoses. However, important differences between eras have been noted. For example, the most common diagnostic category for all veterans (except for OEF/OIF) was depressive disorder closely followed by adjustment reaction. At the same time, almost twice as many veterans returning from Afghanistan and Iraq had adjustment reaction diagnoses, including PTSD, than the next most common diagnostic category – depressive disorder (US GAO, 2011).

High rates of three conditions seriously affecting the emotional, behavioral, and cognitive functioning of the OEF/OIF veterans and closely related to the war zone experiences were found in a study of soldiers previously deployed for OEF/OIF (Schell & Marshall, 2008). PTSD (a reaction to trauma) was diagnosed in 14% of those previously deployed, major depressive disorder and depressive symptoms (a possible reaction to loss) found in 14% of the veterans, and TBI (a consequence of exposure to a blast) found in 19% of the returnees. About one-third of the veterans had at least one of these three conditions, and about 5% reported symptoms of all three. Although the prevalence of PTSD and other mental health problems is much higher among veterans than in the general population, it has been speculated that these numbers are actually underestimations (Marx, 2009). Military personnel and veterans suffering from PTSD and other mental health difficulties might be reticent to disclose their problems as they fear removal from military duties, undermining the military (or civil) career prospects, and delay in returning home.

Another point of concern in relation to veterans returning from Afghanistan and Iraq is the high suicide risk in this group (Bruce, 2010; Kang & Bullman, 2009). Historically, suicide rates among veterans in general have been equal to or lower than that of the United States general population. For example, the crude annual suicide rates among veterans of the Vietnam War and the Gulf War have been between 15.3 and 25.5 per 100,000 per year with comparable rates in the general population between 20 and 24 (Kang & Bullman, 2009). However, the veterans of OEF/OIF have a risk for suicide equal to that of the general United States population, and active duty OEF/OIF veterans have a risk for suicide 33% greater than the general population (Kang & Bullman, 2008).

While serving in an armed conflict is not a suicide risk factor by itself, high levels of combat and war trauma exposure, surviving with an injury or a psychiatric condition, and the availability and knowledge of firearms are suicide risk factors among veterans (Bruce, 2010; Maguen et al., 2011; Pietrzak et al., 2010). Post-deployment readjustment problems, especially marital and financial stress, perceived barriers to care, low resilience, and low levels of social support have also been linked to suicidal ideation in soldiers returning from the war zone (Kline et al., 2011; Pietrzak et al., 2010).

Common Themes and Adjustment Problems

The experience of war leaves no one unchanged, and many of the returning veterans face a number of problems and challenges. However, it should be stressed that, besides several common themes which will be discussed in this section, the war zone and post-deployment experiences of each returning soldier are unique, and the psychosocial needs of every returning veteran should be assessed and addressed individually.

The Emotional Cycle of Deployment

Active duty service members, veterans, and their families go through an "emotional cycle of deployment" including reactions and adjustment tasks related to pre-deployment, deployment and post-deployment (Slone & Friedman, 2008). Pre-deployment is the period between receiving the deployment orders and the day of leaving for the post. It is usually filled with anticipation of departure (and sometimes excitement), frequently mixed with anxiety and distress about the upcoming separation from the family. In case of redeployment, the typical pre-deployment reactions might become even more complicated and difficult to cope with as memories and traumatic experiences from the time spent earlier in the war zone might resurface.

Deployment is the period of 30 continuous days or longer in a land-based location outside the United States. Despite previous training, the first month in the war zone may be particularly difficult as it involves confrontation with new routines and duties in a foreign location with its particular culture, landscape, and climate. Although the troops do adjust to the situation, the extreme stress and hypervigilance do not cease during later months. In such extreme and life-threatening conditions, soldiers establish strong bonds with each other, and "the combat unit becomes a new family in which members depend on each other for physical protection and emotional support" (Slone & Friedman, 2008, p. 10). The last months of deployment are marked by excitement and anticipation, often mixed with anxiety about what will happen after the return, the changed family situation (e.g., birth of a child), or problems preceding the deployment, such as workplace problems or marital discord.

The last element in the emotional cycle of deployment is post-deployment, the period of six to 12 months after returning home from war. Although coming back home means having survived the war and being reunited with family and friends, it is also a period of readjustment to a different lifestyle and environment. The first days and weeks after returning home might be a very positive experience (a "honeymoon period"), often followed by a difficult period of reintegration and readjustment to the family life and the reality outside the war zone. A study of National Guard troops deployed for Iraq (Kline et al., 2011) showed that nearly half of the returnees experienced at least one marital or financial/employment stressor three months after returning home, and these two types of problems were intercorrelated. Marital problems were reported by 34% of married soldiers, and 17% decided to divorce or separate. (The percentages were higher for females than for males.) In addition, 15% of returned troops had serious financial problems, 7% had problems paying their mortgage, and the total unemployment rate in this group increased from 13% to 41%.

The Myths of Homecoming

Slone and Friedman (2008) have described four frequent "homecoming myths," a potential source of stress and conflict for returning veterans and their environment.

Myth 1: My relation with my partner and family will be the same when I get home from war.
Myth 2: My life will be the same as it was before I left for war.

The months spent in the war zone change homecoming veterans. In order to effectively fulfill their duties and to survive, the soldiers have to adopt a special mindset described by the acronym "BATTLEMIND" (Slone & Friedman, 2008). Each letter stands for a particular skill, behavior or attitude expected from the soldiers in the military environment which can become a source of problems of conflicts once reunited with family and in a civilian environment (Table 21-2).

Table 21-2
BATTLEMIND

Skills Related to Survival in the War Zone	Problems Which Might Arise After Returning Home
Buddies (Cohesion)	Withdrawal
Accountability	Controlling
Targeted Aggression	Inappropriate Aggression
Tactical Awareness	Hypervigilance
Lethally Armed	Locked and Loaded
Emotional Control	Detachment
Mission Operational Security	Secretiveness
Individual Responsibility	Guilt
Nondefensive Driving	Aggressive Driving
Discipline and Ordering	Conflict

Soldiers forge strong interpersonal bonds and cohesion with others in their combat units, and the "buddies" become more than a family. Once back home, veterans might miss their war companions or might try to maintain close and exclusive relationships with them at the expense of family and friends. Soldiers' accountability for their weapons and gear, actions, and fellow comrades, as well as adhering to strict discipline and following the chain of command, might evolve into excessive control and conflict back home and an inability to engage in open communication. Individual responsibility for actions in the war zone, including responsibility for one's own life and the life of one's comrades, might lead to survivor guilt and (excessive) guilt for what has happened and for comrades who were wounded or killed in action. Being involved in or exposed to the atrocities of war, including hand-to-hand combat, killing civilians (including women, children, and the elderly) and witnessing carnage, might be other sources of guilt and moral dilemmas. Some veterans use self-medication with alcohol or drugs as a way of escaping the unbearable guilt. Sometimes the guilt has religious connotations and is related to the feeling of having committed a sin and being abandoned by God or being punished by God (Friedman, 2006; Slone & Friedman, 2008).

Soldiers in the war zone always have to be ready for action, forceful, aggressive, and aware of what is happening in their environment. This high level of arousal, aggression, and anger might be difficult to control outside the military environment and lead to risky behaviors, assaults, arguments, and domestic violence. The "tactical awareness" might evolve into hypervigilance, excessive concern for their own safety and the safety of their loved ones. Many veterans experience an "adrenaline train" after returning from the military mission and seek out highly paced or dangerous situations and activities, such as extreme sports, playing violent video games, and buying a new motorcycle or a high-speed boat. In addition, homecoming veterans are used to constantly carrying a weapon (mandatory and necessary in the war zone) without which they may feel vulnerable and unsafe. Having a weapon at home and carrying it around might become a source of stress and concern for the family members (Friedman, 2006; Slone & Friedman, 2008).

Emotional control and not showing any sign of weakness in the war zone might lead to emotional detachment from family members after returning from war. Effective functioning in the war zone requires mission operational security and not talking about the soldier's tasks and experiences. Back home, this might lead to secretiveness, an unwillingness to share the war experiences, and irritation or anger at those who ask questions. Last but not least, the soldiers in the war zone are required to drive in a deliberate and unpredictable manner, full speed ahead to avoid roadside bombs and other explosive devices, including car bombs. In a nonmilitary environment, such nondefensive driving becomes aggressive, unsafe, and irresponsible driving (Friedman, 2006; Slone & Friedman, 2008).

The months of separation, the adoption of BATTLEMIND, and war experiences change soldiers. However, the soldier's family members and their roles do not stay the same during the months of deployment. A partner staying home (usually a woman) becomes a "single parent" and the head of the family who has to take care of the children, finances, and everyday routines. A birth of a child or death of a family member changes the family situation. Returning back home, where things are not the same as they used to be, and renegotiating the family roles might be a challenging task for a veteran (Friedman, 2006; Slone & Friedman, 2008).

Myth 3: All I need is the love and support of my family to get through any post-deployment difficulties.

Friedman (2006) has pointed out that "different individuals manage their passage from the war zone to the home front with various degrees of success. Some accomplish this transition within weeks. Others require more time and, possibly, some assistance. A significant minority fail completely. In other words, readjustment is a complicated process with no clear demarcation points and no consistent time course" (p. 588). Table 21-3 presents "war zone stress reactions" or "combat stress reactions" that are typical psychological, physical, emotional, and interpersonal reactions of veterans retuning home (Slone & Friedman, 2008).

Table 21-3
WAR ZONE STRESS REACTIONS (SLONE & FRIEDMAN, 2008)

Physical reactions and reactions affecting daily activities
- Sleep problems, tiredness
- Stomach and eating problems
- Headaches and sweating when thinking of war
- Nightmares, bad dreams
- Rapid heartbeat or breathing
- Lack of exercise, poor diet, or health care
- Existing health problems becoming worse

Reactions affecting behavior
- Concentration problems
- Jumpy and easily startled
- Hypervigilance
- Excessive smoking, drinking, drug use
- Flashbacks, frequent unwanted memories
- Avoidance of people or places related to the trauma
- Problems with regular tasks at work or school

Emotional reactions
- Anger or irritability
- Experiencing shock, numbness, inability to be happy
- Nervousness, helplessness, or fearfulness
- Sadness, guilt, feeling rejected or abandoned
- Edginess, easily upset or annoyed
- Hopelessness about the future

Reactions affecting relationships
- Withdrawal, detachment, or disconnection
- Emotional shutdown leading to loss of intimacy
- Interpersonal mistrust
- Overprotective or overcontrolling
- Interpersonal conflicts

Given supportive family environment and good communication, many returnees manage to successfully adjust to their family and work situation, and the post-deployment reactions disappear within six to eight weeks. For others, especially veterans who have sustained a physical injury or a handicap and those with PTSD, depression or TBI, the adjustment process may be very difficult and even impossible without professional assistance. There are "red flags" which indicate clinically significant problems in the readjustment trajectory and the need for professional help (Friedman, 2006; Slone & Friedman, 2008). These include anger or aggressive behavior (such as assaults, domestic violence, or threats of harm to others), signs of depression (including self-blame, guilt, shame, and significant changes in mood and behavior), suicidal thoughts or threats of self-harm, and alcohol or drug abuse.

Indentifying the "red flags" and the need for help does not automatically result in seeking or getting support (US GAO, 2011). Many veterans see the need for help as a sign of weakness and loss of control incompatible with the self-image of being strong and the returning "head of the family." The stigma surrounding mental health issues and negative stereotypes of mental health services might hinder veterans of all ages from seeking help, but they may be particularly pertinent to the veterans of World War II and Korea who grew up in a society that considered mental health issues to be a taboo topic. Others, especially Reservists and National Guard members might be concerned about privacy and confidentiality issues and fear that getting professional help might undermine their military or civilian career prospects. Others might distrust mental health services or fear that the mental health providers will not be able to understand their war experiences or believe their stories. They may think that their mental health problems are not severe enough to warrant seeking help or think that such services should be reserved for those most in need and for older veterans. Additionally, young veterans may have other duties and concerns, such as family, school, or work, which make accessing care a lesser priority. Female veterans may face additional barriers to seeking mental health care as they may perceive it as male-oriented or they may not identify themselves as veterans if they did not serve directly in combat. Last but not least, veterans living in rural locations may face serious distance and transportation problems making it impossible to reach mental health services.

Myth 4: Every returning service member wants a large welcoming party.

Although the relieved and happy families and friends often plan a special event to honor the returning soldier, many returnees need personal space, peace and quiet to adjust to the new situation and life outside the war zone (Slone & Friedman, 2008).

Online Psychological Help and Crisis Intervention for War Veterans

The veterans and their families often face serious adjustment challenges in the post-deployment period. The prevalence of post-traumatic stress disorder, traumatic brain injury, depression, substance abuse, suicidality, and other mental health problems is relatively high among the returnees. Many veterans do not need organized help, and time and support of family and friends are sufficient to adjust to life after the war zone. Others struggle hard and might need additional assistance. As discussed earlier, there are many barriers to seeking mental health support, from stigma and taboo to concerns about confidentiality and limited access to resources, especially in cases of veterans living in the rural areas. One of the ways to overcome at least some of these barriers and to meet the needs of those who need help is to offer anonymous telephone and online help free of charge. The US Department of Veteran Affairs and other professional bodies concerned with the well-being of the active military members, veterans, and their families have developed a wide range of resources offering such help. Several of the online nation-wide available resources are presented below.

The Veterans Crisis Line (1-800-273-8255 [TALK], Press 1), previously the National Veterans Suicide Prevention Hotline, was established in 2007 as a part of VA's Suicide Prevention Program. It is a partnership between the VA, the Substance Abuse and Mental Health Services Administration, and the National Suicide Prevention Lifeline. Veterans and their families can receive free and confidential help for problems such as emotional support, crisis and emergency interventions, and referrals to local VA mental health services from trained counselors (many of whom are veterans themselves) 24 hours a day, 7 days a week. Since 2009, the Veterans Crisis Line has been operating online chat services available on its website (www.veteranscrisisline.net). In addition to the online chat, the website offers a self-check quiz regarding signs of stress and depression, a resource locator, links to military specific mental health websites and general mental health and suicide prevention organizations. Since its beginning the Veterans Crisis Line has answered over 500,000 calls and had 28,000 chats with active duty military members, veterans, their family members, and friends (US GAO, 2011).

The US Department of Veterans Affairs general website (www.va.gov) presents information about the VA and services provided by the government to the veterans and their families. It includes a website on mental health issues (www.mentalhealth.va.gov) with information about mental health and well-being, including resources on PTSD, TBI, depression, substance abuse, and suicide risk and prevention. There is also a link to the Veterans Crisis Line, where telephone and online chat support is available 24/7.

The Defense Centers of Excellence for Psychological Health and Traumatic Brain Injury (DCoE) was established in 2007 as collaboration between the Department of Veterans Affairs, civilian agencies, community and advocacy groups, academic institutions, and clinical experts. It aims "to integrate knowledge and identify, evaluate and disseminate evidence-based practices and standards for the treatment of psychological health and TBI within the Defense Department" and "works across the entire continuum of care to promote resilience, rehabilitation and reintegration for warriors, families and veterans with psychological health concerns and traumatic brain injuries." The DCoE website contains information and resources for the military, their families, health professionals, and the media. These include a 24/7 outreach center for service members, veterans, and their families and friends, where professional health consultants provide information on psychological health and traumatic brain injury by phone, e-mail, or online chat free of charge.

The DCoE has launched the Real Warriors Campaign (www.realwarriors.net) and the After Deployment Project (www.afterdeployment.org). The Real Warriors Campaign is an initiative to encourage help-seeking and enhance reintegration of returning service members and veterans with post-traumatic stress and TBI, and their families. Among the campaign materials are real life stories of service members who have successfully sought treatment and who maintain successful military or civilian careers. The After Deployment Project provides information and self-help resources for service members and veterans coping with PTSD, depression, and other mental health issues, as well as for their families. Among the resources are self-assessment tools for a range of mental health problems, including PTSD, depression, anxiety and panic, substance abuse, and sleep problems, and an online workshop on controlling the use of alcohol and drugs.

Make the Connection (maketheconnection.net) is a public awareness campaign launched by the US Department of Veterans Affairs, targeted at veterans and their families, encouraging them to learn about challenging life events, physical and mental health symptoms, and available resources and support. It is based on personal stories and testimonials of both male and female veterans, and the website offers online self-assessment tools for depression, PTSD, alcohol and substance abuse, online information about a range of mental health issues pertinent to veterans, and links to relevant organizations.

The National Alliance on Mental Illness (NAMI), the largest grassroots mental health organization in the US, is operating the Veterans Resources Center online (www.nami.org/template.cfm?section=Veterans_Resources). The website includes a range of online resources, including information on mental health issues, such as PTSD, TBI, and suicide risk, links to other relevant websites, and access to several online discussion groups. The latter include a veterans' forum and an online discussion group focused on living with PTSD.

Conclusion

Homecoming troops and their families face a difficult task of readjustment after the deployment. Veterans of all eras have been exposed to the atrocities of war, risked their lives, and seen their buddies wounded or dying. Some of them have returned from the war zone seriously injured or handicapped, suffering from survivor guilt and other psychological sequelae of the war trauma which has made them vulnerable to suicide, alcohol and drug abuse, social withdrawal, aggression, and other psychological problems. There is evidence showing that veterans of the latest military conflicts in Afghanistan and Iraq run a particularly high risk of post-traumatic stress disorder, traumatic brain injury, and suicide, be it due to the high survival rate of the wounded, the high intensity of deployments, or improved screening and diagnosis of mental health problems.

Not every veteran is ready to admit that there are problems after coming back home, and there are numerous barriers to seeking, asking for, and getting help. The online resources presented in this chapter give some insight into what the veterans and their loved ones can find on the Internet. Although online help is not a panacea for all problems and barriers to help seeking, it has many advantages and unique opportunities. It is usually free of charge, available 24/7, anonymous, and confidential. Many organizations, such as the Veterans Crisis Line, employ veterans as paid staff or volunteers to decrease the threshold for seeking help, and others, such as the Real Warriors Campaign, work with successfully readjusted veterans who serve as role models. Other campaigns, such as Make the Connection, encourage the military and their families to seek help. In the words of Slone and Freedman (2008), "getting assistance from others is sometimes not only the best but actually the *only* way to improve [the veterans'] life and the life of [their] loved ones" (p. 137).

REFERENCES

Bruce, M. L. (2010). Suicide risk and prevention in veteran populations. *Annals of the New York Academy of Sciences, 1208*, 98–103.

Friedman, M. J. (2006). Posttraumatic stress disorder among military returnees from Afghanistan and Iraq. *American Journal of Psychiatry, 163*, 4, 586–593.

Kang, H. K., & Bullman, T. A. (2009). Is there an epidemic of suicides among current and former US military personnel? *Annals of Epidemiology, 19*, 757–760.

Kline, A., Ciccone, D. S., Falca-Dodson, M., Black, C. M., & Losonczy, M. (2011). Suicidal ideation among National Guard troops deployed to Iraq: The association with postdeployment readjustment problems. *Journal of Nervous & Mental Disease, 199*, 914–920.

Kline, A., Falca-Dodson, M., Sussner, B., Ciccone, D. S., Chandler, H., Callahan, L., & Losonczy, M. (2010). Effects of repeated deployment to Iraq and Afghanistan on the health of New Jersey Army National Guard Troops: Implications for military readiness. *American Journal of Public Health, 100*, 276–283.

Maguen, S., Luxton, D. D., Skopp, N. A., Gahm, G. A., Reger, M. A., Metzler, T. J., & Marmar, C. R. (2011). Killing in combat, mental health symptoms, and suicidal ideation in Iraq war veterans. *Journal of Anxiety Disorders, 25*, 563–567.

Marx, B. P. (2009). Posttraumatic stress disorder and Operations Enduring Freedom and Iraqi Freedom: Progress in a time of controversy. *Clinical Psychology Review, 29*, 671–673.

Pietrzak, R. H., Goldstein, M. B., Malley, J. C., Rivers, A. J., Johnson, D. C., & Southwick, S. M. (2010). Risk and protective factors associated with suicidal ideation in veterans of Operations Enduring Freedom and Iraqi Freedom. *Journal of Affective Disorders, 123*, 102–107.

Schell, T. L., & Marshall, G. N. (2008), Survey of individuals previously deployed for OEF/OIF. In T. Tanielian & L. H. Jaycox (Eds.), *Invisible wounds of war: Psychological and cognitive injuries, their consequences, and services to assist recovery*, pp. 87–115. Santa Monica, CA: RAND Corporation.

Schnurr, P. P., Lunney, C. A., Bovin, M. J., & Marx, B. (2009). Posttraumatic stress disorder and quality of life: Extension of findings to veterans of the wars in Iraq and Afganistan. *Clinical Psychology Review, 29*, 727–735.

Slone, L. B., & Friedman, M. J. (2008). *After the war zone. A practical guide for returning troops and their families*. Philadelphia: Da Capo Press.

Sollinger, J. M., Fisher, G., & Metscher, K. N. (2008). The wars in Afghanistan and Iraq: An overview. In T. Tanielian & L. H. Jaycox (Eds.), *Invisible wounds of war: Psychological and cognitive injuries, their consequences, and services to assist recovery*, pp. 19–31. Santa Monica, CA: RAND Corporation.

Tanielian, T., Jaycox, L. H., Adamson, D. M., & Metscher, K. N. (2008). Introduction. In T. Tanielian & L. H. Jaycox (Eds.), *Invisible wounds of war: Psychological and cognitive injuries, their consequences, and services to assist recovery*, pp. 3–17. Santa Monica, CA: RAND Corporation.

US Government Accountability Office (GAO). (2011). *VA Mental Health. Number of veterans receiving care, barriers faced, and efforts to increase access. Report to the Ranking Member, Committee on Veterans' Affairs, House of Representatives*. Retrieved December 15, 2011 from http://www.gao.gov/assets/590/585743.pdf.

Chapter 22

RURAL COMMUNITIES

Danielle R. Jahn

Rural areas present a variety of challenges to the provision of mental health services, as there are often few, if any, mental health professionals in these areas, and access to resources may be limited. In addition, stigma and some of the mindsets of rural dwellers can impede access to services. Telephone and online mental health interventions may provide a way to overcome some of these challenges. In this chapter, I review the characteristics of rural areas and rural dwellers that may create mental health difficulties and crises. I also discuss the difficulties inherent in providing mental health services in rural areas. Finally, I evaluate the positive and negative aspects of using telephone and online services for both crisis intervention and long-term mental health services in rural areas. These topics are augmented with research findings regarding mental health in rural areas and illustrated with case examples based on real cases (with some details changed to protect confidentiality).

Rural Communities and Rural dwellers

More than 20% of the United States population lives in rural areas (US Census Bureau, 2011), and rural dwelling persons live different lifestyles and face different challenges than those living in urban or suburban communities. These differences are particularly evident in terms of mental health issues and access to mental health services. For example, while there do not appear to be significant differences in the rates of depression and anxiety in rural versus urban dwellers, research consistently indicates that suicide rates are higher in rural areas than urban areas (Fiske et al., 2005; Hirsch, 2006). In addition, rural dwellers tend to have less access to mental health services than urban or suburban dwellers (Hirsch, 2006).

The characteristics of people who live in rural areas, as well as the characteristics of the rural areas, contribute to these differences (Judd et al., 2006). First, I examine characteristics of rural areas that may affect psychological health and access to mental health services. In recent years, rural populations have declined as jobs have moved to suburban and urban areas. Additionally, the rural population has aged, meaning that the average age of rural residents has become older because there has been a considerable reduction in the number of young people staying in rural areas (Judd et al., 2006). Much of this loss of population is due to the lack of jobs in rural areas. As weather affects agricultural prosperity and land values decline, there are few opportunities to obtain high-paying jobs in rural areas.

As people move away from rural communities for the aforementioned reasons and there is a downturn in the economy of rural areas, the infrastructures of these areas begin to deteriorate as well. For example, small businesses and hospitals may close, health professionals may be forced to move to suburban or urban areas to keep their practices financially viable, and schools may consolidate because of smaller populations in the areas that they serve. These changes (i.e., loss of services, lower incomes and reduced population), along with others, have led to greater distress in rural dwellers. Higher rates of psychological disorders and elevated suicide rates have also been associated with these types of changes in rural areas (Judd et al., 2006).

Many characteristics of rural dwellers may also increase need for mental health services and crisis intervention. Research has found that people in rural areas tend to drink more heavily, at levels that create risk for alcohol abuse and alcohol dependence (Judd et al., 2006). Substance use in and of itself is an important consideration for mental health providers and may also increase risk for other difficulties among rural residents. Research has linked problems resulting from alcohol use with suicide ideation in rural dwellers (Turvey et al., 2002). Other concerns include psychosocial and health issues. Rural dwellers generally have lower incomes than suburban or urban dwellers, and the aforementioned economic difficulties facing rural areas also mean that many rural dwellers are unemployed. Additionally, in rural areas, residents tend to have more health problems and are older on average than urban or suburban dwellers (Judd et al., 2006). Health concerns and older age have been linked to increased suicide risk in residents of rural areas (Hirsch, 2006).

Rural dwellers are also likely to have little social contact as the population is more dispersed in rural areas. In fact, research has linked smaller populations in rural communities, a measure of social isolation, to higher suicide rates (Hirsch, 2006). The research clearly links each of the previously mentioned issues to greater distress, psychological disorders, and higher risk for suicide in rural dwellers (Turvey et al., 2002) and may provide explanations for the high suicide rates in rural areas (Judd et al., 2006).

Another explanation for the high suicide rates may be that stigma against admitting to mental health difficulties is high, and there is substantial reluctance to seek professional help for psychological disorders in rural areas (Judd et al., 2006; Stark, 2008). This stigma may be linked to the lack of anonymity that exists in small rural communities (Stark, 2008). Because these communities are small, healthcare professionals may be engaged in multiple roles with their patients. For example, a doctor may be friends with his or her patients, may play on community sports teams with patients, may attend the same church as patients, or serve in community agencies with patients. Because of the high likelihood of interaction outside the traditional doctor-patient appointments in a medical office, rural dwellers may be reluctant to discuss mental health issues with their doctors. There may also be a concern that information shared will not be kept confidential. Even though physicians have an ethical obligation to keep patient information confidential, nurses, receptionists, billing specialists, pharmacists, cashiers at the pharmacy, and others may have access to charts, which include diagnoses and medication information. In small rural towns where everyone knows each other, this information may accidentally or intentionally be shared with others.

The stigma regarding mental health disorders may also be linked to some of the traditional beliefs that are often held in rural communities (Hirsch, 2006). In rural areas, value is placed on stereotypical masculinity, particularly for men (e.g., not asking for help, resolving problems without the input of others, and not showing pain or weakness [Judd et al., 2006]). Because relying only on oneself is held in high regard, rural dwellers may be hesitant to discuss their feelings and problems with a healthcare professional. This may be viewed as a sign of weakness and incompetence in rural communities, where people take pride in "pulling themselves up by their bootstraps." In addition, because of the agricultural lifestyle in many rural areas, people may ignore their mental health difficulties because they need to continue working. Agriculture does not provide the luxury of taking paid time off (Hirsch, 2006). Thus, rural dwellers may not see any value in sharing their feelings if they feel powerless to address them because of the demands placed on them by a rural or agricultural lifestyle. Finally, rural areas are often stereotypically viewed as peaceful and idyllic (Stark, 2008), and there is often a desire to reach this ideal. Mental health difficulties and hopelessness do not fit into this ideal. There may be concern that discussing difficulties will be detrimental to the idealized peace in a rural community and will disrupt the tranquil lifestyle that people expect in rural areas.

Another important consideration in rural communities is the lack of access to healthcare services. As mentioned previously, many small rural hospitals closed as the rural population declined and as the economies in rural areas have become depressed. While many rural dwellers utilize a primary care practitioner for health services, they access fewer emergency services or mental health services than suburban or urban dwellers, even though the prevalence of mental health disorders in rural areas is at least at high as the prevalence of such disorders in other areas (Judd et al., 2006). A qualitative study of older adult suicide in a rural community found that only one person out of six who died by suicide was receiving any type of mental health treatment prior to death (Finkel & Rosman, 1996). The lack of utilization of mental health service likely reflects an inability to access these services, as studies have shown that there are fewer mental health professionals per capita in rural areas than in other areas (Fiske et al., 2005).

In addition, primary care practitioners tend to prescribe fewer psychiatric medications and manage fewer psychological disorders in rural areas when compared to suburban and urban areas (Judd et al., 2006). In Finkel and Rosman's (1996) study, four of the six people who died by suicide had seen a primary care practitioner within two days prior to their deaths, and all had seen a primary care practitioner within six months prior to their deaths. Yet, none of the physicians anticipated the suicide deaths of these older adults. Collectively, these results potentially suggest that older adults in this rural community might not have communicated the severity of their issues with their primary care physicians, providing evidence for the points made previously. Another explanation for the lower rate of psychiatric medication prescriptions and psychiatric disorder management by primary care practitioners may be that the primary care practitioners do not recognize the need for such services or are not comfortable addressing these issues.

It is important to note that rural communities are heterogeneous, and the characteristics of rural areas differ greatly in terms of the community mindset, resources available, and access to healthcare. For example, research has shown that crisis services provided through a community mental health clinic in a rural area can be effective when such a clinic is available (Bonynge et al., 2005). In one study, a mental health clinic provided immediate appointments, a crisis hotline, and on-call mental health professionals for after-hours crises. In addition, residential beds were available for psychiatric needs, and a mobile mental health service was available that could go to homes in the community as needed. These services were utilized often and seemed to be effective responses to crises. The clients did not require long-term hospitalization and were able to reside in the community safely (Bonynge et al., 2005). Another study that evaluated an intervention to reduce suicide risk was conducted in a hospital in a rural area. In this case, funding was available to hire a full-time counselor specifically focused on intervening with suicidal rural dwellers, and a hospital existed in the rural community. This study found that the suicide intervention counselor was effective in ensuring follow-up for suicidal people and assisting with communication among the treatment team, community, hospital, and others (Aoun & Lavan, 1998). Thus, for rural communities with more resources, these types of interventions may be practical and effective. However, not all rural areas have mental health clinics, hospitals, or funding to implement these types of interventions. For such rural areas, telephone and online interventions may be more pragmatic and financially viable.

The Case of Jim

Many of the previously discussed issues are illustrated by the case of Jim, a 60-year-old man living in rural west Texas. Jim lived alone on a farm that he owned outside the limits of a small town. (The town had less than 500 residents.) At one point in the 1970s, the town had a population of nearly 1,000, but many people had moved away when the cotton processing plant, which brought a significant number of jobs into the community when it opened in the 1950s, closed in the early 1990s. As the population dropped, the local high school closed, and students were bussed to a town about 30 minutes away each day for school. In addition, the small urgent care clinic in the town closed, leaving a hospital over an hour away as the only option for emergency care. The town had never had a mental health professional working there, and only had two primary care physicians to serve the town and the surrounding areas. The town did not have a community center or other place for social gatherings. The only social events were those held in private homes among small groups of friends.

Jim's small cotton farm had not been doing well for a few years due to a drought and low selling prices. He was at risk of losing his farm and his home because he could not pay his bills. In addition, he was having difficulty managing his farm as he aged and as his health declined. He had no family members who could help him, nor could he afford to hire employees to help him with the daily maintenance and tasks associated with the farm. Jim recognized that he was feeling badly about his life. He felt alone and sad, and hopeless about his financial situation. In recent weeks, he had considered suicide more than once as a way to avoid losing his farm and home. He simply could not see anything positive occurring in his future. He also did not have anyone close to him in his life with whom to share his concerns. He did not want to talk to his doctor about his feelings because he and his doctor occasionally played poker together. He was concerned that he would be viewed as weak or judged badly for admitting that he was having mental health difficulties.

Jim had another concern that is relatively unique to rural areas. He was worried that if he told his doctor he was thinking about suicide, he would end up in jail. Because there was no longer a hospital or urgent care center in his community, if a doctor or police officer thought Jim was at risk for suicide and could not get a transport to the nearest hospital (which was over an hour away), he would be put in one of the two small jail cells at the police station for his safety until transport could be arranged. This was unthinkable to Jim. He was a law-abiding citizen who had never been in jail, and he refused to be put in jail just because he felt sad and hopeless. As Jim's hopelessness about his finances became worse, he felt more isolated and his suicidal thoughts became more frequent and intense. He could not see a way out of his situation and did not think he could talk to anyone about it. Finally, when he received a notice that his farm was being foreclosed on immediately, he lost all hope, went out to his barn, and shot himself. His body was eventually found by a friend after Jim did not show up for the monthly poker game in town.

Crisis Intervention Options

Jim's case, and the statistics discussed earlier, illustrate many of the biggest challenges to crisis intervention in rural areas. There is often a lack of access to mental health services in small rural towns. Stigma regarding mental health issues and lack of anonymity may create an unwillingness to share difficulties with primary care physicians. Yet, just as in suburban and urban areas, people in rural areas experience mental health crises, including suicide ideation, homicidal ideation, manic episodes, and psychotic symptoms. Given these issues, the use of telephone and online crisis intervention in rural areas is critical. Calling a hotline or chatting with a crisis responder through an online service provides a great deal of anonymity. Those in crisis do not have to provide any information about themselves in order to receive these services. This anonymity may decrease the stigma regarding talking about mental health difficulties and asking for help because the conversation cannot be traced back to the person in crisis, and because the information will unquestionably be kept confidential. The anonymity and reduced stigma can increase the likelihood that a rural dweller who is in crisis will reach out and discuss sensitive issues. Rather than being concerned that information about their difficulties will be shared in their communities, or that they will be judged by the people that they interact with regularly, rural dwellers can use telephone and online crisis interventions to share information that they may otherwise not be comfortable discussing. In addition, these services may help rural dwellers feel less alone, as the crisis responder can listen and empathize.

Research has shown that crisis telephone hotlines help those in crisis feel less alone and isolated, and are especially important when other mental health services are not available (e.g., after normal business hours when clinics are closed, and when there are not in-person mental health services in the area [Dalgin et al., 2011]). In addition, crisis hotlines can create short-term reduction in symptoms when the empathy and compassion of the crisis responder helps reduce the distress of the person in crisis (Dalgin et al., 2011). This research was not conducted specifically with rural dwellers, but the results indicate that telephone crisis interventions may be helpful to those in crisis, particularly when mental health professionals are not available in the area.

Rural dwellers may, however, encounter logistical problems. For example, many rural areas do not receive broadband Internet (e.g., DSL or cable) due to the expense of wiring these areas for service when there are relatively few people to utilize the service compared to urban and suburban areas. It is simply not financially pragmatic for cable or telephone companies to provide high-speed Internet in rural areas. This leaves the options of dial-up Internet or no Internet in rural areas. (A rather recent development is satellite Internet, although it is not commonly used or especially affordable at this time.) While online crisis intervention options may still work with dial-up Internet, most were not designed for the slow speeds associated with dial-up Internet. They often rely on software and graphics that do not respond well at dial-up speeds. This means that online chats may be interrupted or slow, which can frustrate those in crisis and potentially lead to more distress and agitation. Slow or interrupted chats may also create more hopelessness and isolation in those in crisis (e.g., "I can't even talk to someone online about my problems, so trying to get help is pointless."). Thus, while the use of online crisis intervention services has potential to benefit people in crisis in rural areas, there are significant limitations that may ultimately make these services impractical in rural areas.

In addition, many rural areas do not have cellular coverage, meaning that telephone crisis interventions are limited to landline telephones. Landline telephones are certainly helpful and effective ways to reach crisis intervention services but may not provide the same flexibility that cellular telephones do. For example, when he decided to kill himself, Jim went to his barn, which did not have a landline telephone. If Jim's area had cellular coverage, he may have been able to call a hotline while in his barn contemplating suicide, and his life could have potentially been saved. People in crisis often leave their homes when they are planning to kill themselves, which means that landlines may not always be available. However, landlines are common in homes and other buildings in rural areas. Given that most rural areas have landline telephone access, telephone hotlines are potentially a more viable way to engage rural dwellers in crisis intervention than online intervention options.

Another issue that may present challenges to the use of telephone and online crisis intervention options is the fact that these options may not be well-known in rural areas. This issue is also present in urban and suburban areas, but may be especially pertinent in rural communities where traditional forms of advertising these services are not available. For example, mental health professionals often provide the telephone numbers and web addresses for crisis response organization to clients, and community centers and schools can also provide this information when a community member or student is in crisis. However, in rural areas, where there are often no mental health professionals, and where schools, community centers and other resources are disappearing, information regarding crisis hotlines and online chats may not be readily available.

Finally, even when crisis intervention options are available and known, they are only designed to be short-term fixes for immediate crises. In general, telephone and online crisis intervention options are designed to help people reduce their critical levels of distress. If the people experiencing crises are willing to share where they live, the crisis responder can provide referrals to mental health services in the area for long-term interventions. However, options for these long-term services are often limited or nonexistent in rural areas. Therefore, while crisis intervention options may be effective in reducing immediate distress, long-term benefits may not be possible because there may not be local options for psychotherapy and medication management to ensure that crises do not continue to occur.

The Case of Emily

Emily was a 30-year-old woman who lived in a rural area in South Dakota. She lived in a small town with a population of about 800 people. She had recently returned to her hometown to help her parents with their dairy after receiving an honorable discharge from the military which she had joined at age 18. During her time in the military, she was deployed to Afghanistan twice, where she witnessed another soldier die after a roadside bomb exploded. During her first deployment, she was also engaged in a fierce firefight with insurgents when out on patrol. This firefight was life-threatening, and Emily's group became trapped and were helpless until other soldiers were able to get to them. After returning from Afghanistan the second time, Emily began experiencing increasing symptoms of post-traumatic stress disorder, including insomnia, hypervigilance, nightmares about Afghanistan, and flashbacks to the firefight. She avoided talking about her time in Afghanistan and did not want to share anything about her memories from her time in the military. It was clear that Emily needed help, as she was unable to help much around the dairy because of her symptoms and would not leave the house to go shopping or to the post office because of her fear of being around groups of other people. There were no mental health professionals practicing in her community, and her only healthcare coverage was through the Department of Veterans Affairs (VA). The closest VA hospital was almost two hours away from her town, making it impractical for Emily to travel there each week for individual psychotherapy. She received a prescription for anxiolytic medications through the VA hospital. These medications were delivered to her home, but she could not go to the hospital regularly for medication management, and she did not feel that her prescription medications were working especially well.

Emily's condition continued to get worse, but neither she nor her parents knew what to do to help her. She was not suicidal or in any real crisis, but could not function and was significantly distressed by her symptoms. Her symptoms finally became so severe that she was admitted to one of the VA's inpatient treatment programs for post-traumatic stress disorder, where she received the help that she needed, processed the traumas that she had experienced in Afghanistan, and returned to her previous level of well-being and functioning.

Mental Health Service Options

Situations like Emily's are often unfortunate realities in rural areas. While some rural areas have mental health professionals practicing in the community, many rural communities do not have any options for long-term psychotherapy or psychiatric medication management. When residents of these communities need mental health services but are not in active crisis, they do not have good options for treatment. They may end up seeking inpatient treatment when their symptoms become overwhelming, as Emily did, or may attempt suicide if they become hopeless and isolated. It is incumbent upon mental health professionals to address the lack of access to services, and one way that they are doing so is through telephone and online intervention options. Telehealth has recently become an important component of mental health services. Telehealth, in which the mental health professional and client interact through web-based audio and video software (e.g., "webcams"), allows rural dwellers to access mental health professionals from their homes or local offices and clinics without the prohibitive time and cost of driving to a larger city where mental health professionals practice. In fact, the VA has begun offering telehealth services to ensure that veterans like Emily, who live in areas that are not convenient to a VA hospital or outpatient clinic, can still receive the services that they need. Other mental health professionals have also recently begun engaging in services via telehealth equipment. The benefits of telehealth extend beyond the convenience of receiving services in the client's local area. Telehealth also allows the mental health professional and client to interact face-to-face in real time, rather than interacting only via voice on the telephone or through texting online. This makes telehealth interactions more like in-person interactions, in which the mental health professional can see the client's facial expressions and reactions to different topics and statements, and the client and mental health professional can also hear the tone in each other's voices as they interact.

Research has shown that telehealth options are practical and well-received (Bhandari et al., 2011). Telehealth psychiatry, in which patients at rural clinics spoke with psychiatrists at a larger hospital, was acceptable to the patients as they were able to easily access knowledgeable psychiatrists. Additionally, it was agreeable to the staff at the rural clinics and large hospital. In this study, there did not appear to be any adverse outcomes associated with telehealth. However, once again, the limitations of rural communities lead to some obstacles in telehealth. As mentioned previously, dial-up Internet is sometimes the only option for Internet, which can make telehealth challenging. In addition, there is not the same anonymity in telehealth as there is in some of the short-term crisis intervention options, which may mean that stigma and reluctance to ask for help are obstacles to seeking telehealth services in rural areas.

Conclusion

Telephone and online interventions are promising developments for mental health service options in rural areas. These types of interventions may be helpful for both immediate crisis intervention and long-term psychotherapy and medication management. However, logistical obstacles, such as lack of broadband Internet and cellular coverage, may create difficulties in implementing these interventions. In addition, stigma regarding admitting mental health difficulties and reluctance to ask for help among rural dwellers may create additional barriers to the utilization of such interventions. There is relatively little research examining the use of telephone and online interventions in rural areas. We do not know how they are received in rural communities and if they are practical and effective. Yet, cases such as Jim's and Emily's suggest a critical need for these interventions. If these interventions are implemented in rural areas, and mental health professionals work to reduce stigma and publicize available interventions, we can begin reaching rural dwellers in need of crisis intervention and other mental health services. While rural areas are heterogeneous and the implementation of interventions must be tailored to the strengths and needs of each community, telephone and online interventions may prove to be a valuable method of reaching rural dwellers in need of mental health services. Ultimately, these interventions may improve the well-being of many rural dwellers and save the lives of those in crisis.

REFERENCES

Aoun, S., & Lavan, T. (1998). Suicide intervention in rural Western Australia: A preliminary report. In R. J. Kosky, H. S. Eshkevari, R. D. Goldney, & R. Hassan (Eds.), *Suicide prevention: The global context*, pp. 231–236. New York: Plenum Press.

Bhandari, G., Tiessen, B., & Snowdon, A. (2011). Meeting community needs through leadership and innovation: A case of virtual psychiatric emergency department (ED). *Behaviour & Information Technology, 30*, 517–723.

Bonynge, E. R., Lee, R. G., & Thurber, S. (2005). A profile of mental health crisis response in a rural setting. *Community Mental Health Journal, 41*, 675–685.

Dalgin, R. S., Maline, S., & Driscoll, P. (2011). Sustaining recovery through the night: Impact of a peer-run warm line. *Psychiatric Rehabilitation Journal, 35*, 65–68.

Finkel, S. I., & Rosman, M. (1996). Six elderly suicides in a 1-year period in a rural Midwestern community. In J. L. Pearson & Y. Conwell (Eds.), *Suicide and aging: International perspectives*, pp. 87–96. New York: Springer.

Fiske, A., Gatz, M., & Hannell, E. (2005). Rural suicide rates and availability of health care providers. *Journal of Community Psychology, 33*, 537–543.

Hirsch, J. K. (2006). A review of the literature on rural suicide: Risk and protective factors, incidence, and prevention. *Crisis, 27*, 189–199.

Judd, F., Cooper, A. M., Fraser, C., & Davis, J. (2006). Rural suicide – people or place effects? *Australian & New Zealand Journal of Psychiatry, 40*, 208–216.

Stark, C. (2008). Suicide in rural areas. In S. Palmer (Ed.), *Suicide: Strategies and interventions for reduction and prevention*, pp. 48–68. New York: Routledge.

Turvey, C., Stromquist, A., Kelly, K., Zwerlig, C., & Kelly, K. (2002). Financial loss and suicidal ideation in a rural community sample. *Acta Psychiatrica Scandinavica, 106*, 373–380.

US Census Bureau. (2011). *United States: Urban/rural and inside/outside metropolitan area geographic comparison table*. Retrieved from http://factfinder.census.gov/servlet/GCTTable?_bm=y&-geo_id=01000US&-_box_head_nbr=GCT-P1&-ds_name=DEC_2000_SF1_U& format=US 1.

Chapter 23

THE ELDERLY

JOHN F. GUNN III

In the most recent statistics on suicide in the United States (for the year 2008), suicide occurred at a rate of 14.8 per 100,000 per year in people aged 65 and older, while the national rate was 11.8 (McIntosh, 2011). In fact, in the United States, older people have the second highest rate of suicide, second only to the rate of suicide in middle age. While the elderly made up 12.7% of the population for the year 2008, they represented 16.0% of suicides. As a result of this high risk of death by suicide in elderly populations, it is important to develop programs and methods for preventing suicide in the elderly and counseling the suicidal elderly. The elderly are clearly at risk for suicide and, therefore, preventive measures must be taken to lower the prevalence of suicide in this population.

However, there are limitations to preventing elderly suicide and counseling elderly individuals who are suicidal through the use of the telephone. One such limitation is the rare use of telephone hotlines by the elderly. Morrow-Howell, Becker-Kemppainem, and Judy (1998), when evaluating Life-Crisis, St. Louis's best-known hotline program, found that only 3% of the callers were over the age of 60. In Adamek and Kaplan's (1996) review of American and Canadian crisis prevention centers, they found as few as 1%-2% of all calls made to the centers were from the elderly. Another problem cited was the lack of suicide prevention programs that targeted elderly populations. At the time their article was written (in 1996), only a few agencies existed that focused on the prevention of elderly suicide, and there are still few programs that focus on elderly suicide prevention. Haas and Hendin (1983) projected that the number of suicides in later life will double by 2030 as a result of the aging "baby boom" cohort. Considering this, and the fact that the elderly already represent one of the most at-risk groups, it is important to focus on this population for future prevention and treatment.

Characteristics of Elderly Suicides

As previously indicated in the introduction to this chapter, the elderly make up a disproportionate number of suicides in the United States. Before entering into a discussion about prevention and treatment of suicidal elderly through the use of the telephone, it is important to examine the characteristics of elderly suicides. Conwell (2001) indicated that elderly suicides were less likely to have a suicide attempt history to such a degree that the ratio of attempted/completed suicide was as high as 200:1 in young adulthood, but as low as 4:1 in the elderly. Conwell noted that "older people have fewer physical reserves and are, therefore, less likely to survive self-damaging acts" (p. 33) as a possible explanation for this trend, along with the fact that they are more isolated and less likely to receive life-saving aid.

In addition, the elderly make fewer warnings to others of their suicidal intent, and use more violent means. Kennedy and Tanenbaum (2000) stated that "[i]t is the greater lethality of methods and lesser likelihood of rescue that distinguishes suicide attempts between the young and old" (p. 351). This is a very important fact to keep in mind when considering prevention and treatment with this population. Conwell also noted that efforts to understand suicide among older persons are often oversimplified, attributing a suicide to a single factor, whereas in fact there are many risk factors for suicide and no single cause. Of these risk factors, psychiatric illness, a past history of suicidal behavior, hopelessness, a characteristic personality style, and physical disorders and impairments should "be the emphases for future preventive efforts" (Conwell, 1997, p. 34).

Psychiatric Illnesses

Research, typically psychological autopsies, shows a close association between suicide in later life and psychiatric illness. Numerous studies have examined the presence of psychiatric illness, and indicate that as many as 90% of suicides may have a diagnosable mental illness (Robins et al., 1959; Dorpat & Ripley, 1960; Barraclough et al., 1974; Chynoweth et al., 1980; Rich et al., 1986; Henriksson et al. 1993; Isometsa et al., 1994; Cheng, 1995). When looking at elderly suicides, between 71%-90% have diagnosable major psychiatric illnesses. Psychiatric illnesses of particular importance in the elderly are alcoholism and other substance abuse disorders and affective disorders, while psychotic illnesses (i.e., schizophrenia, schizoaffective illness, and delusional disorder), personality disorders, and anxiety disorders play a much smaller role (Conwell et al., 1996). Addictive disorders are especially hard to identify in older populations, and treatment options are limited.

Hopelessness

Although hopelessness has been examined to great degree in suicidal populations (Beck, Steer, Kovacs, & Garrison, 1985; Beck, Weissman, Lester, & Trexler, 1974), its role in the elderly has not been addressed thoroughly. When examining the suicide notes of elderly people who died by suicide, Shneidman and Farberow (1957) found that hopelessness was more often present than anger or guilt. Additionally, Hill and colleagues (1988) and Ross et al. (1990) found hopelessness to be a significant predictor of suicide in older outpatients and in retirement communities. However, as Conwell (2001) urged, further research is needed in evaluating the effectiveness of treatments focused on lowering feelings of hopelessness and their impact on suicide risk in the elderly.

Personality Traits

Several personality traits are linked to elderly suicide. These include timidity, shy seclusiveness, a tendency to hypochondriasis, hostility, and an inflexible, independent style (Batchelor & Napier, 1953; Clark, 1993; Farberow & Shneidman, 1970). Furthermore, Duberstein (1995) found that older suicides had higher levels of Neuroticism and lower scores on the Openness to Experience on the NEO Personality Inventory (Costa & McCrea, 1997) and that lower Extroversion scores differentiated those who had made a suicide attempt from those who had not. Personality can play a role in treatment and intervention and, therefore, is an area of interest when evaluating elderly persons at risk of suicide.

Physical Illnesses and Impairments

Physical illnesses and impairments are another area of interest when considering elderly suicides, as they play a large part in later life and offer opportunities for intervention (e.g., in primary care settings) (Conwell, 2001). Physical illness has been estimated to contribute to 35%-70% of suicides in elderly populations (Sainsbury, 1955; Dorpat, Anderson, & Ripley, 1968). Diseases that have been associated with suicide in the elderly include: cancers, diseases of the central nervous system, peptic ulcer, cardiopulmonary complications, rheumatoid arthritis, and urogenital disease in men (Mackenzie &

Popkin, 1987; Dorpat et al., 1968; Whitlock, 1986). Additionally, Conwell et al. (1998) examined physical illness burden, functional impairment, and a history of cancer or cardiovascular disorder and found they distinguished elderly individuals who died by suicide from age-matched controls.

Prevention Programs

To begin this section, consideration of the effectiveness of crisis workers in dealing with elderly callers must be examined. Though elderly callers make up very few of the calls to crisis centers (1%-6%) (Adamek & Kaplan, 1996; Morrow-Howell, Becker-Kemppainem, & Judy, 1998), a certain degree of knowledge about elderly suicide should be expected of crisis counselors. As previously mentioned, Adamek and Kaplan (1996) examined American and Canadian crisis prevention centers in their ability to manage elderly suicidal clients. Through contacting 555 crisis prevention centers in the United States and Canada by mail, of which 268 responded, they were able to gather information concerning the understanding of elderly suicide by the volunteers, staff, and managers. Of those who responded to the surveys, only a quarter of the Canadian centers and a third of the American centers reported having any geriatric-specific programs. Only one in seven managers in Canada indicated having outreach programs for those 65 and over, compared to one in three in the United States. As far as staff training, between 35%-45% of respondents indicated they had had no training with a geriatric focus, no elderly adult case studies, nor any firearm specific training (firearms being the typical method for the elderly). There was no difference in managerial and volunteer/staff training. Approximately a third of the volunteers, staff, and managers indicated a need for further training in dealing with older persons.

In addition to training, the researchers also assessed the basic knowledge of the volunteers, staff, and managers in regard to elderly suicide. The vast majority (80%) of responders felt that the training in elderly suicide needed to be improved. One disturbing finding was that two-thirds of the volunteers and staff and nearly a half of the managers were unaware that elderly populations were the greatest at-risk population (at the time). These researchers concluded that, "a better understanding of elder suicide might enhance older adults' access to prevention services" (p. 129). Further recommendations from the researchers were to move away from traditional approaches to suicide prevention in the elderly.

Additionally, gender also seems to play a part in who uses and does not use crisis hotlines. In their comparison of younger and older clients of crisis intervention services, Winogrond and Mirassou (1983) found that, in every age group, with the exception of the 60-69 age group, calls from females outnumbered calls from males.

Research would seem to indicate that, in their present state, suicide prevention centers are not well equipped to handle elderly callers. However, viewed in light of the fact that as few as 1%-2% of callers to these centers are over the age of 65, it is not surprising that the prevention programs have become better prepared to handle their typically younger callers. Later, recommendations will be made to correct this problem. As previously stated, Adamek and Kaplan (1996) recommended moving away from traditional approaches of suicide prevention to better address elderly suicide prevention. Below, several programs are highlighted that are geared toward elderly populations and that differ from traditional prevention programs. Finally, the findings of Adamek and Kaplan (1996), although thought-provoking, are now over a decade old, and more up-to-date research needs to be done to determine if this is still the current state of crisis prevention centers.

Tele-Help/Tele-Check

From January 1, 1988 to December 31, 1991, over 12,000 elderly (65+ years old) persons were connected to the Tele-Help/Tele-Check program offered in the Veneto region of northern Italy (De Leo, Carollo, & Dello Buono, 1995). The Tele-Help/Tele-Check service connects elderly persons to a center that is open 24/7, via the telephone. The center serves two functions. The first is Tele-Help, a portable device that allows users to "activate a pre-established network of assistance and help" (p. 632). The second is Tele-Check in which trained center workers contact clients on average twice a week to conduct short informal interviews during which emotional support is given. The service is provided by a private organization. Social workers or general practitioners in local health services identify elderly individuals who are in need of home help (e.g., those who are disabled, socially isolated, suffering from a psychiatric disorder, who have difficulty adhering to outpatient care regimens, or who have low income) for enrollment in the program.

De Leo et al. (1995) compared the observed suicide rates among the Tele-Help/Tele-Check users and the expected suicide rate from the Veneto region. In the four-year period studied, only one suicide was observed, which was significantly fewer than the number expected. De Leo et al. (2002) examined the long-term impact of the Tele-Help/Tele-Check program by examining the observed suicide rate and the expected suicide rates in the 18,641 users from January 1, 1988 to December 31, 1998. The researchers found that over this longer time period, only two female users died by suicide and only six males. This was much lower then the expected rates (11.98 in females, 20.86 in males) of suicide for the Veneto region. Both findings suggest that programs, such as the Tele-Help/Tele-Check, offer hope in the prevention of suicide in elderly populations.

Link-Plus

Link-Plus is a program that developed out of Life Crisis, a well-established suicide prevention program in St. Louis (Morrow-Howell, Becker-Kemppainem, & Judy, 1998). Link-Plus was designed to be a means of preventing elderly suicide through the use of the telephone by relieving depression in elderly persons and increasing socialization and independence. Link-Plus is broken into two primary components. The first is focused on clinical case management and the second on supportive therapy. The case management component includes arranging necessary services, confronting the environmental and psychological barriers that prevent service use, ensuring quality and continuity of the services, monitoring the elderly person's changing conditions and needs, and providing supportive counseling and problem-solving as needed in relation to service use. The supportive therapy function focuses on the relieving the symptoms of depression. Link-Plus targets elderly populations, it is provided entirely over the phone, and the program focuses on the use of services available in the St. Louis community.

Morrow-Howell et al. (1998) examined the effectiveness of the Link-Plus program, specifically whether, after a four-month period, the program (1) decreased depressive symptomatology, (2) reduced unmet needs in daily living activities, and (3) decreased social isolation, and (4) whether clients reported improved life situations. A decrease in depressive symptoms was partially supported, a reduction in unmet needs was not supported, a decrease in social isolation was supported in "small part," and that clients would report an improved life situation was fully supported. However, although this study highlighted the improved life situation, no examination was conducted on Link-Plus's ability to prevent suicide. Further research should examine this in order to determine if the program is successful in preventing elderly suicide.

The Friendship Line/Geriatric Outreach Program

The Friendship Line was founded in 1973 in San Francisco by Patrick Arbore. The official website of the Friendship Line[39] indicates that Arbore founded the program after seeing the lack of understanding by some suicide hotline workers for the elderly callers at risk for suicide, a problem discussed above.

Fiske and Arbore (2000) evaluated The Friendship Line, which provides emotional support, crisis intervention, information, and referrals for older adults through the telephone, and the Geriatric Outreach, a program that provides counseling via telephone appointments and home visits to elderly per-

---

[39] http://www.ioaging.org/services/friendline_suicide_hotline_sf.html.

sons at risk for suicide. They found that there was a significant reduction in hopelessness, but there were no changes in depressive symptoms.

Each of the above programs was evaluated by Lapierre et al. (2011) who argued that telephone counseling outreach programs provide essential elements to the prevention of suicide, including "a regular, confiding relationship with a helping person, and a method of increasing the person's sense of mastery, in spite of the physical distance with the healthcare staff" (p. 94). They went on to say that "[o]ne of the important findings of the telecommunication studies is that face-to-face contact may not be required for successful mental health care interventions" (p. 94).

Counseling by Telephone

Telephone services can offer more than just prevention benefits to the elderly who are feeling suicidal. In addition to preventive programs, the telephone can offer therapeutic benefits for the elderly. Evans et al. (1986) examined cognitive telephone group therapy with the physically disabled elderly in Seattle, Washington. Through teleconferencing, this technique provided cognitive therapy for bedridden elderly persons that they would otherwise be physically unable to access. The group met once a week for one-hour sessions. Of the 21 counseling participants, three reported minimal goal achievement, and two reported partial goal achievement, while the rest reported satisfaction with their goal achievement. Evans et al. found also that goal attainment was positively related to reduced loneliness. Loneliness, when examined through the lens of Joiner's (2005) Interpersonal-Psychological Theory of Suicide, can be seen as a vital component of suicidal behavior. Although this study offered telephone group therapy only to the disabled, telephone therapy could be expanded to suicidal elderly clients.

Pearson and Brown (2000) commented on the treatment of elderly persons at risk for suicide based on Shneidman's (1992) theory of suicide in which suicide results from unbearable psychological pain (psychache). They cite the concept of "cognitive constriction" as being particularly applicable to elderly populations. Constriction is the tunneling of vision, or a narrowed view of the range of options. The authors suggest that "[c]linical interventions for suicidal persons, whether they are individual, family, group or pharmacological in nature, must be seen by the patient as providing alternative solutions to suicide to actually diminish its risk" (p. 696). Any program for counseling the elderly at risk of suicide by phone should keep these suggestions in mind.

Recommendations

Prevention

There are several practical recommendations that can be made to improve the welfare of the elderly who are contemplating suicide. One practical consideration is changing the nature of the equipment available that the elderly use to contact hotlines, that is, their telephones. Considering the deterioration in vision and memory as we age, it seems impractical to expect an elderly person to remember a lifeline number that they have probably never dialed before and to which they have probably had very little exposure. This difficulty in memory, coupled with the potential difficulty that an elderly person might have in operating modern telephones, could help contribute to the lack of representation that the elderly have as callers to suicide prevention lifelines. One possibility could be donating telephones with larger and much more visible numbers to the elderly and having a suicide prevention lifeline preprogrammed in so that the elderly can contact the hotline at the click of a button. The less complicated process of contacting the lifelines could potentially increase the use of the lifelines by the elderly population and, in turn, save lives.

In addition to these recommendations, where the elderly spend much of their time must also be taken into consideration. The elderly who are living within healthcare settings (such as senior living facilities and retirement homes) are under more observation and have healthcare more readily available than are the elderly who spend their time isolated at home or in daytime programs. Increasing the knowledge of the workers in daytime programs, and having them inform the elderly of the potentially life-saving lifelines available to them, could lead to an increase in elderly callers to crisis centers. However, unless crisis center volunteers, staff, and managers are better trained in geriatric care, this potential increase in calls may not decrease the suicidality of this population. Training in geriatric suicide should be increased in crisis centers so that, if elderly persons begin to make better use of these prevention programs, they are served better by the crisis workers. Another recommendation could be to promote third-party call-ins. Winogrond and Mirassou (1983) found that half of the calls to Crisis Intervention Hotlines for younger adults were self-referrals while only 9% of the calls from clients 70 years of age and older were self-referred. Such findings support the need for third-party call-ins. Mishara et al. (2005) recommended this, especially for men, as they are at high risk for suicide and are underrepresented in those who make use of the hotlines.

A final recommendation for the prevention of suicide in the elderly would be to take advantage of telephone services to spread understanding about suicide among, not only the elderly, but those who care for them. An example of how an increase in awareness could help to lower suicide rates can be seen in a report from Chiu et al. (2003). In Matsunoyama, a small town in the countryside of Niigata Prefecture, in Japan, there was an annual average suicide rate of 435 per 100,000 per year from 1970-1985. In addition to better depression screening and treatment, nurses contacted the local people and informed them that the problems of the elderly were treatable. Prior to this, local belief was that, once the elderly were ill and could not work, they were worthless. In 1996, the suicide rate in Matsunoyama had dropped to 123.

In 2009, an international expert panel was formed to focus on the key considerations for future prevention in older adults (Erlangsen et al., 2011). The prevention recommendations that came out of this panel were to communicate with elderly suicidal patients prior to treatment and to incorporate family, friends, and caregivers in the treatment talks. These communications could be modeled after the group telephone therapy mentioned previously. Additionally, the panel also recommended regular telephone calls after treatment or postcards that would reassure the participants that their well-being is important. Vaiva et al. (2006) examined the effect of telephone follow-up on further suicide attempts in patients discharged from an emergency department after a suicide attempt involving a drug overdose. They concluded that contacting people by telephone one month after attempting suicide might help to reduce the likelihood of another attempt. Furthermore, they noted that the telephone contact would allow for a reevaluation of suicide risk and allow for referrals for emergency care. However, the effectiveness of follow-up contact has had mixed results. Cedereke, Monti, and Ojehagen (2002) found that a follow-up telephone call did not have any effect on whether or not the subjects attended treatment, nor did it have an effect on suicide reattempt rates. These contradictory findings need to be better examined before any conclusions can be drawn on the effectiveness of telephone follow-up on subsequent suicidal behavior.

Conclusions

The elderly are one of the highest at-risk groups for suicide, and this chapter described existing programs for preventing and treating elderly persons at risk for suicide through use of the telephone. Several programs, such as Tele-Help/Tele-Check, offer some evidence that telecommunication prevention programs can be effective at preventing elderly suicide. Further evidence suggests that the telephone could be a potentially effective tool for providing therapy for home-bound elderly persons. Several recommendations were made concerning what can be done to increase the effectiveness of these programs. First and foremost of these recommendations is increasing the number of elderly persons who use telecommunication prevention and therapy programs through outreach, or perhaps through third-party communications. Finally, it is recommended that several practical changes can be made to increase the use by elderly persons of these programs. Changing the telephones that are used by the elderly and programming in crisis hotlines, so that they can be reached by a single push of a button, could increase the likelihood that these services are used.

REFERENCES

Adamek, M. E., & Kaplan, M. S. (1996). Managing elder suicide: A profile of American and Canadian crisis prevention centers. *Suicide & Life-Threatening Behavior, 26*, 122–131.

Barraclough, B. M., Bunch, J., Nelson, B., & Sainsbury, P. (1974). A hundred cases of suicide: Clinical aspects. *British Journal of Psychiatry, 125*, 355–373.

Batchelor, I. R. C., & Napier, M. B. (1953). Attempted suicide in old age. *British Medical Journal, ii*, 1186–1190.

Beck, A. T., Steer, R. A., Kovacs, M., & Garrison, B. (1985). Hopelessness and eventual suicide: A 10-year prospective study of patients hospitalized with suicidal ideation. *American Journal of Psychiatry, 142*, 559–563.

Beck, A. T., Weissman, A., Lester, D., & Trexler, L. (1974). The measurement of pessimism: The hopelessness scale. *Journal of Consulting & Clinical Psychology, 42*, 861–865.

Cedereke, M., Monti, K., & Ojehagen, A. (2002). Telephone contact with patients in the year after a suicide attempt: Does it affect treatment attendance and outcome? A randomised controlled study. *European Psychiatry, 17*, 82–91.

Cheng, A. T. A. (1995). Mental illness and suicide: A case-control study in East Tawain. *Archives of General Psychiatry, 52*, 594–603.

Chiu, H. F. K., Takahashi, Y., & Suh, G. H. (2003). Elderly suicide prevention in East Asia. *International Journal of Geriatric Psychiatry, 18*, 973–976.

Chynoweth, R., Tonge, J. I., & Armstrong, J. (1980). Suicide in Brisbane: A retrospective psychosocial study. *Australian & New Zealand Journal of Psychiatry, 14*, 37–45.

Clark, D. C. (1993). Narcissistic crises of aging and suicidal despair. *Suicide & Life-Threatening Behavior, 23*, 21–26.

Conwell, Y. (1997). Management of suicidal behavior in the elderly. *Psychiatric Clinics of North America, 20*, 667–683.

Conwell, Y. (2001). Suicide in later life: A review and recommendations for prevention. *Suicide & Life-Threatening Behavior, 31*(supplement), 32–47.

Conwell, Y., Duberstein, P. R., Cox, C., Herrmann, J. H., Forbes, N. T., & Caine, E. D. (1996). Relationships of age and Axis I diagnoses in victims of completed suicide: A psychological autopsy study. *American Journal of Psychiatry, 153*, 1001–1008.

Conwell, Y., Lyness, J. M., Duberstein, P. R., Cox, C., Seidlitz, L., & Caine, E. D. (1998). Physical illness and suicide among older patients in primary care practices. American Psychiatric Association meeting. Toronto.

Costa, P. T., & McCrae, R. R. (1997). Stability and change in personality assessment. *Journal of Personality Assessment, 68*, 86–94.

De Leo, D., Carollo, G., & Dello Buono, M. (1995). Lower suicide rates associated with Tele-Help/Tele-Check service for the elderly at home. *American Journal of Psychiatry, 152*, 632–634.

De Leo, D., Dello Buono, M., & Dwyer, J. (2002). Suicide among the elderly: The long-term impact of a telephone support and assessment intervention in northern Italy. *British Journal of Psychiatry, 181*, 226–229.

Dorpat, T. L., & Ripley, H. S. (1960). A study of suicide in the Seattle area. *Comprehensive Psychiatry, 1*, 349–359.

Dorpat, T. L., Anderson, W. F., & Ripley, H. S. (1968). The relationship of physical illness to suicide. In H. P. L. Resnik (Ed.), *Suicide behaviors: Diagnosis and management*, pp. 209–219. Boston: Little Brown.

Duberstein, P. R. (1995). Openness to experience and completed suicide across the second half of life. *International Psychogeriatrics, 7*, 183–198.

Erlangsen, A., Nordentoft, M., Conwell, Y., Waern, M., De Leo, D., Lindner, R., Oyama, H., Sakashita, T., Andersen-Ranberg, K., Quinnett, P., Draper, B., Lapierre, S., & the International Research Group on Suicide Among the Elderly. (2011). Key considerations for preventing suicide in older adults. *Crisis, 32*, 106–109.

Evans, R. L., Smith, K. M., Werkhoven, W. S., Fox, H. R., & Pritzl, D. O. (1986). Cognitive telephone group therapy with physically disabled elderly persons. *The Gerontologist, 26*(1), 8–11.

Farberow, N. L., & Shneidman, E. S. (1970). Suicide among patients with malignant neoplasms. In E. S. Shneidman, N. L. Farberow, & R. E. Litman (Eds.), *The psychology of suicide*, pp. 325–344. New York: Science House.

Fiske, A., & Arbore, P. (2000). Future directions in late life suicide prevention. *Omega, 42*, 37–53.

Haas, A. P., & Hendin, H. (1983). Suicide among older people: Projections for the future. *Suicide & Life-Threatening Behavior, 13*, 147–154.

Henriksson, M. M., Aro, H. M., Marttunen, M. J., Heikkinen, M. E., Isometsa, E. T., Kuoppasalmi, K. I., & Lonnqvist, J. K. (1993). Mental disorders and comorbidity in suicide. *American Journal of Psychiatry, 150*, 935–940.

Hill, R. D., Gallagher, D., Thompson, L. W., & Ishida, T. (1988). Hopelessness as a measure of suicide intent in the depressed elderly. *Psychology of Aging, 3*, 230–232.

Isometsa, E. T., Henriksson, M. M., Aro, H. M., Heikkinen, M. E., Kuoppasalmi, K. I., & Lonnqvist, J. K. (1994). Suicide in major depression. *American Journal of Psychiatry, 151*, 530–536.

Joiner, T. E., Jr. (2005). *Why people die by suicide?* Cambridge, MA: Harvard University Press.

Kennedy, G. J., & Tanenbaum, S. (2000). Suicide and aging: International perspectives. *Psychiatric Quarterly, 71*, 345–362.

Lapierre, S., Erlangsen, A., Waern, M., De Leo, D., Oyama, H., Scocco, P., Gallo, J., Szanto, K., Conwell, Y., Draper, B., Quinnett, P., and the International Research Group for Suicide among the Elderly. (2011). A systematic review of elderly suicide prevention programs. *Crisis, 32,* 88–98.

Mackenzie, T. B., & Popkin, M. K. (1987). Suicide in the medical patient. *International Journal of Psychiatry in Medicine, 17,* 3–22.

McIntosh, J. L. (1995). Suicide prevention in the elderly (age 65–99). *Suicide & Life-Threatening Behavior, 25,* 180–192.

Mishara, B., Houle, J., & Lavoie, B. (2005). Comparison of the effects of four suicide prevention programs for family and friends of high-risk suicidal men who do not seek help themselves. *Suicide & Life-Threatening Behavior, 35,* 329–342.

Morrow-Howell, N., Becker-Kemppainem, S., & Judy, L. (1998). Evaluating an intervention for the elderly at increased risk of suicide. *Research on Social Work Practice, 8,* 28–46.

Pearson, J. L., & Brown, G. K. (2000). Suicide prevention in late life: Directions for science and practice. *Clinical Psychology Review, 20*(6), 685–705.

Rich, C. L., Young, D., & Fowler, R. (1986). San Diego suicide: Study I: Young vs. old subjects. *Archives of General Psychiatry, 43,* 577–582.

Robins, E., Murphy, G. E., Wilkinson, R. H., Gassner, S., & Kayes, J. (1959). Some clinical considerations in the prevention of suicide based on a study of 134 successful suicides. *American Journal of Public Health, 49,* 888–889.

Ross, R. K., Bernstein, L., Trent, L., Henderson, B. E., & Paganini-Hill, A. (1990). A prospective study of risk factors for traumatic death in the retirement community. *Preventive Medicine, 19,* 323–334.

Sainsbury, P. (1955). *Suicide in London.* London, UK: Maudsley Monographs No. 1.

Shneidman, E. (1992). What do suicides have in common? A summary of the psychological approach. In B. Bongar (Ed.), *Suicide: Guidelines for assessment, management and treatment,* pp. 3–15. New York: Oxford University Press.

Shneidman, E. S., & Farberow, N. L. (Eds.). (1957). *Clues to Suicide.* New York: McGraw-Hill.

Vaiva, G., Ducrocq, F., Meyer, P., Mathieu, D., Philippe, A., Libersa, C., & Goudemand, M. (2006). Effect of telephone contact on further suicide attempts in patients discharged from an emergency department: Randomised controlled study. *British Medical Journal, 332,* 1241.

Whitlock, F. A. (1986). Suicide and physical illness. In A. Roy (Ed.), *Suicide,* pp. 151–170. Baltimore: Williams and Wilkins.

Winogrond, I. R., & Mirassou, M. M. (1983). A crisis intervention service: Comparison of younger and older adult clients. *The Gerontologist, 23,* 370–376.

Chapter 24

INDIVIDUALS WITH DISABILITIES ON CAMPUS

Shelly Meyers

Colleges today are dealing with an increase in the number of students with disabilities who require accommodation in all aspects of campus life. In fact, disability specialists find themselves working more and more with educational, physical, social, and emotional disabilities than ever before. Studies of college students find that, although the number of students with all types of disability is on the rise, the fastest growing disabilities are those in the mental health categories (Belch & Marshak, 2006). In a study of student e-mails, Raskind, Margalit, and Higgins (2006) reported that students with disabilities are more likely to report the experience of peer rejection as well as loneliness, anxiety, low self-esteem, and depression.

Typically, college personnel develop accommodation plans for students with learning, orthopedic, and sensory disabilities that include modifying exams, alternative note-taking practices, response systems, and the physical layout of the classroom. More challenges occur when trying to accommodate students with mental health disabilities. Often mental health issues are comorbid with other disabilities, which require more comprehensive adaptations for students (Chaplin, 2009). In addition, all students, with and without disabilities, experience issues of early adulthood such as ambivalence, instability, stress, and conflict, and they often engage in high-risk behaviors in social contexts. Studies of college students report that 40% of young adults suffer from depression and almost 10% have thoughts of suicide (Hollingsworth, Dunkle, & Douce, 2009). Colleges must be proactive in addressing their social and emotional needs. However because there is stigma associated with mental health difficulties, students are reluctant to disclose any psychiatric disorders.

A critical factor to consider is the legal issues regarding accommodating individuals with disabilities. Colleges no longer have a choice in their decisions to provide services. Section 504 of the Rehabilitation Act of 1973 and the Americans with Disabilities Act 1990 mandate that policies and procedures must be in place so that all individuals with disabilities are given equal opportunity and access as part of the college experience. There are many avenues that colleges can pursue in order to accommodate such students. The most common are classroom interventions, but many colleges are moving in the direction of using computer-related technology aids. Disability services providers find that students turn to technology as a resource and as a means of coping with difficulties because of the ease and convenience of computers. In addition, students have computers readily available to them, and this allows them to avoid face-to-face interaction. This chapter will focus on the types of computer-assisted crisis intervention, noting both their benefits and the shortcomings.

Web-Based Services: Description

The success of computer-assisted technology is attributable to its relevancy and the connection it allows between the individuals and their ecological environments, such as the college campus (Chaffin & Harlow, 2005). Originally, technology helped students manage their cognitive skills, but, with the increased availability of technology services, there is the possibility of more social and emotional support. As students with disabilities discover the purpose and usefulness of technology, they are more apt to employ these resources in crisis situations.

Recently, computer-based counseling services have gained popularity because they are individually-based, with the computer as a mode of communication with the counselor (Efstathiou, 2009). Ideally, the student with disabilities and the counselor begin the session by determining the needs of the student and taking time to develop a specific plan. However, in crisis situations, the counselor does not always have sufficient time to assess the client's needs and, therefore, listens and responds quickly. According to Michaud and Colom (2003), the majority of students using an Internet information and interactive health site were satisfied with the help they received, in particular because the counselor understood their problems.

There are two types of crisis intervention computer-aided technology available to students with disabilities – asynchronous and synchronous. The *asynchronous model* uses written text and includes e-mail, chat rooms and other discussion formats, and the response from the counselor may not always be immediate. In addition, data-bases are available with published answers that address specific needs. Some sites, if the interaction is informational rather than personal, may add the interaction to the database so that others with similar problems may access it. *Synchronous crisis intervention counseling* gives students immediate responses using technologies such as instant messaging. Internet-based counseling includes online peer counseling, peer support, and individual and group counseling. The use of synchronous computer services provides more immediate feedback to students and keeps them more connected to their environment, whereas asynchronous services delay the response (Chaffin & Harlow, 2005).

Gega, Marks, and Mataix-Coles (2004) have gone further and provided computer-aided cognitive behavior therapy via a self-help model with no counselor involved except to occasionally monitor the interactions between the client and the computer program and to provide help, using a telephone help-line, if clients become stuck. In one case, a depressed woman with suicidal ideation was screened initially face-to-face and then chose the self-help program. Over the course of 12 weeks, she completed all of the self-help modules (constructive thinking, behavioral activation and assertiveness training), made 12 telephone calls for technical help, and received seven telephone calls from a live therapist who reviewed her progress and gave support.

Advantages and Disadvantages of Using Web-Based, Computer-Assisted Crisis Intervention

College campuses, communities, and society as a whole tend to isolate individuals with disabilities, resulting in loneliness. The use of Internet-based resources provides a means of communication that lessens the person's loneliness. Students who have access to electronic communication with health professionals are able to receive information that is personally significant, and they are not required to leave their comfort zone (Raskind, Margalit, & Higgins, 2006). Both asynchronous and synchronous models benefit the students because they establish relationships and share their feelings without risk of rejection. The Internet can be confidential and safe, partly because the students can use it while in their own familiar environment. Students with disabilities are able to explore their "true selves" more easily in their own environment where they have established their identities and feel comfortable asking for help (Belch & Marshak, 2006; Raskind et al., 2006). They are more willing to accept help online rather than in face-to-face therapeutic sessions (Margalit & Raskind, 2009). Tate and Zabinski (2009) noted that the benefit of the computer counseling service model is linked heavily to the anonymity of the support. Students are able to access information from home without shame and fear of identification. Services are always available without fighting social and environmental obstacles.

There are some disadvantages to using Internet-based crisis intervention. One is the ease in which a student can break appointments. It is much easier to cancel a session when the counseling services are not face-to-face. In addition, unless the sessions are consistent over time and involve the same counselor, it is difficult to monitor the students' progress and modify intervention treatments as the need arises (Tate & Zabinski, 2009; Efstathiou, 2009).

Ethical Considerations

The benefits of using Internet-based crisis intervention are supported through research, but users of the technology must consider the ethical issues related to this service model (Harvey & Carlson, 2003). In the forefront of such concerns is the Family Education Rights to Privacy Act (FERPA). Campus personnel as well as mental health professionals, disability counselors, administrators, and campus police must adhere to the required components of FERPA which address the confidentiality of educational records, including discipline, mental health and physical health concerns (Hollingworth, Dunkle, & Douce, 2009). The Health Insurance Portability and Accountability Act (HIPAA) also involves confidentiality and, as with FERPA, information may be released only with the patient's consent. The Americans with Disabilities Act and Section 504 of the Rehabilitation Act protect the civil rights of individuals with disabilities. Any college or university that accepts federal funds must comply with this legislation. When developing intervention plans for students with disabilities, counselors must be aware of the possible limitations and challenges they face when maintaining the students' rights.

Besides legal issues, mental health providers must inform the students that Internet-based counseling should not be considered a comprehensive counseling service. Additional intensive services may be called for to aid the student. Furthermore, providers must present their full credentials to the students who request services before counseling can take place (Efstathiou, 2009). The National Board of Certified Counselors (NBCC) has a code of conduct and practice which includes informing Internet clients of possible security issues with the particular website. NBCC also argued that parental consent should be mandatory for minors to receive counseling, but then it becomes difficult to verify the parents' identities. The privacy of students seeking services must be protected, and it is the responsibility of the counselor to inform the student if the site is compromised or inappropriate to meet their needs (Heinlen, Welfel, Richmond, & Rak, 2003).

Discussion

Internet-based crisis intervention for college students with disabilities enables counselors to attend to more students than using face-to-face therapy. Students receive support, and the therapist has computer-aided technology and databases to manage the clerical work, which then provides more time for therapy (Gega, Marks, & Mataix-Cole, 2004). Students report that Internet-based counseling helps alleviate depression and anxiety and enables them to function more effectively in the college environment. Computer systems are cost effective and easier to access for students who need them.

The growing interest in using Internet-based counseling means that mental health professionals and college services providers are obligated to participate in additional training and create more sites for students. Work also needs to be done to educate mental health insurance providers who are not always willing to reimburse Internet-based therapeutic services. There are also ethical considerations. However, as the popularity of Internet-based crisis intervention grows, clinicians should continue to explore Internet-based options and discuss with colleagues how best to service the needs of college students with disabilities (Tate & Zabinski, 2004).

REFERENCES

Belch, H. A., & Marshak, L. E. (2006). Critical incidents involving students with psychiatric disabilities: The gap between state of the art and campus practice. *NASPA Journal, 43*, 464–483.

Chaffin, A. J., & Harlow, S. D. (2005). Cognitive learning applied to older adult learners and technology. *Educational Gerontology, 31*, 301–329.

Chaplin, R. (2009). New research into general psychiatric services for adults with intellectual disability and mental illness. *Journal of Intellectual Disability Research*, 189–199.

Efstathiou, G. (2009). Students' psychological web consulting: Function and outcome evaluation. *British Journal of Guidance & Counseling, 37*, 243–255.

Gega, L., Marks, I., & Mataix-Cols, D. (2003). Computer-aided CBT self help for anxiety and depression disorders: Experience of a London clinic and future directions. *Journal of Clinical Psychology, 60*, 147–157.

Harvey, V. S., & Carlson, V. (2003). Ethical and professional issues with computer related technology. *School Psychology Review, 32*, 92–107.

Heinlen, K. T., Welfel, E. R., Richmond, E. N., & Rak, C. F. (2003). *Journal of Counseling & Development, 81*, 61–69.

Hollingsworth, K. R., Dunkle, J. H., & Douce, L. (Eds.). (2009). *The high-risk (disturbed and disturbing) college student*. Hoboken, NJ: Wiley InterScience.

Margalit, M., & Raskind, M. H. (2009). Mothers of children with LD and ADHD: Empowerment through online communication. *Journal of Special Education Technology, 24*, 39–49.

Michaud, P., & Colom, P. (2003). Implications and evaluations of an internet health site for adolescents in Switzerland. *Journal of Adolescent Health, 33*, 287–290.

Raskind, M. H., Margalit, M., & Higgins, E. L. (2006). "My LD": Children's voices on the internet. *Learning Disability Quarterly, 29*, 253–266.

Tate, D. F., & Zabinski, M. F. (2004). Computer and Internet applications for psychological treatment: Update for clinicians. *Journal of Clinical Psychology, 60*, 209–220.

Laws and Acts

Americans with Disabilities Act of 1990 – ADA – 42 U.S. Code Chapter 126.

Educational Rights and Privacy Act (FERPA) (20 U.S.C. § 1232g; 34 CFR Part 99).

Health Insurance Portability and Accountability Act of 1996 (HIPAA), Public Law 104–191.

Section 504 of the Rehabilitation Act of 1973, Pub. L. No. 93-112, 87 Stat. 394 (Sept. 26, 1973), codified at 29 U.S.C. § 701.

Part V

BEYOND THE TELEPHONE CONTACT

Chapter 25

BEYOND THE TELEPHONE CONTACT[40]

LEE ANN HOFF

Situation 1: Telephone call to the center, wrist-cutting in process, rescue operation, medical treatment, return home, repeat call to the center, wrist cutting in process, and so on.

Situation 2: Telephone call to the center, threat of overdose, face-to-face treatment at the center, failure to involve significant other, overdose of barbiturates, medical treatment, family treatment, broken appointments, repeat calls to the center.

Situation 3: Telephone call to the center, impending plan of carbon monoxide poisoning, acceptance of treatment opportunity at the center, no further calls.

Situation 4: Completed overdose of lethal dose, telephone call to the center, rescue operation, intensive medical treatment followed by long-term comprehensive psychological treatment, no further calls.

Each of these situations includes elements of self-destructive behavior in the patient which are more or less lethal. Which patient represents a high suicidal risk? Who is manipulative as well as suicidal? What steps can be taken to prevent chronicity among callers? The intent in what follows is not to answer these questions as such, but highlight the importance of four questions as they influence what happened after a call, that is, following a call, what are the implications for the caller himself, the significant other, the counselor, and the community at large?

From these brief descriptions, it is already evident that a vicious cycle can occur in relation to telephone calls from would-be suicidal individuals. After

---

[40] This chapter focuses on the client in a suicidal crisis. The concepts and possibilities outlined can, however, easily be extended to clients in a nonsuicidal crisis.

natively, emergency telephone counseling can function as the focal event, launching a network of interaction among persons and agencies: the caller, the counselor, significant other(s), rescue squad, crisis clinic, and so on. Everything that happens after the call is significantly related to the counselor's knowledge of the caller and his psychosocial pattern of behavior and how this pattern influences the counselor, the significant other, and the community at large. The relationship of these variables and how they affect the outcome of calls to a suicide prevention center are explored in what follows. In addition, there is an attempt to delineate some of the problems and limitations intrinsic to the telephone service, as these pertain to the outcome of calls. Illustrative case examples will be cited.

Callers: Who Are They?

The importance of this question can hardly be overemphasized. The identity of callers and their social-psychological patterns of behavior frequently remain ambiguous to the telephone counselor. If this occurs, a vicious cycle can result: call, rescue, symptomatic treatment, discharge, call. Once this cycle develops, the negative effects for the caller himself, significant other, counselor and agencies are difficult to counteract. The identity of callers, then, along with fine discrimination and understanding regarding their overt and covert needs, constitutes the first necessity for developing adequate follow-through after a telephone call. The failure to identify callers and discriminate between their differing needs and levels of lethality can result not only in a possible suicide, which might have been averted, but also in a barrage of undesired results for the significant other, counselor, and various agencies.

Several kinds of callers must be distinguished in order to discuss the outcomes of calls:

1. The caller who is a high suicidal risk, low suicidal risk, manipulative, self-mutilative, or a repeater.

2. The unidentified caller and the identified caller.

3. A significant other calling on behalf of a suicidal person.

The characteristics of callers may often overlap; for example, a highly suicidal person may also be manipulative.

The outcome of anonymous calls may vary considerably from those in which the caller is known. The lack of identification for a caller may be a result of the caller, the counselor or a combination of factors. Some callers who are highly suicidal refuse to give their name until they have tested the counselor's degree of caring and ability to help them discover alternatives to suicide. In most instances this testing is accomplished in the first few minutes of the call, during which the average counselor is able to establish rapport with the caller. The relative ease of this interaction is heavily influenced by the suicidal person's ambivalence about dying which he or she frequently manifests by initiating the call and responding positively to the rescue process. The rescue operation resulting from these calls represents the first step in what should constitute a comprehensive service to the suicidal person. Callers who are less highly lethal, manipulative, and/or self-mutilating demand different responses from counselors as compared to highly lethal callers. Thus, the counselor's ability to discriminate and assess the lethality of callers is a critical factor affecting outcomes of calls.

Factors relative to the identity of callers merit research attention. For example, what is the therapeutic potential in remaining anonymous? Does the caller remain anonymous for his own unexplained reasons or because of the counselor's inattention to identity factors? What are the treatment implications for the caller who uses several names? Are there intrinsic liabilities in a telephone service such as indefinite availability of instant gratification for repeat callers who are not in crisis? Does the value of important emergency services for persons in crisis outweigh these liabilities? Are there other systems in the community which can provide crisis services without these liabilities?

Supportive Services

Regardless of who the caller is, adequate follow-up of the call cannot be accomplished without supportive services functioning interchangeably among the counselor, the center itself, the significant other, as well as the community at large.

Once individuals have made contact with the center and their lethality has been assessed, several things may occur, but in any case the interaction should not end with the telephone contact, which ideally is only the beginning of a comprehensive program of service to the caller and others surrounding them. Suicidal or self-mutilating people are asking for a response not only from the counselor but also from the significant others in their lives which may include agencies they are already in contact with.

In the event that the person has made a potentially lethal suicide attempt, the rescue procedure is fairly obvious and is carried out usually in a straightforward manner with few complications. Medical treatment and/or hospitalization are frequently indicated. This first stage of treatment should be followed by a long-range program focusing not only on the clients themselves but also on the underlying causes and life circumstances influencing their self-destructive behavior. For example, individual psychotherapy and psychotropic drug treatment may be helpful for the depressed person but, if factors such as repeated job failure, inability to develop and sustain satisfying relationships, substandard housing, marital strife, and a role as the family scapegoat are present, a broader treatment approach is indicated. Examples would be family, marital or group therapy, vocational rehabilitation, and social action input to alter a social system which is more destructive than nurturing to the individual. Such a comprehensive program is widely used in many community mental health programs, and its inclusion here may appear to be a statement of the obvious. This is true. However, there are special difficulties in implementing a comprehensive program for the suicidal person, particularly the repeat attempter. Several factors surrounding the repeat attempter seem to militate against the treatment process. These will be examined in some detail as they comprise central issues influencing the outcomes of calls from repeat suicide attempters or self-mutilators.

The social-psychological history of self-mutilators is often characterized by family turmoil, sexual trauma, deficient interpersonal skills, identity problems, social deviancy, and stigmatization. The interpersonal responses are generally inadequate to satisfy their needs. Ordinary communication patterns have been unsuccessful. They often fail to gain the sustained attention of significant others, including treatment agencies, except through some kind of deviant behavior such as self-mutilation. Even in the absence of social deviance and a history of overt family turmoil, self-multilators have, for some reason, been unable to communicate their needs to those around them. After their first suicide attempt, they experience a different response from significant others, not necessarily a positive response, but a different response. Their lethality at this point may be low. They have made no prior attempts, the method is nonlethal, they have clearly provided for rescue, their ambivalence is high and their self-mutilation appears to be directed toward changing their interpersonal field rather than toward death. However, since the self-mutilation is nonlethal, it is easy for significant others and treatment agencies to miss the message of the self-mutilator's behavior. Sometimes, out of shame and stigma, families will shield the self-mutilator and take the risk of rejecting medical treatment.

More typically, there is a response of concern mixed with resentment, anger, and confusion about the meaning of the behavior. The response, however, often remains focused on the symptom itself, namely, self-mutilative behavior, either because the family is unwilling or unmotivated to deal with underlying social and psychological factors, or because treatment personnel likewise miss the meaning of the behavior and focus on a symptomatic approach. When this occurs, clients are almost inevitably left with the option of repeating their self-mutilation.

Successive suicide attempts generally increase in lethality inasmuch as prior attempts fail to accomplish a change in the interpersonal field. At the same time, significant others and treatment agencies become more inured to the attempter's self-mutilating behavior, which in turn perpetuates the behavior. In addition to these factors, the self-mutilator often has personality features which seem to elicit rejection from others. Alternatively, their interpersonal experience includes a pattern of rejection from others so that they are unable to deal with a response of caring and acceptance without extreme testing behavior. This can result in impatience on the part of counselors which, if not dealt with constructively, can further increase the attempter's feelings of rejection. The counselor, on the other hand, can be left with feelings of helplessness, failure, resentment, guilt, and general discouragement in working with these clients. These feelings are often shared by agencies as well.

What happens to clients after a call depends then, not only on who the callers are and what their needs are, but also on the counselor's ability to assess these needs, mobilize client and community resources, and initiate follow-up activity appropriate to the individual situation.

Among these functions, follow-up is perhaps the most challenging. This includes several facets which will be explored especially as they pertain to the function of a suicide prevention center. For clients requiring medical or hospital treatment following a suicide attempt, a comprehensive treatment program may be initiated in the hospital if there is a psychiatric service. If the suicide prevention center is administratively a part of a comprehensive psychiatric service, such as in a community mental health center, there is a natural framework in which to facilitate continuity of treatment between the telephone contact and other services indicated by the client's needs.

When this is not the case, it is important for suicide prevention centers to establish and maintain relationships with the various community agencies necessary to support a total program for clients following their call. Effective interagency communication and coordination is of critical importance in follow-up work with self-mutilators who have a history of repeat behavior of this kind. Given the difficulties of responding therapeutically to these clients, it is readily apparent why these individuals are often active clients with several agencies simultaneously. If this is the case, their suicide potential may increase by virtue of their repeated experience of failure to respond to treatment and inadvertent rejection by the agencies due to the factors described above. When this occurs clients will usually increase their calls to the suicide prevention center where essentially the same result can occur if follow-up and interagency comprehensive treatment planning are lacking. Potentially, then, a vicious cycle can develop: call to suicide prevention center; rescue operation; symptomatic treatment; client's approach to another agency; treatment with little result; feelings of failure by the client, counselor, and agencies; return call to suicide prevention center; and so on.

Effective intervention in this cycle is one of the most challenging problems facing not only suicide prevention centers, but also other helping agencies as well. A comprehensive follow-up program is perhaps the most basic element in such intervention. Suicide prevention centers have a responsibility not only to initiate, implement and evaluate follow-up programs themselves but also to offer consultation and education services to other agencies working with suicidal persons and chronic self-mutilators.

The Significant Other

How does the significant other influence the outcome of a call? How is the significant other influenced by the outcome of the call? How is the outcome influenced by the apparent lack of a significant other in the life of the caller? If a suicide attempt has already been made and a straightforward rescue operation is accomplished by the suicide prevention center, usually the significant other is not on the immediate scene. Depending on the urgency of physical rescue needs, the counselor may or may not have obtained information about the significant others in the caller's life. If such data are not obtained by the telephone counselor, it is, of course, important that the significant other be appropriately included in comprehensive follow-up programs. Failure to do so can contribute to perpetuating the cycle of "call, rescue, failure, call" mentioned above.

In other cases, successful involvement of the significant other necessitates a sensitive, skilled approach by the counselor to a situation in which the latent content and the message of suicide behavior must be understood and dealt with. Sometimes suicidal behavior is a response to the lack of significant others. For callers like this, who either lack resources or are cut off from communication with them, the counselor may become the most significant other. Hopefully the outcome of calls from such persons will result in the mutual discovery of new resources – even if limited at first to a meaningful link with the agency and a counselor – and alternatives to the choice of suicide.

Callers may make the manifest plea to the counselor to not involve the significant other or may threaten to carry out suicidal plans if the significant other is called. When suicidal behavior constitutes a covert message of some kind to the significant other, the counselor is faced with the task of helping callers communicate with significant others at a cost less than the price of their life and not alienating the callers in the process. This is a delicate task involving a clear and secure understanding of confidentiality, the purpose of which is lost, of course, if the counselor colludes with the caller's suicidal plan by dealing only with the manifest plea or threat and promising not to involve significant others.

Most counselors and psychotherapists handle this by a frank explanation of the fact that confidentiality does not apply to information which, if kept confidential, can potentially contribute to the client's death, for example. a lethal suicidal plan. Skillful involvement of significant others by the telephone counselor can lay the groundwork for a comprehensive follow-up program. As noted above, when significant others are not included in the treatment program, not only is self-destructive behavior likely to continue, but also opportunities are lost for working educationally with the problem of taboo. In addition, significant others are an important supportive avenue for suicide prevention workers to address the social and community problems contributing to the self-destructive behavior, such as housing, economic and sexual oppression, and racism.

Significant others are, of course, profoundly affected by self-destructive or self-mutilative behavior, whether this be in the form of disgust, confusion, fear, resentment, concern, or a combination of these feelings. Positive outcomes of calls will hopefully include positive results for significant others as well as for the callers themselves. Ideally this will occur whether the call is from suicidal individuals themselves or from a significant other on behalf of another.

In short, significant others are vital facets in the network of interaction between the caller, the counselor, supportive treatment, and social action agencies in the community. If they are excluded either as potential helpers or as persons to be helped, the self-destructive person will be served less well both during and after the call.

The Counselor

Helping self-destructive persons via the telephone is fraught with difficulties, potential complications, and uncertainties which are much less prevalent in face-to-face counseling situations. Because of this and the fact that the greater portion of telephone counseling in suicide prevention centers is done by lay volunteers, the implications for volunteers after the call deserve serious consideration. Psychotherapists who have worked with suicidal persons are familiar with the emotional energy that can be expended in the process. They also know the importance of sharing responsibility for these clients with other psychotherapists as well as with significant others. As a matter of fact, in the case of a client whose suicidal motivation focuses on otherwise unexpressed anger and revenge toward a significant other and the significant other is a psychotherapist, assumption of therapeutic responsibility by a single psychotherapist can inadvertently increase suicidal potential. During stages of therapy when the client's suicide potential is higher, the psychotherapist often assumes a more active role with the client than is indicated in other therapeutic interactions. This can be both time-consuming and exhausting, and unless colleague and team support is forthcoming, can readily become a source of discouragement and eventual disinclination to work with suicidal persons.

If this is true for the professional psychotherapist, it is doubly so for the volunteer telephone counselor, who is frequently less trained and experienced and also works in physical isolation during the most critical hours of the night. After a call from a self-destructive person, counselors can be left with feelings of isolation, confusion, failure, insecurity, resentment, and guilt, or they may experience a sense of satisfaction in responding effectively to persons in critical need. The counselor's feelings after a call are inevitably affected by the outcome of the call for the client and the significant others. If an adequate treatment program does not follow upon initiation of the rescue and treatment process by the client and telephone counselor, the counselor begins to experience a sense of futility of effort as the client continues to call the telephone service with little or no change in the social and interpersonal field. Counselors may sense vaguely that somehow they are contributing to the perpetuation of dependency on the telephone service which is a less than adequate substitute for a planned treatment program. This is particularly true if the telephone service focuses on emergency and crisis intervention and there is no built-in provision for or expectation of continuity of treatment by telephone.

Follow-up treatment generally includes availability of emergency telephone service for a client who is highly suicidal. In these instances, the client's psychotherapist may advise telephone counselors of factors which would facilitate emergency counseling on the phone. This is particularly important in the case of self-mutilating callers who are also manipulative. Most emergency telephone services are manned by volunteers who work a limited number of hours, which complicates the possibility of providing continuity of service via the telephone. In view of these factors, direction and support of the telephone counselor becomes increasingly important. In fact, the outcome of calls is significantly influenced by the consistency of support to the telephone worker. In instances where the caller's suicide potential is difficult to assess, the counselor needs ready access to consultants who can assist with this task in a skilled manner.

When counselors cannot obtain the identity of the caller and the risk of suicide is high, the counselors will probably experience a sense of failure and insecurity regarding the adequacy of their approach to and management of the situation. When a caller has made a suicide attempt before calling and then lapses into unconsciousness and drops the telephone, the counselor often experiences a sense of helplessness or an unrealistic degree of responsibility for the life of the client. In all of these instances, counselors should have easy access to a consultant on both an immediate and a long-range basis. This provides not only reassurance but also the opportunity to work through feelings of excessive responsibility or neurotically tinged guilt associated with centuries-old societal attitudes regarding suicide and their own possibly unresolved feelings about suicide and death. The consultation and supervisory process also affords telephone counselors a medium for constant evaluation and improvement of their work with suicidal persons.

Obviously, as telephone counselors become more proficient in their role, clients and significant others will be favorably affected following a call to a suicide prevention center. Telephone counseling is an exacting and demanding ingredient in the network of services available for persons in suicidal crisis. The emergency telephone service is regarded by many suicide prevention centers as "the heart of the agency" or the front-line in a network of services to persons in suicidal crises. To maintain this difficult facet of suicide prevention work at a quality level, supportive services must be elicited for counselors as well as callers. This is especially urgent when the counseling is done by volunteers.

It is paradoxical that suicide prevention centers have developed a pattern of work division in which the workers with least preparation, namely, the volunteers, have responsibility for dealing with clients when their suicidal crisis is potentially most critical, and that this same group of workers are frequently barred from participating in face-to-face counseling with suicidal persons, presumably because they lack sufficient skill for this. Yet counseling a person in suicidal crisis on a face-to-face basis is considerably less trying and fraught with uncertainty and risk than is telephone counseling. This fact merits exploration and evaluation by suicide prevention workers.

Summary

Factors influencing the outcome of calls from self-destructive persons have been discussed as they pertain to callers, supportive agencies, significant others, and telephone counselors. Difficulties and problems hindering favorable results are cited. Apropos of these problems, it appears that providing telephone emergency service to potentially self-destructive persons seeking help is a valuable and unduplicated service in most communities. However, suicide prevention workers might address themselves to the question of whether the problems associated with providing such a service are inherent in working with suicidal persons, or whether they are related to organizational and manpower factors such as excessive reliance on nonprofessional workers for the most critical facet of the work. At a time when the manpower shortage in service agencies is more acute than ever, suicide prevention centers have been unique in their extensive and creative use of nonprofessionals. However, it is a well-established fact that, while volunteers offer a distinctive quality that speaks for its own value, the success of their efforts depends on supportive services in whatever setting they work. If and when volunteer counselors work in relative isolation from other facets of the helping network, the outcome of telephone counseling can be seriously jeopardized.

Appendix

The case examples that follow will be illustrative of the factors, issues, and problems inherent in determining what happens "after the call."

Case Situation 1

John, age 31, called the center at 4 a.m. Sunday on a holiday weekend. John was in the process of cutting his wrists when he called. His general message to the counselor was one of desperate loneliness, isolation, helplessness, physical illness, bitterness about past rejections, and extreme dependence on someone to relieve him of his misery. Among the rejection experiences cited, he revealed that the last time he called presenting a similar picture, the counselor had called John's psychotherapist who advised use of the rescue squad. According to John, the rescue squad as well as the psychiatric resident at the local hospital spurned his suicide attempts and left him feeling that they could care less if he killed himself. He was given medical first aid and sent home.

Attempts by the counselor to ascertain the degree of physical injury and need for emergency medical treatment again resulted in evasiveness on John's part. In spite of the counselor's attempt to dissuade John from cutting his wrists and focus instead on underlying problems, John continued with his wrist-cutting behavior. When the counselor discussed rescue possibilities, utilizing the local rescue squad, John announced that he had a gun and would shoot anyone who came to the house. John also stated that his psychotherapist (from a psychiatric outpatient department of a local hospital) "really doesn't understand" and rejects him at times, and that he wanted to speak with the telephone counselor on a face-to-face basis at 4:30 a.m. When the counselor proposed the possibility of seeing the consultant on a face-to-face emergency basis, John insisted that he would talk with no one but the telephone counselor. The interaction between John and the counselor left the counselor with a strong sense of responsibility for John. John had asked for rescue but refused ordinary rescue operations and managed to elicit guilt feelings in the counselor when she explained that she could not see him in person while manning the telephone service.

At this point, the volunteer terminated the call temporarily and advised John that she would call him back after seeking assistance in her efforts to help him. She called the consultant who discussed with her the lethality factors and apparent manipulative elements of the situation. The consultant and counselor agreed to propose to John a crisis home visit by the consultant which would be preceded by the consultant's direct telephone conversation with John. John responded to this plan by stating he would not answer the phone when the consultant called.

After one-half hour of busy signals or no answer, the consultant notified the telephone counselor of the results, having decided not to make the home visit, based on her judgment that the lethality elements were outweighed by manipulative factors. In the event that John called back, he would be told of attempts to reach him. As anticipated, John called back shortly thereafter and was persuaded by the counselor to answer the consultant's call, which he did.

During a 40-minute session, John and the consultant discussed all the foregoing interaction in a very straightforward manner. John's manipulative behavior became clearer, as well as less rewarding, in his interaction with the consultant than with the counselor, at which point it was possible to talk with John about his underlying problems instead of remaining focused on the wrist-cutting behavior. John denied his threats about shooting would-be rescuers and stated he had only scratched his wrists and did not need medical attention. The consultant and John finally agreed on the following plan. Since it was a Sunday night on a holiday weekend, the consultant would call him Monday evening because of the increased anxiety and loneliness he experiences at bedtime, and the following Tuesday a joint conference would be arranged with his psychotherapist, the consultant, and the telephone counselor.

During the ensuing conference, therapy goals were clarified among which were attempts to reduce John's extreme dependency needs and help him meet his attention needs in more satisfying ways than by self-mutilating behavior. Following the conference, John continued to call the suicide prevention center with a presenting behavior pattern similar to that cited above. Telephone counselors, however, were in a more knowledgeable position to respond to him therapeutically, as they had been advised of approaches which led to more positive results and which complemented the overall treatment program directed by his regular psychotherapist. In instances when John's manipulative behavior became extreme, often when talking with a less experienced volunteer, the problem was dealt with by the staff consultant's direct conversation with John. Periodic conferences continued between the psychotherapist and the center staff. Eventually John's physical problems improved with ongoing medical treatment. He became involved in a program of vocational rehabilitation, began to reestablish himself in the community socially, saw his psychotherapist on a gradually decreasing basis, and called the center only rarely. In total, John was in treatment about one year.

Case Situation 2

Karen, age 15, called the center at 8 p.m. threatening to take an overdose of her mother's sleeping pills which were readily available to her. Her presenting difficulty as told to the telephone counselor was a sense of total misunderstanding and unacceptance by her parents. Karen felt unable to communicate her distress to her parents. In fact, she was calling from a local drugstore telephone booth at a shopping center near her suburban home.

After a half-hour discussion with the telephone counselor, Karen felt less reluctant to return home and said she felt she could control herself from taking the pills although she still could not tell her parents how distressed she was. She felt encouraged by the possibilities of help available the next day on a face-to-face basis at the center. Karen refused to give her last name, parents' name, address, or telephone number out of fear that the counselor would involve her parents without her consent. Karen kept her appointment the next day and, after the third session, continued to resist all efforts of the psychotherapist to involve her parents, refusing to give necessary identifying data.

The day following the third session, Karen took an overdose of 20 of her mother's sleeping pills (barbiturates) in school and informed her close girlfriend and a teacher she trusted, who took her to a nearby hospital emergency room. Her parents were, of course, identified and involved at this point. During the course of brief hospitalization, Karen was seen by a psychiatrist. Karen resisted therapy from the psychiatrist, requesting a return to the center. Following this, joint treatment planning ensued between the psychiatrist, Karen, and her parents and the center. Family therapy was decided on with an apparently positive beginning. After three sessions, however, Karen's parents broke the appointments, and Karen began using the telephone and service threatening suicide again.

The center's family therapist attempted by telephone contact to re-engage the parents in therapy with no results, and Karen continued to call. Eventually a home visit was made, and the parents finally began to cooperate in the psychotherapy process after gaining a better understanding of the meaning and seriousness of Karen's suicidal behavior. Among the paradoxes and problems encountered with the parents was their resentment of Karen's use of the telephone, on the one hand, and their refusal to deal with underlying causes on the other. The psychotherapy program included family sessions as well as intermittent individual sessions with Karen over an eight-week period. As treatment proceeded, Karen stopped using the telephone service and was no longer suicidal. Termination included referral and coordinating efforts with Karen's favorite teacher and the counseling service of her private school.

Case Situation 3

Philip, age 52, called the center at 9 p.m. presenting a picture of an acutely suicidal individual. A PhD engineer, he had recently been laid off from his job because of the company's economic straits (a first-time experience for him), was dependent on his wife, an executive secretary, for support, had been told by his wife of her plan to divorce him, was experiencing acute clinical depression with crying bouts, anorexia, and sleeplessness, and felt the strong urge to kill himself by carbon monoxide poisoning.

After a 50-minute session with the telephone counselor, Philip decided against carrying out his suicidal intentions and was willing to work on discovering alternatives to suicide through face-to-face counseling at the center. Two hours after the call, the counselor called Philip in an effort to strengthen his link to the center as a resource since he was considered quite highly suicidal. Philip was feeling less suicidal at this time and was able to share with his wife that he would be seeing a psychotherapist the next day. He was seen in psychotherapy three times a week for four weeks and less frequently for three more weeks. During this time he was able to redirect his energies into developing new potential jobs, changed his way of relating to his wife, but could not deal with the reality of the impending divorce. He continued to blame himself for the apparent failure of the marriage and was obsessed about the thought of suicide which he visualized as the only solution when the divorce eventually was to take place.

He continued treatment very enthusiastically for another six months during which time the divorce was finalized. By this time he had experienced some success in a new job as well as stronger relationships with his two grown children. Upon termination of psychotherapy at the end of eight months, he was still having occasional suicidal ideation but was generally relieved of severe depression and felt a positive link with the center and his psychotherapist in the event of a future suicidal crisis.

Case Situation 4

Susan, age 23, called the center stating she had taken 40 Thorazine tablets one-half hour earlier. She was beginning to experience drowsiness but, in general, presented a picture of great panic about what would happen to her if she were taken to the hospital. She was alone at the time of the call, her two roommates having gone out of town for the weekend. The counselor's attempt to alleviate her fears about the rescue squad[41] were met by a hysterical response, mingled with crying and irrational objections to rescue, while at the same time pleading to be saved. Susan gave her address to the counselor but said she would jump out the window if the fire department rescue squad came.

A telephone counseling colleague called the consultant who arranged to go to Susan's home with the telephone counselor she had talked with. This plan

---

[41] The rescue resource used by the center.

was acceptable to Susan, who also consented to be taken to a private hospital of her choice for medical treatment. There she was admitted to the intensive care unit. Following medical recovery, a comprehensive treatment plan was developed in collaboration with Susan's medical doctor prior to her discharge from the general hospital. Susan's parents and her roommates were included in various facets of the treatment from time to time.

Susan had made three prior suicide attempts, all less lethal than this one, but had always received only emergency medical treatment and was discharged without psychotherapy. After five sessions at the center, Susan was referred for longer-term treatment to the counseling center of a local university where she was a graduate student. She made no further calls to the center.

Chapter 26

BEYOND THE PHONE LINES: NEW AND EMERGING TECHNOLOGIES IN THE FIELD OF CRISIS INTERVENTION

Laura A. Davidson, William P. Evans, and Lorie L. Sicafuse

Since the publication of the previous edition of this book in 2002, the communication landscape worldwide has been dramatically altered by a revolution of new media. Cell phone ownership has doubled in the past decade, and more than 90% of households in the United States now own cell phones (Blumberg & Luke, 2010; Lenhart, 2010b). Internet use has also increased worldwide, with only 45% of individuals using a computer in 2002 compared with 81% in 2010 (Cellular Telecommunications Industry Association, 2011). Not only do most adults in the United States now have cell phones, research suggests that more adolescents and adults *prefer* to communicate through texting and online media than ever before (Lenhart, 2010a; Lenhart et al., 2010). These findings signal a major turning point in the way consumers expect and prefer to contact crisis and counseling services. Roughly six in ten adult Internet users report having gone online to search for health information, and nearly one in three have looked for information on depression, anxiety stress, or mental health issues on the Internet (Fox & Jones, 2009).

Although the use of new media in the field of crisis intervention has somewhat lagged behind its rapid acquisition by consumers, there are a handful of crisis call centers worldwide that have expanded their services to allow individuals to contact them using new media. Data and research emerging from these pilot programs suggest that not only can crisis call centers deliver the same, and sometimes higher, quality of services to users in these new media formats, but new media provides crisis call centers with an opportunity to advertise their services to a broader and younger audience than ever before.

These technological advances are likely to have a profound impact on the way crisis and suicide interventions are conducted in the future, as data on media usage continues to suggest that individuals use their telephones for calling less and less frequently (Lenhart, 2010a). In recognition of the impact of new media on the future of health care, the New Freedom Commission on Mental Health (2003, p. 15) recommended to "Use health technology and telehealth to improve access and coordination of mental health care, especially for Americans in remote areas or in underserved populations." Acknowledging their consumers' changing media preferences and the immense potential for accessing individuals in these remote areas and underserved populations, crisis call centers around the world have begun to expand their technological capacity in order to allow users to contact them via text, chat, and even social networking sites like Twitter and Facebook.

New Media's Capacity to Reach Underserved Populations

Many of the efforts to incorporate new media into crisis intervention have demonstrated promise in their capacity to appeal to underserved populations that have tended to underutilize crisis hotlines in the past. Youths, for example, contact crisis lines in disproportionately low numbers given that as many as 1.5 million students attempt suicide and 2.9 million students seriously consider committing suicide each year (Eaton et al., 2008). Although the exact number of unique calls by youths to crisis call centers is difficult to ascertain (Gould et al., 2006), in Nevada, only 2%-3% of the nearly 100,000 calls to the Crisis Call Center from 2005-2008 were from individuals ages 5-18 (Evans et al., 2009). These statistics parallel those reported by other call centers across the country (e.g., Gould et al., 2006; Offer et al., 1991). Research by Gould et al. (2006) found that the most common reasons youth provide for their unwillingness to use hotlines when in crisis were shame and a belief that they could solve their own problems without outside assistance. However, the underutilization of crisis lines by adolescents also may relate to their communication preferences, as a majority of adolescents now elect to communicate through online or text-based methods rather than the phone. As a result, new media may have the potential to reduce adolescents' feelings of shame for seeking out help and support.

Studies of adolescent media use suggest that texting is the dominant way they prefer to communicate with one another. Of the 75% of 12-25 year-olds with cell phones in the United States, 72% use text messaging, and 54% report that text messaging is the most frequent way they communicate with their friends on a daily basis, more than calling, messaging via social networking sites, instant messaging, or even talking face-to-face (Lenhart et al., 2010). In fact, one-third of teenagers report that they send more than 100 texts each day, and two-thirds of teenagers report sending at least 50 texts per day (Lenhart et al., 2010). These findings suggest that many adolescents communicate via texting with much of the same speed, frequency, and fluidity as would be expected with calling or talking face-to-face.

The popularity of new media among adolescents is attributable to a number of its unique features. Many parents pay for their children's mobile phone use in order to have a way to stay in contact with them (Davie et al., 2004), and many cell phone plans allow for unlimited texting for minimal cost (Faulkner & Culwin, 2005). As a result, the costs associated with texting are often much lower than the costs of calling on a landline or even on a cell phone. In addition to its low cost, youths report that texting is a more immediate, more private, less awkward, less intimidating, and more convenient way of communicating than calling or talking face-to-face (Evans et al., n.d.; Lenhart et al., 2010). Texting and online communication appear to be particularly popular methods of communication among youths who tend to be lonelier and more socially anxious (Pierce, 2009). Youths who report that they preferred texting to calling also report that they were better able to communicate their "real self" via text and online communication than through direct telephone call conversations (Pierce, 2009).

Research by Gilat and Shahar (2007) suggest that online communication, like chatting or social networking, also has immense appeal for adolescents and, most importantly, may promote higher disclosure of suicidal ideation. In a comparison of data collected from a sample of calls, chats, and online support group posts, the researchers found that adolescents were significantly more likely to report suicidal ideation in posts to an online support group than they were to admit suicidal ideation during a telephone call to the hotline or even during one-on-one chat with a call center counselor. The authors identified this phenomenon as the "disinhibition effect" (p. 16), as the increased anonymity associated with online interventions appears to foster increased disclosure of personal information. Similarly, findings from an evaluation of the TextToday program, a text-based crisis line offered in Nevada, suggest that not only do adolescents have more positive attitudes towards a crisis line that offers texting in addition to calling, but adding texting capacity to a crisis call center may also increase adolescents' willingness to seek out and use such services (Evans et al., n.d.). In some schools where the texting crisis line was promoted, as many as 12.3% of students later texted into the hotline to seek information or discuss a crisis. In focus groups with 113 middle and high school students about the texting hotline, students most frequently mentioned the increased anonymity as the greatest benefit of a text-based crisis line over a traditional call line. Thus, preliminary data emerging from crisis call centers that utilize new technologies suggest that, by increasing the anonymity of crisis line services, they may, for the first time in crisis lines' long history, reach one of their most underserved populations.

In response to this changing communication landscape, a number of new crisis intervention programs have emerged that allow users to text, chat, e-mail, or post on crisis centers' social networking sites, organization websites, and online support groups when they are in need of emotional support. These new services can generally be categorized into *synchronous* support services, which provide live and instant back-and-forth conversation with a trained volunteer or counselor (e.g., texting and chatting through instant messaging), and *asynchronous* support services, in which crisis intervention is provided through a process of back and forth responses over time (e.g., e-mail and posts on online support groups or social networking sites). Although some crisis support lines emphasize a particular new technology, like texting or chatting, many other organizations are beginning to provide a continuum of services that include texting, chatting, online support groups, and traditional telephone-based interventions. The following sections provide an overview of some of the different types of new media services currently offered by crisis call centers worldwide followed by a discussion of the opportunities and challenges associated with expanding more of these new technologies into crisis intervention services in the future.

Synchronous Support Services: Texting Hotlines

Samaritans

Samaritans (in the UK) is largely credited as one of the first crisis hotlines in the world to expand the traditional telephone-based crisis call system to include new forms of communication. In 1994, Samaritans was the first to offer emotional support by e-mail, a service that is now available at 193 branches (Samaritans, 2010). In 2006, The Samaritans Crisis line added a text messaging platform to their crisis intervention programs. Samaritans now provide anonymous emotional support via telephone, e-mail, letter, face-to-face visits, and text counseling services and is in the process of expanding their services to include instant messaging (Samaritans, 2010).

Samaritans also was one of the first call centers to demonstrate the immense potential and popularity of providing crisis intervention using nontelephone-based methods. Shortly after expanding their services to include text messaging, Samaritans received over 200,000 text messages with minimal marketing efforts. In fact, shortly after its launch, Samaritans had to cease advertising altogether as the demand for their services overtook their capacity to provide quality services (Substance Abuse and Mental Health Services Association [SAMHSA], 2011). In an early report about the texting program,

Samaritans highlighted its potential to reach more at-risk users when they noted that online and e-mail users reported suicidal ideation more frequently, with 53% of e-mails sent to jo@samaritans.org directly expressing suicidality as compared to 26% of phone calls (Howlett & Langdon, 2004).

TextToday

In May 2010, the Crisis Call Center of Nevada, part of the National Lifeline's network of call centers, piloted one of the first 24-hour, text-based crisis lines in the United States that specifically targeted youth. Posters that included call-line information were posted in the male and female restrooms at 13 middle and high schools in Nevada. Take-away cards with the TextToday number and the numbers for other local crisis resources were attached to each poster display so that youth could take program information home for later use. To access the system, texters type a keyword (e.g., "listen" or "care") to a 6-digit phone number to opt into the Crisis Call Center service. Shortly after, texters receive the following preprogrammed message to notify them that they have successfully opted into the system: "Thank you for texting us. You will be contacted shortly by one of our text message support staff (you may opt out at any time by texting 'stop')."

The TextToday program uses an online system to monitor texts into the Crisis Call Center. Counselors communicate through a computer-based platform to youths on their cell phones. One of the unique features of a text-based platform is that, if texters have opted into the system in the past, counselors can access their previous case history, including a full transcript of all previous text conversations between call center volunteers and youths, what dates and times the texter contacted the center, and any notes other staff have written about the texter.

The TextToday program received a total of 377 texts by 177 individuals from May 6, 2010 when the program was launched at the first school site to June 30, 2011 when the pilot ended. Approximately 53.1% of all text conversations were from "repeat" users who texted into the system on multiple occasions. Approximately 23.8% of youth texted into the system two to three times, and 5.8% of youths texted into the system more than three times (and up to nine times). These findings suggest that not only did the program initially appeal to youth, but most reached out to the system again after having used it.

Most users were not in crisis when they accessed the system. In fact, only 5.8% of all texters were identified as at-risk for suicide, while 60% texted in to receive information or support. In contrast, nearly 10% of all calls to the Crisis Call Center between 2005 and 2008 were from individuals at risk for suicide (Evans et al., 2009). Another 26% of all text conversations ended before a resolution could be reached, often because texters terminated the conversation prematurely. Approximately 7.4% of all text conversations were "pranks," although this might be an underestimate given that it is often more difficult to differentiate between prank and serious texters without any voice or environmental cues.

All staff who were selected to pilot the TextToday system had several years of experience conducting crisis interventions by telephone. During focus groups with counselors about their experiences adapting to the text-based crisis line, counselors noted that their prior experiences with crisis calling provided them with a strong tool-kit of communication strategies and suicide prevention models to rely on when conducting text-based interventions, including how to build rapport, assess suicide risk, and gather demographic information about the user. For example, several counselors had adapted their telephone-based "mirroring" strategies, in which a counselor matches their voice and tone to the client's to help build rapport, for use with texting. "I also think it's really important matching your sentences to them. Like, using abbreviations if they are, or using emoticons if they are. That kind of thing. That's all part of building rapport." Others noted that, rather than relying on voice cues to identify an individual's emotional state, they instead analyzed the speed with which youth texted to assess the seriousness of the text conversation, "The ones who respond quickly seem like they have an idea in mind when they text. Something that they are definitely concerned about." Overall, counselors reported that the transition to text messaging had been relatively smooth, and all expressed excitement about the Crisis Call Center's capacity to reach the previously underserved youth demographic in Nevada for the first time. Detailed findings from the comprehensive, multimethod evaluation of the TextToday program will be disseminated later in 2012. However, initial findings from pilot of the text-based service suggest that previously developed models of identifying and de-escalating individuals in crisis by telephone can be adapted easily to a text-based service.

Mississippi Helpline

In January 2010, the Mississippi Department of Mental Health's statewide Helpline services added the capacity to respond anonymously to text or online messages sent to Helpline staff in partnership with AnComm Inc.'s "Talk About It" program. The program can be accessed by visiting www.dmh.ms.gov and clicking on the "Talk About It" button on the home page. After creating an account, individuals can send anonymous e-mails and text messages to the Helpline. The service provides 24/7 support for mental health issues and suicide intervention, targeted specifically at teenagers and young adults.

Synchronous Crisis Services: Chat-Based Hotlines

Veteran's Crisis Line

In July 2009 the Department of Veterans Affairs launched both a new chat-based and a text-based crisis service through the National Suicide Prevention Lifeline. Both veterans and their friends and families can access the anonymous chat service by texting to a six-digit number, at which point they are connected to a professional counselor at the Department of Veteran Affairs. In addition, two crisis centers that are part of the National Suicide Prevention Lifeline network provide back-up services in cases where the chatter is not in crisis or when the VA lines are busy. The Department of Veteran Affairs is currently evaluating the effectiveness of the line, but has not yet disseminated its findings.

The San Francisco Suicide Prevention, one of the backup sites for the VA chat line, also launched their own counseling service via instant messaging in April 2009 that is available from 3 p.m. to 11 p.m., seven days a week. Through their site, www.sfsuicide.org, consumers may contact counselors via e-mail, chat, or phone. From 2009 to April 2011, the site had received 700 chats through their website sfsuicide.org and another 450 chats that were transferred from the VA chat line (Balch et al., 2011).

SAHAR

In Israel, SAHAR (a Hebrew acronym for "support and listening on the web) launched a similar chat-based crisis line to that of the VA's, but also provided a means for website users to connect with each other via chat rooms or individually with counselors. The website is accessed more than 10,000 times a month, and it is estimated that at least one-third of all contacts with SAHAR are from distressed suicidal persons (Barak, 2007). Trained volunteers and professionals moderate chat conversations, providing support and resource referrals as needed.

Asynchronous Crisis Support Services: E-Mail, Social Networking Sites, and Other Online Services

The majority of both local and national crisis intervention services maintain some type of online profile via a website, social networking site (e.g., Facebook or Twitter), or online blog or chat resource. For example, the National Suicide Prevention Lifeline has an active presence on Facebook through which they regularly post relevant news articles about mental health and suicide, provide information about their services and general education about suicide prevention, and advertise fundraising and social events.

Many crisis support services have reported that having a public website or social networking profile means that many individuals' attempt to contact them online for help and support, regardless of whether they have the capacity to provide crisis services online. As a result, they often forward such requests to the Lifeline's network of crisis response centers, which then attempt to provide telephone-based (and sometimes e-mail) crisis intervention services (SAMHSA, 2011). During the first quarter of 2009, the Lifeline received 261 online messages from individuals in crisis, including e-mails to its own website and messages sent via social networking sites (SAMHSA, 2011). In February 2010, the Lifeline responded to almost 50 individuals whose posts or e-mails indicated at least some risk for suicide.

The Benefits of New Media

New media platforms have the potential to dramatically alter the landscape of crisis prevention and provide a greater range of services to a larger and more diverse group of people. As one counselor from the TextToday program explained, "I think we're connecting with kids we never would have." Several crisis centers have also noted that the additional anonymity provided by chat and text-based services increases individuals' willingness to disclose information about themselves. Furthermore, counselors who were interviewed about their experiences using the text-based line felt that many texters preferred not immediately knowing whether the counselor was male, female, younger, or older. As one counselor commented, "On the telephone, sometimes when you get someone who's maybe from a younger generation they might say to you, 'you have no experience. How can you help *me*?' So on a text, that anonymity really helps."

New media also provides individuals with the opportunity to talk privately wherever and whenever they feel safe and comfortable. Whereas calls made on a landline may be more easily monitored by others, texts, e-mails, and chats may be sent from anywhere. Analyses of timestamps of texts received from adolescents at the TextToday line suggest that some adolescents texted periodically throughout the day, deriving comfort from their brief but regular check-ins with counselors. Finally, whereas few call centers record telephone conversations, many call centers maintain transcripts of back-and-forth chat and text-based conversations for quality control and training purposes. For example, the TextToday program uses real, exemplar transcripts during training sessions with volunteers to demonstrate step-by-step how the ASSIST and other suicide intervention models can be adapted to text format, and to help prepare new staff and volunteers about what to expect in a text-based interventions. Transcripts also help counselors transition between shifts. Because many text conversations span several hours or even days, counselors can more easily "take over" an ongoing text conversation by reading through the back-and-forth that occurred between the texter and counselor in the previous shift with virtually no interruption in service provision.

Challenges in Integrating New Media

Although these new technologies have the potential to reach a wider population than ever before, crisis call centers may face a number of challenges in their attempts to integrate new media into their continuum of services. For one, the demand for text and chat-based crisis services currently exceeds many sites' capacity to provide high quality intervention services. As Laura Balch from the San Francisco Suicide Prevention Center noted in a presentation at the 2011 American Association of Suicidology annual meeting, one of the greatest challenges faced during implementation of their chat-based line was that people now discovered their services "too much" (Balch et al., 2011). The Crisis Call Center of Nevada merely embedded one sentence about their new capacity to accept text messages in the narrative of the "About Us" page of their website and, with no additional advertising, received more than 75 texts in a few months from individuals who found the number online. The majority of these texts were from individuals living outside of Nevada. A number of chats received by the San Francisco Suicide Prevention Center were from other countries. Although most call centers have the capacity to locate local resources outside of their primary region, responding to individuals in crisis from increasingly distant locations creates identification and management challenges for appropriate referral and resource information.

In addition, the lack of voice cues by callers may limit the amount of even basic demographic information call centers are able to collect about users. Of the 377 text conversations that occurred during the first year of the TextToday program, counselors could not identify the texters' gender in 35% of conversations, ethnicity and race in 86% of conversations, and age in 27.3% of conversations. Although research by Barak and Bloch (2006) suggests that counselors are able to reliably distinguish between the writing styles of suicidal individuals in comparison to distressed but *non*suicidal individuals, counselors of the TextToday program reported some difficulty determining the emotional state of texters, particularly when the conversations were shorter in length. Thus, even distinguishing prank texters from texters in true crisis becomes more challenging when voice and environmental cues are not available.

Text and chat-based conversations also tend to span a longer time frame than traditional telephone-based interventions. According to TextToday counselors, a telephone conversation lasting 20 minutes in length, on average, spans several hours using text messaging. In fact, the average text conversation lasted two hours and 46 minutes in length, far longer than a typical telephone call to the Crisis Call Center. Counselors are not necessarily chatting or texting with much intensity during that time, but the longer conversation length often means that staff must continue conversations begun by a different counselor from a previous shift. Although transcripts of the conversation may assist counselors in resuming where another counselor stopped, the longer conversation length does mean that multiple counselors might work with a single texter over the course of a day. The asynchronicity of chats and texts also require counselors to multitask between multiple conversations or, as with the TextToday counselors, even multitask between text and telephone conversations.

In addition, although online and text-based services have the potential to reach more individuals who might be in crisis, some crisis call services are not accessible to the same degree as they are with traditional telephone-based services. For example, call-tracing is not available with online interventions, and sometimes even with cell-phone-based interventions. Although emergency services can trace calls and texts made from a cell phone by determining the cell site closest to someone who might be suicidal, that information may not be specific enough to allow rescue personnel to deliver assistance quickly. Furthermore, calls and texts made from cell phones that do not have a wireless contract typically cannot be traced by emergency services. Many crisis call centers using online and text-based technologies must therefore work without "the safety net" of call-tracing (Balch et al., 2011).

Future Directions

As Kathy Jacobs, the Executive Director of the Crisis Call Center, stated during a 2011 presentation on the TextToday program at the annual meeting of the American Association for Suicidology, "This is not a new service. It is a new technology" (Balch et al., 2011). Indeed, the majority of research and anecdotal evidence from crisis call centers that have added new technologies to their menu of services suggest that they are able to offer the same, if not enhanced, quality of services as they provided with telephone-only interventions. In an age when new technologies have become deeply embedded in our communication norms, more consumers prefer and expect counseling and crisis services to be available digitally. At present, however, only a handful of organizations provide crisis intervention online or via text messaging. As a result, nearly all centers that offer online or text-based support have reported that the demand for these alternative resources far exceeds their capacity to provide targeted services.

Despite a growing movement towards crisis interventions' use of new media and technology, few centers have conducted systematic evaluations of their effectiveness. As with telephone-based crisis interventions, the need to maintain the individual's anonymity and confidentiality creates ethical and legal problems related to data collection. In a recent review of the literature on internet-based crisis services conducted by the Centre for Military and Veterans Health in Queensland (Australia), the authors identified only three papers reporting on the effectiveness of internet-based counseling and only two studies *comparing* features of internet versus telephone-based crisis intervention services (Pietrzak & McLaughlin, 2009).

Although the two landmark evaluations by Gould et al. (2007) and Kalafat et al. (2007) provide some of the first reliable data that crisis call lines are effective in reducing users' suicidal ideation and attempts, rigorous evaluations of call line's effectiveness are still remarkably limited in scope and number given the long history of crisis lines in the United States. Even more limited are evaluations of crisis call lines that use new technologies. Not only are evaluations of these new services crucial to building their credibility as effective and reliable intervention services, but the dissemination of evaluation findings will help accumulate a tool-kit of "best practices" for crisis call centers hoping to expand or improve their new media services. As a result, many centers have had to pilot their services using trial-and-error methods. Findings from the TextToday program and other crisis call centers utilizing new technologies suggest that many suicide intervention and counseling models previously used on telephone-based call lines can be adapted for use with text and chat-based lines. According to focus groups with 14 counselors of the TextToday program, counselors showed remarkable facility in adapting to the text-based communication platform. In the follow-up focus group interview, all counselors reported feeling comfortable with the system, and all reported that they could conduct interventions with texters with roughly the same efficacy that they could conduct interventions with callers to the center. However, a more standardized protocol for delivering services via text and chat would ease crisis call centers' transition to new media to ensure that consumers do not experience any gaps in quality of care.

In addition, there are only a limited number of training guides and courses that specifically train counselors and volunteers how to provide text and chat-based crisis intervention. The QPR Institute recently added a new certification program to become an Online Suicide Counseling and Intervention Specialist (www.qprinstitute.com) that provides training for staff working with suicidal individuals who contact them via text, chat, and Skype. CONTACT-USA, another pioneer in chat-based crisis interventions, also offers crisis call centers a training and accreditation process in Online Emotional Support services through their website. The training can be completed online and teaches counselors to recognize signs of suicide without the assistance of voice cues. Future efforts in the development of training for call centers in how to integrate and adapt to new forms of media will help standardize the practice of care across sites to ensure these new services are as effective and reliable as traditional telephone-based crisis lines.

Conclusion

Given the exponential growth and adoption of new media in our lives during the past decade, it is unlikely that crisis call centers will remain exclusively as telephone-only providers for much longer. Like the concern about telephone-based counseling in the 1950s, there was some initial skepticism about whether crisis intervention services could provide the same quality of care via text, e-mail, and chat as they do with telephone-based interventions. In fact, at the launch of the TextToday pilot, protocol suggested that staff first develop rapport with clients, and then attempt to transfer them to a telephone-based line as quickly as possible under the assumption that texting would merely be the gateway to the higher quality telephone-based service. As the TextToday staff quickly discovered, however, consumers contact the call center in the medium in which they are most comfortable, and the same quality of services *can* be provided by text as by telephone. The more integrated new media becomes in our lives and the more efficacious call centers become at providing services through new media, the clearer it becomes that the field of crisis intervention is on the precipice of a major turning point in its history. As research accumulates about the potential benefits that new media suicide prevention services have to increase users' disclosure, reach previously underserved markets and improve crisis services overall, there is little doubt that the landscape of crisis intervention will look vastly different and more varied in the very near future.

REFERENCES

Barak, A. (2007). Emotional support and suicide prevention through the Internet: A field project report. *Computers in Human Behavior, 23*, 971–984.

Barak, A., & Bloch, N. (2006). Factors related to perceived helpfulness in supporting highly distressed individuals through an online support chat. *Cyberpsychology & Behavior, 9*, 60–68.

Balch, L., Bernik, L., Faler, R., Jacobs, K., & Renenger, L. (2011, April). *Meeting people where they are: Using new technologies to serve at-risk populations* [Powerpoint slides]. Paper presented at the Annual Meeting of the American Association of Suicidology. Portland, OR.

Blumberg, S. J., & Luke, J. V. (2010). *Wireless substitution: Early release of estimates from the National Health Interview Survey, July-December 2009.* Retrieved from http://www.cdc.gov/nchs/nhis.htm.

Cellular Telecommunications Industry Association. (2011). CTIA semi-annual wireless survey. Retrieved from http://www.ctia.org/advocacy/research/index.cfm/AID/10316.

Davie, R., Panting, C., & Charlton, T., (2004). Mobile phone ownership and usage among pre-adolescents. *Telematics & Informatics, 21,* 359–373.

Eaton, D. K., Kann, L., Kinchen, S., Shanklin, S., Ross, J., Hawkins, J., et al. (2008). Youth risk behavior surveillance – United States, 2005. *Morbidity & Mortality Weekly Reports, 57,* 1–131.

Evans, W., Davidson, L., & Sicafuse, L. (2009). *Crisis call center: Data report 2005-2009* [Unpublished internal evaluation report].

Evans, W., Davidson, L., & Sicafuse, L. (n.d.). Someone to listen: Increasing youth help-seeking behavior through a text-based crisis line for youth. Manuscript in preparation.

Faulkner, X., & Culwin, F. (2005). When fingers do the talking: A study of text messaging. *Interacting with Computers, 17,* 167–185.

Fox, S., & Jones, S. (2009). *The social life of health information.* Washington DC: Pew Research Center Publications. Retrieved from http://www.pewinternet.org/Reports/2009/8-The-Social-Life-of-Health-Information.aspx.

Gilat, I., & Shahar, G. (2007). Emotional first aid for a suicide crisis: Comparison between telephonic hotline and internet. *Psychiatry, 70,* 12–28.

Gould, M. S., Kalafat, J., Munfakh, J., & Kleinman, M. (2007). An evaluation of crisis hotline outcomes: Part 2: Suicidal callers. *Suicide & Life-Threatening Behavior, 37,* 338–352.

Gould, M. S., Greenberg, T., Munfakh, J. L. H, Kleinman, M., & Lubell, K. (2006). Teenagers' attitudes about seeking help from telephone crisis services (hotlines). *Suicide & Life-Threatening Behavior, 36,* 601–613.

Howlett, S., & Langdon, R. (2004). Messages to Jo: The Samaritans' experience of email befriending. In G. Bolton, S. Howlett, C. Lago, & J. K. Wright (Eds.), *Writing cures: An introductory handbook of writing in counselling and psychotherapy,* pp. 160–167. New York: Brunner-Routledge.

Lenhart, A. (2010a, September). *Adults, cell phones and texting.* Washington, DC: Pew Research Center Publications. Retrieved from http://pewresearch.org/pubs/1716/adults-cell-phones-text-messages.

Lenhart, A. (2010b, September). *Cell phones and American adults.* Washington DC: Pew Research Center Publications. Retrieved from http://www.pewinternet.org/Reports/2010/Cell-Phones-and-American-Adults.aspx.

Lenhart, A., Ling, R., Campbell, S., & Purcell, K. (2010, April). *Teens, cell phones and texting: Text messaging becomes centerpiece communication.* Washington, DC: Pew Research Center Publications. Retrieved from http://www.pewinternet.org/Reports/2010/Teens-and-Mobile-Phones.aspx.

New Freedom Commission on Mental Health. (2003). *Achieving the promise: Transforming mental health care in America: Final report* (DHHS Pub. No. SMA-03-3832). Rockville, MD. Retrieved from http://www.scribd.com/doc/24874379/Achieving-the-Promise-Transforming-Mental-Health-Care-in-America-July-2003.

Offer, D., Howard, K. I., Schonert, K. A., & Ostrov, E. (1991). To whom do adolescents turn for help? Differences between disturbed and non-disturbed adolescents, *Journal of the American Academy of Child & Adolescent Psychiatry, 30,* 623–630.

Pierce, T. (2009). Social anxiety and technology: Face-to-face communication versus technological communication among teens. *Computers In Human Behavior, 25,* 1367–1372.

Pietrzak, E., & McLaughlin, R. (2009, April). *The effectiveness of online suicide prevention programs: A literature review.* Queensland, Australia: Centre for Military and Veterans Health. Retrieved from http://www.cmvh.org.au/docs/ehealth/Effectiveness_of_Online_Suicide_Prevention_Programs_Literature_Review_April_2009.pdf.

Public Technology. (2008). Case study: Samaritans SMS text messaging project. Retrieved from www.publictechnology.net/content/14736.

Samaritans UK. (2010). *Information resource pack 2011.* Retrieved from http://www.samaritans.org/pdf/Samaritans%20Info%20Resource%20Pack%202011.pdf.

Substance Abuse and Mental Health Services Association. (2011, May). *Using new media in suicide prevention: Existing efforts and future opportunities* [Whitepaper]. Retrieved from http://newmediawhitepaper.wordpress.com.

Chapter 27

CRISIS INTERVENTION BY E-MAIL[42]

GERALDINE WILSON AND DAVID LESTER

Although the traditional mode for psychotherapy and counseling is a face-to-face interaction, alternative modes of communication have been explored, including communication by closed-circuit television, telephone, tape recorder, books, and computers (Lester, 1977; Wagman, 1988; Zarr, 1994). In particular, as we have already seen in this book, the use of the telephone as a mode of communication between client and counselor has become widespread for crisis intervention in general and for suicide prevention in particular. Most suicide prevention and crisis services maintain a telephone counseling service, seven days a week, 24 hours a day (Lester & Brockopp, 1973; Roberts, 1995; Waters & Finn, 1995).

Counseling by letter has a history going back to Freud who wrote to the father of "Little Hans" advising him on how to deal with Hans (Freud, 1959). Grotjahn (1953) exchanged letters with an adolescent female client when their psychoanalysis was interrupted, with the aim of supporting her and encouraging her to stay in contact with him until she could return to proper psychoanalysis. Alston (1957) conducted psychotherapy with a client whose voice was weak and whose tuberculosis prevented her from visiting his office. They exchanged letters daily for two years. Alston noted that the disadvantages were that the letters involved delays between the client reporting an emotionally laden experience and receiving Alston's reply, and the letter writing eliminated the nonverbal cues available to the face-to-face counselor. On the other hand, the letter writing helped overcome the client's fear of psychotherapy and minimized possible disruption from her hostility.

---
[42] Modified from Wilson and Lester (1998).

Farber (1953) was a deaf psychotherapist who was forced to use written communications with his clients. He had clients write during the counseling sessions, while he was able to speak his responses. Farber felt that the slower tempo of the sessions gave him more time to digest what the client was "saying," and the written communications helped clients with a preference for visual memories to remember what had transpired in the sessions. Ellis (1965) reported using a similar technique when he had laryngitis or had deaf clients.

Over the years, "advising" people by means of advice columns in newspapers and magazines has become common. Kesen (1962) noted that this type of communication differs greatly from traditional counseling, for the communication is a one-time message and the solution comes from the advisor rather than from the client. However, some clients feel freer in expressing themselves in such letters than in face-to-face relationships.

More recently, Morita therapy in Japan has used letter writing to continue communication between therapists and clients (France et al., 1995). Modeling their approach on Morita therapy, France et al. suggested the following structure for conducting counseling by letter: (1) summarizing the contents of the previous letter, (2) exploring feelings and thoughts, (3) positively reinforcing the client's progress, and (4) giving homework assignments and advising on activities and thoughts. In an example of letter therapy with a client, France et al. identified several stages in their five-month interaction with the client: opening up, focusing on life themes, redirecting the client toward her strengths, reinforcing actions, and affirming a positive attitude.

Some researchers have evaluated the effectiveness of counseling by letter. For example, Bastien and Jacobs (1973) found that behaviorally-oriented therapeutic responses by letter over a period of four months to college students with problems was more effective than letters in which the counselor expressed simple reassurance and a control group who simply completed and mailed problem-check lists to the counselor regularly.

Three sets of conditions typically lead to the use of written communications in counseling (Burnell & Motelet, 1973):

1. When there are limitations in physical circumstances, such as the absence of client or counselor, a client living in an isolated area, or when the counseling is mediated by friend or relative.

2. When the transference or countertransference creates problems, as when the client is fearful or hostile.

3. When there are communication problems, such as when the client or counselor is deaf or unable to speak.

Suicide Prevention by E-Mail

Although crisis intervention involving the internet has been reported in situations where an individual reports on the internet having attempted suicide and someone elsewhere on the internet responds immediately by calling emergency services in the attempter's neighborhood, we are concerned here with sustained counseling using e-mail communications.[43] In these situations, a client contacts the suicide prevention center by sending an e-mail communication. Within 24 hours, a counselor reads the communication and writes and sends a response. This exchange may continue for a period of time.

For the Samaritans, there is a central "address" for e-mail messages from clients (Morgan, 1996). The central computer then assigns the message to one of more than 20 centers around the world. The crisis intervention is then handled by the center to which the client has been assigned. Encryption (scrambling) of the letters is possible if clients desire this.[44]

The Client

Suicide prevention centers using the telephone as the mode for communication have noted that their typical caller is a young female. Males are much less likely to use these services even though they have the higher suicide rate. Men are less likely to seek assistance, and they rarely telephone or walk into suicide prevention centers. Computers and the Internet are used extensively by men and especially by men in their twenties and thirties, a group which suicide prevention centers would like to target. Based on data collected so far on clients whose gender is known, men and women were equally often callers on the telephone service, whereas men outnumbered women two-to-one using e-mail.

As in counseling by letter, e-mail offers advantages to clients who would find telephone communication difficult, such as hearing-impaired and speech-impaired clients. E-mail provides ease of access in general and to the disabled in particular (as does the telephone). E-mail provides privacy as to the identity of the client, even more so than the telephone, since with e-mail, the gender of the caller can be disguised if desired. Students often have their tele-

---

[43] Similar dramatic "crisis intervention" has been reported by Jacobs and Mack (1986) who received a letter from a suicidal woman. They wrote back to the local mental health center and to her husband and her stressing the importance of the situation and urging them to seek help. The husband received the letter, and his wife was hospitalized that day.

[44] Access is currently limited to a Web site (http://www.compulink.co.uk/~careware/samaritans/) and Internet e-mail. This is always answered by real volunteers; there are no "automatic" response. Other Internet techniques, such as Telnet or anonymous ftp will not work.

phone usage monitored by their parents, which inhibits their use of telephone crisis services, but parents are less likely to monitor their children's use of the Internet. Furthermore, whereas caller ID (unless blocked by the caller) identifies from where the client is calling, e-mail can be sent via a service which removes the Internet address of the client. E-mail is also appealing to clients who have a lack of trust and who fear loss of face in calling a suicide prevention center. As with telephone counseling, clients find safety in their increased control over the process, and they are working with a medium with which they are familiar.

The Process

Suicide prevention by e-mail permits a time lapse between each communication. This time lapse (24 hours or less) is not as long as that required for mail sent by postal services (several days to more than a week). This time allows a period for the client and the counselor to consider what is happening in the client's life. There is time for the counselor to consult with peers and supervisors before sending the reply. There is an opportunity for the client to study the counselor's response.

Suicide prevention by e-mail elicits more comments from the counselor, since a simple "hmm-hmm" no longer suffices. Counselors have to show that they are listening carefully in other ways. Just as telephone counseling can degenerate into conversation (see Chapter 8), counselors using e-mail can easily forget that they are engaged in crisis intervention and suicide prevention. In particular, it is easy for the counselor to make errors such as diagnosing and advising.

In contrast to counseling by e-mail, telephone counseling is immediate, feedback is obtained from the client quickly, and there is opportunity to correct mistakes. Counselors can hear the client's voice and realize if they have touched an area which is sensitive for the client. There are many cues, such as the tone of voice, silence, and crying, and these cues can guide counselor responses.

When using e-mail, it is harder to avoid direct questions from the client. Whereas, in telephone counseling, client-centered responses often by-pass answering questions, e-mail makes a stronger demand for counselors to answer. A question such as "Am I being selfish?" requires that the counselor answer "Yes" or "No." However, it is possible to acknowledge the question without directly answering – for example, "You ask if you are being selfish? As you have asked, that seems to indicate that it has crossed your mind as a possibility, but only you can really answer. The fact of it crossing your mind tells me that you are willing to consider other views and this says a lot of good things about you."

Counselors sometimes find it hard to zero in and, for example, directly ask about "suicide" – typing it seems harsher than asking about suicidal thoughts during telephone counseling, and so a gentler, more caring lead-in is required. Furthermore, since the counselor cannot be sure about the client's age, and since children use the Internet quite easily, counselors must be a little more cautious about inquiring about suicidal inclinations, with this one proviso. The Samaritans feel that they fail their clients if the opportunity to acknowledge and discuss suicidal thoughts and feelings is not actively sought and encouraged.

The language used in e-mail counseling is another area in which the counselor can have difficulties. In telephone counseling, it is easier to give the nuances of meaning by the tone of the voice. E-mail requires simpler more straightforward language in order to avoid any confusion. Using the word "we" for example can be interpreted as you (the client) and me, suggesting togetherness and support; or it can mean me and my associates in the counseling center. Similarly, "they," an important word, which, if used without care, as in "You'd think they would do something about. . ." might encourage the client to blame the group of people referred to as "they" rather than face his or her own problems and situation.

A Simulated Example

Because the Samaritans are committed to maintaining confidentiality for their clients, it is not possible to reproduce an actual exchange of messages here. However, we have created a simulated exchange which is very similar to the actual kind of exchanges that take place.

Hello. I don't know if this is going to work or if it some kind of rip-off. Anyway who cares? I'm so down right now all I want to do is die. Don't even know why I'm saying this. Are you guys really there? Ross.

Hello Ross. To answer your last question first, yes I am really here, and it's not a rip off. I don't know if it's going to work either, but I'm glad you mailed me, and I'd like to try. Please will you try too? Can you tell me more about what is going on with you? Your words "all I want to do is die" sound so desperate and make me feel that you are very alone and isolated.

The wish to die may have been with you for a long time or something may have happened recently to make you feel this way. Please can you tell me? Are you thinking or planning to act on your wish to die? Contemplating suicide? To answer your other question, I do care. Mail me soon, Ross. I'll be thinking of you. I'm sending you the Samaritan faq list so you'll know a bit about us and what we do. Jo.

faq list: Our mailbox is read every day of the year by a group of trained vol unteers – all using the pseudonym "Jo." Callers are offered absolute confidentiality, and do not lose the right to make their own decisions (including the decision to end their own lives). Your messages (and our replies) will be kept for 30 days at most. You may ask for earlier deletion of a message.

Hi Jo: I've been feeling really bad for months. I broke up with my girlfriend and don't seem to be able to forget her. I had a go at suicide right after the break-up, but I couldn't even do that right. We'd been together six years, and I thought everything was ok. Sometimes we'd fight a bit, especially if I'd had a few beers, but everybody fights sometimes, right? Now she won't even speak to me. My job is the pits as well. I hate it. Sometimes I feel like I hate the whole world, especially my boss. She's a bitch, and here's the sick bit. She has the same name as my girl. Susan. What a bummer! Ross.

Hi Ross. Things sound really tough for you, and you are very unhappy and also angry. The break-up with Susan has hit you hard, and you are hurting, possibly feeling rejected too? I am worried about how down you sound and about your suicidal feelings. Can you tell me about them and about what you did after you and Susan broke up? Do you have any plans for suicide now?

I would like to hear about Susan, and it might help you to talk about her, if you feel you can trust me with your thoughts and feelings. It seems there are some strong feelings about your boss as well. Perhaps you and I could discuss these, and your job. Jo.

This correspondence hopefully would continue along the lines of getting Ross to pour out all of his feelings about both Susans and working through his hurt, with a view to talking about how he has coped with trouble and disappointment in the past. By providing emotional support throughout this period, it is hoped that he may find his way through his suicidal crisis. The time frame can be anywhere from a few weeks to several months.

Discussion

Experience with crisis intervention by e-mail has been limited at present. Within 15 months of going online, the Hong Kong Samaritan branch had 467 total e-mail contacts, including repeat contacts. Worldwide, in the first three months of 1997, there were 1,157 contacts, of which 35% were new contacts. At the Hong Kong Samaritan branch, the length of contact varied from once, to daily for two or three weeks, all the way to intermittent contacts over a period of months.

A greater proportion of the writers appeared to be suicidal than those contacting centers by telephone or by visiting. Many e-mail writers had a local telephone crisis counseling nearby, but they preferred the Internet. For example, one writer could not bring himself to contact his local crisis intervention center, writing of his loneliness and his feelings of despair, partly because of his homosexuality and partly because of his low self-esteem (Scott, 1996). The counselor and he discussed options and how he might go out and meet people and make friends. When asked what stopped him from doing this, he wrote "I can't because I'm B-()))) and I want to X-(." (He meant that he was ugly and very fat and that he wanted to kill himself.) Thus, even writing does not always make it easy to express oneself directly.

It is evident from our discussion that many of the skills and styles of telephone crisis intervention do transfer to e-mail crisis intervention, but that modifications are necessary because of the type of communication. It is also clear that the use of this medium for crisis intervention may provide counseling for those who might not otherwise use face-to-face or telephone counseling. Furthermore, other possibilities exist for crisis intervention via e-mail, including informational messages on improving social skills, assertive behavior, and relaxation techniques.

This form of crisis intervention appears to be viable and useful. It stands on its own as an accepted service alongside telephone and face-to-face contacts, and it can also serve as a stepping stone to telephone contacts. E-mail clients tell the centers that they have been helped by their interaction with the counselor and, accepting their judgments, the centers are endeavoring to encourage others to use the service.

REFERENCES

Alston, E. (1957). Psychoanalytic psychotherapy conducted by correspondence. *International Journal of Psychoanalysis, 38*, 32–50.
Bastien, S., & Jacobs, A. (1974). Dear Sheila. *Journal of Consulting & Clinical Psychology, 42*, 151.
Burnell, G., & Motelet, K. (1973). Correspondence therapy. *Archives of General Psychiatry, 28*, 728–731.
Ellis, A. (1965). Some uses of the printed, written, and recorded word in psychotherapy. In L. Pearson (Ed.), *The use of written communication in psychotherapy*, pp. 23–36. Springfield, IL: Charles C Thomas.
Farber, J. (1953). Written communication in psychotherapy. *Psychiatry, 16*, 365–374.
France, M. H., Cadieax, J., & Allen, G. E. (1995). Letter therapy. *Journal of Counseling & Development, 73*, 317–318.
Freud, S. (1959). Analysis of a phobia in a five-year-old boy. *Collected Papers, Volume 3*, pp. 149–289. New York: Basic Books.
Grotjahn, M. (1955). *Six letters to an analyst by an adolescent girl.* Unpublished.
Jacobs, D., & Mack, J. E. (1986). Case report of psychiatric intervention by mail. *American Journal of Psychiatry, 143*, 92–93.
Kesen, S. (1962). The advice column as a means of counseling. *Japan Christian Quarterly, 28*, 168–171.

Lester, D. (1977). *The use of alternative modes for communication in psychotherapy*. Springfield, IL: Charles C Thomas.

Lester, D., & Brockopp, G. W. (1973). *Crisis intervention and counseling by telephone*. Springfield, IL: Charles C Thomas.

Morgan, C. (1996). Befriending by Email. *Befriending Worldwide, 49*, 11.

Roberts, A. R. (1995). Crisis intervention units and centers in the United States. In A. R. Roberts (Ed.), *Crisis intervention and time-limited cognitive treatment*, pp. 54–70. Thousand Oaks, CA: Sage.

Scott, V. (July, 1996). Listening to the silence. Paper presented at the Befrienders International Conference, Kuala Lumpur, Malaysia.

Wagman, M. (1988). *Computer psychotherapy systems*. New York: Gordon & Breach.

Waters, J., & Finn, E. (1995). Handling client crises effectively on the telephone. In A. R. Roberts (Ed.), *Crisis intervention and time-limited cognitive treatment*, pp. 251–289. Thousand Oaks, CA: Sage.

Wilson, G., & Lester, D. (1988). Crisis intervention by e-mail. *Crisis Intervention & Time-Limited Treatment, 4*, 81–87.

Zarr, M. (1994). Computer-aided psychotherapy. *Psychiatric Annals, 24*, 42–46.

Chapter 28

COUNSELING THE CLIENT IN CRISIS BY LETTER[45]

DMITRI SCHUSTOV AND DAVID LESTER

We have seen in Chapter 27 that the use of letters for counseling was first demonstrated by Freud who wrote to the father of "Little Hans" advising him on how to deal with Hans (Freud, 1959). Grotjahn (1953) exchanged letters with a female client when their psychoanalysis was interrupted, with the aim of supporting her and encouraging her to stay in contact with him until she could return to proper psychoanalysis. Alston (1957) conducted psychotherapy with a client whose voice was weak and whose tuberculosis prevented her from visiting his office. France et al. (1995) suggested the following structure for conducting counseling by letter: (1) summarizing the contents of the previous letter, (2) exploring feelings and thoughts, (3) reinforcing positively the client's progress, and (4) giving homework assignments and advising on activities and thoughts.

In Russian culture, letter writing traditionally enables the writer to be more open, frank, and direct than in face-to-face direct communication. In order to explore whether this tradition would facilitate counseling conducted by letter, a service was established in 1992 in Ryazan, Russia, which was advertised via radio, television, and the newspapers, encouraging people to write to the service with their problems. Contracts were sent to those who wrote, outlining the service and its limitations, specifying a time limit for responses to client letters, and noting possible actions which the client might be asked to undertake. There was no charge, and the salary for the counselors came from private sources.

---

[45] Modified from Schustov and Lester (1999).

The first 81 clients wrote 200 letters. Twenty-two percent of these initial clients were men and 78% women. The mean age of the respondents was 44 years (standard deviation = 18), with an even distribution from age 15 though 80. The mean number of letters written was 1.7 (SD = 2.3), but 73% of the respondents wrote only one letter. Nineteen percent had suicidal ideation, and 5% had attempted suicide. Twenty-six percent were judged to be depressed in mood or by diagnosis, 12% schizophrenic or psychotic and 2% alcohol abusers. The only associations between these variables were that the alcohol abusers were primarily male, and the depressed correspondents were older and had more often attempted suicide.

Case Study

The following presents two letters from a suicidal client and the responses by the counselor.

Letter 1

Dear Doctor:

I read about the "Confidence Post" in our town in a newspaper a while back, but decided to write to you only now. Perhaps you can help me. First, something about myself.

I'm sixteen, and I have been working as a sewing-machine operator for six months. When I left secondary school, I entered a specialized college, after which I returned to work immediately. I had to work because my father has been seriously ill for a long time, and my mother's salary is too low. There are four children in our family. I'm the second child. My older brother is a loafer and a thief. I think he began stealing when he was in second grade. At first he took money from our mother, then my silver earrings. He sells these things and lives off the money. Don't think too badly of him – he steals only from his home and from relatives. That's enough about my family.

The point is that I'm only sixteen, but I have no will to go on living. When I was twelve, my mother scalded me with boiling water in the bath by accident. After three or four months, some white spots began to appear on my skin, beginning on my legs. At first, I didn't understand what was happening. Then the torture began. I can't swim in the river. I can't wear shoes on my bare feet – I wear pants or tights in summer. My relationships with friends at school began to become limited. I feel defective, and this feeling never leaves me. Sometimes I feel like committing suicide, but I'm afraid of the pain and having a long, agonizing death. And I fear for my father. If I do this, then he might follow me for my death would kill him. So I did not. I don't want to be a burden to anyone. I feel that even my relatives are ashamed of me. I feel very bad. I'm human, you know. I'm a woman, and I'd like to have a boyfriend who could love me. But I realize that I'll never have this. I have no hope. Some time ago, I had a boyfriend at school, my first love, but it ended when he saw my spots. I loved him, you know – maybe in a childish way. Our friends teased us and called us the bride and bridegroom. My God, why did it happen to me? What for? I don't go anywhere because I'm afraid to fall in love. Everything would end when he saw me naked. And nothing will stop me after that.

What am I to do? I beg you, help me for God's sake. I rely on you, and I'm looking for your response.

Very truly yours,
Mary.

Reply 1

Dear Mary:

We have received your letter, and we would like to thank you for your sincerity and confidence. We would like to know more about you, your family, your work, and your friends. We need this information to get a full picture of your life. Every person's life is unique, mysterious, and interesting, you know. Yes, it is really interesting. I am not afraid of this word.

As soon as I began reading your letter, even before I got to the part describing your troubles, I realized that I was reading the letter of an interesting and extraordinary girl. Your letter aroused my sympathy for you and confidence in your thoughts and feelings. I have the impression that I have known you for many years, for a friend of mine experienced similar feelings some time ago. That is why I think I am able to understand you.

And now I have to be brief and rather rigid. This is the requirement of my profession as a counselor. I am ready to work with you. I am sure that we will be able to work efficiently together with your problem. But I am obliged to set a tough condition which, in case of failure to do so, would make our work together senseless. You have put me in a very uncomfortable position by your letter or, to be more precise, you have placed me in a state of dependence. You said the following in your letter: "I am appealing to you, but you should bear in mind that, whatever you do, I have reserved a way out – at any moment I can commit suicide if this or that happens to me." I cannot be open and sincere with you in our work while I have the possibility of your suicide in mind. And I think you can help me with this. I respect all of your thoughts, but I know too well that there are some thoughts which cannot be opposed or vanquished. I would like to ask you not to contemplate suicide for the period of our joint work. I hope you understand this.

Please write to us whether this condition is acceptable to you. Or is it too distressing for you to give up these thoughts and be responsible for the alternative choice?

Yours faithfully,
Dmitri Ivanovitch

Letter 2

Dear Doctor:

What a surprise to get your letter. Of course, I was waiting for it with impatience, and curiosity. Yes, that's it exactly, curiosity. It was very interesting to find out what the reply or advice might be. The fact is, this was my first appeal to a counselor, even though it was in a written form. But I never expected an immediate response. I didn't reply to your letter at once. I was seized with the feeling that my letter might be insincere, false, and wrong if I wrote immediately. Why do such things happen to me? I can't find an answer. Can you?

When I reached the suicide part of your letter, I was frightened. I stumbled on the word as it were a stone on a smooth road. And I vow, with all my responsibility, that I shan't think about it any more. Please, believe me. I shan't. You may rely on me.

At the beginning of your letter, you wrote that I am an interesting and extraordinary girl. I don't consider myself that way, and I don't think anybody does. I guess I am quite ordinary. There are thousands of such people in this town. But perhaps you wrote those words to support me. If this is the reason, I am very grateful to you, Dmitri Ivanovitch! If not, please don't feel hurt.

After that, you write that you can understand me because a friend of yours had a similar experience. Why do you write that he "had" such an experience – the past form? I am sorry, but I am interested in learning the rest. Did he recover, or is he gone?

Please forgive me for all my "why's" but I would be grateful for your answers to my questions. And one more request. I'd like to ask you to address me as "tu." I guess I'm much younger than you. And besides, I paid attention at the beginning of your letter that your typewriter was typing "tu" and not "vous" now and then. Maybe you prefer to address me as "tu" but your politeness does not permit this. Well, I don't care a damn for manners! You want some confidence between us, don't you?

I'll be waiting for your response.
Mary

Reply 2

Dear Mary:

It is really more convenient for me to address you with "tu" but this is not because of our disparity in age. There was something in your first letter that made such a form of address possible for me.

I was pleased with your response and your decision. I do believe you.

Now some answers to your questions. I do not think there are thousands of people like you in town. Your style of writing is nice, you can clearly express your feelings, and the most important thing is your ability to understand other people.

As far as that friend of mine is concerned, he is alive, of course, and is quite well now. Five years ago, or so, he began to lose his hair. He was twenty then. His head was going bald, and not in spots, but along the same lines as his father's head. The boy was upset, he could not sleep, and he didn't want to meet people or get acquainted with girls. And the more nervous he got, the more hair he lost. Now he lives a full life, and he has a family and a little daughter.

Mary, in my previous letter, I asked you to tell me about your friends and parents in more detail. This is important.

And one more thing. Please make a copy when writing a letter to me (using carbon paper). This will help you to keep your questions in mind.

My best regards.
Dmitri Ivanovitch.

Comments on this Case

The correspondence ended at this point, and information about the girl's progress is unavailable. The counselor did have a current address for the girl, but it was felt that to write to her without receiving a new letter would be an unwarranted intrusion.

In some countries, such as the United States, parental permission is needed in order to counsel adolescents under the age of 18 in face-to-face psychotherapy or psychiatric treatment. Parental permission is not, however, required for telephone counseling on a "teen hotline." In Russia, the law requires parental permission for treatment only for formal psychiatric patients under the age of 15. The Confidence Post has had only a few letters from adolescents and so has not deemed it necessary to set up a special service for adolescents.

Counseling Techniques

The first task, of course, with a client is simply to listen to them and to acknowledge that we have heard what they have said. An effort is made to give nurturing support and occasional recommendations. Aside from this, the counselors utilize techniques based on transactional analysis (Berne, 1961) and Frankl's (1960) paradoxical intention.

The major counselor tactics include:

1. *Informing* – The counselor can answer concrete questions, such as with respect to diagnosis. What to do? How to act? Where to go?

2. *Supporting* – The counselor can offer support to the client, especially when clients express confusion, depression, helplessness, and low self-esteem. Encouragement and praise are frequently given to such clients.

3. *Strengthening the Adult Ego State* – The acts of organizing one's thoughts and putting them down intelligibly on paper for someone else to read forces the Adult ego state to assume control, temporarily suppressing the Child and Parent ego states. In contrast, writing one's thoughts down in a diary that only will be read by oneself permits the Child or Parent ego states to stay in control. In the second response from the counselor in the example above, the client was asked to make copies of her letters so that she could refer back to them. This too will increase the likelihood that the Adult ego state will be in control when the letters are written.

4. *Decontamination* – Once the Adult ego state has assumed control in the counseling process, the counselor can then point out where intrusions from the Child and Parent ego states have occurred into the thinking and written content of the client.

5. *Confrontation* – After good rapport has been established with the client and there is a strong therapeutic alliance, the counselor can begin to confront the client about dysfunctional thought or behavior patterns. Passivity and chronic suicidal ideation are often the targets for this confrontation.

6. *Contracts* – It is useful to suggest contracts and to request that clients agree to them and honor them. In the case of the adolescent above, the counselor proposed a "No suicide" contract (Drye et al., 1973), to which the client agreed.

7. *Transference* – There is great opportunity for transference to occur in counseling by mail. As compared to face-to-face counseling, counseling by mail, in a similar fashion as does telephone counseling, removes counselor stimuli, and permits the client to fantasize about the counselor. Telephone counseling removes the visual impression of the counselor, and counseling by mail removes the voice. The transference may be useful. Williams and Douds (Chapter 3) pointed out with regard to telephone counseling, that perhaps clients can imagine the counselor to be the kind of person they need at that point in time – "positive transference."

Final Comments

The average number of letters is about two. The exchange ends usually with no further communication from the client or with resolution of the problem from the client's point of view. The service never initiates the end of the correspondence – termination is always the client's choice. Although the service does not contact clients unless the client writes to the service, further communication is always possible at the client's instigation.

Is the service effective? No efficacy studies have been conducted because to do so would violate the contract between the client and the service. Clients do not expect the service to contact them outside of the letter exchanges initiated by them.

The text of the formal contract between the service and writers has been published several times in the local newspapers. The contract notes that the service is free of charge, anonymous, and ensures secrecy of all information. The service promises to reply within two to four weeks of receipt of a letter to the address indicated in the letter. All the counselors treat clients and their problems with respect and have a right to receive respect. The service promises to (1) listen to clients (without comments if appropriate), (2) discuss with the clients their problems if the problems are in the area of competence of the counselor (and, if not, the counselor will indicate this), (3) endeavor to help clients by means of this correspondence, and (4) invite clients for face-to-face counseling if the clients wish this.

If the writer shows signs of depression, the writer is encouraged to visit a physician for antidepressants. If the depression appears to be mild, then the counselor uses the strategies discussed above to deal with the underlying problems causing the depression, supplemented by cognitive therapy tactics if irrational or distorted thinking is evident.

In the United States, there is some doubt as to the efficacy of no-suicide contracts and some question as to whether they provide any legal protection from malpractice suits in the event that the client commits suicide (Stanford et al., 1994). However, this may be true of many counseling tactics, but this does not prevent their use when deemed appropriate for particular clients.

The American Psychological Association's Board of Professional Affairs and Ethics Committee has questioned the use of telephone therapy (Haas et al., 1996), and their concerns could apply also to correspondence therapy. The Committee has noted that there is little evidence pertinent to the efficacy of telephone therapy and difficulty in enforcing ethical standards. Their concerns apply primarily to psychologists providing formal psychotherapy via the telephone rather than in face-to-face sessions. In contrast, crisis intervention (rather than psychotherapy) by telephone continues to be a widely offered service in many nations of the world and is not (and should not) be subjected to the same criteria as formal individual psychotherapy. Crisis intervention by correspondence should be viewed as similar in nature to crisis intervention by telephone. It provides a source of help for clients who are unable or unwilling to enter into a formal psychotherapeutic relationship with a psychotherapist. As such it can provide a useful service for a community.

REFERENCES

Alston, E. (1957). Psychoanalytic psychotherapy conducted by correspondence. *International Journal of Psychoanalysis, 38*, 32–50.

Berne, E. (1961). *Transactional analysis in psychotherapy.* New York: Grove.

Drye, R. C., Goulding, R. L., & Goulding, M. E. (1973). No-suicide decisions. *American Journal of Psychiatry, 130*, 171–174.

France, M. H., Cadieax, J., & Allen, G. E. (1995). Letter therapy. *Journal of Counseling & Development, 73*, 317–318.

Frankl, V. E. (1960). Paradoxical intention. *American Journal of Psychotherapy, 14*, 520–535.

Freud, S. (1959). Analysis of a phobia in a five-year-old boy. *Collected Paper, Volume 3*, pp. 149–289. New York: Basic Books.

Grotjahn, M. (1955). Six letters to an analyst by an adolescent girl. Unpublished.

Haas, L. J., Benedict, J. G., & Kobos, J. C. (1996). Psychotherapy by telephone. *Professional Psychotherapy, 27*, 154–160.

Schustov, D., & Lester, D. (1999). Counseling the suicidal client by letter. *Crisis, 20*, 127–131.

Stanford, E. J., Goetz, R. R., & Bloom, J. D. (1994). The no harm contract in the emergency assessment of suicidal risk. *Journal of Clinical Psychiatry, 55*, 344–348.

Part VI

THE TELEPHONE COUNSELOR

Chapter 29

THE CASE FOR NONPROFESSIONAL CRISIS WORKERS

RICHARD K. McGEE AND BRUCE JENNINGS

At the beginning of the 1970s there could be no mistaking the full force of the nonprofessional revolution in the helping services. Extensive reviews of the role for new, lesser trained manpower in nearly all areas of health, educational, social, and humanitarian enterprises had been provided by both scientific researchers and casual observers (Ewalt, 1967; Grosser, Henry, & Kelly, 1969; Guerney, 1969; Reiff & Riessman, 1965; Sobey, 1970). Nowhere had the role of the nonprofessional been more in evidence, nor more fully utilized than in the growing field of suicide prevention and crisis services (Heilig et al., 1968). Anyone who reflects upon the development of suicide prevention and crisis services during the 1960s may arrive at his own personal opinion as to the most important factor which permitted or stimulated this social service phenomena. However, in the opinion of many, the present writers included, it was the repeated success of the nonprofessional volunteers in the Los Angeles Suicide Prevention Center which made possible the development of a new form for delivering helping services to persons suffering an acute personal crisis. It was the eminent Louis Dublin (1969) who made the point, with his usual dramatic eloquence, at the first annual conference of the American Association of Suicidology: "The lay volunteer was probably the most important single discovery in the fifty-year history of suicide prevention. Little progress was made until [they] came into the picture."

So enthusiastic has been the acceptance of the nonprofessional in some quarters of the crisis intervention movement that there has been a tendency to conclude that the nonprofessional is clearly and unequivocally superior to the professional person from any discipline for this particular role. Such a position should not be espoused without careful study and evaluation of many issues, both theoretical and practical, together with an objective analysis of empirical data. At least two positions may be taken on the continuum of attitudes toward the volunteer. At one extreme is the position just mentioned, that the nonprofessional is basically superior to the professional in the delivery of crisis services. Another position is that the professional is clearly the superior person but that, due to the shortage of professional manpower and the great demand for services, our society will have to accommodate by accepting inferior services where the alternative may be no service at all. Such a position holds that, if there are sufficient professional personnel, they should perform the functions but, in their absence, the nonprofessional may be used as an aide to assist the professional caregiver.

The purpose of this chapter is to examine these issues and some data and offer a rational base upon which to draw an informed conclusion in favor of the nonprofessional as the most appropriate crisis intervention worker. The arguments come from various sources: dogma, precedent, practical considerations, and laboratory research.

Dogma

Students who attended one of the semiannual training institutes at the Los Angeles Suicide Prevention Center (Heilig, 1970) became familiar with an oft-quoted principle known as "Litman's Law." Briefly stated, this law holds that: The more severe and acute the suicidal crisis is, the LESS one needs to be professionally trained to manage it effectively. This principle is not merely idle talk, articulated for its "shock value," although it does produce an element of surprise in the neophyte upon first encounter. Rather, Litman's Law is the result of serious reflection upon the observations and experiences of the staff at the Los Angeles center, both in their own work with acutely suicidal people and in their supervision of nonprofessional volunteers performing the same clinical functions. Litman and his colleagues have found that, whereas both professional clinicians and the lay volunteers can manage acute crises effectively, the skills, training, theory, and other characteristics which distinguish the professional from the layman are simply unnecessary for the task. What matters most, especially in the more acute cases, are the traits of human concern for people, good judgment, and a determination to intervene, traits which cut across disciplines or professional-nonprofessional categories.

Farberow (1966) leant more toward the nonprofessional in his evaluation of the first year's experiences with the Los Angeles volunteers. He says,

> We found that they were often able to offer a relationship to the client which was on a more direct and a more friendly level than that of the professionals. There seems at times . . . a sense of professional detachment which is de-

veloped by professionals. This, we find, often gets in the way. The volunteers did not have this kind of barrier. (p. 12)

Caplan (1961) has described this barrier as the "professional armor" developed during and as a result of professional training. It serves to protect the clinician from the vulnerability which arises when his own personal identification with the problems of the client interferes with the professional work of being a therapist. Caplan further sees this professional distance as a distinguishing feature of the professional. "An essential difference between an amateur and a professional is that the professional has this distance, and deals objectively rather than subjectively with the problems of his clients" (p. 24).

Farberow is not alone in the belief that the professional persona or armor is a disadvantage in crisis intervention work. Edwards (1970) described the result of using full-time, paid nonprofessional counselors in the Fulton-DeKalb County (Georgia) Emergency Mental Health Service. Many of these counselors had been on the job for 12 to 15 months and had logged over 2,000 calls. He reported that they had lost their original anxiety over taking emergency calls from suicidal people, and consequently, in his opinion from monitoring their work, they had lost their effectiveness as crisis counselors. According to Edwards, "They have begun to sound just like a psychiatrist on the telephone." Edwards further declared that the nonprofessional counselors are "the real professionals" in the crisis intervention field. As a psychiatrist charged with the awesome responsibility of establishing and directing a suicide and crisis intervention program to serve the entire metropolitan Atlanta area, Edwards is in a position to make valid judgments in such matters.

Caplan (1964) has described the theory and technique for crisis intervention therapy, and he shows why professional-level expertise is unnecessary. He argues that the crisis is a present, real life drama in which the client is struggling with stressors in the here-and-now environment. It is not necessary nor appropriate to handle such cases by delving into the deeper layers of the unconscious or by probing the childhood and other earlier experiences for symbolic or latent meanings. Primary process data are irrelevant. Hence, much of the area in which a professional clinician is accustomed to working, and the avenues to understanding problems wherein he is most comfortable, are not the ones which offer him or the client the best chance for healthy resolution of the crisis. In a sense, the professional clinician is disarmed and forced to take on a role which does not utilize his years of training and skill. He is forced to take on the role which the nonprofessional is already best equipped to play. The latter, by definition, lacks the skills and knowledge and the habitual tendency to be led into a deep interpretative inquiry of the psychodynamic etiology of the client's problem.

To completely understand this position, it is necessary to escape from the cognitive trap which places personal crises, sometimes called "problems of living," in the category of psychopathological disorders. Whereas neurosis or schizophrenia may require the application of specialized types of treatment program, a personal crisis is a different type of human ailment and correspondingly requires a different type of amelioration. Elsewhere, Caplan has warned that the symptoms of a crisis, namely, increased anxiety, signs of depression, agitation and confusion, may mimic the symptoms of mental illness, but they are not the same and should not be confused with them.

To summarize, the opinions and attitudes of some of the outstanding authorities in the field of suicide prevention and crisis intervention have assigned to the nonprofessional an unequaled value in this form of helping service. It must be recognized that this position takes nothing away from experienced professional clinicians. In fact, it recognizes them even more for their special skills which other lesser trained personnel cannot perform; it recognizes that the society needs such skills in quantities which far exceed the supply. The position merely states that there are some problems that people face which can be handled better by nonprofessional personnel because of the nature of the problem, the appropriate form of treatment, and the nature of the helper. Acute suicidal cases and personal crises require, not the expertise of diagnosticians and therapists, but the availability of immediate warmth, personal involvement, firm direction, and gentle but forceful action. Such behaviors are not generally in the clinical repertoire of professionals when they are acting in their professional role. This is not to say that professionally-trained persons cannot be as warm, sensitive and involved as the nonprofessional. It is the professional role which inserts the armor or distance between the helper and the client. The dogma resulting from these attitudes of prominent leaders of suicidology – all of them professional persons – holds that nonprofessional volunteers are free of these barriers and are, therefore, best equipped to use their lesser training in more effective intervention as crisis workers.

Precedent

One of the arguments which speaks most heavily for the nonprofessional person is that she has emerged in so many centers around the country as the only person willing to take on the task. Resnik (1964) argues that the professional practitioners failed to pick up the challenge when it was presented and, therefore, the nonprofessional moved in to fill a vacuum which was created by an expanding need and a professional resistance to meeting it. Even the very early programs used nonmental health personnel. The National Save-A-Life League in New York began in 1906 with the support of the clergy. While they were certainly professional persons, these ministers pioneered a new form of finding cases and serving suicidal people. To be sure, they had the cooperation of local psychiatric practitioners when needed. While some may argue about how often such support is needed, the fact remains the league began a new form of service. Dublin (1963) reported that some churches in Chicago began operating telephone lines for suicidal people. Not much is known about these programs, and one can assume that, due to changes in leadership, the impetus behind the program was lost. However, in 1959, FRIENDS in Miami developed the first program which was clearly based upon the power of the involved nonprofessional in helping relationships. Resnik (1964, 1968) has described the FRIENDS program in detail.

Almost simultaneously with the development of FRIENDS, Chad Varah began writing of his success with the Samaritans in England. That program has spread throughout the United Kingdom, due primarily to the ability of the nonprofessional in extending a befriending relationship to whomever is in need (Varah, 1965).

In the mid-1960s, when the suicide prevention center movement was first getting started, one concentration of activity could be found in Florida and the Southeast. The establishment of WE CARE in Orlando, Florida, in 1965 marked the beginning of a type of crisis service designed to become a component of the local community mental health services (McGee & McGee, 1968). Soon after WE CARE was started, other programs were initiated on the same model. The Brevard County Suicide Prevention Center was the second example (McGee, 1968), and the Lifeline program in Miami followed. By 1970, there were suicide prevention services in 19 cities of six states in the Southeast. All but two of these programs used nonprofessionals as the primary crisis workers.

Two surveys were taken of the centers around the country (McGee, 1967). Questionnaires were mailed to all known centers operating in November of 1967 and in March of 1969. Returns from both of these surveys revealed that over 80% of all suicide and crisis intervention programs utilized nonprofessionals in some direct service capacity with people who call the publicized telephone number.

Consequently, the history of the suicide prevention center movement shows that the volunteer is a most significant factor in permitting such programs to be developed. Had volunteer nonprofessionals been found unacceptable and unable to meet the challenge, the programs could not have survived and multiplied as they have. Some communities such as Halifax County, North Carolina, which had no local professional manpower in the mental health field, were nevertheless able to begin and maintain a viable crisis intervention service because of the availability of the nonprofessional (Altrocchi & Batton, 1968; Altrocchi & Gutman, 1968). It is especially noteworthy that the Suicide Prevention Center in Knoxville, Tennessee, began its service utilizing the professional members of the local mental health clinic staff. After little more than a year of operation, it began recruiting some nonprofessional personnel to take over. The professionals who began and operated the service came to realize that their services could be better used as consultants, and they went looking for nonprofessionals to assume their role. One can hardly conclude that these professionals deliberately elected to begin providing an inferior service to their community. Rather, the conclusion is obvious that they recognized that the nonprofessional could do the job as well, if not better than they could. However, if nonprofessionals can do the job as well as professionals, but do it on a volunteer basis rather than for extensive fees or salaries, that does seem preferable for most communities. The precedent established by the early centers and continued throughout the massive spread of new centers across the nation clearly implies the advantage of nonprofessionals.

Practical Considerations

Of course, an obvious observation is that nonprofessional volunteers eliminate the costs of salaried professionals. While this is certainly true to some extent, it is neither completely accurate that the volunteer is cost-free to a program, nor is this economic argument the most important of the practical considerations. In the first place, the volunteer must have some professional guidance in the form of clinical case consultation or administrative management. The programs using volunteers exclusively have found that they must employ a person just to coordinate the activities of the nonprofessional staff. Volunteers are by no means a free or even inexpensive way to operate a crisis intervention program. The distinct advantage in communities where there are professional personnel already working in clinics and other settings is that the professionals are freed to utilize their time for consultation activities, program development activities, and other professional tasks which are becoming recognized as more appropriate for professional practitioners than one-to-one client care. This was the original rationale for the use of nonprofessionals in the Los Angeles Suicide Prevention Center (Heilig et al., 1968), and it is still a major advantage of the system.

In addition, there are more potential volunteers available in every community than there are professional personnel. Between 10 and 90 persons must be available to be scheduled for duty shifts each week in 24-hour crisis intervention services. The actual number needed depends upon the length of the shift per day and the number of shifts covered by each person per week. In the Suicide and Crisis Intervention Service in Gainesville, Florida, the schedule required the filling of 69 time periods each week. This is a difficult task even with nonprofessional workers who volunteer their time for community service. It would be impossible if professional personnel were required.

Some efforts have been made to add crisis intervention duties to the workload of professional personnel who are already on duty in other roles. Such attempts have been made using nurses and aides in hospital emergency rooms, nurses or residents on psychiatric units of inpatient settings, and the professional staff of outpatient mental health clinics. Typically, such efforts have been unsatisfactory, and the practice has been to bring in nonprofessional volunteers to handle the crisis intervention and suicide prevention functions.

A third practical consideration is related to the fact that professional personnel are rarely adequately trained for crisis intervention. Each psychologist who has successfully dealt with a suicidal depressed client in psychotherapy, or every psychiatrist who has capably managed antidepressant medication to control a personal crisis is not, thereby, automatically an authority in suicidology. There are very few university graduate or medical schools in the nation which have established even one course in crisis intervention or suicidology. The social work profession has been the group most identified with the practice of crisis therapy, but psychology and psychiatry have tended to overlook such training, both in didactic and experiential form. Naturally, both psychiatric residents and psychology interns have been trained in psychotherapy with depressed and sometimes suicidal clients, but these clients come from a far different population than the typical individual who calls the suicide or crisis telephone line. Developments at the Center for Studies of Suicide Prevention at NIMH were in the direction of establishing a national curriculum in suicidology (Resnik, 1971), but the consequences of awakening academic institutions to the need for, as well as the availability of, such educational material for professional trainees was not apparent in even the current students, much less the already graduated practitioners.

Finally, a further practical consideration of using nonprofessionals relates to the healthy skepticism which still prevails concerning them. Such skepticism is felt not only by the professionals who look askance at their competence, but also by the community at large which generally responds with stereotyped concepts about personal misery. The nonprofessional, being a part of the general public, feels and shares this skepticism about his own ability to handle acute personal crises. All of these attitudes contribute to a readiness for thorough screening and continuous evaluation of on-the-job performance. It is true that not all suicide and crisis centers perform as extensive or as elaborate performance evaluations as are desirable, but the fault here lies in the lack of suitable performance criteria and measurement methods (McGee, 1971). Nearly every center performs some type of routine screening, even perfunctorily, and some have instituted very elaborate screening programs. On the other hand, it is rare to find such careful screening of professional people in community mental health agencies. Until recently, when academic programs have begun to produce more professional people than the available public money permits to be employed on limited budgets, mental health professionals were in complete control of the marketplace. Only the curriculum vitae was important, and that was most often a formality used to exclude the most inadequately trained. The vitae reveals only experience, with no comment on competence. The general rule was that a clinic in need of a psychiatrist, or a hospital in need of a psychologist, would take the first one who was willing to work for the low salary they had to offer. Furthermore, who has ever heard of on-the-job quality control of professional competence? Unless individuals are so noxious and inept in their personal style that even the secretaries can detect their danger to clients, there is no formal system whereby professional clinicians must account to their superiors for what they do during the 50-minute client hour. Of course, there are the state licensing boards and the national specialty boards which certify competence – at one time only. Who is to say how well some competencies are preserved 15 or 30 years later? All professionals resent being supervised by or responsible to members of other disciplines and, in the interests of harmony, such procedures are not found in the typical community mental health agency.

This is not the case in the suicide prevention or crisis intervention center which utilizes nonprofessional workers. These people are tenacious in their demands for supervision and feedback from consultants or staff supervisors. It has been observed in several centers that the lack of satisfactory amounts of evaluation and in-service training will result in a marked diminution of volunteer morale and enthusiasm for the task. They will drop out if they are not given the kind of continuous overseeing from more experienced personnel which permits low levels of anxiety to be maintained. Rarely does a system develop with a built-in quality control phenomena such as is found in the use of nonprofessionals in the helping services. It is a distinct practical advantage over the use of professional workers who ordinarily eschew supervision and evaluation of their clinical work as soon as they leave the training role.

Empirical Data

With the generally recognized manpower shortage in all areas of mental health care, a number of investigators began experimenting with the use of lay persons in a wide variety of client relationships. Knickerbocker and McGee (1973) and Knickerbocker and Fowler (1971) have reviewed the literature on the measurement of therapist behavior which facilitates effective outcomes in therapy. There is now extensive evidence that lay persons can offer moderately high levels of warmth, empathy, and genuineness in several client populations, including hospitalized and outpatient neuropsychiatric clients, normals, juvenile delinquents, and children (Carkhuff, 1968). Truax and Carkhuff (1967) have shown that, of these three therapist-offered conditions, warmth is the most potent factor as a predictor of successful outcome.

Inasmuch as these dimensions had not been previously observed systematically with volunteers in the role of crisis intervention telephone workers, Knickerbocker and McGee (1973) compared their performance with that of professional persons working in the same center, under the same work conditions. All subjects, whether professional or nonprofessional, had received the same basic training course before becoming workers in the center. Their ratings were made blindly by groups of raters who had no knowledge about the purposes of the investigation or the professional status of the worker being rated. Ratings of empathy, genuineness and warmth were made using the Truax method (Truax & Carkhuff, 1967) and the method developed by Lister (1970).

The results revealed clearly that in all three dimensions, the nonprofessionals were as high in their scores as the professionals. There were no significant differences between the two groups in amount of empathy or genuineness as measured by the Lister ratings or in the amount of genuineness as measured by the Truax method. However, on both rating methods, the lay volunteers were significantly superior to the professionals in amount of warmth they offered to callers.

Such data offer an unequivocal verification of the impression that Farberow (1966) reported when he said the volunteers offered "a relationship which was on a more direct and a more friendly level than that of the professionals." It is important to note that it is in the dimension which counts the most towards successful outcome of the helping relationship that the nonprofessional is most clearly superior, under the conditions observed in this study.

Summary and Conclusions

There was a time when volunteer nonprofessionals were valued because they were more plentiful than professionals. If they were given some supervision and careful training, it was felt that they would probably do little harm, and they might do some good in helping relationships. It was a time of consciously altering the strategy of mental health service delivery. The original strategy had been to train as many highly competent professional people as possible to staff the mental health services which began developing in more affluent communities in the 1940s to facilitate rehabilitation of GIs and their families following World War II. The goal was to minimize the number of losses due to inadequately trained personnel. In recent years, the strategy has required modification because of the great number of people needing many more kinds of help than the former model can provide. The goal has become to maximize the number of wins. So the volunteer nonprofessional was seen as a person who could possibly add a few more wins than losses to the accounting of services delivered.

Almost immediately, nonprofessionals began to attract the attention of some of the professional community with the fact that they have something unique to offer in a situation which may be especially suited to their own talents. Rather than be a substitute for unavailable professionals, nonprofessionals became recognized as necessary and valuable in their own right. In some fields more than others, nonprofessionals are considered even more useful than the professionals whom they replace. Suicide prevention and crisis intervention is such an area of activity. The evidence is overwhelming. There are practical advantages, there is a substantial theory or impressionistic opinion resulting in a dogma, and there are empirical research results which demonstrate that nonprofessionals are superior to professionals in these functions. With such evidence in the field of suicidology, the movement to nonprofessionals is the only rational response that the profession can make in its ascent to higher levels of service.

REFERENCES

Altrocchi, J., & Batton, L. (March, 1968). Suicide prevention in an under-populated area. American Association of Suicidology, Chicago, IL.

Altrocchi, J., & Gutman, V. (April, 1968). Suicide prevention in an under-populated area. Southeastern Psychological Association, Roanoke, VA.

Caplan, G. (1961). *An approach to community mental health.* New York: Grune & Stratton.

Caplan, G. (1964). *Principles of preventative psychiatry.* New York: Basic Books.

Carkhuff, R. R. (1968). Differential functioning of lay and professional helpers. *Journal of Counseling Psychology, 15,* 117–126.

Dublin, L. I. (1963). *Suicide: A sociological and statistical study.* New York: Ronald Press.

Dublin, L. I. (1969). Suicide prevention. In E. S. Shneidman (Ed.), *On the nature of suicide,* pp. 43–47. San Francisco: Jossey-Bass.

Edwards, C. H. The identification, training and utilization of paraprofessional key personnel in the delivery of crisis intervention services in non-metropolitan areas. Mid-South Conference on Crisis Intervention and Suicide Prevention, Athens, GA, January 1970.

Ewalt, P. L. (Ed.). (1967). *Mental health volunteers.* Springfield, IL: Charles C Thomas.

Farberow, N. L. (April, 1966). The selection and training of nonprofessional personnel for therapeutic roles in suicide prevention. Southeastern Psychological Association, New Orleans, LA.

Grosser, C., Henry, W. E., & Kelly, J. G. (1969). *Nonprofessionals in the human services.* San Francisco: Jossey-Bass.

Guerney, B. G. (Ed.). (1969). *Psychotherapeutic agents: New roles for nonprofessionals, parents, and teachers.* New York: Holt, Rinehart & Winston.

Heilig, S. M. (1970). Training in suicide prevention. *Bulletin of Suicidology,* No. 6, 41–44.

Heilig, S. M., Farberow, N. L., Litman, R. E., & Shneidman, E. S. (1968). The role of nonprofessional volunteer in a suicide prevention center. *Community Mental Health Journal, 4,* 287–295.

Knickerbocker, D. A., & Fowler, D. E. (March, 1971). A system for evaluating the performance of crisis workers. American Association of Suicidology, Washington, DC.

Knickerbocker, D. A., & McGee, R. K. (1973). Clinical effectiveness of nonprofessional and professional telephone workers in a crisis intervention center. In D. Lester & G. W. Brockopp (Eds.), *Crisis intervention and counseling by telephone,* pp. 298–309. Springfield, IL: Charles C Thomas.

Lister, J. L. (1970). A scale for the measurement of accurate empathy, facilitative warmth, and facilitative genuineness. Unpublished paper, University of Florida, FL

McGee, R. K. (1967). A community approach to crisis intervention. In R. K. McGee (Ed.), Planning emergency services for comprehensive community mental health centers. Unpublished, Gainesville, University of Florida, FL.

McGee, R. K. (1968). Community mental health concepts as demonstrated by suicide prevention programs in Florida. *Community Mental Health Journal, 4,* 144–152.

McGee, R. K. (March, 1971). Assessing the performance of suicide prevention center programs and personnel. American Association of Suicidology, Washington, DC.

McGee, R. K., & McGee, J. P. (1968). A total community response to the cry for help: We Care, Inc. of Orlando, Florida. In H. L. P. Resnik (Ed.), *Suicidal behaviors: Diagnosis and management,* pp. 441–452. Boston: Little, Brown.

Reiff, R., & Riessman, F. (1965). The indigenous nonprofessional. *Community Mental Health Journal Monograph,* No. 1.

Resnik, H. L. P. (1964). A community anti-suicidal organization. *Current Psychiatric Therapies, 4,* 253–259.

Resnik, H. L. P. (1968). A community antisuicide organization: The friends of Dade County, Florida. In H. L. P. Resnik (Ed.), *Suicidal behaviors: Diagnosis and management,* pp. 418–440. Boston: Little, Brown.

Resnik, H. L. P. (March, 1971). Critical issues in suicide prevention. American Association of Suicidology, Washington, DC.

Sobey, F. (1970). *The nonprofessional revolution in mental health.* New York: Columbia University Press.

Truax, C. B., & Carkhuff, R. R. (1967). *Toward effective counseling and psychotherapy: Training and practice.* Chicago: Aldine.

Varah, C. (1965). *The Samaritans.* New York: Macmillan.

Chapter 30

THE USE OF THE PROFESSIONAL IN TELEPHONE COUNSELING

ANN S. MCCOLSKEY

In considering crisis intervention models, one is met with a bewildering variety of examples, serving a variety of purposes and value systems under that broad rubric. If, however, the various models are arrayed along two dimensions, a professional-lay dimension and a volunteer-compensated dimension, some order is introduced into the universe, and rational comparisons can more readily be made. These distinctions are not always clearly rendered. For example, "volunteer" is sometimes loosely contrasted with "professional" in discussion of crisis intervention models, as if these were antonyms. It should be clearly kept in mind that they are not and that two orthogonal, unrelated dimensions are involved. Volunteers may be professionals, sub-professionals, pre-professionals, and para-professionals – every variant of trained worker – as well as lay helpers, in crisis intervention programs.

The professional-lay dimension is, of course, the primary dimension, insofar as the character of a particular crisis intervention program is concerned. The volunteer-compensated dimension is a secondary utilitarian dimension. There are other secondary descriptive continua that can be introduced in schematizing crisis intervention programs. There is a continuum of breadth or comprehensiveness of services, for example, ranging from narrowly conceived, brief, superficial intervention in suicidal crises (limited to rescue efforts and referrals to other agencies) or stopgap drug therapy at one end of the continuum to continued psychotherapeutic care and comprehensive, social-environmental management at the other end. There is also a continuum of directness-indirectness (of intervention efforts), ranging from direct, face-to-face encounters to indirect phone contacts.

If crisis intervention models, extant and theoretical, are arrayed along the primary professional-lay dimension and categorized as broadly professional or nonprofessional in character, the other three dimensions can be utilized to pinpoint secondary differentiating characteristics of programs to facilitate comparative analysis.

Nonprofessional Crisis Intervention Programs

Considering first the broad category of nonprofessional crisis intervention programs, it may be stated that, from a theoretical point-of-view, the concept of a program of this type represents a contradiction in terms – that there is no logical justification for an emergency service manned by unskilled workers. Logically, if professional training in one of the mental health disciplines is considered a requisite for management of psychological problems of any degree of severity, then adjustment crises or acute problems demand the utmost, not the least, in expertise. Conceptually, the notion of using untrained persons to intercept crisis reactions is as illogical and hazardous as attempting to stem a massive hemorrhage with a Band-Aid.

Suicide Prevention Programs

The argument has been advanced, nevertheless, that in a specific type of adjustment crisis, namely a suicidal crisis, untrained persons can be taught specific responses or that naïve caring is enough (McGee, 1966a). As a result, suicide prevention programs, soliciting suicidal calls and deploying benevolent lay people to intercept them by telephone, have sprung up with accelerating frequency over the past decade and a half, inspired chiefly by the establishment of the Los Angeles Suicide Prevention Center in 1958. This pioneer center was founded by the NIMH as a support facility for the groundbreaking research efforts of Farberow and Shneidman in the previously tabooed area of suicidal behavior. Subsequently, the LASPC staff cautiously began to experiment with the use of volunteer nonprofessionals with their suicide prevention program (Shneidman et al., 1970) to relieve the staff of some of their burgeoning clinical responsibilities and to facilitate research, and this feature of the program caught the public fancy. A grass-roots suicide prevention movement resulted, sweeping the country with near-evangelical fervor and little rational restraint. It unfortunately has not been clearly recognized that the popular variant of the LASPC suicide prevention model bears little resemblance to the original – that the nonprofessional volunteers at the LASPC executed a restricted function (answering phone calls during the day) under the watchful eye and direct supervision of the professional staff, and also that there was a little-touted cadre of pre-professional graduate students who handled all the night calls, so that the total LASPC operation was a complexly organized, highly professional, research-oriented suicide prevention program which has little in common with the popular, free-standing, lay-operated answering services bearing the same generic name.

The contagion of the popular suicide prevention movement, even if transitory, demands careful, critical study of the phenomenon. It may be noted, first, that an earlier survey (McGee, 1968) of 40 programs across the country (about a 75% sample) revealed that only 31% were now operating with a wholly nonprofessional staff, and that over two-thirds of the programs had become in part or entirely professional in composition, providing empirical evidence that the basis concept of a nonprofessional emergency service was not viable. Concomitantly, another more detailed appraisal of a smaller sample of suicide prevention programs (Whittemore, 1970) revealed the same trend toward professionalization and a related change in the direction of broadening of the original suicide prevention base to embrace crisis intervention. Most of these programs have expanded their titles to include crisis intervention or have given up the narrower suicide prevention appellation entirely. At the same time, utilization statistics demonstrate that less than 10% of the calls to these ostensible suicide prevention centers involve suicidal attempts, and only one-fourth involve either attempts or threats. (Nearly 40% of the tiny fraction of calls involving actual attempts are placed by third parties who happen to be on or come on the scene, rather than by the person attempting suicide.) Subsequent data from the LASPC (Shneidman et al., 1970) demonstrated the same paradox more emphatically. Less than 2% of the calls to that prototypical suicide prevention involved actual attempts, and only 10% involved either attempts or impulses. This ubiquitous finding puts in clear question the theoretical rational for suicide prevention as a unique type of clinical operation, identifiably different from crisis intervention and, therefore, supports the argument that there is no logical substitute for wide-ranging professional skills in this or any type of emergency mental health program.

Another line of evidence challenging the rationale for suicide prevention is one that emerged from research on the apparent antithesis between the suicide attempter and the suicide completer or the unsuccessful and the successful suicide, to put it in paradoxical terms. A number of studies (e.g., Beall, 1969) described the typical attempter in statistical language as a woman who tends in personality pattern to be a dependent hysteric, protesting against the actual or threatened loss of or rejection by a significant other, and employing nonlethal methods. The typical completer is described statistically as a man who manifests independence in interpersonal relationships and underlying feelings of alienation and who employs lethal methods. It has been remarked that the act of suicide, for the completer, represents an assertive rather than a defeatist action – an active, ideological commitment to death; while, on the other hand, the attempter's suicidal gesture represents an attention-getting "cry for help," as Farberow and Shneidman (1961) have poetically termed it – a desperate but self-aborting effort to escape life stress while clinging to life. It follows (as Seiden [1971] and others have recognized) that it is the attempter, not the completer, who is attuned and responds to the naïve helping efforts of a suicide prevention service while, ironically, the completer, the putative target of such service, is unaffected.

The so-called helping efforts of the lay suicide prevention worker, which are necessarily circumscribed and have become somewhat ritualized, and which include attempts to ascertain the lethality of suicidal intent by direct questioning, followed by either rescue efforts or referral to mental health professionals, may be worse than ineffectual with the genuinely suicidal individual. They may be offensive, further alienating potential suicides and firming their suicidal resolve. Szasz (1971) and others (e.g,. Macks, 1971) have protested against the coercive intervention of zealous suicide prevention workers and have questioned the ethics and clinical propriety of involuntary rescue or referral. The practice of direct interrogation regarding the lethality of a caller's suicidal intentions appears particularly suspect. Such questioning may alienate the genuinely suicidal individual, or it may have a dangerous power of suggestion for the hysteric (as may the overly enthusiastic promotion of a suicide prevention service).[46]

At the same time, there is evidence that lethality ratings by untrained workers have poor predictive power and, therefore, no utility, for they have been found to vary directly with and to reflect the degree of inexperience and level of anxiety of the worker rather than the gravity of the suicidal crisis. It has been demonstrated, conversely, that lethality can be assessed with a very high degree of precision by an experienced psychologist (Shneidman, 1971), and the unarguable conclusion is that professional competence is a requisite for the practice of any of the functions subsumed under suicide intervention, and that there is no mechanical shortcut to nor substitute for professional competence.

It has also been found (Murphy et al., 1969) that many or most of the callers to a suicide prevention center have previously had or are currently receiving some type of professional help, which is consistent with the hypothesis that the actual consumers of this type of service are dependent-hysteric suicide attempters rather than completers. This finding suggests that the lay worker's practice of automatically referring these already psychiatrically or psychologically sophisticated callers for professional help is redundant, and

---

[46] Callers have been known to profess to be suicidal in order to justify use of suicide prevention services (McGee, 1966a)

the concomitant finding that follow-through on such referrals is limited (Murphy et al., 1969) supports this judgment.

Apart from consideration of the theoretical or clinical implications of lay-operated suicide prevention services, there is, of course, a pragmatic question of economy. The appeal of volunteer nonprofessionals lies at base in the low cost, on paper, of their services. There are high, indirect or intangible costs of utilizing untrained volunteers, however, to substitute for or supplement professionals in the delivery of critical emergency services. The involved professionals paradoxically spend as much or more time in recruiting, selecting, training, and supervising nonprofessionals as they would in providing direct services, and there is simply an indirect rather than a direct expenditure of professional time and skill. If the nonprofessionals are uncompensated volunteers, there is also a cost in morale of the workers over a period of time, compounding the problems of recruitment, training, and supervision. There is invariably a very high turnover and attrition rate among voluntary nonprofessionals. The absence of compensation inevitably affects worker morale, particularly when there are compensated as well as uncompensated staff, and there is also a subtle morale factor involved in the covert role conflict that is typically induced in the fledgling, nonprofessional mental health worker in the course of his brief training and exposure to acute adjustment problems and crisis situations in the lives of others. As they gain experience, however superficial or peripheral, a sense of professional pride and ambition is prematurely awakened and they come to think of themselves as part of a professional service, and yet they have no licit professional status. At the least, suppressed frustration and envy of legitimate (and adequately compensated) professionals are felt, while ultimately many are driven to abandon their anomalous roles. The position of unpaid nonprofessionals in an emergency mental health service becomes, in time, untenable.

A parenthetical observation from the LASPC experience and two other experimental projects in nondegree training of ancillary mental health personnel is that a minimum of two years of study and training (involving both course work and field training) is apparently required (McGee, 1966b; Rioch et al., undated). Since, in each of these three experimental projects, the trainees were college educated (or better) and the training was at a graduate level, a master's degree in psychology or social work could have been earned in the same time or less, and the conclusion again appears to be that there is no shortcut to professional competence in this field.

This complex of theoretical, empirical, and pragmatic arguments against the use of nonprofessionals in crisis intervention programs comprises virtually a mandate to base whatever model is adopted at or near the professional end of the professional-lay descriptive dimension.

Professional Crisis Intervention Programs

Suicide Counseling Associations

Turning to consideration of professionally-staffed crisis intervention programs, there are, first, voluntary associations of professionals in suicide counseling which have emerged spontaneously in this country and abroad at intervals over the second half of the twentieth century (Farberow & Shneidman, 1961). These are at base social welfare programs with a religious flavor, usually sponsored by social agencies or church-related organizations. They frequently include mental health paraprofessionals (ministers, physicians, nurses, lawyers, and educators) along with social workers, psychologists, and psychiatrists as mental health professionals. There sometimes is a nucleus of paid professionals as a regular staff. Short-term, emergency counseling is offered either indirectly (by telephone) or directly (in person) for identified suicidal crises. These programs are narrow in reach by definition and are limited in an operational sense by their voluntary and loosely organized character. The use of volunteer professionals represents, of course, a significant paper economy, but entails a devitalizing sacrifice of efficiency and control. Attrition among the volunteer professionals is high, and the viability of programs of this ilk is a direct function of the degree of dedication and emotional stamina of their leadership. Typically, there is a low survival rate.

Emergency Psychiatric Services

A different crisis intervention model utilizes professionals on a compensated basis, providing for better coordinated services and more sustained participation. One variant of the compensated professional model is the emergency psychiatric services type of program (Furman, undated; Lamb et al., 1969; Weisz et al., 1968). These services are typically linked to a hospital inpatient facility and are based in the hospital emergency room and patterned after ER services. The staff ordinarily consists of psychiatric residents who provide brief diagnostic screening for hospital admission or stopgap chemotherapy to ER walk-ins or via home visitations. The model is superficial and limited in its conceptualization of crisis intervention in terms of rudimentary, medically-oriented surveillance rather than broader, psychotherapeutic management. Programs of this type have been inspired (in the financial as well as ideological sense) chiefly by the Community Mental Health Services Act of 1963 which stipulated that emergency mental health services must be provided in order for any facility to qualify for federal funds as a community mental health center, and they proliferated in the following decade as a kind of bandwagon phenomenon without a great deal of conceptual programming.

Crisis Counseling Programs

An alternative model involving compensated professionals is what may be termed a crisis counseling model. In contrast to the emergency psychiatric services type of program, this is a conceptually broader, psychotherapeutically-oriented rather than medically-diagnostically-oriented model, with a concomitant focus on indirect, verbal intervention by telephone rather than direct, face-to-face encounters, with at the same time a focus on more in-depth, psychological response to acute adjustment problems or crisis situations. There are few unequivocal examples to date of this progressive model but, as previously intimated, many suicide prevention programs appear to be evolving into a broader, compensated-professional-crisis intervention format and hence converging on the crisis counseling model. None of the contemporary crisis counseling programs, however, satisfies a criterion of comprehensiveness of care, although there is conceptual breadth, for none can be classified as comprehensive because of the short-term, time-limited character of their psychotherapeutic services. Invariably, they depend upon referral to other professionals or mental health services for longer-term or follow-up counseling. In a rare instance, provision for continued psychological care is made in indirect fashion, by housing separate crisis intervention and regular outpatient services under the same programmatic roof, so that crisis cases can be followed at least within the same facility if not by the same professional (cf. the program of the Massachusetts Mental Health Center),[47] but there is still in such a case a clinically inefficient break in the continuity of care and an artificial, conceptual distinction between crisis counseling and regular psychotherapy. Ideally, the crisis counseling model should provide for continuity of care by utilizing the same professional staff for emergency and follow-up psychotherapy and thus will satisfy the threefold criterion of comprehensive, compensated, professional service.

A Comprehensive Crisis Counseling Program

One program in Florida emulated the comprehensive crisis counseling model: the Escambia County Community Mental Health Center in Pensacola. So far as can be determined, it was unique in this respect and, therefore, bears detailed examination and description for heuristic purposes.

At the core of the Escambia County program was a duality of roles assumed by the professional staff of the outpatient unit of the center as a logical consequence of the fact that emergency mental health services are conceptu-

---

[47] See Emergency Services. U.S. Government Printing Office. USPHS Publication #1477.

alized as an integral aspect of or an extension of regular outpatient services, and not as a discontinuous system. In this program, every staff member in rotation took a shift on a 24-hour emergency or crisis intervention schedule which was labeled "Crisis Call." The professional on Crisis Call was responsible for managing all calls received during his shift, whether day or night and whatever the nature of the call or contact (whether emergency or routine, by telephone or walk-in). No operational distinction was made between after-hours calls and calls during center office hours, as is necessarily made when services are provided by different emergency and regular outpatient staffs. Day or night, the staff member on Crisis Call executed the same, full range of professional functions, assessing the degree of urgency and the psychological needs in each case, responding as immediately and actively (in a psychotherapeutic sense) as was required, and offering further counseling or consultation as needed.

The telephone is the preferred medium for crisis counseling (or crisis consultation) within this framework, bridging physical distance and the ritualistic delays of traditional scheduling-by-appointment; immediately clarifying needs and coordinating helping efforts in the course of third-party referral or consultation; and dispelling some of the stigma and negative mystique of mental health services for the naïve caller. Walk-in crisis cases were also seen at the center during the day, but were not solicited actively, for experience demonstrated that the typical walk-in client was not in crisis and was more likely to have stopped by the center out of curiosity or on idle impulse, or to have been arbitrarily referred to the center by another social or health agency or private professional in a mechanical fashion for no clear reason. If a crisis was experienced in a walk-in case, it was frequently experienced by a third party (parent, teacher or spouse) who conveyed the resisting patient into the august presence of the professional for judgment (as "crazy" or "sick") and treatment (perceived as magical exorcism or as restraint, by confinement or chemical means). Partly for this reason, counseling and psychotherapy in this program were family and relationship centered, rather than individually focused, and consultation with allied "caretaker" agencies and paraprofessionals was emphasized. The program was comprehensive in this sense as well as in the sense of continuity of care.

At night, the telephone was the exclusive medium for Crisis Call, and reliance was placed explicitly and realistically on indirect, verbal intervention rather than direct confrontation. If, however, physical intervention in some form was required (e.g., in the event of a serious suicidal attempt), the Crisis Call staff member could, of course, call on other emergency resources in the community.

Crisis Call had its own telephone number to enhance the visibility of the service in the community and to identify and expedite urgent calls. All calls were screened through the center switchboard and receptionist during daytime office hours and through a commercial answering service at night and on weekends. The staff member on call, day or night, remained accessible by telephone at all times. At night, however, he or she took calls in his home, relayed by the answering service.

The mode of reimbursement for night Crisis Call was via compensatory time. This means of reimbursement was not only enormously economical (128 hours a week of professional time on night Crisis Call costs but 21 hours of compensatory time), but also appeared to have some psychological advantages over monetary compensation from the staff's point of view. Time off from daily responsibilities is highly valued by professionals, and it also appears to lend a certain dignity to overtime work. From an accounting and administrative point of view, compensation in the form of time is a more flexible commodity than money, and it has the distinct advantage of being an invisible and readily absorbed expense, requiring no direct, budgetary defense or justification. This highly effective system of compensation, of course, was an outgrowth of the unique duality of roles assumed by the outpatient staff in this program.

It may be concluded that the comprehensive crisis counseling model functions in an efficient manner from both clinical and mechanical points of view. The only drawback, if it be such, is a subtle one that arises from the overlapping roles played by the staff. Some center clients perceive the night Crisis Call staff as being "on call" for other staff (in the medical, group practice tradition) rather than as providing an ancillary outreach service, and this results occasionally in abuse of the service and exploitation of the night staff – in the latter's opinion. The problem is, however, resolved on an individual basis by the night Crisis Call staff member, with the caller and/or his or her regular therapist, when it occurs.

Preliminary utilization statistics on night Crisis Call tended to validate the conceptual underpinnings for this crisis intervention model and confirmed the impression of clinical effectiveness. The average frequency of calls per evening was two (which was consistent with projections from other crisis counseling programs, taking into account a local population of about 200,000). This rate appeared to reflect a sufficient need for and use of the service without overburdening the night Crisis Call staff. More significantly, virtually all (90%) of the night calls were appropriate, in the sense that they were of a clinical rather than information-giving character and required half to three-quarters of an hour of telephone counseling or consultation on average. Furthermore, fully half of the calls were classified as "extremely urgent," and three-quarters were classified as either "moderately" or "extremely urgent." Night Crisis Call therefore appeared to answer a genuine and unique need, and the impression was that the active and appropriate use of and positive response to the service by the local community was a direct consequence of its professional character and the feature of continuity of care. It is of interest, in this regard, that in over two-thirds of the cases, follow-up counseling was planned, while in 20%, a single intensive, telephone counseling or consultation session sufficed. Only about 12% of the calls entailed referral to other emergency resources in the community. It may also be noted, incidentally, that some callers explicitly recognized and made use of the protective shield of anonymity that can be offered by a phone counseling service, and that some also used night Crisis Call on a repeated basis to the exclusion of other, direct modes of psychotherapeutic help – providing testimony for the unique effectiveness of indirect telephone counseling.

It may further be noted that fewer than half of the night callers (41%) were new to psychotherapeutic help, while the majority had had some prior contact with mental health professionals (at the center or elsewhere). It could be argued from this that this program was tapping a population of already identified consumers of mental health services and that its value, therefore, was attenuated. This, however, is a common finding among crisis intervention programs of all types, as previously has been suggested, and appears to bear out the axiom that most individuals making an unstable adjustment have a history of unstable adjustment.

The conclusion from this comparative analysis of contemporary crisis intervention models and detailed exposition of the comprehensive crisis counseling model is that this model, satisfying as it does the criteria of compensated professionalism and breadth of concepts and services and featuring telephone counseling or indirect intervention, approximates an ideal type of crisis intervention.

REFERENCES

Beall, L. (1969). The dynamics of suicide. *Bulletin of Suicidology*, March, 2–16.
Farberow, N. L., & Shneidman, E. S. (1961). *The cry for help*. New York: McGraw-Hill.
Furman, S. S. (undated). *Community mental health services in Northern Europe* Washington, DC: US Government Printing Office. USPHS Publication #1407.
Lamb, H. R., Heath, D., & Downing, J. J. (1969). *Handbook of community mental health practice*. San Francisco: Jossey-Bass.
Macks, V. W. (1971). Suicide prevention. Mental health 'oppression.' *Social Work, 16*, 102–104.
McGee, R. K. (1966a). Development and organization of suicide prevention centers. Community Mental Health Services Symposium, Atlanta.
McGee, R. K. (1966b). Non-professionals as mental health workers in counseling and testing. American Psychological Association, New York.

McGee, R. K. (1968). The manpower problem in suicide prevention. In N. L. Farberow (Ed.), *Proceedings of the 4th International Conference for Suicide Prevention*, pp. 98–103. Los Angeles: Delmar.

Murphy, G. E., Wetzel, R., Swallow, C., & McClure, J. N. (1969). Who calls the suicide prevention center? *American Journal of Psychiatry, 126*, 314–324.

Rioch, M. J., Elkers, C., & Flint, A. A. (undated). *Pilot project in training mental health counselors*. U.S. Government Printing Office. USPHS Publication #1254.

Seiden, R. (March 29, 1971). Quoted in *Behavior Today*, page 3.

Shneidman, E. S. (1971). Perturbation and lethality as precursors of suicide in a gifted group. *Life-Threatening Behavior, 1*, 23–45.

Shneidman, E. S., Farberow, N. L., & Litman, R. E. (1970). *The psychology of suicide*. New York: Science House.

Szasz, T. (1971). The ethics of suicide. *Intellectual Digest, 2*, 53–55.

Weisz, A. E., Staight, D. C., Houts, P. S., & Voten, M. P. (1968). Suicide threats, suicide attempts, and the emergency psychiatrist. In N. L. Farberow (Ed.), *Proceedings of the 4th International Conference for Suicide Prevention*, pp. 227–251. Los Angeles: Delmar.

Whittemore, K. (1970). *Ten centers*. Atlanta, GA: Lullwater Press.

Chapter 31

SELECTING THE TELEPHONE COUNSELOR

GENE W. BROCKOPP

Crisis intervention is hard work. To do a competent job, the most highly trained professional needs to use all of her skill and experience in the fast-moving, arduous process of assisting an individual who has come to her with a critical life problem. To engage in the same process over the telephone is often more difficult because the interviewer must base her decisions on only the overt and covert verbal cues. Each center has the task of finding people who will be able to perform this task with understanding skill, objectivity, and involvement. From the population of the community, each center must select individuals who can feel and express the basic human qualities which will enable them to relate to and work with a person in crisis. In this chapter we will discuss some of the problems related to the selection of individuals who work on a telephone emergency service.

Professional Versus Nonprofessional

One of the first decisions that a crisis service needs to make is whether or not the individuals answering the telephone will be selected from a professional population or from the general population of the community. Almost all of the more than 200 centers in the country at the time of writing used volunteers to work on the telephone. A few programs used only professional individuals who were specifically trained in one of the mental health disciplines. The question of which group functions better on the telephone has not been definitely answered. There is no sound empirical evidence to indicate that professional individuals function better than nonprofessional individuals on a crisis intervention telephone service. The few studies that have been completed are on such highly specific and unique groups that it is questionable whether the data from the studies can be applied to any other group in the country. In the cities where only professional individuals are used on the telephone service, justification for this practice is stated in terms of opinion and subjective experience, rather than in terms of actual data. At the same time, there is also no scientific basis or justification for the use of volunteers in a center. This decision is often based on the judgment that these individuals can do an adequate job on the telephone and that, since they are volunteers, they reduce the cost of the operation. To further blur the line between these two groups, Dublin stated that the nonprofessional is the true "professional" of the suicide prevention movement and that the so-called mental health professional is really the untrained individual in the field. With very little data to indicate which is the true "professional" or which group is most effective in working with this population, I would like to state my opinion regarding the relative use of professional or nonprofessional as a worker in the emergency telephone service.

At the Buffalo Suicide and Crisis Service, we trained more than 400 volunteer counselors over a period of three years for our 24-hour telephone service. About one-half of these can be classified as professionals, that is, individuals who are presently practicing in one of the mental health professions, such as social workers, psychologists, nurses, or advanced students in these fields. The other half were either undergraduate students in a variety of subject areas, people from the community who maintained a regular job in the community, or housewives who worked at the center on a part-time basis. Our experience has been that there is very little difference between the work of the professional and the nonprofessional person when they use a crisis intervention model in working with a client on the telephone. Professionals have some advantages in that they have a theory to guide them in their counseling relationships with people. They also have an understanding of dynamic psychology and, therefore, some method of placing the behavior of the client into a meaningful context. Their diagnostic skills may assist them in determining the severity of the person's problems and increase their ability to evaluate the client's need for assistance. At the same time, these skills can often be a hindrance because telephone crisis intervention work forces professionals out of the traditional therapeutic model into a much more problem-solving type of relationship. Their training, which is designed to assist them in working with "sick" people, may result in them being unable to see the client in terms of his strengths rather than his weaknesses. Also, as mentioned in previous chapters, it is most important that the person working on the telephone be able to relate to the client through his "humanness." Often the academic training and therapeutic techniques that individuals acquire in the process of professional training reduce their ability to relate in a "real" way with the client.

Nonprofessionals also have difficulties. Although they do not need to unlearn specific therapeutic techniques, they must do something equally difficult – they must learn to "listen with their gut" and respond to the feelings that they have about the individual in crisis, for they do not have the technical skills that professional have and, therefore, cannot rely on academic knowledge about the individual. Being untrained in mental health and being told for many years that only professional people can handle individuals in difficulty, nonprofessionals are often quite anxious and concerned whether or not they are doing a good job. This increased anxiety may cause them more problems and greater difficulty in doing a good job than any other single thing.

Given a nonprofessional individual who is mature in his feelings, has sufficient sensitivity to develop good interpersonal relationships, and enough intelligence to act judiciously, we feel that the quality of the crisis counseling is about the same as that of a professional person who is open and has not lost his "humanness." Either of them can develop the technical skills necessary to work on an emergency telephone service and do so with the concern, intelligence, and objectivity that are necessary in crisis intervention work.

In the Buffalo Suicide and Crisis Service, we did not differentiate between the so-called professional and the nonprofessional person on any of our services. We classified all individuals who worked on the telephone as volunteers. Our criteria for selecting them were not in terms of their professional background, but in terms of their characteristics as human beings and their ability to relate to people in a positive and innovative manner. Regardless of their background or previous experience in the mental health or other related areas, they had to go through the same selection process, the same training program, and be subject to the same type of supervision, scrutiny, and regulations. The experiential evidence we had indicated to us that this basis for selection resulted in highly qualified and responsive telephone workers.

Methods for Finding Volunteers

Initially, the center had difficult recruiting sufficient volunteers to maintain the telephone service. To reach the widest number of potentially good volunteers, speeches were given in several classes in psychology, social work, medicine, and nursing at the universities and colleges in Erie County. In addition, each time a speech was made in a community organization or business group, a request for volunteers was made. This resulted in sufficient individuals being recruited for the telephone service. We were, however, quite concerned about attracting individuals to the center who would have opinionated points of view, or people who would not have the basic personality traits that would allow them to work effectively at the center, but who might want to engage in this type of activity for the personal therapeutic value it would have for them.

As the service continued, our confidence in our ability to select individuals and to train them for the telephone service increased, and we began to explore different means of recruiting volunteers. For example, an ad was placed in the local newspaper under the "Personal" column which read as follows:

> Part-time counselors for day work with telephone counseling service. Work 4-8 days per month, 1/2 day shift ok. No salary but $1.00 per hour expense money. We provide training and supervision. We are looking for warm, sensitive people who can relate to others and who are open to learning. Some college desirable. Age no factor except must be over 18. Call Miss Hanon, Suicide Prevention & Crisis Service. Mon. through Fri. 9 a.m. to 5 p.m. 854-1966.

At the same time, ads were placed under "Help Wanted – Male" and "Help Wanted – Female" columns which would direct the individual to the larger, more inclusive ad in the "Personal" column. We ran the ad for a three-day period of time and obtained more than 180 responses. Each person was sent an application form to complete and return to the center. Over 90 applications forms were completed and returned to the center.

As a result of the high quality training programs we established and the increased visibility of the center in the community, we had more individuals who wished to work for the center than we could train and use. Virtually every day brought additional applications from people who had heard about the service and who wanted to work at the center. As a result, the process of finding volunteers changed into a process of selecting volunteers from the many individuals who applied for training.

Criteria for Selecting Volunteers

We felt that the criteria for the initial selection of volunteers should be extremely broad and should be restricted by only a few conditions. For example, we did not allow anyone under 18 years of age to work on the telephone service. Although this minimal age was initially an arbitrary one, we felt that it was justified for the following reasons. It was difficult to find individuals below 18 years of age who had sufficient maturity of thought and action to enable them to work on a telephone crisis intervention service. Their experiential background, both with life in general and with crises in particular, was naturally quite limited. Although they responded quite freely and innovatively to individuals in crisis, their background often hindered their seeing clients' problems in the perspective of a chronic life situation and understanding the difficulties which they may have been having for a long period of time. In addition, we found that the majority of individuals under 18 who were working on a crisis intervention telephone service were those who had a history of positive experiences, a sense of mastery over their environment, and a future which looked bright. The result was that they sometimes adopted a flippant view toward individuals who were in chronic serious crisis situations. Another reason for not using the individual under 18 was the legal problems that could arise from having an underage person working in a crisis service, giving advice and direction to an individual who is in a serious situation. It was felt by our insurance underwriter that the service itself could be faulted and possibly sued if it used individuals on the telephone service who were not of legal age.

The second criterion that we used to exclude individuals from the telephone service was personal characteristics that may hinder their active and objective participation as volunteers. We were concerned about a number of areas, such as questionable emotional stability as evidenced by the previous behavior of the individuals or their active involvement as a client in psychotherapy. If they had made a suicide attempt in the past three years, they were automatically excluded from the volunteer service until the seriousness of the attempt and the means by which they had resolved the difficulty which resulted in their making the suicide attempt could be ascertained by a careful evaluation of their behavior. The same was true of individuals who were in psychotherapy. We did not allow any individuals to work on the telephone service who were presently in a therapeutic relationship unless (1) the therapists with whom they were working agreed to their employment as a volunteer, and (2) after an intensive evaluation, we felt that the individuals would be able to undertake the stress of working on the telephone service and not be a deterrent to individuals who are calling the center, or have their involvement result in exacerbation of their emotional problems. Each of these cases was evaluated individually. No one who had made a suicide attempt or was in therapy was automatically excluded. We were equally concerned about individuals who had a heart condition, had been subject to epileptic seizures, or had a speech impediment or a physical handicap which might hinder their effective operation on the telephone service. Each special condition was evaluated in terms of both the impact of the continuous emotional stress on the person and the potential effect of the condition on the client who is calling the center.

The other criteria we used for selecting volunteers were (1) the individuals, if selected and trained, would work at the center for a period of time; (2) the individuals must agree to the process of continued supervision of their work at the center and be able to maintain a schedule whereby they can put in a minimum of one six hour shift every two weeks; and (3) they had to agree to sign a pledge of confidentiality and an agreement that their work at the center could be used in the ongoing research program of the center.

The Process of Selection

As the first step in the selection process, individuals who wished to work at the center were sent an application form to complete and return to the center. Shortly after the application form was received and reviewed by the supervisor of the volunteer program, a call was made by her or by another clinical staff to the individual, at which time additional information about the person's interest in the center, reasons for wanting to work at the center, or questions raised by the application form were discussed with the individual. At the same time, the person calling from the center was listening to the characteristics of the applicants' telephone voice, their ability to "come across" over the telephone as a person, and the quality of their voice (such as timbre and tone). We were looking for individuals whose enthusiasm for life and concern for the other could be transmitted through their voice, individuals who could transmit through their nonverbal communication a sense of hope and expectancy, and individuals whose speech impediments, if any, would not detract from the communication to the point that they would call attention to themselves.

On the basis of this short interview, most individuals who applied as volunteers were requested to come to the center for a personal interview with the Supervisor of Volunteer Services. This interview was the first of two, each conducted by a different individual on the clinical staff. The initial interview focused on giving prospective volunteers information on the center, their work as volunteers, the expectations of the center for them, the responsibilities that they would have as volunteers, and an evaluation of their potential as a telephone workers. The second interview focused much more on a clinical evaluation of their ability to work as crisis interveners on the telephone. The questions that were raised on the application form were brought to their attention, and they were given an opportunity to expand or enlarge on the items in question. At the end of the second interview, the applicants were informed that they would be contacted within a few days as to whether or not they would be accepted for one of the training programs. Using the four pieces of information (the application form, the evaluation of the individual's telephone voice, and the two clinical interviews), the supervisor, together with the clinical person who had interviewed the applicant, determined whether or not the individuals were qualified and suitable for working on the telephone on the basis of the collected data and their "gut" responses to them. Although this selection process might appear to be arbitrary and somewhat unsystematic, we found that obtaining individuals who are successful at working on the telephone was more efficiently accomplished by this method than by giving the applicants a series of psychological tests and a psychiatric examination. To our knowledge, no set of tests or evaluations had been devised which would adequately predict success in working on a telephone crisis intervention service.

Our experience indicated that a multiple clinical evaluation was the most efficient selection process for volunteers who would be successful crisis interviewers.

The selection process, however, was not completed when the individual was permitted to enter the training program. We emphasized to the applicants that the process of selection continued through the training program. We also told them that they were under no obligation to work at the center after they had completed the training program (although we used this as one criterion for their selection). At the same time, we informed them that we, through the training program, were continually evaluating their work and their suitability for working at the center so that through the process of training they must select us and we must select them. The training program itself was designed to help weed out individuals who were able to verbalize or intellectualize but who were unable to function in real counseling situations. Using role play situations, people were asked to confront some of the problems they had difficulty resolving. Through this process, approximately 10% of the individuals who began the training program decided not to continue to work at the center as volunteers.

After they had completed the training program, they were placed on a probationary status for a period of six weeks. During this period of time, they had to work under the supervision of a senior volunteer. Calls, worksheets, and contacts with clients were carefully evaluated and analyzed with them, and suggestions were made by supervisors regarding improvements they could make in their telephone work. The quality of their work was also evaluated by both the clinical director and the supervisor of volunteers. After the six-week probationary period, they became regular volunteers at the center.

If their work continued at a high level of competence, and they showed an ability to be a supervisor of volunteers, they could be selected by their clinical supervisor as a candidate for the position of senior volunteer. To be placed in this position, a person again needed to move through a selection process whereby both a supervisor and at least five volunteers recommended the individual for this senior position. Once selected, the volunteer went through an advanced training program on supervising volunteers.

Criteria for Firing Volunteers

Even though it is most disagreeable, each center needs to prevent certain individuals from continuing as telephone crisis interveners. Relieving a volunteer of his duties is extremely difficult, perhaps even more difficult than relieving a person from a paid position. We strongly felt that volunteer workers at a center should be treated in the same way we treated paid workers. Their selection, training, and supervision should be of a high quality. If their level of performance deteriorates or for some reason becomes destructive to individuals calling the center, their services, like those of any other person, need to be terminated. To facilitate this process and to decrease the negative elements, we instituted the following criteria for releasing an individual from the volunteer service at the center: (1) poor quality performance on the telephone after direction and supervision had been given to the volunteer; (2) consistent failure to show up for supervision, or inability to utilize supervisory sessions; (3) attitudes which interfered with or were opposed to the philosophy and purpose of the center; (4) irresponsibility, especially as indicated by a failure to be present for the shift accepted by the volunteer; (5) violation of the confidentiality code of the center; and (6) refusal to give sufficient time to perform the required functions of the volunteer.

If volunteers violated any of the above stated principles, they were called in by the supervisor of the volunteer services, informed of the apparent violations, given an opportunity to correct any misconceptions or to express their feelings about their violations of the code and their willingness to improve their performance at the center. If the supervisor felt that there was some justification for the individual violating the above policies, the volunteer was placed on inactive status for a short period of time, after which the volunteer was allowed to return to full status. If the violations continued, the volunteer was dismissed from the service.

By placing responsibility on each of the volunteers for maintaining excellence and respectability, we are able to provide a high quality service to the community. The volunteers "police" each other to a high degree and were quick to call attention to violations of rules and regulations committed by their fellow volunteers, since they were concerned about the well-being of the clients calling the center and the need for them to obtain service of the highest quality at the time of their crises. The result is an elite corps of individuals who measured up to the highest standards of the words "professional volunteer."

Chapter 32

TRAINING TELEPHONE COUNSELORS

John Kalafat

This chapter describes a training program that is designed to systematically and efficiently prepare individuals to provide basic helping skills and crisis intervention to the wide variety of callers who present to a typical hotline or telephone counseling service (TCS). While there are solid conceptual and empirical bases for the training approaches described here, it is important to note that they have been developed, tested, and endorsed by experienced trainers and staff in operating TCSs over a period of years. Trainees have also consistently rated this training program as one of their most positive and effective training experiences.

First, the basic training approaches, strategies, and techniques are described, followed by an overview of the training program. The training program is not described in greater detail than an overview and outline as this would amount to a training manual, which is beyond the scope of a single chapter.

Training Overview

The training program is a competence-based, criterion-referenced program that consists of the following elements:

- Conduct ongoing training needs assessment
- Screen and engage trainees
- Create a learning community
- Employ validated instructional principles and training strategies
- Develop training content and sequence
- Evaluate training process and outcomes

Competence-based training (CBT) involves the ongoing identification of specific behaviors, knowledge, and attitudes that characterize effective job performance. These competencies are identified through a task-analysis that specifies the nature of the job and the specific demands involved in carrying out the job. A task analysis of crisis intervention indicates that it demands an individual who is fully prepared to respond immediately to a wide variety of unselected clients and situations. The crisis worker must respond as part of an interdisciplinary team, or as an independent helper who has less opportunity for review or extensive data gathering than in other helping situations. The job calls for an active approach that has as its aim the development of a collaborative relationship with an essentially healthy individual or the search for competence in an acutely or chronically dysfunctional individual. It also entails the liaison with and mobilization of a variety of institutional and/or interpersonal support systems. In addition, crisis workers must be able to engage in this problem-solving in a wide variety of stressful situations, while resisting the temptation to assume complete responsibility for confused individuals in crisis. This calls for considerable ego strength as well as awareness of one's own weaknesses, concerns, and needs. The training must provide opportunities for development of this awareness, and it must teach individuals to be both active and collaborative with clients. The crisis worker must not become overwhelmed with anxiety and must learn to assess rapidly the situation and avoid pathologizing, if he/she is to take advantage of the opportunity to affect positive change in a short period of time.

In addition to task-analyses, competencies are also identified by worker analyses which consist of observing what can be agreed on as effective performers and specifying what they do and do not do, as compared to less effective performers. This calls for ongoing observation of and discussion with experienced workers, and infusion of their experiences and insights into the training program. In most settings, it is fairly easy to obtain consensus as to who the superior performers are, based on both their observable helping repertoire and the results that they achieve. An example of this is the development of a Trainer Behavior Checklist (Appendix A) that reliably distinguished between trained and untrained trainers in a telephone crisis service (Lay, 1979). The checklist was based on the compilation of five years of written trainee feedback, and experienced trainers' ratings of videotapes of training sessions.

These training needs assessments have led to a training program that addresses skills such as effective questioning, confrontation, reflection, and summarization; strategies such as a generic helping strategy, assessment of suicide risk, and responding to borderline individuals (Shinefield & Kalafat, 1996); self awareness, such as one's attitudes toward types of individuals (e.g., elderly or religious individuals), or needs (e.g., to be liked or to be in control); and substance, or knowledge bases, such as how children grieve, risk factors for suicide, and the cycle of domestic abuse.

In CBT, trainees are trained to an acceptable level of performance (criterion). TCSs generally evolve their own criteria as to acceptable performance and can reliably assess such performance (Boroto et al., 1978). This usually involves a trainee initially being cleared for supervised telephone duty during which training is continued through silent monitoring and feedback on actual calls, and then cleared for solo telephone duty with intermittent review and training updates. The practicalities of operating crisis services place a limit on the amount of time that can be invested in training an individual, so that they must reach the criterion level of performance within a given time period. Care must be taken to provide specific and respectful feedback to individuals who must be "screened out."

Screen and Engage Trainees

Trainees should be pre-screened according to specific criteria maintained by the crisis service for at least three reasons. First, crisis services provide complex, critical services that can only be carried out by highly trained and qualified individuals. This requirement does not exclude paraprofessionals without advanced degrees, as research has consistently demonstrated their efficacy as crisis workers. Second, there are limited training resources, such as time and personnel, and these must be devoted to those candidates who are most likely to profit from intense, concentrated training. Third, training seems to be most effective when carried out through a cooperative learning process in which trainees feel both valued and encouraged to take risks in order to discover the strengths and gaps in their helping repertoires. Although no screening is foolproof, a "weeding out" process during training substantially undermines the efficiency and learning atmosphere of the training.

While a detailed discussion of screening criteria is beyond the scope of this chapter, it is recommended that the following areas should be explored. First, inquire about some significant crisis that the applicant has experienced in his/her life. The crisis need not be completely resolved, but should not be so active as to interfere with the applicant's general functioning or ability to respond to a similar concern. A blank stare in response to this query is not a good sign, as the initial telephone call should not be the first crisis the person has ever encountered. Early research on paraprofessional helpers indicated that those who had experienced and dealt with crises in their own lives were better able to handle others' crises. Second, it is important to assess the applicant's ability to hear and incorporate feedback on their performance. The applicant can be engaged in a brief role-played vignette. She/he is told that it is not necessary to display polished skills. Rather, the purpose of the role-play is to provide a sense of how the training is done and how the applicant responds to feedback The role-play is followed by feedback on some specific aspect of the applicant's response and an invitation to try again. Does the applicant understand and attempt to incorporate the feedback? Again, we are assessing the degree to which the feedback is "heard," rather than demonstration of a particular helping skill level.

During an evaluation of this training program, a group of selected trainees participated in a set of brief (five to seven minutes) role-plays of typical crisis calls in order to obtain a baseline or pre-training performance sample. No performance feedback was provided. We discovered that this experience created some mild anxiety among the trainees and heightened their motivation to learn the skills required to deal with such calls. Subsequently, we incorporated three to four brief pre-role-plays into our training sequence in order to heighten the salience of the training and engage the trainees.

Create a Learning Community

Returning to the task for which trainees are being prepared, there is evidence that effective crisis workers must be active, autonomous problem-solvers, and such helpers cannot be developed through a process that places trainees in a passive, recipient role. Also, through our efforts to identify generic helping approaches, we have found a growing consensus for a helping approach that favors a decrease in the separation between the providers (agencies, helpers, and trainers) and consumers (communities, clients, and trainees) by drawing on the resources of the consumers and actively involving them in the resolution of their own concerns. The goal of this approach is to teach problem-solving rather than offering solutions to passive or helpless clients. The provider seeks to become a transitional figure for clients by helping them recognize and utilize resources in themselves and their environments. Given that efficient training parallels or models the interventions that are being taught, the goal of training is to create an atmosphere in which trainees and staff assume a shared responsibility among themselves and with the trainers to identify and develop their helping skills on an ongoing basis.

Thus, the training program emphasizes active participation by the trainees in mutual exploration and training, as opposed to functioning as passive recipients of pre-digested training content. In addition to instructors, trainers serve as facilitators who encourage exploration, intercommunication, and the development of personal styles among trainees. Trainees are encouraged to observe, learn from, provide, and receive feedback from each other's efforts and varied styles as much as from the trainers and supervisors.

A TCS-wide learning community is forged through careful screening and selection, guidelines for providing specific, behavioral feedback, and a participatory, experiential/didactic training sequence consisting of an initial one-day workshop, followed by small group-training sessions. These sessions, as described below, adhere to a specific format that incorporates validated instructional principles and a structure designed to promote nondefensive exploration and practice of helping skills and strategies.

It should be noted that there appears to be a dilemma presented by this training philosophy. On the one hand, trainees are told that they must learn to think on their feet, develop a personal helping style, and use themselves as a helping instrument. On the other hand, they are presented with an explicit set of strategies from the helping literature and the experience of the trainers.

The apparent contradiction between encouraging trainees to find a personal style while following a specific helping strategy may be resolved by Ivey's (1974) distinction between intention and action. Ivey contended that an aim of training is to develop intentional individuals, that is, those who are clearly aware of their intentions and can translate those intentions into behaviors (actions) that can (1) effectively carry out the intent and (2) be altered on the basis of feedback from the environment.

Ivey noted, "A central part of growth is intentionality – the blending of intent and behavior, thought and action" (1974, p. 181). In this training program, the helping model represents the proper intention (effective helping strategy) and the trainee's personal style represents the action (his/her way of carrying out that intention in a congruent style). The task of the training program becomes one of clearly presenting the intervention models and then providing the appropriate atmosphere, opportunity for practice, and helpful feedback that facilitate the development of trainees' styles.

Training Strategies

The goal of the program is to train individuals to perform helping behaviors rather than simply understand or become aware of such interventions. Skill training requires the use of an instructional sequence developed by Gagne (1985) that contains the following elements:

1. Clear specification of the skills: e.g., a brief lecture identifies the given skill and gives the rationale and objective for the skill.
2. Modeling of the skill: e.g., trainers give examples and live or taped demonstrations of the skill; trainees model skills for each other in role-plays.
3. Practice: e.g., skills are practiced chiefly through role plays.
4. Feedback: e.g., trainer and trainees provide verbal and written feedback.
5. Practice: e.g., continued role-plays, supervised telephone work, and in-service training.

The second training strategy employed is the use of experiential exercises. These are exercises designed to give the trainee the experience of a client in a given situation. Our experience, as well as psychotherapy process research (Hill et al., 1988; Horvath et al., 1990), has indicated that, if a trainee, or any helper, has a sense of what the client is experiencing, they can usually generate effective helping responses.

What is being recommended here is a generic training strategy that is best used in combination with a more structured approach such as the instructional sequence described earlier. In other words, if one wishes to teach individuals a given approach, such as responding to the panic response of a person overwhelmed in a crisis, or effective interventions in family disputes, an important part of that training is to simulate that situation and require the trainee to respond. An even more effective training device is to place the trainee in the role of the client in these situations as a means of generating helping responses. It appears that responses learned from this direct experiencing are more congruent and generalized than those taught through passive shaping of overt behavior (e.g., helpful verbal responses) or an intellectual grasp of helping interventions. Moreover, it seems that this is the way that helpers learn through their applied experience, so they are also obtaining practice in the process by which they will be monitoring and learning from their ongoing experience throughout their careers.

A sample experiential exercise is included in Appendix B, and trainers are encouraged to devise their own exercises in order to address specific training needs. The basic question presented to trainees in these exercises, as well as when assisting a trainee who is stuck in a particular role-play, is, "What do you think or feel the client is experiencing or trying to express right now?" To the extent that the helper can begin to sense this, they can begin to generate their intentions. Thus, the next question when processing an experiential exercise or when assisting in a role-play is, "What would you like to do now, or what do you feel would be helpful now?" This question is followed by one that aims to generate helper actions: "What could you do to accomplish this?"

Feedback: An Interpersonal Skill

The process of giving and receiving feedback is an integral component of training as well as of helping. It is through feedback that individuals can discover how their behavior is perceived by others, or whether it corresponds to their intentions. In order for feedback to be helpful, it must have certain characteristics. If an individual receiving feedback is made to feel personally attacked or threatened, she/he will naturally become defensive. The more defensive she/he becomes, the less able or willing he/she is to accurately perceive the message of the sender. The less defensive he/she is, the more able he/she is to concentrate on the content and cognitive meaning of the message. Being observed and receiving feedback on one's behavior is threatening under the best of circumstances and cannot help but result in the receiver feeling anxious. By structuring feedback in a helpful manner, this threat is substantially reduced and the opportunity for the receiver to be open to hearing and accepting feedback is enhanced. The receiver will also be more apt to try out new ideas and be more spontaneous in developing an effective helping style if she/he feels those observing are doing so with an attitude of understanding and a desire to help rather than criticize.

It is not the feedback givers' responsibility to make a judgment as to how "good" or "bad" they thought the performance of their peer was, but rather to express the impact of the peer's specific interventions on them. Feedback is given on specific behaviors that can be modified or maintained. For example, in a training group, telling an individual that she "was helpful," or "did a good job," or "was too directive," or "was condescending" does not tell her what she must do or avoid doing in order to be helpful. How does one "do a good job" or "be less condescending" the next time? On the other hand, telling her that her calm voice tone was perceived as helpful because it helped assure the client, identifies behaviors that can be practised and maintained in her repertoire.

The job of the feedback givers is to structure their feedback in such a way that the person receiving it can hear it in the most objective and least distorted way possible, and understand it and choose to use it or not use it. Guidelines for feedback are available from a variety of sources (e.g., Turock, 1980). The following are sample guidelines:

1. Feedback should be based on what the person giving it is feeling or thinking. (This is unimpeachable, for the feedback receiver cannot say, "No you weren't feeling that.")

Example: "When you began with a rapid series of questions, I felt pressured."
Versus: "You seemed to be in a hurry at first."

2. Feedback should be focused on behavior rather than on the person or on inferences.

Example: "When you said that it sounded as if I felt betrayed, I really felt understood."
Versus: "You were empathic."
Example: "At times when you paused for a long time after I said something, I felt concerned that I wasn't getting across to you."
Versus: "You seemed confused or lost at times."

3. Feedback should be specific, rather than general.
Example: "Your voice felt warm and calming to me, and your pauses allowed me time to think."
Versus: "I liked your style."

4. Feedback should be limited to what the receiver can absorb at the moment.
Example: "When you asked if I thought that my mother was an alcoholic, I was shocked – I couldn't think about that."
Versus: "It's not a good idea to get too far ahead of the client without laying some groundwork, for you might overload them cognitively."

5. Trainer feedback should initially facilitate exploration, rather than give advice.
Example: "What could you do that might help you find out what the client was feeling?"
Versus: "Why don't you just ask the client what he was feeling?"
Example: "What are some strategies that you can think of for dealing with this kind of manipulative caller?"
Versus: "I've found the best way to handle a manipulative caller is . . ."

This does not mean that the trainers cannot give advice or share their experience with trainees after trainees have had the chance to brainstorm and explore strategies. This advice can be on intentions (e.g., "I think that it is helpful to couch your strategies in terms that the caller seems to value, such as the 'brave' or 'caring' thing to do"), or on actions (e.g., "Sometimes a confrontation can be quite brief, such as 'why not?'").

Note that, in the group, feedback concerning a given intervention need not agree because any given intervention may strike different clients in different ways. For example, in #3 above, another's feedback might have been "I found your voice tone calming, but I began to get anxious during the pauses." Also, feedback that the client felt uncomfortable, as in #4 above, does not necessarily mean that the intervention was inappropriate or that the impact was unintended. It is not the job of a helper to make the client comfortable at all times. The issue is the congruence between the helpers' intentions, actions, and impact.

Most, if not all, TCS training programs employ role-plays and feedback. However, such feedback is commonly given by instructors and peers from the standpoint of observers of the interaction between the helper and the client, and usually consists of suggestions for alternate interventions or critiques of the helper's interventions from the standpoint of another helper or counselor. (Some student trainers have called this type of feedback "I would haves.") While such cognitively and strategically oriented feedback is a useful component of training, it is not the most crucial element in the development of an intentional helping repertoire. Any trainee can listen to a tape of his/her helping and come up with plenty of "I would haves." What trainees and helpers rarely get is feedback from their clients as to their impact on them. The most critical aspect of the counselor's intentions is their impact on the client, and counselors must learn to continually assess these impacts and adjust their intentions accordingly.

Moreover, feedback given from the standpoint of the client's experience is not only unimpeachable but also seems to generate less defensiveness on the part of the helper because instead of hearing "you," they are hearing the client's experience. For those giving feedback, it provides valuable practice in empathizing with the client and experiencing the impact of various interventions (e.g., "Now I know what it feels like to be asked a long series of questions!"). It also provides practice in the important dual role that the helper must assume as both empathic participant and objective observer in the helping interaction.

While this departure from usual feedback was prompted by trainers' attempts to create a less threatening atmosphere and provide trainees with practice in empathizing with clients' experience and in generating helping interventions based on this empathy, research on psychotherapy process has also supported the importance of the client's experience. Based on their program of counseling process and outcome research, Hill et al. (1988) emphasized the importance of feedback from the client. Hill et al. noted that "if therapists automatically assume that they know how the client is reacting without verifying their perceptions, they may be operating on faulty assumptions," and, that "feedback from the client can be a potent tool in correcting misperceptions" (p. 34). They concluded that "In the long run, the development of techniques that permit one to value the client's contribution to the therapy process should enhance psychotherapy research and practice" (p. 35).

Summarizing their process and outcome research, Horvath et al. (1990) came to a similar conclusion:

> From the therapist's point of view, what may be important is the accuracy of the therapist's estimate of the client's understanding of a particular intent. Using this information, the therapist could proceed with new intentions, resolve misperceptions by reiterating the intention, or use alternative intentions to achieve the desired goal. (p. 620)

Again, client feedback is not proposed as substitute for, but rather can be supplemented by, feedback from the observer standpoint. After feedback is given from the client's standpoint, the trainer and trainees can discuss alternate intentions and strategies for given call situations.

These, then, are the training foci (skills, strategies, self, and substance) and core strategies or techniques (role-plays, feedback, and experiential exercises) employed. Additional training approaches include lectures, written materials, on-line supervision, and silent call-monitoring. The next section describes the training program in which these foci and techniques occur.

Training Content and Sequence

Pre-role-plays

As previously noted, pre-role-plays establish the salience of the training and provide a baseline estimate of the trainees' performance for training and program evaluation purposes. Pre-role-plays can be done in a variety of formats. Trainees can be given a brief series of two or three seven to ten minute role-plays in a row, each provided by a different experienced worker presenting common nonacute call situations such as interpersonal conflict or loss. This simulates, to some degree, a typical telephone shift in which multiple calls must be handled with little or no feedback. These role-plays can be recorded, and trainees can be provided with brief, written critiques of their performances. These role-plays can be completed with small groups of trainees by placing one trainee per room and having three to four trainer "callers" rotate through the rooms providing presenting problems; or, by placing role-played "calls" by telephone to trainees. Another less complicated approach is to assign one experienced worker to each trainee. The worker "calls" the trainee either by telephone or in a room in which the caller and trainee are separated by a screen or work back-to-back to eliminate visual cues. This single, 15-minute role-play is recorded, and the trainee writes a transcript and brief (one to two page) critique of the role-play. The trainees are informed that the role-play and critique should focus on establishing rapport and beginning to identify the caller's concern(s). Trainers then provide brief written comments on the role-play and the trainee's critique.

Workshop

The material included in the workshop can be provided in a series of individual training sessions, but the workshop format helps to forge the trainees and trainers into a learning community. TCSs can include content of their choosing, and the following is a suggested workshop content.

1. Ice-Breaker Exercise (20–25 minutes)

In this writer's opinion, ice breaker exercises that are unrelated to training objectives waste precious training time and are often experienced as irrelevant, if not condescending, to adult learners. Therefore, an exercise that also addresses such content as listening skills is recommended. An example is provided in Appendix C, Opening Exercise.

2. Personal Problems Exercise (Appendix B). (25 minutes)
3. Exercises in Communication Skills (25–40 minutes)

These exercises are designed to introduce and review communication skills that will be practiced as part of the role-plays. These include the use of open and closed questions; avoiding multiple and either-or questions; the use of "why" as a confrontation, not a question; and reflections or summary statements that attempt to capture and check the helper's understanding of the content and feelings expressed by the caller. There are numerous sources that address these communication skills (e.g., Benjamin, 1987; Brammer, 1998). The amount of time spent on them depends on the level of experience of the trainees. For example, first-year graduate students in core helping disciplines such as psychology or social work usually need only brief (e.g., one to two hours) review exercises.

4. Feedback Training (25 minutes)

This provides an overview and demonstration of the type of feedback used in the training program. Trainers will continue to shape trainees' feedback (structure, more than content) during the training sessions until trainees learn to give feedback in the appropriate form. For this training, a trainee is asked to play a caller while a trainer plays the helper. While generally helpful, the trainer includes some intentional mistakes such as asking "why" early on, giving lengthy self-disclosure, and gently telling the caller that she should not feel that way. Another trainer gives feedback to the helper, and in a supportive tone, breaks feedback rules by generalizing ("You sounded supportive"); making an inference ("You seemed to feel the need to get close to the caller quickly by your disclosure"); lecturing ("I know you were trying to get at the caller's concern, but 'why' questions tend to make people defensive . . .").

Trainees are asked to respond to the feedback and, while some may have a negative reaction to the feedback, they generally assess it as helpful. The trainer then tells them that s(he) has broken a number of feedback rules and, after reviewing them, demonstrates appropriate feedback and hands out the feedback guidelines.

5. Overview of Helping Model (30–40 minutes)

A brief lecture, accompanied by demonstration tapes or role-plays, provides an overview of the basic helping strategy.

6. Organizational Orientation (30 minutes)

This includes any organizational information, policies and procedures that trainees should know at this time.

Training Sessions

Training sessions are generally scheduled for two hours. Sessions can be devoted to brief overviews and demonstrations to introduce a helping strategy and or role playing. A typical training sequence is presented in Table 32-1. The actual amount of time spent on topics and role plays depends on the ra

Table 32-1
TRAINING SEQUENCE

Training session	Activity	Method	Time
I. Workshop.	Workshop led by all trainers; covering topics reviewed in text, or added by TCS.	Exercises, role-plays, lecture discussion.	4–5 hours, including lunch and breaks.
II. Overview of crisis intervention.	Definition, development, common causes of crisis and implications for crisis intervention.	Lecture, discussion, audiotapes.	2 hours.
III. Establishing the relationship.	Trainer reviews goals of this segment of the helping model, and engages trainees in brief (7 min.) role-plays of reluctant, questioning, hostile callers. Trainees learn how to describe what they do and their qualifications.	Lecture, role-plays, discussion.	2 hours.
IV. Defining the problem(s).	Trainer reviews goals of this segment, leads discussion in criteria for deciding how to prioritize call concerns; demonstration of defining problem and maintaining focus.	Lecture, discussion, taped or live demonstration; if time, role-play.	2 hours.
V. Defining the problem(s) cont.	Role-plays selected for practice in defining problems.	Role-plays.	2 hours.
VI. Exploring feelings.	Trainer reviews goals and rationale for this segment; reviews different types of feelings and when/when not to address them; demonstration of addressing feelings.	Lecture, discussion, taped or live demonstration; if time, role-play.	2 hours.
VII. Exploring feelings, cont.	Role-plays selected for practice in exploring feelings.	Role-plays.	2 hours.

Table 32-1 – Continued

Training session	Activity	Method	Time
VIII. Exploring past coping and developing alternatives	Trainer reviews goals for this segment; reviews solution-focused approaches; demonstration of exploring past coping and alternatives	Lecture, discussion, taped or live demonstration; if time, role-play	2 hours
IX. Putting it all together	Role-play practice incorporating all segments of helping model	Role-plays, usually continuation of previous role-plays	Two 2-hour sessions
X. Acute crises	No introduction or demonstration is provided prior to role-plays. After role-plays, discussion and demonstration of dealing with acute crises	With no warm-up, trainees are individually presented with caller in acute crisis (e.g., highly anxious, hostile, or abusive situation)	2 hours
XI. Special topics	Series of sessions covering special topics such as suicide, drugs and alcohol, psychosis, borderline, grief, repeat caller procedures, callers currently in treatment, etc Some of these sessions, such as suicide, must occur prior to supervised telephone duty; while others can be included in ongoing training for telephone workers	Overview, demonstration, role-play feedback, and discussion	Open-ended

tio of trainers to trainees. Generally, a minimum of 30 hours of training before supervised telephone duty is recommended. Additional special topics can be covered during ongoing training available to telephone workers.

The central method for helping trainees develop an effective helping approach is small-group role-play sessions. These sessions provide an opportunity to identify and practice helping behavior in an open learning atmosphere. The ideal group size is five to six trainees, which permits role-players to receive feedback from the trainer and at least three peers. Each trainee should have the opportunity to role-play a helper twice during a typical 15-week training program.

The groups should be mixed each session to ensure maximum exposure to a variety of feedback and helping styles, and to attenuate group process issues such as falling into set roles (e.g., "rescuer" or "critic"). Exposure to a variety of reactions to a trainee's helping style and skills provides important preparation for the actual counseling situation in which the helper must deal with a variety of callers but may not receive clear feedback as to their different reactions. The group setting also presents trainees with a variety of models of helping approaches that can maximize the generalizability from the role-play sessions to actual counseling situations. The role-plays become quite realistic, and trainees gain particularly useful insight and empathy from playing clients (e.g., "Now I know what it feels like to be feeling something and to be acknowledged").

Role-plays are all developed from actual clients and are chosen to emphasize a particular skill or strategy, such as exploration of feelings or choosing a concern on which to focus. Role-plays last about ten minutes. The trainer stops the role-play when there is sufficient material (helping behavior) on which to give feedback. At times the helper may become "stuck," and the trainer can stop the role-play for a moment and take the helper outside the room for a brief consultation that focuses on what is going on and what the helpers' strategy and intention should be. The role-play is then resumed for a few exchanges to obtain some closure.

Trainees do not volunteer for the helper roles. The trainer chooses role-players to ensure that each trainee plays a helper at least twice. Based on prior knowledge or pre-role-plays, more skilled trainees are generally chosen for the first two to three role-plays to model appropriate interventions and provide an opportunity for vicarious learning. As the training progresses, a trainee may be given a particular role-play to provide practice in a given area, such as dealing with anxious callers.

For the first few role-plays, the trainer feedback places more emphasis on positive or effective interventions in order to help trainees identify and develop the foundation of an effective helping repertoire. Later, the trainers' feedback becomes more balanced (some trainees say more "picky") as trainees approach supervised telephone duty. Trainees are informed of this process.

At times, after the feedback has been given, the trainer can continue the role-play with the trainee who played the caller to demonstrate a particular point or strategy. Early in training, role-plays are chosen that emphasize particular phases of the helping model such as exploring feelings and, later, trainees can be provided role-play practice in "putting it all together." Role-plays provide effective practice for the first four phases of the helping model, but less so for the last phase because this phase depends on more extensive and intensive previous experience with the client. Early role-plays can be continued in later sessions in order to provide trainees with some practice in exploring alternatives and developing plans.

Table 32–2 depicts a typical role-play session. Again, during the role-play, the other trainees are to identify with the client's role, not the counselor's. They are encouraged to make brief notes because their feedback must be specific (e.g., "When you said 'It must be frustrating when your husband does that,' I really felt understood" versus "You really connected well with me"). The trainer takes extensive notes – usually writing most of the helper's interventions verbatim because she/he must model appropriate feedback and must complete detailed Progress Forms which are described below. The Progress Forms reinforce the learning and help trainees to identify the more effective components of their helping repertoire. A tape recorder could be used, although the instructor must then go over the tape. While tape recordings might enhance training and counseling, in actual practice, helpers must rely on their ability to listen and capture with some immediacy what is happening in a session without such aids.

At the conclusion of the role-play, the helper is asked to report his/her dominant feeling at that moment. Any attempt to discuss the role-play is cut off, and the helper is asked to report one feeling. This procedure provides practice for students to attend to their feelings as a cue to what is happening in the session. Often, the feeling reported captures the overall sense of the interaction to that point. For example, the helper may say "confused," "frustrated," or "connected."

Following these comments, the client always gives feedback first, because his/her feedback tends to consist of more immediate and affective reactions than the other trainees' feedback, even though all are giving feedback from the standpoint of a client. Often, the client can initially share only his/her experience and impressions of the interaction, which are later affirmed and fleshed out by the feedback of other students in the group. Clients can add feedback as others' feedback reminds them of impressions that they experienced during the role-play.

Table 32-2
ROLE-PLAY TRAINING SESSION

Approximate time in minutes	Activity
5	A. Trainer assesses group: asks for comments or questions from last session
10–15	B. Trainer provides brief description of and rationale for skill or strategy to be covered
5–10	C. Trainer gives brief demonstration of skill/strategy by means of role-play or tape. (Note: B and C can be done in a didactic session for the entire group of trainees before breaking up into smaller role-play groups.)
	D. Role-play
5–7	1. Trainer excuses counselor from room and warms up client for his/her role. Trainer provides overview of problem to be initially presented and added aspects if counselor explores further; asks client why she or he called now and what she or he wants.
3	2. Trainer warms up counselor outside the room, asking how she or he is feeling and how the "shift" has gone so far.
10–15	3. Role-play occurs during which the trainer and the group observe and take notes.
2–3	4. Trainer stops role-play and asks counselor how she or he is feeling. Trainer gives client a moment to "come down" from the role.
2–3	5. Client feedback first. All feedback directed at counselor, not trainer. "When you said, I felt/thought"
10–15	6. Group feedback follows, one at a time, no repetition of previously given feedback, except to note agreement or different reaction; client allowed to insert any further feedback/reactions recalled during the feedback.
2–3	7. Trainer feedback given last; then trainer summarizes feedback (optional)
5	8. Counselor responds to feedback.
10	9. General discussion/questions about role-play. Trainer keeps it focused on relevant helping issues.
5–10	10. 1–9 repeated for second role-play.
5–10	E. Wrap-Up 1. Trainer requests general feedback on session. 2. Each trainee notes one thing from session that he or she wants to particularly recall for him/herself.

While the helper receives feedback from the group members and the instructor, she/he cannot respond. This accomplishes two things. First, since they cannot respond, the helpers focus on the feedback, rather than thinking up responses. Second, the feedback is then based solely on the impacts of the interventions, uncontaminated by post hoc explanations. The helper needs to learn if he/she was able to communicate his/her intentions during the helping interaction. After the feedback, the helper responds to the feedback, reporting what he/she heard and sharing his/her intentions. This promotes a group discussion of intentions and a variety of possible alternate interventions. The instructor uses this discussion to make points about helping strategies and relates the discussion to the helping literature and telephone situations.

During a typical two-hour training session, an experienced trainer can usually complete two role-plays. The trainer ends the session by asking that each trainee identify one thing that she/he will take from that day's session (e.g., "I learned that you don't have to respond always right away to the caller; you can take a moment to think, and you can ask the caller to give you a moment to think about what they just said"). The trainer then ends the session by asking if there are any other questions or issues to be discussed. Table 32-3 summarizes the trainer's tasks during a role-play session.

After the session, it is recommended that trainers complete Progress Forms (Appendix D). This form is used to summarize the feedback that is given to a

Table 32-3
TRAINER TASKS DURING ROLE-PLAY SESSIONS

1. Chooses and briefs role-players

2. During role-play
   - Monitors own reactions as client
   - Takes note of helper's responses
   - Monitors progress of role-play and helper's performance
   - Determines length of role-play

3. Monitors forms (feedback guidelines) and content of group feedback

4. Gives own feedback and summarizes group feedback

5. Elicits helper reactions to feedback

6. Leads discussion of role-play relating points to call situations and helping strategies

7. After role-plays, elicits trainees' closing thoughts/questions and summarizes session

8. Prepares notes for Progress Forms

trainee during a role-play training session. The form is filled out each time a trainee role-plays a counselor. Trainers have found it most efficient to take notes during the training and then to transpose these notes onto the form. The forms are maintained in a file that is kept on each trainee. As the trainee's progress during training is reviewed among trainers and between the trainer and the trainee, a written summary of this review is also inserted into the trainee's file. Thus, at any point in training, theoretically at least, the trainee knows where she/he stands in training. She/he knows what her/his helpful behaviors are and what she/he must be changing or developing in order to progress through training. Trainees not only have access to their files, but they are requested to review them on a weekly basis. The trainees may insert into their file comments on their feedback and share these with a trainer.

Any training program, no matter how well it is organized, depends substantially on the quality of the trainers. This training program requires sophisticated trainers. Among the competencies that trainers should possess are:

1. Being well-versed in providing constructive feedback and summarizing and clarifying trainees' feedback.

2. A basic understanding of group process. Even though the training is designed to minimize some of the issues that arise in groups, trainers must be able to monitor the mood of the group and address any confusion or concerns about the training process or content. As is true of any instructor, they must maintain the safety of the class and sensitively address such (rare) critical incidents as argumentative, defensive, overly talkative trainees; or trainees who appear to be lost or overwhelmed by their role-play experience. They must also be able to involve the group in problem-solving around some helping issues rather than always attempting to provide resolutions themselves.

3. Thorough familiarity with the helping model, crisis intervention approaches, and other training content. This is critical since, in our experience, trainers who are not well-versed in the training content tend to be more rigid in what they consider acceptable performance (i.e., they "go by the book" more). For example, when an intervention is experienced as unhelpful by the role-played client, trainers must be able to explore and distinguish between a helpful intention that may simply require brainstorming other actions or ways to carry out the intent on the one hand and, on the other hand, interventions that are unhelpful because the helper has misread the client or whose intention may not be helpful (e.g., to give premature advice or reassurance). In this way, trainers can encourage the exploration of a variety of helping approaches or styles, rather than push conformity to a single "correct" approach

Again, Appendix A summarizes helpful and unhelpful trainer behaviors that were identified by trainees and experienced trainers. Many telephone counseling services could add to this list of necessary trainer qualifications. It is assumed that services also continuously update their training content based on their own evolving caller and community profiles, the accumulating experience of their staff, and systematic perusal of the counseling, crisis intervention, suicide prevention, and other relevant literature. The aim of this chapter has been to provide a framework of training strategies for effectively developing and maintaining the knowledge, skills, and attitudes necessary for effective telephone interventions.

REFERENCES

Benjamin, A. (1987). *The helping interview.* Boston: Houghton-Mifflin.

Boroto, D. R., Kalafat, J., & Cohen, L. E. (1978). Client versus rater judgments of counselor effectiveness. *Journal of Clinical Psychology, 34*, 188–194.

Brammer, L. (1998). *The helping relationship: Process and skills.* Boston: Allyn & Bacon.

Gagne, R. M. (1985). *Conditions of learning and theory of instruction.* Fort Worth, TX: Harcourt College.

Hill, C. E., Helms, J. E., Speigel, S. B., & Tichenor, V. (1988). Development of a system for categorizing client reactions to therapist intervention. *Counseling Psychology, 35*, 27–36.

Horvath, A. O., Marx, R. W., & Kamann, A. R. (1990). Thinking about thinking in therapy: An examination of clients' understanding of their therapists' intentions. *Journal of Consulting & Clinical Psychology, 58*, 614–621.

Ivey, A. E. (1974). Microcounseling and media therapy: State of the art. *Counselor Education & Supervision, 3*, 174–183.

Lay, J. M. (1979) Training for trainers: Development and evaluation of a training program. *Dissertation Abstracts International, 39* 11B, 5564.

Shinefield, W., & Kalafat, J. (1996). Effective management of borderline individuals in crisis. *Crisis Intervention & Time-Limited Treatment, 2*, 273–287.

Turock, A. (1980). Trainer feedback: A method for teaching interpersonal skills. *Counselor Education & Supervision, 9*, 216–222.

Appendix A

TRAINER BEHAVIORS AFFECTING THE LEARNING CLIMATE

PART OF GROUP

Willing to share own feelings, reactions
Participates in group and gives feelings
Open to questions and feedback – elicits feedback
Gives honest feedback and encourages this among participants
No hesitation to share own experiences

ACCEPTING

Accept trainees and different attitudes
Understanding when someone is not getting a point
Nonjudgmental, noncritical
Doesn't talk down to "lowly" trainee as expert and authority
Supportive of trainees' struggles
Ask question only to clarify, not to put on the spot

INVOLVED/CONCERNED

Enthusiastic
Willing to listen to questions and concerns
Will stay after group
Won't move on until everyone finished with point

SENSITIVE

Is aware of feelings and concerns as they arise in the group; acknowledges and responds
Moves with current group feeling
Talks to everyone in the group
Flexible as to pace, process, etc.
Tuned into what trainee is saying
Explains what is doing (e.g., stopping role-play for a consult) to allay concerns, confusion

CALM/RELAXED

Puts group at ease
Uses humor
Accepts distractions
Seems comfortable in the group

LEADER

Sets appropriate pace – establishes proper flow in group (slows down/speeds up)
Task-oriented but not rigid, authoritative
Keeps focused but allows group to experience feelings, finish discussions
Clarifies points and confusion
Summarizes material to reduce confusion
Highlights important material
Responds to critical incidents (e.g., hostile, challenging, anxious, lost trainees)
Takes work seriously
Displays confidence
Gives clear task directions
Gives clear criteria for success
Raises questions that promote learning and challenges

EXPERT

Gives good examples (specific, relevant); relates material to real world situations
Shares own experience in relation to material
Emphasizes practical vs. theory, abstract
Provides good alternatives; clarifies difficult issues

NEGATIVE TRAINER BEHAVIOR

Self-deprecating comments
Nervous
Comes on too strong; directive rigid
Dogmatic (i.e., one "right way")
Task-oriented to exclusion of current feelings
Too neutral
Feedback unclear, too general
Too abstract vs. clear application of content
Glosses over problems or issues
Ignores trainee
Acknowledges trainee but moves on without answering
Gives punishment (criticism, mocking)
Says or implies "I'm lost" (Can say "I don't know," but not too much)
Allows discussion, distraction that bogs down training (loses control of group)
Always gives own answer versus drawing out group

Appendix B

PERSONAL PROBLEMS EXERCISE

Introduction

There is a tendency for a gap to develop between helpers and those whom they seek to help, such that the latter are thought of only as clients, problems, or cases, rather than as people who are experiencing difficulties. By getting in touch with themselves and their peers as persons with problems, trainees develop greater empathy for those who are seeking help. In so doing, they also share a variety of preferences and expectations that people have about the nature of helping and helpers, as well as different ways of responding to help seekers that enable them to feel more at ease.

Purpose

The purpose of this exercise is for trainees to use their own feelings associated with times when they are dealing with personal concerns as a guide for responding appropriately to clients in crisis.

Method

It is important in introducing the exercise that an atmosphere of trust and relaxation be developed. It must be made clear that trainees will not be asked to reveal any personal concerns, nor will they be expected to do anything that the trainer will not also be doing.

The exercise starts with a private fantasy that serves as a common baseline for a group discussion organized around a series of specific questions concerning help-seeking. The trainer begins by requesting that group members close their eyes and focus on a specific personal problem. The following instructions can serve as a guideline for helping trainees focus on the concerns. (Note: trainer should pause for 20-30 seconds where the dots appear).

> I want you to think of a personal problem that has caused you some concern. It can be a problem that you are currently experiencing or one that you've dealt with in the past. It is important to focus on a specific problem. . . . What is the nature of the concern? Who else is involved? What have you done about it? . . . . Now, what are the feelings associated with this concern? Not what you think about it or what you did or would like to do, but what are the feelings involved? . . . . Get in touch with these feelings. Label them and hold onto them for the following discussion. Again, you will at no time be asked to share what your concern is. . . . Now, keeping these feelings in mind, open your eyes and let's begin to respond to some questions.

At this point the larger group should be broken into groups of about eight people, each led by a trainer. The groups should disperse to break-out rooms or to places in the room where they can work without too much interference from one another.

The trainers should not spend too much time on each of the questions. The pacing will depend on the group in terms of allowing adequate coverage of each question. Notice that the questions are presented in a logical order. The trainers should write on their pads, not on the easel, what people say in response to each question.

The trainers should take a level of risk in sharing that serves as an example of what they expect from the group. It is up to the trainers to keep the participants on a personal level (i.e., no generalizations allowed; say "I", not "you" or "people"). Not everyone will talk, and that is okay. Trainers do not have to put a lot of energy into the quiet ones. The group will tend to stray, and the trainer should keep them focused on the question, and reflect, clarify, and summarize what has been said. Each question should be read and followed by about five to seven minutes of discussion. The trainer should allow all those who want to speak to make their points while only providing the usual reflection to be sure he/she understands what was said.

1. How do you feel about yourself when you have a problem – not your feelings about the problem, but about having the problem?

2. In what ways are you different from when you don't have a problem?

3. What hints do you give to people around you that you have a problem? How do they know when you are having a problem?

4. What do you want from them?

5. If you feel like talking to someone about your problem, think of a specific person that you would talk to. What is it about that person that makes you feel okay to talk with them? Let's identify some specific characteristics.

For each question, as each trainee offers a response, the trainer should just reflect or clarify to be sure that she/he understands what has been said. After all the responses have been given to a particular question, the trainer should go back and ask trainees to expand on some of their responses. For example, "You said 'angry.' Can you tell me a little more about that anger? What is it about?" Or, "What is that scared feeling about? Oh, you mean scared because you don't know if you can resolve the problem?" The trainer is modeling how helpers must clarify clients' thoughts and feelings. After all the questions have been answered, the trainer should ask the group if anyone noticed the trainer's behavior during the questions. Often, some notice the reflection and clarifications, while few notice the effort to clarify thoughts and, in particular, feelings. The trainer should point these out and indicate how this is modeling an important helping behavior.

After the questions have been covered, the trainer brings the groups back together (or trainees can remain in smaller break-out groups) and asks participants to share what they have discovered about helping and about clients. Among the points that the trainer should raise, if they do not come out in discussion, include:

• (Trainer should read the feelings given in response to the first question.) We now have a sense of what feelings clients bring to the helping contact, and we can use this understanding to facilitate rapport with clients and help them to open up about their concerns.

• (Trainer should read the descriptions trainees gave in response to the second question. These usually include unflattering characteristics as self-involved, moody, not thinking clearly, not working efficiently, overly sensitive, and withdrawn. Trainer comments on what an unpleasant person that sounds like.) We would not want people to form opinions of us based only on how we are when we're having a problem. People who are having problems are often behaving at their worst. They are feeling bad about themselves, functioning less effectively than they normally can and, in general, are putting their worst foot forward. It is the naïve helper who shares in clients' belief they are helpless or stupid, and who doesn't recognize that they are seeing the person at their worst.

- Having a concern doesn't diminish one as a person. Clients are people with concerns, not just categories of problems.
- (Trainer should read responses to the fourth question.) People have varying expectations about how others should respond to them and experience different interventions as helpful.
- (Trainer should read responses to the fifth question.) Beyond some basic considerations, there are many ways to be helpful.
- We now have many answers to the question as to what is helpful and not helpful, based on our own experiences.
- Trainees should have a sense of their own attitudes about seeking help and how these affect their helping.

Appendix C

OPENING EXERCISE

Rationale

This is the first in a series of experiential exercises through which certain feelings are created that serve as guides for increasing the trainees' understanding of what is going on in a helping contact. The feelings elicited may be those experienced by the client, thus increasing the trainees' awareness of their impact on the client; or the feelings may be those that often arise in the helper, thus increasing the trainees' awareness of their own feelings that may help or hinder their helping efforts.

The exercises teach the trainees to use themselves (their feelings, reactions, etc.) as a resource for understanding others; and to look upon the training group as a resource for understanding themselves and their impact on others, and as a means of providing some insight into the variety of reactions they can expect in helping interactions.

Method

(The trainer should participate in these exercises.)

The trainer should arrange the group (this can be done with 8-10 people) into dyads, Partners should be assigned rather than asking trainees to choose. Each trainee is to take five minutes to tell his/her partner how he/she got to be who he/she is right now. The trainer is to provide no more structure concerning the topic than the preceding statement. This allows trainees to address the topic in any way or level they choose. While one trainee is speaking, his/her partner can only listen – no comments or questions. They then switch roles for the next five minutes, again avoiding comments or questions. The time limits should be adhered to strictly.

At the end of this time, have the sets of dyads come together into groups of six to eight. One at a time, each person is to describe the significant things about his/her partner to the new group members. Again, no comments or questions are permitted. It is important that the trainees not know that they are going to be doing this, in order to ensure spontaneity.

The trainer next addresses the trainees in the following manner. I would like you to take a few minutes and get in touch with some of the feelings you may have been experiencing during this exercise (after each question pause for about 20 seconds to let participants think about the questions. They are not to respond to the questions yet). First, be aware of how it felt to simply listen without talking. . . . Was it difficult to suppress comments or questions? One of the most helpful things you can do with someone is to simply listen while they talk out their concerns or explore their conflicts. You should be able to listen for five minutes without interrupting.

Next, recall how you felt while you talked. . . . If you had some difficulty filling the five minutes, you have a sense of how difficult it can be to share. Think about what you shared. Did you stick pretty much to facts? Did you share feelings? Did you stay pretty much on the surface? . . . These statements are not meant in an evaluative sense. It is simply helpful to be aware of the levels on which we commonly function. While these may be in contrast to the level of communication aspired to in helping, they are not "better" or "worse" in themselves.

Next, recall how you felt in the group of six to eight. How did you feel while the other dyad was reporting? Were you listening? Were you anticipating your own reporting? How did you feel while your partner talked about you? How does it feel to be heard? How does it feel not to be heard? . . .

Now, invite the group to share some of these feelings and reactions for about 10-15 minutes or whatever seems necessary.

Finally, share the general purpose of the exercise in the following manner. (This is meant to be a guideline, not verbatim instructions.)

Each of you should have some idea as to how he/she listens, how difficult it is to concentrate on listening, and how much can be learned just by listening. You may also be aware of how being heard can be a positive experience and how not being heard can have a negative impact. You will be expecting your clients to share or self-disclose. You may see how difficult this can be and may understand what you are asking of them and how important your response (e.g., listening or not) can be to maintain this trust and encourage this process.

An equally important outcome of this exercise is getting to know some other trainees better. This is important because other trainees will be an important source of learning in this program. Through the sharing of everything that each person brings to training, the group will become an important resource with considerable expertise. Toward this end, trainers will attempt to bring out in the group what individuals already know, rather than functioning solely as experts who must provide all the answers.

Appendix D

PROGRESS FORM

(Filled out after every role-play)

Counselor _____ Trainer _____

Client _____ Date _____

Problem given:

How did the counselor establish the relationship:

How did the counselor define the problem (and maintain focus):

How did the counselor explore and deal with feelings (persist):

How did the counselor explore past coping and alternatives:

In general, how was the counselor helpful:

In what ways did the counselor fail to be helpful:

Specifically, how can the counselor go about improving any of the aforementioned:

Group's feedback:

Chapter 33

IDENTIFYING AND RESPONDING TO BURNOUT

JAMES R. ROGERS AND BARBARA MEDLOCK

Workers, whether paid or volunteers, who provide crisis intervention and counseling by telephone are susceptible to a variety of cognitive and emotional reactions as a result of these activities. Similar to other workers in the mental health fields who come into contact with clients in a face-to-face environment, telephone counselors can find themselves emotionally impacted in ways that can negatively influence their effectiveness and negatively impact their mental and physical health. The term *burnout* has come to be used to describe this reaction and has been defined by Pines and Aronson (1988) as "a state of physical, emotional, and mental exhaustion caused by long term involvement in situations that are emotionally demanding" (p. 9). Collins and Long (2003) and Conrad and Keller-Guenther (2006) have suggested that burnout is the result of a process of gradual wearing down of energy and a sense of feeling overwhelmed by client problems, and this results in exhaustion, cynicism, and disengagement from work-related responsibilities.

Since the term was coined by Freudenberger in 1975, a considerable theoretical and empirical literature has emerged in this area, with the most commonly used definition of burnout coming from Maslach (1986). According to Maslach, "Burnout is a syndrome of emotional exhaustion, depersonalization and reduced personal accomplishment that can occur among individuals who work with people in some capacity" (p. 61). More specifically, Maslach and Schaufeli (1993) identified five elements of burnout common across definitions:

1. burnout includes symptoms of mental and emotional exhaustion, depression, and fatigue,

2. although reactions may include physical symptoms, the emphasis is on behavioral symptoms,
3. the symptoms are work-related,
4. symptoms occur in individuals without previous mental health problems, and
5. burnout results in decreased professional effectiveness and work performance.

Beyond defining and describing burnout, Pines and Aronson (1988) theorized about the cause of the syndrome. According to them, "The root cause of burnout lies in our existential need to believe that our lives are meaningful, that the things we do are useful, important, and even heroic" (p. 11). Thus, perhaps even more than it is for other mental health workers, who often have an opportunity to follow up with their clients, telephone crisis intervention and counseling workers may struggle with questions regarding the meaningfulness and usefulness of their efforts because of a lack of ability to evaluate the effectiveness of their work once the call has ended.

The purpose of this chapter is to provide a brief overview of the literature on burnout as it relates to the provision of mental health services, discuss some of the potential warning signs, and offer some suggestions for responding to burnout in the telephone counseling milieu. As a precursor to our overview of the literature, it is important to note that we were unable to locate any published studies of burnout specific to telephone counseling and crisis intervention, and this is clearly an area for future research. Consequently, we draw on the more general empirical literature related to burnout including burnout in the mental health professions. The relatively limited research into burnout has typically focused on specific populations and is based on self-reported symptoms of burnout.

Burnout Research Overview

In their review of several longitudinal studies of burnout and its associated negative impact on work performance and behavior, Maslach and Schaufeli (1993) found burnout to be related to a number of negative responses. They indicated that there was considerable evidence that burnout leads to absenteeism, job turnover and physical symptoms. Similarly, in more recent research, Maslach and Leiter (2008) found burnout to be related to low job satisfaction, poor commitment to the organization, and high intentions to leave one's job.

Sprang et al. (2007) assessed burnout in a sample of psychologists, psychiatrists, social workers, marriage and family counselors, professional counselors, and drug and alcohol counselors. In looking at differences within these samples, these authors found that women generally reported higher levels of burnout than did males and that those professionals working in inpatient settings reported higher levels than those in private practice. They also found that being younger, having less clinical experience, and having more difficult clients predicted higher levels of burnout.

What may be most relevant to burnout in telephone crisis workers is the finding by Sprang et al. (2007) that clinicians working with a high volume of clients who are reacting to trauma-related experiences reported higher levels of burnout. Thus, it is likely that telephone counselors, who respond to higher numbers of calls from clients reacting to traumatic events, including significant suicidal ideation or intent, may be particularly at risk for experiencing burnout.

In a study similar to Sprang et al. (2007), Linely and Joseph (2007) looked at occupational and personal factors associated with burnout in a sample of professional therapists. Linely and Joseph found that being engaged in their own personal therapy served as a "protective" factor for burnout, while adhering to a cognitive-behavioral orientation in their work was related to increased burnout. In terms of psychological factors, these authors found that having a strong sense of self, purpose, and meaning, and positive attachments with their clients was related to lower levels of burnout.

In summary then, burnout is characterized by emotional, mental, and physical exhaustion resulting from high levels of engagement in emotionally demanding situations (Pines & Aronson, 1988). For telephone counselors, these situations are intimate interpersonal communications with callers struggling with often complex scenarios that are sometimes life-threatening in nature. Complicating the experience for telephone counselors, in contrast to mental health providers who have direct contact with their clients, telephone counselors are limited in their ability to more directly influence callers' behaviors in the moment, as well as following up with callers to evaluate the effectiveness of their efforts at helping. Thus, the context of crisis intervention and counseling by telephone may in and of itself exacerbate the potential for burnout. Burnout is important to consider as it has been shown to relate to negative physical and psychological symptoms, poor work performance and satisfaction, and high turnover.

Identifying Burnout in Telephone Counselors

With little research directly investigating the experience of burnout in telephone counselors, we next draw form the early work of Freudenberger and North (1985) and clinical experience to identify potential signs of burnout in telephone crisis counselors.

Freudenberger and North (1985) theorized that burnout processes in general could be considered to consist of 12 phases, some of which may be taken as signs of burnout. The signs that may be most relevant for understanding burnout in the telephone intervention and crisis counseling context include:

1. working harder perhaps to convince oneself that he or she is effective
2. neglecting needs outside of the workplace because of the increased effort needed to perform work responsibilities
3. social withdrawal as a response to increased stress, self-doubt and related psychological reactions
4. emptiness related to a sense of loss of meaning in work, and
5. depression as a function of exhaustion, feelings of hopelessness, and low self-efficacy.

These five signs are seen as general characteristics of burnout that likely cut across work environments and, although they may be useful in identifying burnout in telephone crisis intervention and counseling workers, we have identified a number of warning signs that may additionally be useful for identifying potential burnout in this context. As a caveat, our experience has been in the context of work in a crisis intervention suicide prevention hotline staffed primarily by trained volunteers. However, we believe that many of these warning signs will generalize to other organizations where providers, either volunteers or mental health practitioners, engage in crisis intervention and counseling by telephone.

With this caveat, the following are signs that we have experienced as potential markers or warning signs for burnout in telephone workers:

- changes in scheduling patterns which may include
  - increased requests for changes,
  - frequent cancellations of work shifts
  - procrastination in scheduling
    requests for long absences
- incomplete documentation
  - specifically, a negative change in quality of documentation over time
- changes in time perception
  - as a function of boredom or frustration, calls feel longer than they are
  - losing track of time on calls (i.e., not actively managing calls)
- changes in attention to detail and in following policies and procedures
- decreased confidence in skills
- changes in way callers are characterized reflecting frustration with callers such as referring to caller "types" rather than individuals
- changes in energy or enthusiasm and level of engagement with callers
- demonstrating a more judgmental attitude toward callers

- avoiding high volume shifts in scheduling hours
- poor communication with staff
- signs of changes in physical health
- avoiding suicide risk assessment or incomplete suicide assessments
- over or under-reaction to high risk calls

As evidenced in this list, some of these warning signs can be identified through monitoring calls for quality assurance, others through discussions with workers, and still others through more objective indicators such as scheduling changes, chart reviews, and observable behaviors such as withdrawal from work-related social interactions, decreased energy, and call-offs. Additionally, although much of the literature we have presented focuses solely on the impact of the work environment on the development of burnout, it is clear that what happens outside of that environment may also exacerbate individual responses or buffer against its development. The following case examples will serve to demonstrate some of these issues.

Three Case Examples

The following three case examples represent actual scenarios encountered on a suicide and crisis intervention hotline. The examples are based on actual experiences with volunteer telephone counselors, but names and identifying information have been changed.

Case #1

Jim is in his late twenties and has been with the hotline for three years. He holds down a full-time job and is taking classes part-time toward a degree. He shared that his ex-wife of two years was depressed, struggling with suicidal thoughts, and leaning on him for help. Over the next three months, there was a gradual change in his scheduling patterns, such as more sporadic scheduling, procrastination in responding to scheduling requests, last minute call-offs, and choosing less busy shifts. He said that he was having difficulty scheduling shifts with his work and school schedule, but this had not been a problem for him in the past. When asked, he minimized the stress of the situation with his ex-wife. Eventually, he told staff that he planned to resign. He was feeling a lot of pressure from family to help his ex-wife because of his hotline experience, and he felt responsible for her well-being. The situation was made even more difficult because of his ambivalent feelings about her and the end of the marriage. He was feeling helpless and ineffective, and the thought of talking to a caller at risk for suicide made him depressed and fearful. He began counseling during which he realized that he was avoiding the hotline because he felt overwhelmed. He apologized for not telling staff earlier, but it had been a gradual process for him and he was too embarrassed to share his fears.

This case demonstrates the impact of events in the outside world in the development of burnout. In fact, one of the issues identified here was the interaction of the telephone counseling position and what was happening in his life. Specifically, the counselor had an expectation of himself, supported by his family, that he had a special responsibility to help his ex-wife with her mental health concerns by virtue of his training, thereby creating more stress. Here the most obvious warning signs were emergent problems in scheduling shifts, calling off more frequently, opting for shifts that were during slower times, and feelings of helplessness and decreased confidence in his skills. The case of Wendy next highlights some additional warning signs of burnout.

Case #2

Wendy is a college senior in a psychology program. She plans on applying for a doctoral program and joined the hotline hoping to gain experience in crisis intervention. She is very dependable, eager, and a quick learner. After about eight months of solid performance, the staff noticed that the calls she took seemed to be shorter and shorter although her estimate of the call length was often overestimated. Her overall call documentation became more cursory and occasionally contained some judgmental language. She seemed less active in engaging callers, less attentive, and less likely to use available tools to assist with managing calls from repeat callers. At times, risk assessments were not done, were incomplete, or the level of risk was minimized. She expressed her frustrations with other workers. She was starting to feel irritated with callers and felt that her efforts to help repeat callers were futile.

As suggested previously, burnout in this situation was identifiable by observing a rather drastic change in the volunteer's work behavior. Over time, she became less engaged in calls, increasingly frustrated and judgmental with repeat callers, and avoided giving appropriate levels of attention to suicide risk. Additionally, Wendy's documentation suffered and she began sharing her frustrations with coworkers. This case in particular shows that evidence of potential burnout can be gleaned from multiple sources, and it can be important for supervisors to pull that information together in order to identify problems early on if possible. The final case presents a scenario in which the potential signs of burnout may be predominately physical in nature although additional warning signs emerged as well.

Case #3

Sarah is a middle-aged woman who was a reliable crisis worker for seven years. She was married with teenage children and worked part-time as a cashier. Periodically, she would begin a pattern of last-minute cancellation or rescheduling of shifts because of medical appointments or an ER visit the day before. When she did come to work during those times, she often looked tired and reported that her mind felt "fuzzy," and there was often an increase in complaints about head and muscle aches and upper respiratory infections. On calls, she was generally more impatient with callers, less attentive to details and had difficulty remembering or laxness in following policies and procedures, resulting in frequent phone consultations with staff. These episodes seemed to occur in conjunction with reports of increased stress in her personal life.

Clearly in this final case example, it would be difficult to determine whether Sarah's physical symptoms contributed to her burnout or whether they were symptoms of burnout. Nevertheless, it seems clear that there was an interaction with the physical symptoms co-occurring with other warning signs such as frustration with callers, lowered attention to administrative details and lowered confidence, which could be inferred from the more frequent consultations with staff. What the example does point out is that it is important for supervisors to consider not only performance on the job but also, to the extent possible, the counselors' health status and external stressors when evaluating the potential for burnout.

In summary, there are many potential signs of burnout and likely many potential contributors. Despite both Pine and Aronson (1988) and Maslach (1986) offering definitions of burnout that focus on the stress of work with people in emotionally demanding situations, it is clear that what is happening in an individual's outside life, including his or her health, will contribute to burnout in the telephone crisis intervention and counseling milieu. In consideration of this, we next offer some suggestions for responding to telephone counselors who may be at risk for burnout or who may be evidencing significant warning signs of burnout. From this perspective, we see burnout as existing on a continuum from perhaps one or a few warning signs on one end to significant impairment in job performance on the other.

Responding to Burnout

Considered on a continuum, the earlier the identification and response to potential burnout symptoms, the greater the likelihood of effectively addressing the related issues before significant impairment occurs. Thus, our first recommendation is that organizations that offer crisis intervention and counseling services by telephone should develop a plan of action for identifying and addressing burnout in counselors. The plan should include strategies for the early identification of warning signs and policies and procedures to follow up on those signs in counselors. In line with this strategy, it may be useful to educate counselors about the warning signs of burnout in an attempt to normalize some of those initial reactions. In this way, telephone counselors may feel less threatened by going to supervisors and discussing their reactions and may be in a better position to help coworkers who may also be struggling.

Beyond developing an a priori approach to identifying and addressing burnout through policies and procedures, we offer the following suggestions. The first few suggestions may best be considered as "protective" strategies that could help lessen the development of burnout, and the remainder are suggested responses or strategies to employ when burnout is identified in a telephone counselor.

Protective Strategies

As indicated above, we believe that these administrative strategies may be helpful in preventing burnout in telephone crisis intervention counselors. One strategy is to insure that there is a mutual understanding with regard to role expectations, including a realistic discussion of the limitations of telephone counseling as compared to face-to-face services. Frequent discussions with counselors related to potential discrepancies between what they hope for in terms of helping callers and what they may experience in their work may serve as a buffer to frustration, meaninglessness, and a sense of lack of confidence that may accrue from work with difficult callers. Similarly, as we mentioned previously, periodically reminding counselors about warning signs of burnout in a way that normalizes those symptoms may serve a protective function in that counselors may be more likely to discuss their reactions with supervisors if those reactions are not seen as pathological or abnormal. Also, having a well-developed and consistent system of strategies and limits for managing calls from repeat callers can alleviate some of the stress that comes from working with chronic callers that can lead to burnout. Finally, increasing the focus on self-care strategies in initial training modules, and continuing to reinforce the importance of self-care through in-service training, can help counselors maintain balance and reduce the negative impact of engagement with challenging callers.

Response Strategies

Despite our best efforts at attempting to prevent the development of burnout, telephone counselors may struggle in their work of providing crisis intervention and counseling. This is especially true given the likely reality that the development of burnout is influenced not only by stressful experiences with callers, but also by other stressful life experiences outside of the workplace. Next are a few response suggestions that we have identified through experience as potential ways to help counselors who are exhibiting signs of burnout. Of course, we recognize that the viability of these strategies may be limited by organizational constraints. However, a consideration of these responses or some version of them may prove to be useful.

- Provide for more frequent contact with workers who are experiencing personal issues that may affect their objectivity,
- Provide additional or more regularly scheduled individual and group supervision time,
- Temporarily provide supervisor or staff monitoring of calls with immediate feedback until confidence returns,
- Temporarily offer more flexible scheduling options to accommodate the counselor's needs,
- Work with the counselor to frame, or reframe as necessary, the value of his or her interventions with difficult callers (such as acceptance, empathy, contact with others, reassurance, consistency, honesty, trust, etc.),
- Design multiple mechanisms for both worker and staff-initiated communications related to their reactions to callers (e-mail, telephone, face-to-face, communication book, chat-board, call report feedback, etc.), and finally,
- Consider the possibility of the need for short or extended leave of absence as an option (the earlier the better) or, in extreme cases, a shift in duties or resignation.

Conclusion

Despite attention to burnout in the organizational literature and the mental health fields, there has been little specific attention to the issue as it relates to crisis intervention and counseling by telephone. We believe that this is a critical oversight as telephone counselors are often faced with stressful caller concerns including rape and other forms of violence, suicidal ideation and intent, unemployment and poverty, and chronic mental illness. For many of these concerns, there is a complex set of personal, interpersonal, and environmental causes resulting in behavioral and emotional difficulties for which crisis intervention and counseling by telephone can offer some relief. However, providing these services can be highly stressful for counselors in that complex problems often require sustained and complex solutions, efforts beyond the ability of the counselor to provide over the telephone. Added to this, the likelihood that telephone counselors may never know the outcome of their efforts with callers because of anonymity, it is easy to see how telephone counselors may become physically, emotionally, and mentally exhausted through their work. Thus, we believe that it is important for telephone counselors, their supervisors, and administrators to be aware of the warning signs of burnout and to develop both preventive and response strategies to address it in the work environment.

Although we have offered some examples of strategies to identify, prevent, and respond to burnout in workers involved in crisis intervention and counseling by telephone, it is important to keep in mind that there is very little, if any, empirical literature on burnout specific to telephone counseling. We believe that it is critical to begin to look at this issue in a systematic way in telephone counseling environments in order to determine the extent of the experience of burnout in counselors and to empirically assess the appropriateness of specific approaches to prevention and intervention. Here we suggest that researchers interested in this area consider using the *Maslach Burnout Inventory* (3rd ed.) (Maslach et al., 1996) since this measure (and earlier versions) is generally viewed as one of the leading measures of burnout in the field. A concerted effort to address burnout clinically and systematically from a research perspective should result in a better understanding of the issue in this setting, improve services to callers, and protect workers from the potential negative effects of providing crisis intervention and counseling by telephone.

REFERENCES

Collins, S., & Long, A. (2003). Working with the psychological effects of trauma: Consequences for mental health-care workers: A literature review. *Journal of Psychiatric & Mental Health Nursing, 10,* 417–424.

Conrad, D., & Kellar-Guenther, Y. (2006). Compassion fatigue, burnout, and compassion satisfaction among Colorado child protection workers. *Child Abuse & Neglect, 30,* 1071–1080.

Freudenberger, H. J., & North, G. (1985). *Women's burnout.* Garden City, NY: Doubleday.

Linely, P. A., & Joseph, S. (2007). Therapy work and therapists' positive and negative well-being. *Journal of Social & Clinical Psychology, 26,* 385–403.

Maslach, C. (1986). Stress, burnout, and workaholism. In R. R. Kilburg, P. E. Nathan, & R. W. Thoreson (Eds.), *Professionals in distress: Issues, syndromes, and solutions in psychology,* pp. 53–75. Washington, DC: American Psychological Association.

Maslach, C., Jackson, S. E., & Leiter, M. P. (1996). *The Maslach Burnout Inventory* (3rd ed.). Palo Alto, CA: Consulting Psychologists Press.

Maslach, C., & Leiter, M. P. (2008). Early predictors of job burnout and engagement. *Journal of Applied Psychology, 93,* 498–512.

Maslach, C., & Schaufeli, W. B. (1993). Historical and conceptual development of burnout. In W. B. Schaufeli, C. Maslach, & T. Marek (Eds.), *Professional burnout: Recent developments in theory and research*, pp. 1–16. Washington DC: Taylor & Francis.

Pines, A., & Aronson, E. (1988). *Career burnout: Causes and cures.* New York: Free Press.

Sprang, G., Clark, J. J., & Whitt-Woosley, A. (2007). Compassion fatigue, compassion satisfaction, and burnout: Factors impacting a professional's quality of life. *Journal of Loss & Trauma, 12,* 259–280.

Part VII

EVALUATING TELEPHONE COUNSELING SERVICES

Chapter 34

THE EFFECTIVENESS OF SUICIDE PREVENTION AND CRISIS INTERVENTION SERVICES

DAVID LESTER

Since one of the central goals of suicide prevention centers is, obviously, to prevent suicide, it is important to examine whether they do so. Lester (1997) carried out a meta-analysis of ecological studies (studies comparing regions with different numbers of suicide prevention centers) conducted for Canada, England, and the United States and time series studies for England, Germany, Japan, Taiwan, and the United States. Reducing the results of each of these studies to a common statistic (a Pearson correlation coefficient) and then averaging these statistics produced an average correlation of -0.16 with 2,549 degrees of freedom, which indicates an overall statistically significant preventive effect, although the effect is modest in size.

Thus, there is reason to be optimistic about the success of suicide prevention centers in preventing suicide, although it is important that more researchers focus on the problem of evaluating the effectiveness of suicide prevention centers and devise new ways and new sources of data to evaluate their effectiveness.

While some suicide prevention centers include the term "crisis intervention" in their name, others label themselves solely as crisis intervention services. Thus evaluating such services simply by focusing on the mortality of the clients is a rather narrow approach.

It is becoming increasingly important in mental health programs to evaluate the services provided. Partly because funding sources, public and private, are demanding feedback as to how beneficial their money has been for the community, and partly because in the past, too many programs made claims for their usefulness that were undocumented or, when documented, found to be unsubstantiated; few programs can exist today without advancing some data to justify their continued funding.

On the other hand, faced with the demand that a program be evaluated, administrators are often hard pressed to find meaningful ways to do so. Inspection of the annual reports of telephone counseling services reveals that the most common way of demonstrating the effectiveness of the service is to present data on its activity. If an agency made contact with N clients, then this is seen as evidence of its usefulness to the community and justification of its continued funding. The astute observer who compares several annual reports will quickly note that the number N varies between 50 and 25,000 among different telephone counseling services, and yet each agency is satisfied with its performance.

A documentation of activity, although of interest, will not do as a measure of effectiveness for several reasons. First, the services rarely if ever have any notion of what the need of the community might be. Although the service may be counseling 100 clients a month, there may be 1,000 or even 10,000 people in the community in need of help. Second, the service may not be counseling those to whom it is directed. Suicide prevention centers counsel large numbers of clients, but the available evidence indicates that they rarely receive calls from the individuals in the community who are about to complete suicide (rather than those who are experiencing suicidal ideation or planning to attempt suicide). Third, there is no indication that those clients counseled received adequate, beneficial counseling. The clients calling the service might conceivably be helped more were there no telephone counseling service to call. Finally, telephone counseling services might be doing harm in the community, for example, by impeding the development of independence in its clients.

The presentation of data on the volume of activity of the service by itself is insufficient to answer these points. Better methods of evaluation must be used.

The Objectives of the Service

It is obvious that in order to evaluate a program, its objectives must be clearly stated. Although obvious, this is rarely the case. Occasionally, the name of the agency implies an objective. A suicide prevention center has the unavoidable implication that, at the least, it will prevent suicide in the community. (That this implication is unavoidable may account for why many suicide prevention centers have reoriented themselves as crisis clinics.) Other services, such as teen hotlines, have no objectives implied in their title.

It would be a useful exercise for a telephone counseling service to try to formulate its idealized objectives, as Suchman (1967) has called them. What changes does the agency hope to effect in its community? The suicide prevention center might reduce the community's suicide rate or its attempted suicide rate; the teen hotline might reduce drug use, illegitimate births, absence from school for emotional reasons, or the incidence of delinquency; the crisis intervention service might reduce admissions to psychiatric facilities, reduce recidivism in former psychiatric clients, or speed up the referral process in which a distressed individual in the community is referred to an appropriate helping agency.

For an agency to be forthright enough to state its idealized objectives is a courageous act, for most likely these objectives may not be reached. (It would be wise, nonetheless, to be aware of the idealized objectives, even though they are not advertised.) The experience of telephone counseling services indicates that they release a flood of response from the community which indicates a vast amount of emotional distress among the members of the community who hitherto had no resources to which to turn. However, there are no data yet that counseling these clients has any general or specific effect on the mental health of the community.

Lesser Objectives

A telephone counseling service can formulate lesser objectives for itself. For example, if a service addresses itself to a particular subgroup of the population, several possibilities are available.

1. The potential clientele can be asked whether they have heard of the service, whether they have used it, and what their image of it is. For example, Motto (1971) found that 80% of a sample of depressed and suicidal clients admitted to a psychiatric unit had heard of the local suicide prevention center, but that only 11% had called it. Evidence from Los Angeles (Weiner, 1969) indicated that only 2% of completed suicides had called the suicide prevention center.

2. Who calls the center? If the center is addressed to a particular clientele, do these people call the service? For example, the typical completed suicide is old, white, and male. The typical caller to the Chicago suicide prevention center was young, black, and female (Maris, 1969).

3. Are the calls coming from the appropriate areas of the community? For example, if the suicide rate is high in a particular locale in the community, does the center receive a high proportion of calls from that locale. In Buffalo, Lester (1971) was able to demonstrate that this was occurring. The monitoring of the areas where calls come from to the agency enables the agency, if it desires, to adjust its advertising and out-reach activities accordingly and so provides useful feedback to the agency.

Categories of Evaluation

Aside from the objectives of a program, Suchman (1967) noted that programs can be evaluated in terms of the different types of effect that they have on the community. These categories represent different criteria by which a program may be judged. To date, very little research or evaluation of telephone counseling services has been conducted for any of these criteria. However it may be informative to list the criteria mentioned by Suchman.

1. *Effort.* What is the quantity and the quality of the activity that takes place and how does this compare to the counseling resources? This, of course, varies from service to service. The suicide prevention and crisis service of Buffalo served a community of about one million and received some 24,000 client calls a year on its three telephone services (suicide prevention service, teen hotline, and problems-in-living service). The service was staffed by about 75 volunteers. The quality of the service was unknown.

2. *Performance.* What is the effect of the effort put out by the service? Do people receive help from the service? A few studies have attempted to follow up callers to telephone counseling services and assess the impact of the service. For example, Murphy et al. (1969) interviewed a sample of callers to a suicide prevention center who had called on their own behalf and found that only about half had followed through on the advice given to them by the counselor.

3. *Adequacy of performance.* Is the performance of a service sufficient to cope with the community need?

4. *Efficiency.* Could the service provided by the agency be better provided by a different kind of agency or by an agency with a different structure?

5. *Process.* How does the agency produce the results that it does?

Evaluating the Internal Operations

So far, the methods of evaluation discussed have been unsuitable for the majority of telephone counseling services. To evaluate idealized objectives is a gamble. To evaluate lesser objectives is expensive. To evaluate in the areas suggested by Suchman is to break new ground for telephone counseling services, and most services are not equipped to do this. What can telephone services do in order to evaluate their services if these alternatives are not feasible?

A number of telephone counseling services that do evaluate their performance focus upon low-level objectives concerned primarily with the internal operation of the agency, the administrative functions, and the performance of the counselors. There are many possibilities here and a number of them are described below.

The Internal Operation of the Agency

1. How long does it take to obtain a counselor at a telephone counseling service? Lester (1970a) called a telephone counseling service at different hours during the week and noted how long it took a counselor to answer the telephone and how often he obtained a busy signal. In this way, a center can identify peak periods of activity and monitor the performance of its counselors. McGee et al. (1973) called different centers in the southeast United States and noted the time that passed until a counselor was obtained. This latter study provided data on the speed with which a center could respond to a call depending upon its system for answering calls: an answering service, use of a local agency such as the fire station, locating the counselors at their homes or in the center, and so forth.

2. The success in referring clients to other resources can be noted by finding out the proportion of referrals who show at these resources. The Suicide Prevention and Crisis Service in Buffalo referred clients to its own crisis clinic, and Lester (1970b) studied the proportion of referrals who showed. Over several months, this varied from 29% to 56%. The success in referring clients can also be noted for each counselor. Following up on this finding, Lester (1970c; Lester and Priebe, 1971) tried to identify from the data on the initial contact sheets, completed by the counselors when a client first called, those characteristics that distinguished shows from no-shows. The shows were older, less likely to be single, and more likely to be calling on the suicide prevention line than on the other lines (teen hotline and problems in living line).

Slaikeu et al. (1973) pursued this issue by carrying out a content analysis of the telephone calls during which shows and no-shows were referred to the crisis clinic. The major finding was that clients who themselves suggested a referral were more likely to show.

In this way it is possible to provide feedback to the counselors as to the factors likely to lead a client to follow through with the referral made for him.

3. The completeness with which client records are kept can be assessed. Do counselors obtain the information from clients that the center requires? Kolker and Katz (1971) found at their suicide prevention center that, if a counselor fails to note down the age of the caller, then he is also less likely to collect information necessary to recontact the client if this is necessary (if the client hangs up, if the line inadvertently gets disconnected, or for a follow-up contact). Whittemore (1970) compared samples of initial contact sheets at different centers and noted that whereas the sex of the client was noted in 99.9% of the calls he checked, the age was not noted for 16.9% of the callers, marital status was unknown for 10.4%, and religion was unknown for over 75%.

4. Whittemore (1970) in his comparison of ten centers provided data on the kinds of callers and calls that different centers receive. For example, Whitte-

more found that the proportion of anonymous calls at the ten centers varied from 18% to 63%. The proportion of calls with no suicidal involvement varied from 43% to 79%. Telephone counseling services can easily collect their own data and compare the data to those from the ten centers studied by Whittemore.

5. Many centers ask counselors to rate the improvement of the clients as a result of the telephone contact. This rating can provide some data as to how well the counselors feels that they are performing.

6. Although it is obvious that the cost of the service is not necessarily related to the adequacy and quality of the service, the cost per telephone contact can easily be computed and compared with other centers.

7. Motto (1969) devised a set of standards for suicide prevention centers in terms of the adequacy of the administration, staffing, and evaluation of the program, the training and supervision of counselors, consultation resources, and ethical standards. The American Association of Suicidology now has a formal program in place to evaluate crisis intervention services to see whether they meet these standards (www.suicidology.org).

Lester (1970a, 1970b, 1970d) provided sample data for many of these criteria for the internal functioning of a center from the suicide prevention and crisis service of Buffalo and these data can be used for comparison.

The Adequacy of the Counselor's Performance

A separate and crucial area for evaluation is the adequacy of the counseling provided by the staff of a telephone counseling service. Most centers require some kind of supervision of counselors, and this is, of course, crucially important. However, it is also necessary to devise standardized means of evaluating the effectiveness of counselors. Not all centers can obtain adequate supervisors for counselors, and not all supervisors are competent. The availability of standardized evaluation procedures would enable centers to make additional checks on the competence of their staff and, furthermore, enable centers to compare their performance with that of other centers.

Knickerbocker and McGee (1973) trained judges to make ratings of concreteness, empathy, warmth, and genuineness, as defined by Carkhuff (1969), and then gave them written excerpts from actual conversations between telephone counselors and clients to rate. Interestingly, Knickerbocker and McGee found that lay volunteers obtained higher scores than professional volunteers on these dimensions, but both groups performed at an acceptable level. Applying these to the functioning of a sample of counselors at the Suicide Prevention and Crisis Service in Buffalo, Lester (1970d) found that the only dimension that appeared to be related to whether a client shows or fails to show for an appointment at the center was the dimension of concreteness.

Fowler and McGee (1973) developed a "technical effectiveness" scale that measures the performance of the counselors at the tasks they are supposed to do, including:

1. Can the caller be immediately recontacted?
2. Did the volunteer ask for or obtain specific information regarding significant others?
3. Were specific problems identified?
4. Did the volunteer communicate that he/she is willing to help?
5. Did the volunteer develop a structured plan of action or help the caller develop one?
6. Did the caller agree to the action plan?
7. Was it determined whether or not this was a suicide case?
8. Did the volunteer ask about a suicide plan?
9. Or, if the caller voluntarily disclosed the information, did the volunteer inquire for further details?
10. Was it determined if the caller had made prior suicide attempts?

Fowler and McGee had judges make these ratings from recordings of actual telephone calls made by clients and showed that the scale could be employed meaningfully to compare counselors and to monitor the progress of individual counselors over time. Rogers and Subich (1990) have also explored the usefulness of a standardized means of data collection and risk assessment of clients by telephone counselors.

Mishara and Daigle (1992) had observers listen in to actual calls at two suicide prevention centers in Quebec. The observers classified the types of statements made by counselors, finding that the most frequent response was *acceptance*, followed by *orientation-investigation* (asking direct questions). The observers also rated changes in the depression level of the client (about 14% of the clients were judged to have become less depressed by the end of the call), changes in the probability of suicidal behavior in the client (27% of the clients were judged to have a lower suicidal risk at the end of the call), and whether the counselor and client reached an agreement (which happened in 68% of the calls).

Others have made simulated crisis calls to telephone counselors. Williamson et al. (1973) devised a series of simulated client calls. In these, an actor calls the counselor (who may or may not be informed that the call is a test call) and presents a rehearsed role. The response of the counselor to this standardized call can then be evaluated.

Bobevski and McLennan (1998) had counselors come into the clinic and handle calls from people they knew to be role-playing. Bobevski and McLennan found that the effectiveness of the counselors, as rated by the callers, was related to the level of the counselors' expertise, the cognitive effort they put into the counseling, the level of emotional involvement with the caller and their level of anxiety.

Do these simulated calls assess behavior when taking real calls? Garrett et al. (1993) had counselors take a simulated call and then real calls while an evaluator listened in. They found that performance on the simulated call predicted performance on the real calls quite well.

Research to explore which traits predict performance as a telephone counselor would be useful in helping crisis service staff select new counselors. Along these lines, Tekavcic-Grad and Farberow (1989) asked telephone crisis counselors in Ljubljana (Yugoslavia) and Los Angeles (USA) to list the traits which a good counselor should possess. Both sets of counselors rated motivation to work and being a good listener as the most important traits. However, while the counselors in Los Angeles felt that they possessed the desirable traits for being a good counselor, counselors in Ljubljana did not. Research to identify traits which actually predict good counselor performance would be useful for those involved in the selection and training of telephone counselors.

In order to explore reasons for the high drop-out rate of telephone counselors (Mahoney & Pechura, 1980), Mishara and Giroux (1993) explored determinants of the stress level experienced by telephone counselors. They found that experience as a counselor, the urgency of the call, and inappropriate coping mechanisms on the part of the counselors contributed to their stress level, and they made recommendations for the selection and training of counselors based on their findings. The adequacy of the training program for telephone counselors can also be evaluated (Tierney, 1991).

Several recent studies have explored how attempted suicides rate the treatment they received at the hospitals to which they went or were taken (Grootenhuis & Papp, 1993; Kocmur & Zavasnik, 1991; Treloar & Pinfold, 1993). For example, Grootenhuis and Papp (1993) found that their sample of suicide attempters wished that they had been treated in a "more human way." It would be of interest to follow-up clients of suicide prevention centers to see how they evaluate the service.

Discussion

Traditional crisis counseling is based on the person-centered system of therapy devised by Carl Rogers. Rogers always advocated the importance of formulating goals for counseling and of evaluating whether these goals were met. Rogers and his staff and students at the counseling center which he established at the University of Chicago recorded and analyzed interviews with clients, followed-up clients to see whether they improved, and devised ways of testing whether one method or another was better for producing change in their clients (Kirschenbaum, 1979). For Rogers, research was not incompatible with providing excellent services. Indeed, without research, he could not be sure that the center provided excellent services!

Staff in suicide prevention centers need to become more active in this scientific endeavor. They should be encouraged to formulate their goals, both at the community level and for the individual clients they counsel, and they should decide how they might evaluate whether these goals are being met. How can the center attract more of the potential suicides in their community to use the resources provided by the center? What are the different approaches that might be used with suicidal clients and which approaches are more effective with which types of clients? Which counselors work most effectively with suicidal clients and what makes them so effective?

Asking these kinds of questions and seeking ways of answering them would advance crisis intervention and suicide prevention efforts tremendously in a few years. The antipathy that some counselors have toward research needs to be challenged, for counselors are in the best position both to formulate hypotheses about suicide prevention and to test the validity of these hypotheses.

At the suicide prevention conferences each year, I am struck by the lack of research specifically focused on the evaluation of the effectiveness of suicide prevention efforts in general and suicide prevention counseling in particular. If Carl Rogers had assumed that the way he counseled in 1930 was the best possible, he would never have developed person-centered counseling. If we assume that the activities taking place in suicide prevention centers today are the best possible, then we will never improve those services.

REFERENCES

Bobevski, I., & McLennan, J. (1998). The telephone counseling interview as a complex, dynamic, decision process. *Journal of Psychology, 132*, 47–60.

Carkhuff, R. (1969). *Helping and human relations.* New York: Holt, Rinehart, & Winston.

Fowler, D. E., & McGee, R. K. (1973). Assessing the performance of telephone crisis workers. In D. Lester & G. W. Brockopp (Eds.), *Crisis intervention and counseling by telephone*, pp. 287–297. Springfield, IL: Charles C Thomas.

Garrett, C. R., Teare, J. F., Reed, C. R., Shanahan, D. L., & Coughlin, D. D. (1993). Counselor evaluation. In D. Lester (Ed.), *Suicide '93*, pp. 109–111. Denver, CO: American Association of Suicidology.

Grootenhuis, M. A., & Papp, R. P. (1993). How do suicide attempters evaluate the treatment in a general hospital? *Italian Journal of Suicidology, 3*, 25–28.

Kirschenbaum, H. (1979). *On becoming Carl Rogers.* New York: Delacorte.

Knickerbocker, D. A., & McGee, R. K. (1973). Clinical effectiveness of nonprofessional and professional telephone workers in a crisis intervention center. In D. Lester & G. W. Brockopp (Eds.), *Crisis intervention and counseling by telephone*, pp. 298–309. Springfield, IL: Charles C Thomas.

Kocmur, M., & Zavasnik, A. (1991). Patients' experience of the therapeutic process in a crisis intervention unit. *Crisis, 12*(1), 69–81.

Kolker, H., & Katz, S. (1971). If you've missed the age you've missed a lot. *Crisis Intervention, 3*, 34–37.

Lester, D. (1970a). Steps toward the evaluation of a suicide prevention center: Part two. *Crisis Intervention, 2*(supplement to 1), 12–18.

Lester, D. (1970b). Steps toward the evaluation of a suicide prevention center: Part one. *Crisis Intervention, 2*(supplement to 2), 42–45.

Lester, D. (1970c). A comparison of patients who show for appointments and those who do not show. *Crisis Intervention, 2*, 75–76.

Lester, D. (1970d). Steps toward the evaluation of a suicide prevention center: Part four. *Crisis Intervention, 2*(supplement to 4), 20–22.

Lester, D. (1971). Geographical location of callers to a suicide prevention center. *Psychological Reports, 28*, 421–422.

Lester, D. (1997). The effectiveness of suicide prevention programs. *Suicide & Life-Threatening Behavior, 27*, 304–310.

Lester, D., & Priebe, K. (1971). Patients who show for therapy and those who fail. *Crisis Intervention, 3*, 69–72.

Mahoney, J., & Pechura, C. (1980). Value and volunteers. *Psychological Reports, 47*, 1007–1012.

Maris, R. (1969). The sociology of suicide prevention. *Social Problems, 17*, 132–149.

McGee, R. K., Richard, W. C., & Bercun, C. (1973). A survey of telephone answering systems in suicide prevention and crisis intervention agencies. In D. Lester & G. W. Brockopp (Eds.), *Crisis intervention and counseling by telephone*, pp. 24–40. Springfield, IL: Charles C Thomas.

Mishara, B. L., & Daigle, M. (1992). The effectiveness of telephone interventions by suicide prevention workers. *Canada's Mental Health, 40*(3), 24–29.

Mishara, B. L., & Giroux, G. (1993). The relationship between coping strategies and perceived stress in telephone intervention volunteers at a suicide prevention center. *Suicide & Life-Threatening Behavior, 23*, 221–229.

Motto, J. (1969). Development of standards for suicide prevention centers. *Bulletin of Suicidology*, March, 33–37.

Motto, J. (1971). Evaluation of a suicide prevention center by sampling the population at risk. *Life-Threatening Behavior, 1*, 18–22.

Murphy, G., Wetzel, R., Swallow, C., & McClure, J. (1969). Who calls the suicide prevention center? *American Journal of Psychiatry, 126*, 314–324.

Rogers, J. R., & Subich, L. M. (1990). Reliability analysis of the crisis line suicide risk scale. In D. Lester (Ed.), *Suicide '90*, pp. 223–224. Denver, CO: American Association of Suicidology.

Slaikeu, K., Lester, D., & Tulkin, S. R. (1973). Show versus no show. *Journal of Consulting & Clinical Psychology, 40*, 481–486.

Suchman, E. A. (1969). *Evaluative research*. New York: Russell Sage Foundation.

Tekavcic-Grad, O., & Farberow, N. L. (1989). A cross-cultural comparison of ideal and undesirable qualities of crisis line workers. *Crisis, 10*, 152–163.

Tierney, R. J. (1991). Suicide intervention training evaluation. In D. Lester (Ed.), *Suicide '91*, p. 113. Denver, CO: American Association of Suicidology.

Treloar, A. J., & Pinfold, T. J. (1993). Deliberate self-harm. *Crisis, 14*, 83–89.

Weiner, I. W. (1969). The effectiveness of a suicide prevention program. *Mental Hygiene, 53*, 357–363.

Whittemore, K. (1970). *Ten centers*. Atlanta: Lullwater Press.

Williamson, J. W., Goldberg, E., & Packard, M. (1973). Use of simulated patients in evaluating patient management skills of telephone counselors. In D. Lester & G. W. Brockopp (Eds.), *Crisis intervention and counseling by telephone*, pp. 310–322. Springfield, IL: Charles C Thomas.

Chapter 35

REFLECTIONS FROM A CALLER

CARA ANNA[48]

When David Lester circulated the table of contents for this latest edition, I noticed that it had several chapters on problem callers but no chapter by *The Caller*. David kindly allowed me to write one. I have called three kinds of crisis lines in the past few years: a therapist-staffed service offered under my insurer's Employee Assistance Plan, the National Suicide Prevention Lifeline, and the Samaritans.

I have not been a frequent caller, but I have thought about suicide frequently during the past few years. I had always believed that such feelings could be avoided if I was disciplined, worked hard, didn't burden myself down with possessions, and didn't stay anywhere too long. That changed when the way I felt about myself began to affect my job as a reporter. Agreeing to take such risky steps as talking to a psychotherapist, taking medication, and confiding in others was not easy, and I felt ashamed. The transition continues, with plenty of mistakes.

As for crisis lines, I started calling because I was cheap. Psychotherapy was expensive, and my insurance plan allowed just five free face-to-face sessions per year. Calls to the Employee Assistance Program help line were free. I didn't mind talking to a stranger on the telephone as my job often required it. I also didn't have to worry about the person looking at me and taking into account any negative impressions into the way they dealt with me. Furthermore, I could, if needed, cry without them noticing.

---

[48] Cara Anna has been a China-based foreign correspondent for The Associated Press, a Peace Corps volunteer in Africa, and an English teacher in rural Pakistan. She is currently applying to public interest law schools.

I had always assumed that psychotherapists were blank slates with a dry manner, but the ones who answered the telephone had at least a glimmer of personality that made them real. I remember them as alert individuals who could think on their feet and have a proper conversation. There was no script. One was surprisingly chatty and told me about his own past with suicidal thinking and what steps he had taken to turn things around. His style was that of a street-smart urban preacher, and he made an impression because of his enthusiasm and because he didn't fit the mold. Whether he made it up or not, he told me his first name. It was Tom.

For a while, I considered asking for him if I needed to call again, but that struck me as awkward. What if he remembered me? Or not? What if he wasn't as enthusiastic as before? What if he didn't have as compelling a message for someone who spoke with him a second time? There were too many chances for disappointment, some of which I might be able to blame on myself. The next time I called, I simply talked with whomever answered.

Next was the National Suicide Prevention Lifeline. I'm sorry to be blunt, but the experience was irritating and almost insulting. As we know, suicide isn't yet a topic that one can discuss openly. There's too much potential for freaking out the other person or, as happened with me, getting yourself committed. (That's another story.) I know better than to tell a psychotherapist or psychiatrist too much about suicidal thinking, especially any reference to having a plan, unless they've assured me otherwise, and I feel I can trust them. Under these circumstances, there are hardly any outlets for sharing thoughts that are far better aired than hushed up inside like some dirty sin.

I would like to think I simply got a bad Lifeline counselor, perhaps a new trainee. It made me think of a news interview where the interviewee keeps trying to open up about something and introduces a number of topics worthy of exploring, but the reporter sticks to his or her prepared list of questions and plods woodenly on.

Just as a good interview finds a flow of give-and-take (or at least of question-and-evade), a crisis line call ought to feel its way along with the caller's cues instead of going down a list of questions. I felt I was talking to a clipboard, not a human being. I was being triaged, not listened to, and I just wanted a human being to listen to me and respond in a thoughtful way. The advice didn't have to be ground breaking. I was prepared for the usual, "Have you tried yoga, meditation, dancing" etc? But it is human to at least offer advice, and I wanted to speak to a human. I wanted to share my thoughts, however ineptly, and be reassured that someone was trying to be there with me.

As for the Samaritans, I had tried to volunteer for them before ever calling them. I had formed a good impression, perhaps based on the understanding that they don't call the police on you. I also had heard that they are good listeners. While I was recovering from my latest suicide attempt, I thought volunteering with the Samaritans would be a fitting transition from focusing on suicide issues to helping others. I was open during the volunteer interview, and they didn't back away from questions. I was turned down, but one interviewer was kind enough to hint that it might just be too soon.

On a low and lonely evening a few months later, I finally gave them a call. I was, to my disappointment, uncomfortable with their approach. The idea of confiding in someone who listens and doesn't judge sounds like a relief until you find that it comes with another set of restrictions. The woman on the other end of the line was careful to restate the main idea of anything I said in slightly different terms. She may have proved that she was paying attention, but she wasn't responding. The restraint was obvious. Real people don't talk that way. I wondered what I could say to make her express an opinion or give advice. I was able to confide, but it was like a one-sided game of catch. She never threw me the ball.

Then, to my surprise, she announced that she had to go in a minute. This was a new one. I hadn't expected that a crisis line worker would cut off a conversation that couldn't have lasted more than ten minutes. Had she been keeping a triage checklist too? Was I not compelling? Couldn't she have mentioned a time limit at the beginning? I hung up and wondered who else was left to call.

These days, I see a social worker. We meet once a week, but I know that moods don't keep a regular schedule. There will be times when I will be tempted to call a crisis line again. I hope I get someone who is unrestrained, intelligent, and calm, a good listener with the confidence and grace to express emotions and opinions without drama. Someone who has digested the training and ethics of the world of crisis lines without letting them replace intuition and the human touch.

I'd also like to make a suggestion. I think the world of suicide prevention, and especially crisis lines, needs to incorporate a new message. In my suicide attempts, I exhausted myself trying to find an utterly foolproof method. The more I researched, the less confident I became. Perhaps I'm a perfectionist, or chicken, but I wanted to be certain that I would either die or emerge unscathed. I found that every method has its weaknesses, even those endorsed by the right-to-die groups. At the time, I very much wanted to try some method, but I didn't want it to fail because I was scared of the way that failure could affect me. Would I be paralyzed? Would I destroy my liver? Would I suffer brain damage? Would I lose control over part of me when I already felt so helpless? I found those fears stopped me from jumping, putting a gun to my head, or doing anything powerful and risky that could result in me emerging more limited than I already felt.

I believe suicide prevention efforts should include a simple message: Nothing you are thinking of doing is guaranteed. Anything can fail. There is absolutely nothing romantic, quick, and painless. Anything can risk messing you up even more, perhaps forever. Strangely enough, you need to tell people who want to end their lives that they risk ruining them instead. You don't have to get into the details of certain methods. You don't have to mention certain methods. You don't even have to ask the caller what they have in mind. Just make that blanket statement, and make it as convincingly as you know how.

I've been surprised by how little suicide prevention efforts use suicide attempt survivors in their outreach and prevention work. Why not have a campaign in which survivors who have been impaired by their attempts speak out about the misconceptions they had before they tried, about the mistaken ideas, and the notion of simply drifting off to sleep? I believe people will be deterred by this knowledge and the uncertainty it brings. I believe that speaking up about this doesn't cancel out existing suicide prevention messages. I believe that people who have gone through the usual concerns ("Think about your family") are focusing solely on themselves but still have room for a deterrent, one that addresses them alone. I don't know whether anyone else feels this way, largely because suicide isn't an easy topic of conversation, but I think the idea should be put out there and explored, and not just dismissed automatically with fear.

You may be wondering if any of my crisis line calls came just before a suicide attempt. They didn't. For me, making these calls occurs when I am losing confidence in my usual ways of coping and pick up the phone to see what happens. That's still a spark of hope. When that spark disappears, I'm not going to call. I enter a period of shutting down and making plans, and by then I don't want to talk to anyone.

Aside from my proposal above, I wish I could tell you what crisis line workers ought to say. I can only offer some advice to make the connection smoother. First, follow up. As far as I know, the only action a crisis line worker might take is calling 911. There should be a way to contact every caller again, even just a call or two to check in over a certain period of time.

In addition, find a way to address the caller's underlying problems. Refer them to a social worker, case manager, or person who can help with the issues that have made life overwhelming. Eventually a crisis line call must end, and the caller is left alone again with a silent telephone. It would be of some comfort to know that something more will happen, and the wait for that something can be enough to keep the person going.

It was such a relief to learn recently about an Australian, David Webb, who is the first openly admitted suicide attempt survivor to get a PhD in suicidology. In his book *Thinking About Suicide*, he writes, "For real suicide prevention, that is, to minimize suicidality arising rather than just treating it after it has already arisen, we need to stop blaming the victim so much and address issues such as social isolation, poverty, homelessness, domestic violence, and the institutionalized abuse of our children."

In Chapter Four, he mentions the intriguing idea of a Crisis Assessment and Treatment team that follows up on a call with an immediate visit and guidance on how to get help. I suggest reading his book for his thoughts on suicide prevention and bringing the voices of other attempt survivors into the open. I also suggest looking at the website of the Aeschi Working Group, a collection of suicidologists pursuing similar goals.

Some people benefit from lists, and most of us are busy people. Here is some final advice:

• If you have to ask a certain set of questions, say so and say why. The caller will better understand what you're doing, and after that, you're free to simply talk.

• Don't be afraid to react like a normal human being. If the caller shares something startling or moving, express that, even if in a low-key way. Don't simply respond with a dry, mechanical, "And how did that make you feel?" Even an "I'm so sorry" will help.

• Follow up. At least express interest in checking in with the person again soon and ask for a way to contact him/her. Some people will refuse, but at least you've tried.

• Don't be afraid to admit your limitations. Admit when you feel uncomfortable and when you're hearing something that you find hard to understand.

• Don't blame. Don't bullshit. Never dismiss. People can be tied so tightly to their feelings that in dismissing their feelings, you're dismissing the person.

• Pay attention.

• Remember that not all people can articulate their feelings in a graceful way.

• Remember that your crisis line may be the only place the person can go to talk.

• Don't pretend to understand if you don't. Just be there.

• If fitting, ask the person to tell you more about their life outside whatever drove them to call.

• You're not going to have a cure, or sometimes even good advice. But simply being an engaged listener can help the caller find their own way out of their tangle.

• At the end of the day, talk with someone yourself. You're doing a difficult job, and I know I haven't done enough to thank you in this essay. Secondary trauma can be painful, so don't neglect or fear your own feelings.

• Finally, please talk about your work with others. Conversation that mentions the normality of having and dealing with suicidal feelings is one way to lessen the taboo of suicide.

I attended the American Association of Suicidology conference in 2011 to witness history. It had the first plenary session that featured suicide attempt survivors. It was my first such conference, and I was struck by how the vast room of clinicians, academics, and crisis line workers seemed riveted as these people told their stories. How could it have taken decades for this to happen? How many people in the room, despite their work, still didn't dare to speak out about their own experience with suicidal actions and thinking? After I spoke out myself in some of the sessions, some people quickly, quietly told me, "Thank you for being here."

Speak out. It's too risky *not* to do so. Our conversations must move beyond hushed crisis line calls and away from a sense of shame. I hope this chapter contributes somehow, and I'm happy for the chance to write it.

NAME INDEX

A

Abel, G. G., 142, 153
Ackerman, G. L., 229, 243
Adamek, M. E., 274, 277, 278, 283
Adams, P. F., 320
Adams, S., 247
Adamson, D. M., 262
Alarcon, R. D., 244
Albers, E. C., 187, 192
Albert, D., 244
Albert, P., 248
Alcorn, J., 73
Alegre, C., 26
Alexander, C., 249
Alexander, J., 25
Alford, G. S., 142, 153
Allen, G. E., 329, 338
Allman, C., 244
Almansi, R. J., 149, 153
Alston, E., 323, 329, 331, 338
Altrocchi, J., 345, 350
Ameratunga, S., 26
Andersen-Ranberg, K., 284
Anderson, W. F., 276, 284
Antonioni, D. T., 15, 21
Aoun, S., 267, 273
Apter, A., 245, 246, 247
Apter, M. J., 154
Arbore, P., 279, 284
Arkin, A., 21
Armstrong, J., 283
Aro, H. M., 284
Aronson, E., 398, 399, 400, 408
Aronson, J. K., 5, 21
Ashdown-Lambert, J., 24
Auerbach, S. M., 23

Austin, M. J., 6, 25
Awad, G. A., 142, 156

B

Bajaj, P., 244
Baker, C. D., 5, 21
Baker, S., 245
Balach, L., 244
Balan, B., 83, 247
Balch, L., 315, 317, 318, 320
Ballard, E. D., 233, 244
Barak, A., 315, 317, 320
Barber, J. G., 20, 21
Bardon, C., 83, 247
Barmann, B. C., 19, 21
Barnes, G., 119
Baron, A., 18, 21
Barraclough, B. M., 275, 283
Bastien, S., 324, 329
Batchelor, I. R. C., 276, 283
Battin, D., 6, 15, 21
Batton, L., 345, 350
Bauer, D., 246
Baugher, M., 244
Bauman, K. E., 248
Beall, L., 354, 361
Bearinger, L. H., 248
Bearman, P. S., 229, 244, 248
Beaulieu, C., 225, 246
Beautrais, A. L., 23, 228, 229, 231, 244
Beck, A. T., 104, 110, 276, 283
Becker, J. V., 153
Becker-Kemppainem, S., 274, 277, 279, 285
Bedrosian, R. C., 110
Beebe, J. E., 11, 21
Behrendt, A. E., 231, 248

Belch, H. A., 286, 288, 290
Bellamy, G. T., 26
Belliveau, G., 178, 180, 189, 192
Benedetti, P., 6, 21
Benedict, J. G., 338
Benjamin, A., 381, 389
Bercun, C., 28, 38, 420
Bergin, A. E., 77, 82
Bergman, J. N., 249
Berman, A. L., 33, 37, 83, 234, 236, 244, 246, 247
Berne, E., 111, 115, 119, 336, 338
Bernik, L., 320
Bernstein, L., 285
Beuhring, T., 248
Bezencon, E., 31, 37
Bhandari, G., 272, 273
Bickman, L., 246
Bishop, J., 205
Black, C. M., 261
Blackman, E. K., 21
Blair, G., 244
Blakemore, S. J., 248
Bloch, N., 317, 320
Blodgett, A., 17, 25
Bloom, J. D., 338
Blum, R. W., 248
Blumberg, H. P., 245
Blumberg, S. J., 309, 321
Blumenthal, J., 245, 247
Bobevski, I., 417, 419
Boehm, K. E., 244, 258
Bolling, D. Z., 227, 244
Bolton, G., 321
Bongar, B., 285
Bonneson, M. E., 19, 21
Bonynge, E. R., 266, 273
Borders, L. D., 19, 21, 148, 153
Borofsky, L. A., 247
Boroto, D. R., 373, 389
Borowsky, W., 223, 229, 230, 248
Bosk, A., 244
Bostwick, D., 26
Bovin, M. J., 262
Brammer, L., 381, 389
Brand-Gothelf, A., 245
Brent, D. A., 227, 228, 230, 244
Bridge, J., 229, 244
Broadbar, D., 200, 205
Broadhead, R. S., 6, 21

Brockopp, G. W., 5, 15, 16, 23, 38, 48, 54, 61, 65, 83, 120, 132, 159, 164, 181, 192, 323, 330, 419, 420
Brodish, P. H., 246
Bromley, J. L., 73
Brossart, D. F., 25
Brown, G. K., 280, 285
Brown, M., 115, 119
Brown, S., 154
Bruce, M. L., 253, 261
Brumbaugh, L., 82
Brunet, A. F., 178, 180, 185, 186, 189, 191, 192
Bryant, B. K., 72
Bryant, R. A., 18, 19, 20, 21
Buck, W., 144, 153
Bullman, T. A., 253, 261
Bunch, J., 283
Burnell, G., 324, 329
Burns, D., 104, 110

C

Cadieax, J., 329, 338
Caine, E. D., 283, 284
Callahan, J., 67, 68, 70, 71, 72
Callahan, L., 261
Camasso, M. J., 18, 25
Campbell, J. K., 83, 244
Campbell, N. B., 238, 244
Campbell, S., 321
Cantor, D., 141, 153
Caplan, G., 49, 60, 65, 68, 72, 343, 350
Card, A. L., 24
Carkhuff, R. R., 53, 66, 77, 82, 83, 99, 100, 349, 350, 351, 416, 419
Carlson, V., 284, 290
Carollo, G., 278, 284
Caruth, E. G., 199, 205
Cash, S. K., 229, 244
Casselman, J., 153
Castellanos, F. X., 245
Cedereke, M., 282, 283
Chaffin, A. J., 287, 288, 290
Chagnon, F., 83, 247
Chandler, H., 261
Chantana, N., 24
Chaplin, R., 286, 290
Charlton, T., 321
Chatterton, M., 153
Checkley, K. I., 153

Chein, J., 226, 244
Chen, H., 7, 21
Chen, R., 248
Chen, T., 244
Cheng, A. T. A., 275, 283
Chenkin, C. G., 24
Chiappetta, L., 244
Chicz-DeMet, A., 24
Chiles, J. A., 10, 21
Chiu, H. F. K., 282, 283
Christensen, E. R., 77, 83
Chynoweth, R., 273, 283
Ciccone, D. S., 261
Clark, D. C., 276, 283
Clark, J. J., 408
Clark, S. P., 18, 21, 144, 148, 153
Clarke, R. V., 144, 153
Clasen, L. S., 245, 248
Cloudman, D., 25
Coffman, D., 6, 23
Cohen, L. E., 389
Cohen, R. A., 321
Cohen, R. B., 21
Cole, W., 21
Collins, D. L., 247
Collins, M., 150, 154
Collins, S., 398, 407
Colom, P., 287, 291
Combs, D. C., 6, 21
Comstock, B. S., 245
Connell, C. M., 7, 22
Conoley, C. W., 35
Conrad, D., 398, 407
Conwell, Y., 275, 276, 277, 283, 284, 285
Coombs, D. W., 223, 244
Cooper, A, M., 273
Cooper, J., 19, 22
Cooperman, S., 9, 15, 22
Corbett, M. M., 77, 83
Costa, P. T., 276, 284
Cote, J., 246
Cotler, S., 238, 248
Coughlin, D. D., 419
Cox, C., 283, 284
Craft, L., 230, 248
Crawford, M. J., 233, 244
Crocker, P. J., 77, 82
Crowell, F. A., 26
Crowley, M. J., 244
Culwin, F., 311, 321

Cunningham-Rathner, J., 153
Cyr, C., 22

D

D'Augelli, A. R., 77, 82
D'Augelli, J. F., 82
Daigle, M., 5, 20, 24, 34, 35, 36, 37, 38, 56, 57, 66, 77 ,83, 178, 179, 181, 185, 186, 190, 192, 247, 417, 420
Dalby, J. T., 142, 144, 153
Dalgin, R. S., 268, 269, 273
Daniel, L. S., 15, 22
Dapretto, M., 247
Dattilio, F. M., 67, 72, 105, 110, 120, 132
David-Ferdon, C., 237, 244
Davidoff, M., 7, 22
Davidson, L., 321
Davie, R., 311, 321
Davies, M., 246
Davies, P. G., 19, 22
Davis, J., 273
de Anda, D., 179, 185, 192, 238, 245
De Leo, D., 5, 23, 278, 284, 285
de Sola Pool, I., 23
Deen, B., 244
DeJulio, S. S., 77, 83
Dello Buono, M., 278, 284
di Fabio, M., 21
Diaz, C., 26
Dimalanta, A. S., 10, 22
Dingus, T. A., 248
Dogan-Ates, A., 24
Doherty, I., 26
Dolan, F. B., 236, 245
Dominish, C., 31, 37
Donovan, J., 22
Dooley, D., 77, 83
Doonan, R., 23
Dorey, F., 26
Dorpat, T. L., 275, 276, 277, 284
Douce, L., 286, 289, 290
Downing, J. J., 361
Dowrick, P. W., 22
Draper, B., 284, 285
Draper, J., 246
Driscoll, P., 273
Drye, R. C., 116, 119, 130, 132, 336, 338
Du Pont, N., 24
Duberstein, P. R., 276, 283, 284

Dublin, L. I., 341, 344, 350
Dubren, R., 8, 22
Ducrocq, F., 285
Dumontheil, I., 248
Dunkle, J. H., 286, 289, 290
Durocq, F., 26
Dwyer, J., 284

E

Eaton, D. K., 310, 321
Ebberline, J., 144, 153
Echterling, L. G., 52, 66
Edirippulige, S., 24
Edmonton, E. E., 227, 245
Edwards, C. H., 343, 350
Efstathiou, G., 287, 289, 290
Eisenberger, N. I., 247
Elkers, C., 362
Elliot, C. A., 249
Elliot, R., 64, 66
Ellis, A., 101, 107, 110, 324, 329
Ellis, C., 248
Elson, M., 199, 205
Emery, G., 108, 110
Emmison, M., 21
English, F., 116, 119
Ensidler, B., 83
Erikson, E., 224, 245
Erlangsen, A., 282, 284, 285
Eshkevari, H. S., 273
Evans, A. C., 245, 247, 248, 249
Evans, M. O., 6, 22
Evans, R. L., 11, 22, 23, 280, 284
Evans, W., 310, 311, 313, 321
Everly, G. S., 67, 71, 72
Ewalt, P. L., 341, 350

F

Fagan, J., 132
Fakhoury, W. K. H., 182, 192
Falca-Dodson, M., 261
Faler, R., 320
Farber, J., 324, 329
Farberow, N. L., 245, 276, 284, 285, 342, 349, 350, 351, 355, 357, 361, 362, 418, 421
Faulkner, X., 311, 321
Fergus, E. O., 7, 22

Finkel, S. I., 266 273
Finn, E., 323, 330
Firth, A., 21
Fisher, G., 262
Fisher, P., 248
Fiske, A., 263, 266, 273, 279, 284
Flay, B. R., 24
Flint, A. A., 362
Flory, M., 248
Fogel, G. I., 154
Folkman, S., 105, 110
Forbes, N. T., 283
Ford, C. A., 246
Foster, S. L., 187, 192
Fowler, D. E., 348, 351, 417, 419
Fowler, R., 285
Fox, H. R., 22, 284
Fox, S., 309, 321
France, M. H., 324, 329, 331, 338
Frankenfield, D., 223, 245
Frankl, V. E., 336, 338
Franklin, J. L., 238, 245
Fraser, C., 273
Frauenfelder, J., 17, 22
Frauenfelder, K., 17, 22
Frederick, C. J., 238, 245
Freedman, M., 5, 24, 253
Freeman, A., 67, 105, 110, 120, 132
Freeman, E. W., 11, 26
Freud, S., 323, 329, 331
Freudenberger, H. J., 398, 400, 401, 407
Freund, K., 142, 153
Friedman, M. J., 253, 254, 255, 256, 257, 258, 261, 262
Friedman, R. J., 119, 132
Furman, S. S., 357

G

Gagne, R. M., 375, 389
Gahm, G. A., 262
Galambos, N. L., 224, 245, 247
Gallagher, D., 284
Gallo, J., 285
Garfield, S. L., 77, 82
Garrett, C. R., 418, 419
Garrison, B., 276, 283
Gassner, S., 285
Gatz, M., 273
Gega, L., 288, 290

Gendrich, J., 26
Gerrity, E. T., 26
Gesten, E., 17, 26
Ghosh, P., 244
Giedd, J. N., 225, 245, 247, 248, 249
Gielen, A., 245
Gilat, I., 6, 23, 311, 321
Gilliland, B. E., 68, 72
Gingerich, W. J., 19, 22
Girardi, P., 247
Giroux, G., 18, 24, 178, 186, 193, 418, 420
Giulani, M., 21
Goetz, R. R., 338
Gogtay, N., 225, 245, 248
Gohr, V. M., 192
Goldberg, E., 421
Goldberg, I., 27
Goldberg, R., 145, 153
Goldblatt, M. J., 116, 119
Goldfried, M. R., 58, 66
Goldney, R. D., 273
Goldstein, M. B., 262
Goldston, D. B., 231, 245
Goodman, G., 77, 83
Goodman, P., 120, 132
Gordon, F., 244
Gordon, T., 100
Gorrell, J., 120, 132
Gothelf, D., 232, 245
Goud, N., 6, 16, 22
Goudemand, M., 26, 285
Gould, M. S., 19, 178, 179, 192, 228, 229, 231, 233, 238, 239, 245, 246, 248, 310, 314, 321
Goulding, M. E., 116, 119, 130, 132, 338
Goulding, R. L., 116, 119, 130, 132, 338
Grant, P. R., 178, 180, 186, 192
Gravitz, M. A., 9, 22
Greenberg, L. S., 58, 66, 77, 83, 131, 132
Greenberg, T., 245, 246, 321
Greenstein, D., 245, 248
Gregg, M. E., 231, 249
Grier, M., 6, 24
Grootenhuis, M. A., 48, 419
Grosser, C., 341, 351
Grotjahn, M., 323, 329, 331, 338
Grumet, G. W., 11, 22
Guiney, J., 245
Guerney, B. G., 341, 351
Guerney, L. F., 6, 22

Gunnell, D., 22
Guo, B., 67, 71, 72
Gurney, R. J., 22
Gutman, V., 345, 350
Guyer, B., 247

H

Haas, A. P., 274, 284
Haas, L. J., 337, 338
Halar, E. M., 22
Hall, B., 177, 179, 180, 181, 183, 185, 187, 189, 190, 191, 192
Hallfors, D. D., 228, 246
Hallstrom, K., 192
Halpern, C. T., 246
Handis, M. H., 82
Hankoff, S., 83
Hanna, J., 26
Hannell, E., 273
Harlow, S. D., 287, 288, 290
Harmon, M., 6, 23
Harris, K. M., 248
Harris, T., 115, 119
Harstall, C., 67, 72
Hartsough, D. M., 19, 21, 62, 66, 71
Harvey, A. G., 19, 20, 21
Harvey, V. S., 289, 290
Hassan, R., 273
Hawkins, J., 321
Hawton, K., 22
Hayashi, K. M., 245
Hayward, A., 22
Haywood, C. H., 148, 153
Heath, D., 361
Hefferline, R. F., 120, 132
Heikkinen, M. E., 284
Heilig, S. M., 341, 342, 346, 351
Heinlein, K. T., 289, 290
Helms, J. E., 389
Henderson, B. E., 285
Hendin, H., 274, 284
Henriksson, M. M., 275, 284
Henry, W. E., 341, 351
Herlihy, C., 244
Herman, D. H., 245
Herrmann, J. H., 283
Hertz, M. F., 237, 244
Hess, A. K., 26
Hess, K. D., 26

Hess, T. H., 26
Hides, L., 246
Higgins, E. L., 286, 288, 291
Hightower, N. A., 10, 22
Hill, C. E., 77, 83, 205, 376, 379, 389
Hill, F. E., 6, 23
Hill, R. D., 276, 284
Hiner, S. L., 26
Hinson, J., 19, 22
Hirsch, J. K., 263, 264, 265, 273
Hirsch, S., 77, 83
Hitlin, P., 247
Hochstadt, N. J., 6, 23
Holinger, P. C., 226, 246
Hollingsworth, K. R., 286, 289, 290
Hollon, S. D., 110
Holmes, C. J., 248
Hornblow, A. R., 19, 23
Horowitz, L., 244
Horvath, A., 376, 379, 389
Houle, J., 285
Houts, P. S., 362
Howard, K. L., 322
Howlett, S., 313, 321
Hribersek, E., 143, 153
Hucker, S., 153
Huff, C. O., 231, 246
Huige, K., 119
Hunter, C., 22
Husting, S. R., 247
Huston, P., 16, 23
Hymer, S. M., 9, 12, 13, 15, 23

I

Ialongo, N. S., 24
Illig, V., 82
Inayatullah, M., 249
Ingram, S., 177, 179, 185, 192
Ireland, M., 248
Iritani, B., 246
Iscoe, I., 6, 23
Ishida, T., 284
Isometsa, E. T., 275, 284
Ivey, A. E., 375, 389

J

Jackson, S. E., 407
Jacobs, A., 324, 329

Jacobs, D., 325, 329
Jacobs, K., 320
Jacobsen, L. K., 233, 246
James, R. K., 68, 72
Jaureguy, B. M., 11, 22, 23
Jaycox, L. H., 262
Jeffries, N. O., 245
Jernigan, T. L., 248
Jiffry, M. T. M., 24
Jobes, D. A., 244
Johnson, D. C., 262
Johnson, S. M., 131, 132
Joiner, T., 19, 223, 231, 246, 280, 284
Joines, V., 119
Jones, J., 248
Jones, S., 309, 321
Joseph, S., 400, 407
Josse, G., 248
Judd, F., 264, 265, 266, 273
Judy, L., 274, 277, 279, 285

K

Kalafat, J., 19, 54, 66, 178, 179, 187, 192, 246, 319, 321, 372, 389
Kamann, A. R., 289
Kang, H. K., 253, 261
Kann, L., 321
Kaplan, M. S., 224, 277, 278, 283
Kapur, N., 22
Katz, J. E., 139, 153
Katz, M. M., 119, 132
Katz, R., 7, 22
Katz, S., 415, 420
Kavanagh, D., 24
Kayes, J., 285
Kehoe, S., 178, 180, 186, 192
Kellar-Guenther, Y., 398, 407
Kelly, J. G., 341, 351
Kelly, K., 273
Kennedy, G. J., 275, 284
Kerr, J. H., 154
Kesen, S., 324, 329
Keyl, P., 245
Kiesler, D. J., 77, 83
Kilburg, R. R., 407
Kinchen, S., 321
King, G. D., 17, 23, 238, 246
King, R., 225, 238, 246, 247
Kinzel, A., 18, 23, 177, 178, 180, 186, 192

Kirschenbaum, H., 418, 419
Kisker, G. W., 147, 153
Klauer, S. E., 248
Kleespies, P. M., 72
Kleinman, M., 178, 179, 192, 245, 246
Kline, A., 251, 253, 254, 261
Knickerbocker, D. A., 77, 83, 348, 349, 351, 416, 420
Knudson, M., 153, 246
Kobos, J. C., 338
Koch, S., 100
Kocmur, M., 418, 420
Koetting, M. G., 205
Kolker, H., 415
Kolloerstrom, N., 20, 23
Korb, M. P., 120, 132
Kosky, R. J., 273
Kovacs, M., 276, 283
Kral, M. J., 249
Kramer, R. A., 228, 229, 231, 246
Kroger, W. S., 9, 23
Krone, K., 6, 25
Krysinska, K., 5, 23
Kuoppasalmi, K. I., 284

L

Ladany, N., 199, 200, 205
Lago, C., 321
Lake, C., 223, 246
Lamb, D. H., 201, 205
Lamb, H. R., 357, 361
Lambert, M. J., 77
Lane, R. C., 200, 205
Lang, R. A., 142, 153
Langdon, R., 313, 321
Langevin, R., 153
Lapierre, S., 280, 284, 285
Larkin, G. L., 18, 23
Larsen, H. B., 140, 153
Latzer, Y., 6, 23
Laust, A. K., 24
Lavan, T., 267, 273
Lavoie, B., 285
Lay, J. M., 372, 389
Lazarus, R. S., 105, 110
Leadbeater, B. J., 224, 245
Lebel, C., 225, 246
Lee, J. M., 244
Lee, K. H., 52, 54, 56, 57, 64, 66

Lee, R. G., 273
Lee, S. E., 248
Leenaars, A. A., 119
Leff, J. A., 9, 23
Leising, P., 141, 144, 148, 149, 153
Leiter, M., 399, 407
Leitner, L. M., 67, 71, 72
Lelliott, P., 24
Lemay, L., 178, 180, 189, 192
Lenhart, A., 223, 237, 247, 309, 310, 311, 321
Lenroot, R., 248
Lerch, J., 248
Lerner, R. M., 224, 247
Lester, D., 5, 12, 15, 16, 19, 23, 30, 36, 37, 38, 65, 83, 119, 120, 132, 159, 164, 181, 192, 199, 205, 276, 283, 323, 330, 338, 411, 413, 415, 416, 419, 420, 421
Leth, I., 153
Levitt, H. M., 200, 205
Lewis, M. M., 69, 72
Libersa, C., 26, 285
Liegner, E., 199, 200, 201, 205
Light, L. S., 230, 249
Lindner, R., 284
Linely, P. A., 400, 407
Ling, R., 321
Lister, J. L., 349, 351
Litman, R. E., 245, 284, 351, 362
Liu, H., 245
Liu, X. X., 21
Long, A., 398, 407
Lonnqvist, J. K., 284
Losee, N., 17, 23
Losonczy, M., 261
Lowinger, P., 16, 23
Lubell, K., 245, 246, 321
Luke, J. V., 309, 321
Lunney, C. A., 262
Lusk, L., 245
Luxton, D. D., 262
Lyness, J. M., 284

M

MacDonald, D., 249
MacDonald, M. L., 7, 25
Mack, J. E., 325, 329
Mackenzie, T. B., 276, 285
MacKinnon, C., 177, 178, 180, 192
MacKinnon, R. A., 13, 24

Macks, V. W., 355, 361
Madden, M., 247
Madoc-Jones, I., 6, 24
Maguen, S., 253, 262
Maher, B. A., 153
Mahoney, J., 17, 24, 418, 420
Maline, S., 273
Malley, J. C., 262
Maltsberger, J. R., 119
Mancinelli, I., 247
Maples, M. R., 73
Marcoux, I., 83, 247
Marek, T., 408
Margalit, M., 286, 288, 291
Maris, R., 413, 420
Marks, I., 24, 288, 290
Marmar, C. R., 262
Marrocco, F. A., 246
Marshak, L. E., 286, 288, 290
Marshall, G. N., 251, 252, 262
Marasinghe, R. B., 7, 24
Marttunen, M. J., 284
Marx, B. P., 252, 262
Marx, R. W., 389
Masi, D., 5, 24
Maslach, C., 398, 399, 404, 407, 408
Mason, M., 245
Masten, C. L., 227, 247
Mataix-Cols, D., 288, 290
Matek, O., 145, 149, 153
Mathews, T. J., 223, 247
Mathieu, D., 26, 285
Mathis, J. L., 150, 154
Mayes, L. C., 244, 245
Mazure, C. M., 245
Mazziotta, J. C., 247
McCarthy, G., 27
McClure, J. N., 362, 420
McCrae, R. R., 276, 284
McDonald, J., 7, 26, 178, 193
McDowell, H., 26
McFall, S. L., 6, 24
McGee, J. P., 345, 351
McGee, R. K., 28, 32, 77, 83, 345, 347, 348, 349, 351, 353, 354, 355, 356, 361, 362, 415, 416, 417, 419, 420
McGlynn, F. D., 8, 24
McGowen, R., 23
McIntosh, J. I., 274, 285
McKeon, R., 246

McLaughlin, R., 319, 322
McLennan, J., 417, 419
McNamee, G., 9, 24
McNealy, K., 247
McNees, M. P., 26
Mead, B. T., 141, 154
Merkel, W. T., 154
Merry, S., 26
Methuen, C., 244
Metscher, K. N., 262
Metzler, T. J., 262
Meyer, P., 26, 285
Meyersberg, G., 6, 24
Michaud, P., 287, 291
Michaels, R., 13, 24
Michiner, A., 24
Mickelson, D. J., 6, 25
Miller, H. L., 244
Miller, W. B., 8, 13, 14, 15, 24
Miniño, A. M., 247
Mirassou, M. M., 277, 281, 285
Mishara, B. L., 5, 18, 19, 20, 21, 24, 34, 35, 36, 37, 38, 56, 57, 66, 77, 78, 83, 177, 178, 179, 181, 185, 186, 190, 192, 193, 223, 247, 281, 285, 417, 418, 420
Mitchell, K. J., 239, 247, 249
Mittelman, M. S., 153
Moergen, S. A., 142, 148, 154
Monk, B. J., 24
Monti, K., 282, 283
Moody, J., 229, 244
Moreau, D., 248
Moreland, H., 6, 24
Morgan, C., 325, 330
Morgan, G., 22
Morgenstern, A., 201, 205
Moritz, G., 244
Morra, N. N., 140, 142, 154
Morrison, D. P., 244
Morrow-Howell, N., 274, 277, 279, 285
Mostkoff, K., 246
Motelet, K., 324, 329
Motto, J., 413, 416, 420
Munfakh, J. L. H., 178, 179, 192, 245, 246, 321
Murgatroyd, S., 145, 154
Murphy, G. E., 285, 355, 356, 362, 414, 420
Murphy, W. A., 201, 205
Murphy, W. D., 153
Murray, F. S., 15, 24, 141, 134

Murray, J. N., 231, 248
Myers, W. A., 147, 154

N

Nadler, R. P., 146, 154
Nanson, J., 18, 23, 177, 178, 180, 186, 192
Napier, M. B., 276, 283
Nathan, P., 16, 24, 407
Neimeyer, R. A., 119
Neinstein, L. S., 247
Nelson, B., 283
Nelson, E. L., 6, 24
Newcomb, A. F., 6, 24
Nishimoto, K. P., 24
Nordentoft, M., 284
Norman, K. P., 247
North, G., 400, 401, 407
Noy, B., 6, 25
Nugent, T. F., 245
Nurcombe, B., 246

O

O'Brien, K. M., 205
O'Brien, L., 244
Oberg, C. N., 231, 249
O'Connell, V. F., 120, 132
Ofek, H., 245
Offer, D., 310
Offer, N., 245, 322
Ojehagen, A., 282, 283
Orten, J. D., 117, 119, 120, 132
Osann, K., 24
Ossip-Klein, D. J., 6, 25, 26
Osterman, M. J., 247
Ostrov, E., 322
O'Sullivan, G., 24
Ottens, A. J., 69, 72
Ouimet, M. C., 248
Owens, H. E., 9, 25
Owen-Smith, A., 22
Oyama, H., 284, 285
Ozer, E., 223, 247

P

Packard, M., 421
Paganini-Hill, A., 285
Pakhomou, S. M., 143, 144, 154

Palmer, S., 273
Panting, C., 321
Pao, M., 244
Papp, R. P., 418, 419
Parad, H. J., 66
Parag, V., 26
Parham, I., 23
Parker, S., 246
Parry, O., 24
Paterson, H., 20, 25
Paus, T., 225, 245, 247
Payne, D. S., 148, 154
Pearce, D. C., 26, 178, 193
Pearson, J. L., 280, 285
Pearson, L., 329
Pease, K., 140, 153, 154
Pechura, C. M., 17, 24, 418, 420
Peck, M. L., 245
Pelphrey, K. A., 244
Perls, F. S., 120, 121, 132
Perper, J., 244
Pfeffer, C. R., 228, 231, 232, 233, 234, 245, 246, 247
Pfeifer, J. H., 247
Philippe, A., 26, 285
Piaget, J., 232, 247
Pierce, L. H., 6, 25
Pierce, R. L., 6, 25
Pierce, T., 311, 322
Pietrzak, E., 319, 322
Pietrzak, R. H., 253, 262
Pines, A., 398, 399, 400, 404, 408
Pinfold, T. J., 418, 421
Pinsof, W. M., 77, 83
Pitskel, N. B., 244
Polster, E., 120, 132
Polster, M., 120, 132
Pompili, M., 228, 231, 247
Popenhagen, M. P., 227, 231, 247
Popkin, M. K., 277, 285
Poppe, H., 153
Popper, M., 246
Praderas, K., 7, 25
Price, C. J., 248
Priebe, K., 415, 420
Pritzl, D., 22, 284
Pudlinski, C., 188, 193
Pugh, G., 153
Purcell, K., 321

Q

Qualley, R. M., 227, 231, 247
Quinnett, P., 284, 285

R

Rabinowitz, I., 246
Radzik, M., 224, 226, 247
Ragle, J., 6, 25
Rak, C. F., 289, 290
Ramsden, S., 227, 248
Ranan, W., 12, 25
Range, L. M., 73, 118, 119, 131, 132
Rapoport, J., 245, 247, 248
Rapoport, L., 49
Raskind, M. H., 286, 288, 291
Raymond, S., 83, 247
Reardon, R., 25
Reed, C. R., 419
Reese, R. J., 19, 25
Reger, M. A., 262
Reid, W., 246
Reiff, R., 341, 351
Reina-Patton, A., 24
Reinecke, M. A., 107, 110
Renenger, L., 320
Reniers, R., 25
Resnick, M. D., 229, 248
Resnik, H. L. P., 284, 344, 345, 347, 351
Rich, C. L., 275, 285
Richard, W. C., 28, 38, 420
Richardson, F. M., 248
Richars, C. S., 9, 26
Richmond, E. N., 289, 290
Rickert, V. C., 7, 25
Riessman, F., 341, 351
Rincon, E., 23
Ringle, J. L., 192
Rioch, M. J., 356
Ripley, H. S., 275, 276, 284
Rivera, H., 23
Rivers, A. J., 262
Roach, D., 6, 25
Robertiello, R. C., 9, 25
Roberts, A. R., 18, 25, 29, 38, 67, 69, 71, 72, 105, 110, 120, 134, 323, 330
Robins, E., 275, 285
Rodgers, A., 26
Rogers, C. R., 76, 77, 83, 94, 98, 100

Rogers, J. R., 67, 69, 71, 72, 73, 417, 420
Rohrbaugh, A. H., 249
Roiser, J. P., 248
Rosen, I., 149, 154
Rosenbaum, M., 8, 12, 25
Rosenfield, M., 5, 10, 25
Rosenthal, H., 118, 119, 120, 132
Rosman, M., 266, 273
Ross, J., 244, 321
Ross, R. K., 276, 285
Rossi, A., 24
Roth, C., 244
Rouleau, J. L., 153
Roy, A., 285
Ruben, H. L., 6, 25
Ruberto, A., 247
Rubin, D., 24
Ruchkin, V. V., 246
Rueter, M., 231, 249
Rutter, P. A., 231, 248

S

Saebel, J., 21
Safran, J. D., 58, 66
Sainsbury, P., 276, 283, 285
Sakashita, T., 284
Sanders, P., 5, 25
Saul, L. J., 9, 25
Saunders, E. B., 142, 154
Schafer, D. W., 9, 15, 22
Schaufeli, W. B., 398, 399, 408
Schell, T. L., 251, 252, 262
Scher, H., 153
Schill, D. E., 192
Schlosar, H., 177, 179, 180, 181, 183, 185, 187, 189, 190, 191, 192
Schmidt, C. M., 6, 25
Schmitz, M. B., 6, 25
Schnelle, J. F., 6, 26
Schnurr, P. P., 262
Schonert, K. A., 322
Schustov, D., 331, 338
Schwab-Stone, M. E., 246
Schwartz, E., 27
Schweers, J., 244
Schweibert, D., 23
Scocco, P., 285
Scott, V., 30, 38, 199, 205, 330
Searer, R., 82

Sebastian, C. L., 227, 248
Seeley, M. F., 180, 186, 193
Seghier, M. L., 248
Seibel, M., 231, 248
Seiden, R., 355, 362
Seidlitz, L., 284
Seligman, M., 117, 119, 123, 132
Shaffer, D., 230, 246, 248
Shahar, G., 311, 321
Shakeshaft, C., 248
Shanahan, D. L., 419
Shanklin, S., 321
Shapiro, R. M., 25, 26
Shaw, P., 227, 248
Sheerin, D. F., 6, 26
Sheffield, C. J., 140, 154
Shepard, P., 12, 26
Shepherd, M., 26
Shepherd, I. L., 132
Sherer, S., 247
Shew, M., 248
Shinefield, W., 54, 66, 372, 389
Shneidman, E. S., 56, 58, 66, 67, 72, 125, 132, 276, 280, 284, 285, 350, 351, 353, 354, 355, 357, 361, 362
Sicafuse, L., 321
Sieving, R. E., 248
Silbereisen, R. K., 224, 248
Silverman, M. M., 244
Simmons, J. T., 245
Simons-Morton, B. G., 226, 248
Sinha, R., 245
Skopp, N. A., 262
Slaikeu, K., 49, 56, 64, 66, 72, 415, 420
Slem, C. M., 238, 248
Slone, L. B., 253, 254, 255, 256, 257, 258, 261, 262
Smiga, S. M., 247
Smillie, E., 10, 25
Smith, A., 24
Smith, C. H., 8, 26
Smith, K. M., 284
Smith, M. A., 179, 185, 192, 238, 245
Smith, M. D., 140, 142, 154
Smith, S., 24
Smyer, M. A., 7, 22
Snowdon, A., 273
Snyder, D., 244
Sobey, F., 341, 351
Sokol, M. S., 246

Sollinger, J. M., 262
Solomon, R. J., 246
Southwick, S. M., 262
Sowell, E. R., 225, 248
Soyka, K. M., 67, 71, 72
Spear, L. P., 227, 248
Speigel, S. B., 389
Spevak, P., 9, 26
Sprang, G., 399, 400, 408
Staight, D. C., 362
Stanford, E. J., 337, 338
Stanle, S. V., 244
Stanton, E. E., 9, 26
Stark, C., 265, 273
Stasiak, K., 26
Steer, R. A., 276, 283
Steffert, B., 20, 23
Steinberg, L., 244
Steley, J. R., 19, 26, 147, 154
Stelzer, J., 249
Stern, D., 23
Stewart, I., 116
Stiggins, J., 25, 26
Stokes, H., 246
Stone, C. R., 142, 148, 154
Strobino, D. M., 247
Stromquist, A., 273
Subich, L. M., 69, 72, 417, 420
Suchman, E. A., 412, 414, 421
Suh, G. H., 283
Sussner, B., 261
Swallow, C., 362, 420
Szanto, K., 285
Szasz, T., 355, 362

T

Tabor, J., 248
Takahashi, Y., 283
Talbot, C., 21
Taliaferro, L. A., 223, 229, 230, 248
Tan, G. C. Y., 248
Tanenbaum, S., 275, 284
Tanielian, T., 251, 252, 262
Tatarelli, R., 247
Tate, D. F., 288, 289, 290, 291
Taussig, J. E., 11, 26
Taylor, I., 9, 26
Teach, S. J., 244
Teare, J. F., 419

Tekavcic-Grad, O., 19, 26, 418, 421
Thana, L., 244
Thomas, J. C., 67, 71, 72
Thomas, J. G., 246
Thomas, M. M., 26
Thomas, M. S. C., 248
Thompson, B. J., 205
Thompson, L. W., 284
Thompson, M. P., 230
Thompson, P. M., 225, 245, 248, 249
Thompson, R. W., 192
Thoreson, R. W., 407
Thurber, S., 273
Tichenor, V., 289
Tierney, R. J., 418, 421
Tierney, W. M., 26
Tiessen, B., 273
Todt, E., 224, 248
Toga, A. W., 245, 248, 249
Tonge, J. I., 283
Toumbourou, J. W., 231, 249
Trautman, P., 248
Treloar, A. J., 418, 421
Trent, L., 285
Trexler, L., 276, 283
Trowell, I., 75, 83
Truax, C. B., 77, 83, 349, 351
Trybula, J., 6, 23
Tulkin, S. R., 420
Turner, D. W., 82
Turner, J. E., 7, 25
Turock, A., 377, 389
Turvey, C., 264, 273
Tyano, S., 245

U

Uckert, K., 244
Udry, J. R., 248

V

Vaituzis, A. C., 245
Vaiva, G., 6, 26, 282, 285
van de Riet, V., 120, 132
van de Voorde, H., 153
VandenBos, G. R., 72
Varah, C., 345, 351
Velting, D. M., 246
Viding, E., 248

Vollm, B., 25
Voten, M. P., 362

W

Waern, M., 284, 285
Wagman, M., 323, 330
Waldvogel, J. L., 223, 231, 249
Walfish, S., 17, 18, 26, 144, 154
Waller, M. W., 246
Wang, F., 245
Wang, J., 248
Ward, J. T., 200, 205
Wark, V., 149, 205
Warren, E., 24
Waters, J., 223, 330
Watson, R. J., 18, 26, 178, 180, 185, 193
Webster, J. S., 153
Weich, M. J., 145, 154
Weinberger, M., 6, 26
Weiner, I. W., 413, 421
Weisman, A. D., 201, 205
Weissman, A., 276, 283
Weissman-Frisch, N., 6, 26
Weisz, A. E., 357, 362
Welfel, E. R., 289, 290
Weller, E. B., 227, 231, 249
Weller, R. A., 249
Wenk, R., 6, 26
Wenzel, L. B., 24
Werkhoven, W., 22, 284
Werthamer, L., 245
Westefeld, J. S., 68, 73
Wetzel, R., 362, 420
Wharff, E. A., 244
Wheeler, G., 120, 132
Whitlock, F. A., 277, 285
Whittaker, R., 7, 26
Whittemore, K., 354, 362, 415, 421
Whitt-Woosley, A., 408
Wibbelsman, C. J., 247
Wiener, A., 21
Wilkinson, R. H., 285
Williams, E., 24
Williams, T., 13, 27
Williamson, J. W., 417, 421
Willis, M. A., 56, 64, 66
Wilson, G., 323, 330
Wilson, K. G., 228, 249
Winogrond, I. R., 277, 281 285

Wirtz, T. S., 22
Wise, T. N., 145, 153
Wiser, S., 58, 66
Wissow, L., 245
Wolf, A., 7, 27
Woods, R. P., 249
Woollams, S., 115, 119
Worsley, K., 247
Wright, J. K., 321

X

Xu, H., 23

Y

Ybarra, M. L., 239, 247, 249

Young, D., 285
Young, K. M., 249
Young, L., 120, 132
Young, R., 19, 27, 56, 66
Yufit, R. I., 119, 132

Z

Zabinski, M. F., 288, 289, 290, 291
Zaccarelli, M., 21
Zahnd, E., 247
Zarr, M., 323, 330
Zavasnik, A., 19, 26, 418, 420
Zeligs, M. A., 199, 205
Zhang, Z., 248
Zijdenbos, A., 245, 247
Zwerlig, C., 273

SUBJECT INDEX

A

accreditation, 35, 319
active listening, xi, 71, 77, 79, 80, 94, 100, 106, 186, 188, 234
administration, 34, 78, 258, 416
adolescents, xii, 7, 46, 106, 141, 189, 223, 309, 310, 311, 316, 335
Adult ego state, 109, 112, 113, 114, 115, 116, 117, 336
agoraphobia, 9
AIDS, 6
American Association of Suicidology, 33, 35, 317, 341, 416
anger, 12, 18, 58, 97, 106, 108, 118, 124, 125, 135, 136, 140, 144, 145, 146, 147, 151, 157, 158, 171, 177, 179, 180, 197, 199, 208, 236, 256, 257, 258, 276, 298, 301, 393
anonymity, 11, 13, 16, 43, 44, 45, 81, 137, 143, 236, 240, 241, 265, 268, 272, 288, 311, 316, 319, 361, 407
anonymous callers, 77, 161
anorexia, 8, 307
answering services, 354
antidepressants, 109, 203, 337
anxiety, 6, 8, 9, 12, 13, 14, 33, 49, 50, 56, 58, 64, 69, 90, 95, 96, 98, 101, 104, 106, 121, 122, 136, 145, 146, 149, 151, 167, 190, 199, 200, 201, 213, 215, 253, 254, 260, 263, 276, 286, 290, 305, 309, 343, 344, 348, 355, 365, 372, 374, 418
aphasic patients, 7
assertiveness training, 288
asynchronous communications, 287, 312, 315

B

Befrienders International, 30, 35, 36
behavior therapy, 8, 94, 103, 148, 288
behaviorist perspective, 147
bereavement, 15
blame, 60, 62, 104, 155, 258, 307, 327, 423, 426
blind clients, 11
blind therapist, 15
borderline personality disorder, 199
burnout, 18, 177, 398

C

California Psychological Inventory, 17
Caller ID, 13, 36, 326
calls by third parties, 354
career counseling, 6
cell phones, 7, 189, 237, 269, 309
Child ego state, 112, 113, 114, 115, 116, 117
chronic callers, 16, 33, 159, 160, 161, 162, 163, 164, 166, 167, 168, 169, 170, 173, 175, 177, 178, 179, 180, 181, 182, 183, 184, 185, 186, 187, 188, 189, 190, 191, 192, 218, 405
clergy, 29, 344
client control, 13, 42
client-centered therapy, 94, 96, 98, 99, 100, 120
coaching, 7
cognitive behavior therapy, 288
cognitive constriction, 50, 280
cognitive therapy, 8, 9, 101, 105, 106, 107, 109, 280, 337

competence-based training, 372
conditions of worth, 95, 96, 99
confluence, 56, 126, 128
confrontation, 90, 91, 103, 146, 149, 151, 152, 167, 254, 336, 359, 360, 361, 384, 404, 416
consultation, 6, 7, 78, 168, 300, 302, 346, 359, 360, 361, 384, 404, 416
Contact, 31
contact between self and environment, 122
contamination, 113, 114, 115, 336
conversation, 15, 36, 53, 89
coping, 8, 18, 31, 49, 50, 51, 52, 61, 67, 68, 69, 70, 96, 106, 149, 191, 203, 228, 232, 234, 235, 260, 287, 283, 397, 418, 425
cost, 30, 32, 159, 290, 311, 346, 356, 360, 364, 416
counselor performance, 19, 418
countertransference, 10, 15, 98, 158, 324
covert cry for help, 194, 196
crises, acute, 50, 188, 383
crises, nature of, 49, 51, 55

D

deaf clients, 324
deaf counselors, 324
defense mechanisms, 122
depression, 7, 30, 37, 63, 69, 70, 78, 101, 106, 108, 111, 113, 117, 170, 179, 186, 190, 227, 228, 230, 239, 251, 252, 257, 258, 259, 260, 263, 279, 282, 286, 290, 307, 309, 336, 337, 344, 398, 401, 417
disabled clients, 11, 286
discharged patients, 6
"Don't exist" injunction, 115, 116

E

ego states, 109 112, 113, 114, 115, 116, 336
ego-dystonic, 114
ego-syntonic, 114
elderly, 274
e-mail, ix, 7, 16, 31, 36, 82, 189, 190, 237, 260, 286, 312, 323, 406
emergency psychiatric services, 357, 358
empathy, 15, 17, 20, 53, 71, 77, 80, 81, 96, 126, 130, 186, 241, 269, 348, 349, 379, 384, 392, 406, 416
episcript, 116

errors made by counselors, xi, 84, 102, 326
ethos, 113
evaluation, ix, 13, 17, 19, 29, 35, 71, 76, 77, 82, 99, 104, 116, 142, 163, 189, 191, 192, 218, 302, 303, 311, 314, 319, 341, 342, 347, 348, 367, 368, 369, 374, 380, 412, 414, 416, 419
exhibitionists, 141
experiential exercises, 376

F

family therapy, 10, 306
feedback, 19, 48, 88, 288, 326, 348, 372, 406
feelings, exploring, 58, 324, 331, 385
firing volunteers, 369
follow-up, 6, 9, 19, 52, 56, 58, 64, 76, 130, 179, 189, 235, 266, 282, 297, 299, 319, 358, 415, 418
functional pathology, 114
funding, 30, 34, 187, 266, 411
futility suicides, 115

G

genuineness, 77, 97, 348, 416
Gestalt therapy, 120
Goals of centers, 35, 411
grounding, 129
group therapy, 10, 11, 150, 169, 199, 280, 298

H

hang-ups, 211
helping model, 51, 64, 375, 381
hiccups, 9
hopelessness, 58, 70, 107, 117, 239, 257, 265, 276, 280, 401
humanistic approach, 94, 149
hypnosis, 9

I

id, 113
IFOTES, 31
implosive therapy, 9
incomplete calls, 213
injunctions, 115
insomnia, 9, 270
insurance, 18, 236, 289, 367, 412

Subject Index

internal operations of centers, 414
Internet, ix, 28, 74, 223, 250, 263, 286, 309, 323
irrational thinking, 101
isolates, 46, 106

L

learned helplessness, 117, 123
letter writing, 12, 16, 19, 169, 189, 312, 323, 331
Lifeline, 8, 18, 31, 78, 231, 235, 259, 313, 315, 422
locus of control, 123, 129
loneliness, 6, 19, 127, 143, 161, 167, 170, 179, 280, 286, 304, 328
Los Angeles Suicide Prevention Center, 48, 76, 78, 341, 353

M

mania, 113
manipulative callers, 124, 213, 295
masturbators, 135
melancholic suicides, 116

N

nail-biting, 9
naming services, 33
national curriculum in suicidology, 347
National Save-a-Life League, 344
neurosis, 95, 114, 344
neurosis, transference, 9
nondirective therapy, 76, 94
nonprofessionals, 32, 77, 303, 341, 352
No-Suicide contracts, 116, 130, 337
nuisance calls, 141, 175, 201, 211

O

obesity, 9
objectives, 29, 191, 380, 412
obscene calls, 15, 33, 135
one-counselor callers, 215
opening exercise, 380, 395

P

palliative care, 6
paradoxical intention, 336
Parent ego state, 109, 112
pathos, 113
personal problems exercise, 380, 392
person-centered therapy, 94
perturbation, 58, 123
poison control center, 6
professionals, 352
projection, 96, 123, 163
psychoanalysis, 9, 17, 94, 111, 200, 323, 331
psychodynamic approach, 145, 148, 152, 343
psychotics, 217, 223, 230, 383

R

radio, 6, 29, 138, 331
rape, 6
rapport, 52, 106, 233, 296, 314, 320, 336, 380, 393
rational emotive therapy, 101
record keeping, 33
recruiting, 346, 356, 365
redecision, 116
relaxation training, 9, 329, 392
repeat attempts, 296
repressing emotions, 124
role plays, 103, 108, 369, 373, 384, 417
rumors, 6
rural residents, 234, 258, 263

S

Samaritans, 7, 30, 35, 75, 312, 325, 345, 422
schizophrenia, 10, 11, 14, 33, 69, 113, 190, 199, 200, 275, 331, 343
screening, 17, 53, 233, 252, 261, 282, 347, 357, 372, 374
script, 115
selecting counselors, 363
self-disclosure, 98, 164, 239, 381
sex information, 6
sexual abuse, 6, 36
silent callers, 16, 140, 199
smart phones, 7
smoking, 6, 8, 257
social skills training, 148
staffing, 32, 236, 416
standards for centers, 19, 31, 35, 68, 155, 223, 231, 259, 347, 370, 416
stress, for counselors, 18, 398

structural analysis, 111
structural pathology, 113
substance abuse, 30, 50, 179, 185, 228, 230, 251
supervision, 17, 32, 76, 176, 342, 348, 353, 356
supportive services, 297, 303
synchronous communications, 287, 312, 315

T

technical effectiveness, 17, 417
teen hotlines, 6, 412
texting, 7, 82, 189, 237, 271, 309
toll-free lines, 36, 78
tracing calls, 82, 144, 152, 158, 318
trainer behaviors checklist, 372
training counselors, 1, 17, 18, 30, 32, 54, 75, 88, 89, 90, 99, 148, 175, 201, 215, 277, 316, 319, 347, 356, 364, 371
transactional analysis, 109, 111, 120, 336
transference, 9, 12, 16, 91, 103, 200, 324, 336
transference, positive, 13, 44, 219

trauma, 6, 36, 101, 112, 114, 121, 149, 223, 234, 251, 271, 298, 400, 426

U

unconditional positive regard, 76, 95

V

veterans, 250
violence, 29, 50, 181, 223, 256, 406, 525
volume of calls, 33
volunteers, 17, 29, 75, 165, 177, 215, 235, 261, 277, 301, 313, 315, 341, 352, 363, 398

W

war, 6, 250
warmth, 77, 171, 199, 344, 348, 416
wrist-cutting, 10, 33, 209, 295, 304
writing therapy, 169, 189, 323, 331
wrong numbers, 195, 206

CHARLES C THOMAS · PUBLISHER, LTD.

**THE HANDBOOK
OF CHILD LIFE** (2nd Edition)
by Richard H. Thompson
642 pp. (7 x 10) • 7 illustrations • 14 tables
$59.95 (paper) • $59.95 (ebook)

**PRESCRIPTIONS FOR CHILDREN
WITH PSYCHOLOGICAL AND
PSYCHIATRIC PROBLEMS** (4th Edition)
by David F. Bogacki, Ralph F. Blanco,
Michael Roberts, Basant Pradhan,
Karim Sedky, and Andres Pumariega
278 pp. (7 x 10) • 1 table
$42.95 (paper) • $42.95 (ebook)

CHOOSING TO LIVE
by Cliff Williams
204 pp. (7 x 10) • 1 illustration
$28.95 (paper) • $28.95 (ebook)

**ART THERAPY WITH
STUDENTS AT RISK**
(3rd Edition)
by Stella A. Stepney
344 pp. (7 x 10)
39 (12 color) illustrations • 27 tables
$44.95 (paper) • $44.95 (ebook)

INTRODUCTION TO ART THERAPY
(3rd Edition)
by Bruce L. Moon
284 pp. (7 x 10) • 28 illustrations
$37.95 (paper) • $37.95 (ebook)

**INTRODUCTION TO
HUMAN RELATIONS STUDIES**
by George Henderson and
Wesley C. Long
364 pp. (7 x 10)
$62.95 (paper) • $62.95 (ebook)

TECHNOLOGY IN MENTAL HEALTH
(2nd Edition)
by Stephen Goss, Kate Anthony, LoriAnn
Sykes Stretch, and DeeAnna Merz Nagel
456 pp. (7 x 10) • 12 illustrations • 6 tables
$81.95 (paper) • $81.95 (ebook)

ART-BASED GROUP THERAPY
(2nd Edition)
by Bruce L. Moon
258 pp. (7 x 10) • 26 color illustrations
$38.95 (paper) • $38.95 (ebook)

**PRIMER ON EFFECT SIZES,
SIMPLE RESEARCH DESIGNS, AND
CONFIDENCE INTERVALS**
by Marty Sapp
196 pp. (7 x 10) • 1 illustration • 7 tables
$32.95 (paper) • $32.95 (ebook)

**UNDERSTANDING
PARENTAL ALIENATION**
by Karen Woodall and Nick Woodall
252 pp. (7 x 10)
6 illustrations
$39.95 (paper) • $39.95 (ebook)

**CHILDREN IN THE
URBAN ENVIRONMENT**
by Norma Kolko Phillips and
Shulamith Lala Ashenberg Straussner
358 pp. (7 x 10) • 1 illustration
$49.95 (paper) • $49.95 (ebook)

**COMBINING THE CREATIVE
THERAPIES WITH TECHNOLOGY**
by Stephanie L. Brooke
332 pp. (7 x 10)
48 illustrations • 3 tables
$49.95 (paper) • $49.95 (ebook)

SPIRITUAL ART THERAPY
(3rd Edition)
by Ellen G. Horovitz
230 pp. (7 x 10)
47 illustrations • 3 tables
$37.95 (paper) • $37.95 (ebook)

COMPUTATIONAL ART THERAPY
by Seong-in Kim
318 pp. (8.5 x 11)
358 (266 in color) illustrations • 37 tables
$49.95 (hard) • $35.95 (ebook) • $14.95 (dload)

**PSYCHIATRIC ASPECTS
OF CRIMINAL BEHAVIOR**
by Louis B. Schlesinger
280 pp. (7 x 10) • 10 tables
$32.95 (paper) • $32.95 (ebook)

**SPIRITUALITY AS A WORKING MODEL
IN BRIEF PSYCHOTHERAPY**
by Richard H. Cox
202 pp. (7 x 10) • 11 illustrations
$32.95 (paper) • $32.95 (ebook)

Find us on: facebook
FACEBOOK.COM/CCTPUBLISHER

FREE SHIPPING ON ORDERS OVER $50! USE PROMO CODE: SHIP50
Available on retail purchases through our website only to domestic shipping addresses in the United States

TO ORDER: www.ccthomas.com • books@ccthomas.com • 1-800-258-8980

Sign up for our e-Newsletter for e-Only Specials! Go to: www.ccthomas.com